P9-CRM-276

JOHN WILLIS'

SCREEN WORLD

1977

Volume 28

CROWN PUBLISHERS, INC.

ONE PARK AVENUE

NEW YORK, N.Y. 10016

Copyright © 1977 by John Willis. Manufactured in the U.S.A.
Library of Congress Catalog Card No. 50-3023

TO

ALFRED

HITCHCOCK

the ingenious director of practiced professionalism who, for over fifty years, has entertained millions of viewers with his enthralling masterpieces of suspense that are deliciously flavored with his legendary humorous approach to the macabre.

SYLVESTER STALLONE and TALIA SHIRE in "ROCKY"
1976 ACADEMY AWARD FOR BEST PICTURE

CONTENTS

Dedication: *Alfred Hitchcock* 3

Top Boxoffice Stars of 1976 6

Domestic Films released in the United States from January 1 through December 31, 1976 8

Promising New Actors of 1976 151

Academy Awards ("Oscars") for 1975
          presented Monday, March 29, 1976 154

Academy Award Winners of previous years 160

Foreign Films released in the United States
          from January 1 through December 31, 1976 162

Biographical Data on film actors 215

Obituaries from 1976 232

Index 238

EDITOR: JOHN WILLIS

Assistants: Alberto Cabrera, Ron Reagan

STAFF: Joe Baltake, Scott Chelius, Mark Cohen, Frances Crampon, Miles Kreuger, Gino Moya, Don Nute, Stanley Reeves, William Schelble

ACKNOWLEDGMENTS: This volume would not be possible without the generous cooperation of Ted Albert, David Bannon, Michael Berman, Allen Bornstein, Barry Brown, Linda Calabro, Philip Castanza, Mary Dolan, Burton Elias, Jackie Epstein, Stuart Fink, Barry Fishel, Rene Furst, Joseph Green, Dawn Hauraman, Dennis Holly, Roger Karnbad, Mari Kirnan, Andrew Lamy, Ruth Levinson, Bryan Lindquist, Arlene Ludwig, Sam Madell, Kip Miller, Michael Miller, Eric Naumann, Ronald Perkins, Arthus Rubine, Suzanne Salter, Michael Scrimenti, Robert Shaye, Eve Siegel, John Sutherland, John Wiencko, Sandra Wixon, Kurt Woolner, and many secretaries and assistants whose names we failed to record. To the above, we are gratefully indebted.

1. Robert Redford

2. Jack Nicholson

3. Dustin Hoffman

4. Clint Eastwood

5. Mel Brooks

6. Burt Reynolds

7. Al Pacino

8. Tatum O'Neal

9. Woody Allen

10. Charles Bronson

11. John Wayne

12. Barbra Streisand

13. Robert DeNiro

14. Walter Matthau

15. Liza Minnelli

16. Paul Newman

6 **TOP 25 BOX OFFICE STARS OF 1976**

17. James Caan

18. Charlton Heston

19. Peter Sellers

20. Gregory Peck

1976 RELEASES

January 1 through December 31, 1976

21. Faye Dunaway

22. Jan-Michael Vincent

23. Marlon Brando

24. Gene Hackman

25. Gene Wilder

Lee Remick

Billy Dee Williams

Rita Moreno

TAXI DRIVER

(COLUMBIA) Producers, Michael and Julia Phillips; Director, Martin Scorsese; Screenplay, Paul Schrader; Music, Bernard Herrmann; Associate Producer, Philip Goldfarb; Photography, Michael Chapman; Art Director, Chuck Rosen; Editor, Marcia Lucas; Assistant Director, Peter Scoppa; Costumes, Ruth Morley; In Panavision and color; Rated R; 113 minutes; February release.

CAST

Travis	Robert DeNiro
Betsy	Cybill Shepherd
Wizard	Peter Boyle
Iris	Jodie Foster
Tom	Albert Brooks
Palantine	Leonard Harris
Sport	Harvey Keitel
Charlie T	Norman Matlock
Doughboy	Harry Northrup
Personnel Officer	Joe Spinnell

Left: Robert DeNiro

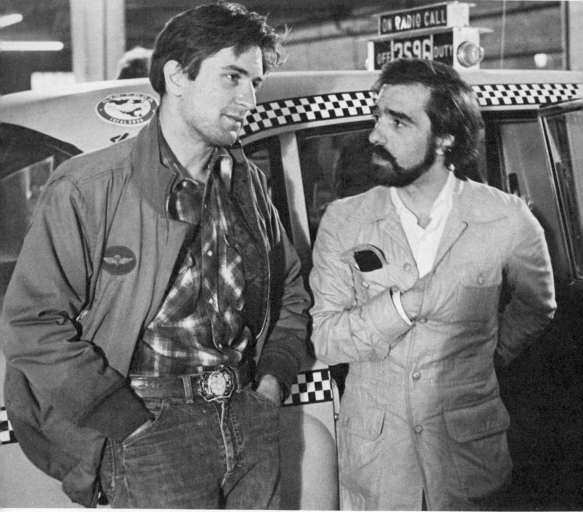

Robert DeNiro, Martin Scorsese

Jodie Foster Top: Robert DeNiro
Top Right: Leonard Harris

Harvey Keitel, Jodie Foster
Above: Jodie Foster, Robert DeNiro

Vic Tayback, David Niven Above: Kim Richards,
Darren McGavin Top: John Williams, David Niven

NO DEPOSIT, NO RETURN

(BUENA VISTA) Producer, Ron Miller; Co-Producer, Joe McEveety; Director, Norman Tokar; Story, Joe McEveety; Screenplay, Arthur Alsberg, Don Nelson; Photography, Frank Phillips; Music, Buddy Baker; Art Directors, John B. Mansbridge, Jack Senter; Editor, Cotton Warburton; Assistant Directors, Arthur J. Vitarelli, William St. John; Costumes, Chuck Keehne; In Technicolor; Rated G; 112 minutes; February release

CAST

J. S. Osborne	David Niven
Duke	Darren McGavin
Bert	Don Knotts
Sgt. Turner	Herschel Bernardi
Carolyn	Barbara Feldon
Tracy	Kim Richards
Jay	Brad Savage
Jameson	John Williams
Longnecker	Charlie Martin Smith
Big Joe	Vic Tayback
Peter	Bob Hastings

Top: Don Knotts, Kim Richards, Brad Savage,
Darren McGavin Below: Herschel Bernardi,
David Niven, Barbara Feldon

Charlie Martin Smith, Herschel Bernardi *Above: David Niven, John Williams Top: Don Knotts*

Kim Richards, Brad Savage
Above: Don Knotts, Darren McGavin   **11**

NEXT STOP, GREENWICH VILLAGE

(20th CENTURY-FOX) Written, Produced and Directed by Paul Mazursky; Photography, Arthur Ornitz; Co-Producer, Tony Ray; Editor, Richard Halsey; Music, Bill Conti; Design, Phil Rosenberg; Assistant Director, Terry Donnelly; In DeLuxe Color; Rated R; 111 minutes; February release

CAST

Larry Lapinsky	Lenny Baker
Mrs. Lapinsky	Shelley Winters
Sarah	Ellen Greene
Anita	Lois Smith
Robert	Christopher Walken
Connie	Dori Brenner
Bernstein	Antonio Fargas
Herb	Lou Jacobi
Mr. Lapinsky	Mike Kellin
Herbert	Michael Egan
Ellen	Denise Galik
Producer Weinberg	John C. Becher
Barney	John Ford Noonan
Herb's Wife	Helen Hanft
Neighbor Tupperman	Rashel Novikoff
Poet Jake	Joe Madden
Cop	Joe Spinell
Abortionist	Rochelle Oliver
Marco	Gui Adrisano
Southern Girl	Carole Manferdini
Actor Clyde	Jeff Goldblum
Party Guest	Rutanya Alda

Left: Lenny Baker

Ellen Greene, Dori Brenner, Lois Smith, Christopher Walken, Antonio Fargas, Lenny Baker

Lois Smith, Christopher Walken
Top: Ellen Greene, Lenny Baker

13

LEADBELLY

(PARAMOUNT) Producer, Marc Merson; Executive Producer, David Frost; Director, Gordon Parks; Screenplay, Ernest Kinoy; Photography, Bruce Surtees; Editor, Harry Howard; Music, Fred Karlin; Design, Robert Boyle; Assistant Director, Reuben Watt; In Eastmancolor; Rated PG; 126 minutes; March release

CAST

Huddie Ledbetter	Roger E. Mosley
Wes Ledbetter	Paul Benjamin
Miss Eula	Madge Sinclair
Prison Chief Guard	Alan Manson
Dicklicker	Albert P. Hall
Blind Lemon Jefferson	Art Evans
John Lomax	James E. Brodhead
Governor Neff	John Henry Faulk
Old Lady	Vivian Bonnell
Margaret Judd	Dana Manno
Gray Man	Timothy Pickard
Sally Ledbetter	Lynn Hamilton
Lethe	Loretta Greene
Amy	Valerie Odell
Sugar Tit	Rozaa Jean

Roger E. Mosley

Top: Roger E. Mosley

Roger E. Mosley, Art Evans
Top: Roger E. Mosley, Madge Sinclair

ONE SUMMER LOVE

(AMERICAN INTERNATIONAL) formerly "Dragonfly"; Producer-Director, Gilbert Cates; Associate Producer-Art Director, Peter Dohanos; Screenplay, N. Richard Nash; Photography, Jerry Hirschfeld; Editor, Barry Malkin; Costumes, Ruth Morley; In Movielab Color; Rated PG; 100 minutes; March release

CAST

Jesse Arlington	Beau Bridges
Chloe	Susan Sarandon
Mrs. Barrow	Mildred Dunnock
Gabriel Arlington	Michael B. Miller
Willa Arlington	Linda Miller
Lonnie Arlington	Martin Burke
Clifford	James Otis
Dr. Le Cooper	James Noble
Pearlie Craigle	Ann Wedgeworth
Walter Craigle	Fredrick Coffin
Mrs. Patterson	Harriet Rogers

Right: Beau Bridges, Susan Sarandon

Susan Sarandon Above: Beau Bridges, Ann Wedgeworth

Beau Bridges, Mildred Dunnock Above: Beau Bridges, Ann Wedgeworth

DEADLY HERO

(AVCO EMBASSY) Producer, Thomas J. McGrath; Executive Producers, Robert Liberman, Stanley Plotnick; Director, Ivan Nagy; Screenplay, George Wislocki; Photography, Andrzej Bartkowiak; Editor, Susan Steinberg; Music, Bard Fiedel, Tommy Mandel; Art Director, Alan Herman; Assistant Director, Jack Baran; In Movielab Color; Rated R; 99 minutes; March release

CAST

Ed Lacy	Don Murray
Sally Devereaux	Diahn Williams
Rabbit	James Earl Jones
Mrs. Broderick	Lilia Skala
Reilly	George S. Irving
Billings	Treat Williams
Baker	Charles Siebert
Buckley	Hank Garrett
D. A. Winston	Dick A. Williams
Arco	Mel Berger
Ellie	Virginia Sandifur
Capt. Stark	Ronald Weyand

Right: Don Murray, Diahn Williams

Don Murray, Diahn Williams
Above: Diahn Williams, James Earl Jones

Lilia Skala, Dick A. Williams
Above: Don Murray

17

ALL THE PRESIDENT'S MEN

(WARNER BROS.) Producer, Walter Coblenz; Director, Alan J. Pakula; Screenplay, William Goldman; Based on book of same title by Carl Bernstein and Bob Woodward; Music, David Shire; Photography, Gordon Willis; Designer, George Jenkins; Editor, Robert L. Wolfe; Associate Producers, Michael Britton, Jon Boorstin; Assistant Directors, Bill Green, Art Levinson; A Wildwood Enterprises production; In Panavision and Technicolor; Rated PG; 138 minutes; April release

CAST

Carl Bernstein	Dustin Hoffman
Bob Woodward	Robert Redford
Harry Rosenfeld	Jack Warden
Howard Simons	Martin Balsam
Deep Throat	Hal Holbrook
Ben Bradlee	Jason Robards
Bookkeeper	Jane Alexander
Debbie Sloan	Meredith Baxter
Dardis	Ned Beatty
Hugh Sloan, Jr	Stephen Collins
Sally Aiken	Penny Fuller
Foreign Editor	John McMartin
Donald Segretti	Robert Walden
Frank Wills	Frank Wills
Arresting Officer #1	F. Murray Abraham
Bachinski	David Arkin
Barker	Henry Calvert
Martinez	Dominic Chianese
Arguing Attorney	Bryan E. Clark
Markham	Nicholas Coster
Kay Eddy	Lindsay Ann Crouse
Miss Milland	Valerie Curtin
Tammy Ulrich	Cara Duff-MacCormick

Gene Dynarski (Clerk), Nate Esformes (Gonzales), Ron Hale (Sturgis), Richard Herd (McCord), Polly Holliday (Secretary), Kames Karen (Lawyer), Paul Lambert (Editor), Frank Latimore (Judge), Gene Lindsey (Baldwin), Anthony Mannino (Officer), Allyn Ann McLerie (Carolyn), James Murtaugh (Clerk), John O'Leary (Attorney), Jess Osuna (FBI Man), Neva Patterson (Angry Woman), George Pentecost (George), Penny Peyser (Sharon), Joshua Shelley (Al), Sloane Shelton (Sister), Lelan Smith (Officer), Jaye Stewart (Librarian), Ralph Williams (Ray), George Wyner (Attorney), Leroy Aarons, Donnlynn Bennett, Stanley Clay, Carol Coggin, Laurence Covington, John Devlin, John Furlong, Sidney Ganis, Amy Grossman, Cynthia Herbst, Basil Hoffman, Mark Holtzman, Jamie Smith Jackson, Barbara Litsky, Doug Llewelyn, Jeff MacKay, Irwin Marcus, Greg Martin, Ron Menchine, Edward J. Moore, Christopher Murray, Jess Nadelman, Noreen Nielson, Florence Pepper, Barbara Perlman, Louis Quinn, Peter Salim, Shawn Shea, Marvin Smith, Pam Trager, Carol Trost, Richard Venture, Bill Willens, Wendell Wright

1976 Academy Awards for Best Supporting Actor (Jason Robards), Best Screenplay, Best Art Direction, Best Sound

Robert Redford, Dustin Hoffman
Above: Robert Redford, Jack Warden, Jason Robards, Dustin Hoffman

Nicolas Coster, Robert Redford
Top Left: Robert Redford, Dustin Hoffman

Robert Redford, Dustin Hoffman
Top: Jack Warden, Martin Balsam

Dustin Hoffman, Penny Fuller, Robert Redford
Above: Dustin Hoffman Top: Jack Warden,
Jason Robards, Martin Balsam

19

Billy Barty, Bernadette Peters

W. C. FIELDS AND ME

(UNIVERSAL) Producer, Jay Weston; Director, Arthur Hiller; Screenplay, Bob Merrill; Based on book by Carlotta Monti, Cy Rice; Photography, David M. Walsh; Designer, Robert Boyle; Editor, John C. Howard; Music, Henry Mancini; Costumes, Edith Head; Assistant Directors, Frederic Brost, Gary D. Daigler; In Panavision and Technicolor; Rated PG; 111 minutes; April release.

CAST

W. C. Fields	Rod Steiger
Carlotta	Valerie Perrine
Bannerman	John Marley
John Barrymore	Jack Cassidy
Melody	Bernadette Peters
Dockstedter	Dana Elcar
Ziegfeld	Paul Stewart
Ludwig	Billy Barty
La Cava	Allan Arbus
Chasen	Milt Kamen
Gene Fowler	Louis Zorich
Claude	Andrew Parks
Leon	Hank Rolike
Parker	Kenneth Tobey
Edward	Paul Mantee
Woman Patient	Elizabeth Thompson
Private Detective	Eddie Firestone
Ingenue	Linda Purl
Assistant Director	Clay Tanner
Schmidt	George Loros

Top: Rod Steiger, Valerie Perrine

Buff Brady, Dana Elcar, Rod Steiger,
Billy Barty Above: Rod Steiger,
Valerie Perrine

Elizabeth Thompson, Rod Steiger
Top: Valerie Perrine, Jack Cassidy

21

STAY HUNGRY

(UNITED ARTISTS) Producers, Harold Schneider, Bob Rafelson; Director, Bob Rafelson; Screenplay, Charles Gaines, Bob Rafelson, Based on novel by Charles Gaines; Photography, Victor Kemper; Editor, John F. Link II; Music, Bruce Langhorne, Byron Berline; Design, Toby Carr Rafelson; Assistant Director, Michael Haley; In DeLuxe Color; Rated R; 102 minutes; April release

CAST

Craig Blake	Jeff Bridges
Mary Tate Farnsworth	Sally Field
Joe Santo	Arnold Schwarzenegger
Thor Erickson	R. G. Armstrong
Franklin	Robert Englund
Anita	Helena Kallianiotes
Newton	Robert E. Mosley
Craig's Uncle	Woodrow Parfrey
Butler	Scatman Crothers
Dorothy Stephens	Kathleen Miller
Amy Walterson	Fannie Flagg
Joe Mason	Joanna Cassidy
Hal Foss	Richard Gilliland
Lester	Ed Begley, Jr.
Halsey	John David Carson
Jabo	Joe Spinell
Walter, Jr	Cliff Pellow
Bubba	Dennis Fimple
Packman	Mayf Nutter

Below: Joanna Cassidy, Jeff Bridges, Kathleen Miller Right: Arnold Schwartzenegger, Jeff Bridges Top: Jeff Bridges, Sally Field

Goldie Hawn, George Segal

THE DUCHESS AND THE DIRTWATER FOX

(20th CENTURY-FOX) Producer-Director, Melvin Frank; Screenplay, Melvin Frank, Barry Sandler Jack Rose, From story by Mr. Sandler; Photography, Joseph Biroc; In DeLuxe color; Rated PG; 105 minutes; April release

CAST

Charlie Malloy	George Segal
Amanda Quaid	Goldie Hawn
Gladstone	Conrad Janis
Widdicombe	Thayer David
Trollop	Jennifer Lee
Bloodworth	Roy Jenson
Dance Hall Girl	Pat Ast
Rabbi	Sid Gould
Bloodworth Gang	Bob Hoy, Bennie Dobbins, Walter Scott, Jerry Gatlin

THE LAST HARD MEN

(20th CENTURY-FOX) Producers, Walter Seltzer, Russell Thacher; Executive Producer, William Belasco; Director, Andrew V. McLaglen; Screenplay, Guerdon Trueblood from novel "Gun Down" by Brian Garfield; Photography, Duke Callaghan; Editor, Fred Chulack; Music, Jerry Goldsmith; Art Director, Edward Carfagno; Assistant Director, Jack Roe; In DeLuxe Color; Rated R; 103 minutes; April release

CAST

Sam Burgade	Charlton Heston
Zach Provo	James Coburn
Susan Burgade	Barbara Hershey
Cesar Menendez	Jorge Rivero
Sheriff Noel Nye	Michael Parks
Mike Shelby	Larry Wilcox
Portugee Shiraz	Morgan Paull
George Weed	Thalmus Rasulala
Lee Roy Tucker	Bob Donner
Will Gant	John Quade
Hal Brickman	Christopher Mitchum

Right: Charlton Heston, Barbara Hershey

Christopher Mitchum, Michael Parks, Charlton Heston Above: Jorge Rivero, James Coburn

Charlton Heston, Michael Parks Above: James Coburn, Barbara Hershey

FAMILY PLOT

(UNIVERSAL) Producer-Director, Alfred Hitchcock; Screenplay, Ernest Lehman; From novel "Rainbird Pattern" by Victor Canning; Photography, Leonard J. South; Designer, Henry Bumstead; Editor, J. Terry Williams; Costumes, Edith Head; Music, John Williams; Assistant Directors, Howard G. Kazanjian, Wayne A. Farlow; In Technicolor; Rated PG; 120 minutes; April release

CAST

Fran	Karen Black
Lumley	Bruce Dern
Blanche	Barbara Harris
Adamson	William Devane
Maloney	Ed Lauter
Julia Rainbird	Cathleen Nesbitt
Mrs. Maloney	Katherine Helmond
Grandson	Warren J. Kemmerling
Mrs. Clay	Edith Atwater
Bishop	William Prince
Constantine	Nicholas Colasanto
Vera Hannagan	Marge Redmond
Andy Bush	John Lehne
Wheeler	Charles Tyner
Parson	Alexander Lockwood
Sanger	Martin West

Left: Barbara Harris

William Devane, Karen Black

Barbara Harris, William Devane
Top: Ed Lauter, Bruce Dern

LIPSTICK

(PARAMOUNT) Producer, Freddie Fields; Director, Lamont Johnson; Screenplay, David Rayfiel; Photography, Bill Butler, William A. Fraker; Editor, Marion Rothman; Music, Michel Poinareff, Jimmie Haskell; Design, Robert Luthardt; Assistant Director, Mickey McCardle; In Technicolor; Rated R; 89 minutes; April release

CAST

Chris McCormick	Margaux Hemingway
Gordon Stuart	Chris Sarandon
Steve Edison	Perry King
Carla Bondi	Anne Bancroft
Nathan Cartwright	Robin Gammell
Martin McCormick	John Bennett Perry
Kathy McCormick	Mariel Hemingway
Photographer	Francesco
Judge	Bill Burns
Sister Margaret	Meg Wylie
Sister Monica	Inga Swenson

Margaux Hemingway, Mariel Hemingway
Above: Margaux Hemingway, Chris Sarandon

Top: Margaux Hemingway, Chris Sarandon
Left: Margaux Hemingway

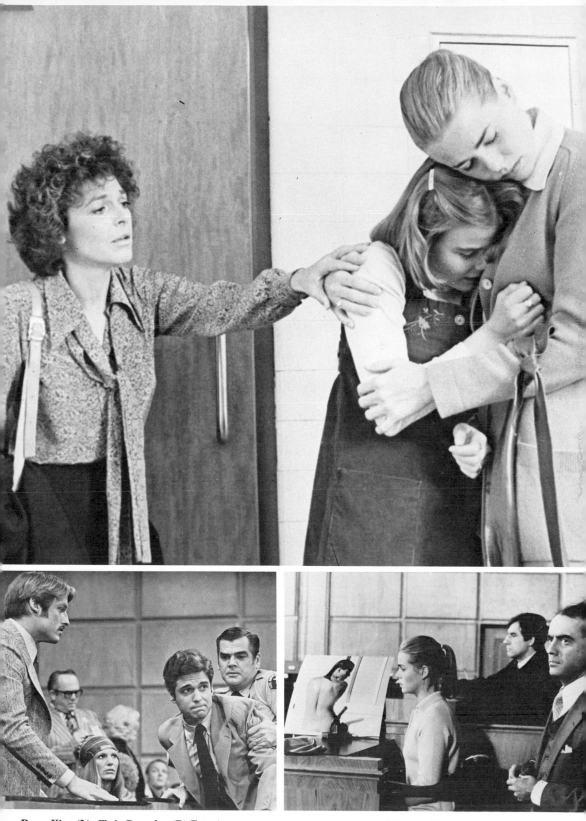

Perry King (L), Chris Sarandon (R) Top: Anne
Bancroft, Mariel Hemingway, Margaux Hemingway

Margaux Hemingway

27

THE BAD NEWS BEARS

(PARAMOUNT) Producer, Stanley R. Jaffe; Director, Michael Ritchie; Screenplay, Bill Lancaster; Photography, John A. Alonzo; Editor, Richard A. Harris; Music, Jerry Fielding; Design, Polly Platt; Assistant Director, Jack Roe; In Movielab Color; Rated PG; 102 minutes; April release

CAST

Coach Buttermaker	Walter Matthau
Manda Whurlizer	Tatum O'Neal
Roy Turner	Vic Morrow
Cleveland	Joyce Van Patten
Councilman Whitewood	Ben Piazza
Kelly Leak	Jackie Earle Haley
Ogilvie	Alfred W. Lutter
Joey Turner	Brandon Cruz
Mrs. Turner	Shari Summers
Umpire	Joe Brooks
Announcer	Maurice Marks
Lupus	Quinn Smith
Engelberg	Gary Lee Cavagnaro
Ahmad	Erin Blunt
Toby Whitewood	David Stambaugh
Agilar Boys	Jaime Escobedo, George Gonzales
Other Bears	David Pollock, Chris Barnes, Scott Firestone, Brett Marx

Left: Tatum O'Neal, Walter Matthau

Vic Morrow, Joyce Van Patten
Top: Walter Matthau, Tatum O'Neal

Tatum O'Neal, Walter Matthau

29

HAWMPS

(MULBERRY SQUARE) Producer-Director, Joe Camp; Co-Producer, Ben Vaughn; Story, William Bickley, Michael Warren, Joe Camp; Screenplay, William Bickley, Michael Warren; Assistant Director, Terry Donnelly; Music, Euel Box; Photography, Don Reddy; Designer, Harland Wright; Art Director, Ned Parsons; Executive Producer, A. Z. Smith; Associate Producers, H. T. Ardinger, Jr., Glenn C. Amon; In color; Rated G; 126 minutes; May release

CAST

Howard Clemmons	James Hampton
Uriah Tibbs	Christopher Connelly
Naman Tucker	Slim Pickens
Col. Seymour Hawkins	Denver Pyle
Hi Jolly	Gene Conforti
Jennifer Hawkins	Mimi Maynard
Fitzgerald	Lee de Broux
Smitty	Herb Vigran
Mariachi Singer	Jesse Davis
Cook	Frank Inn
Cpl. LeRoy	Larry Swartz
Logan	Mike Travis
Higgins	Tiny Wells
Drake	Dick Drake
Col. Zachary	Henry Kendrick

and Don Starr, Cynthia Smith, Roy Gunzburg, Rex Janssen, Catherine Hearne, Larry Strawbridge, James Weir, Alvin Wright, Lee Tiplitsky, Joey Camp, Perry Martin, Richard Lundin, Charles Starkey

Right: Christopher Connelly, Gene Conforti, James Hampton

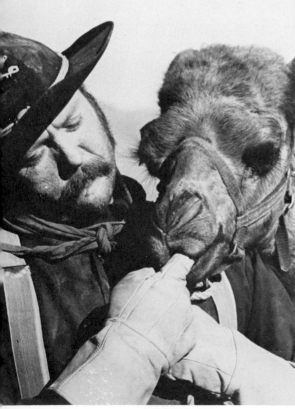

Lee de Broux

James Hampton, Christopher Connelly
Above: Herb Vigran, Slim Pickens

BIRCH INTERVAL

(GAMMA III) Producer, Robert B. Radnitz; Director, Delbert Mann; Screenplay from her novel, Joanna Crawford; Photography, Urs B. Furrer; Music, Leonard Rosenman; Designer, Walt Scott Herndon; Editor, Robbe Roberts; In color; Rated PG; 104 minutes; May release

CAST

Pa	Eddie Albert
Thomas	Rip Torn
Marie	Ann Wedgeworth
Jesse	Susan McClung
Samuel	Brian Part
Esther	Jann Stanley
Charlie	Bill Lucking
Hattie	Margaret Leary
Mrs. Tanner	Anne Revere
Aaron Byler	George Ebeling
Mrs. Byler	Eunice Lehman
Josh	Doug Fishel, Jr.
Martha	Patricia Elliott
Andrew	William Morgan, Jr.
Mason	Andrew Gates
Boorsy	John Keffer
Pissy	David Gates
Crazy Girl	Robin Strosnider

Henry Strozier (Ben), Catherine Knox (Mrs. McBride), Joe Whitaker (Doctor), Madelyn Coleman (Nurse), Mildred Harman, Patrick Reynolds, Amos King, Ken Reed, Rev. William Barr, Maria Deeds, Lori Cole, Cassandra Stouck, Joanna Crawford

Right: Susan McClung, Eddie Albert

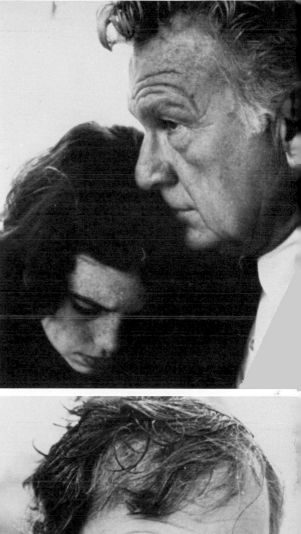

Eddie Albert, Ann Wedgeworth
Above: Rip Torn, Susan McClung

Rip Torn

31

BREAKHEART PASS

(UNITED ARTISTS) Executive Producer, Elliot Kastner; Director, Tom Gries; Screenplay, Alistair MacLean; Producer, Jerry Gershwin; Photography, Lucien Ballard; Music, Jerry Goldsmith; Editor, Buzz Brandt; In color; Rated PG; 95 minutes; May release

CAST

John Deakin	Charles Bronson
Nathan Pearce	Ben Johnson
Richard Fairchild	Richard Crenna
Marcia	Jill Ireland
Frank O'Brien	Charles Durning
Maj. Claremont	Ed Lauter
Dr. Molyneux	David Huddleston
Banlon	Roy Jenson
Jackson	Casey Tibbs
Carlos	Archie Moore

Left: Charles Bronson

Richard Crenna, Charles Durning, Ben Johnson

Jill Ireland, Charles Bronson Top: (L) Charles Bronson
(R) Charles Bronson, Archie Moore

THE MISSOURI BREAKS

(UNITED ARTISTS) Producers, Elliott Kastner, Robert M. Sherman; Director, Arthur Penn; Screenplay, Thomas McGuane; Photography, Michael Butler; Editors, Jerry Greenberg, Stephen Rotter, Dede Allen; Associate Producer, Marion Rosenberg; Music, John Williams; Costumes, Patricia Norris; Designer, Albert Brenner; Assistant Directors, Malcolm Harding, Cheryl Downey; Art Director, Stephen Berger; In color; Rated PG; 126 minutes; May release

CAST

Lee Clayton	Marlon Brando
Tom Logan	Jack Nicolson
Little Tod	Randy Quaid
Jane Braxton	Kathleen Lloyd
Cary	Frederic Forrest
Calvin	Harry Dean Stanton
David Braxton	John McLiam
Si	John Ryan
Hank Rate	Sam Gilman
Lonesome Kid	Steve Franklin
Pete Marker	Richard Bradford
Hellsgate Rancher	James Greene
Rancher's Wife	Luana Anders
Baggage Clerk	Danny Goldman
Sandy	Hunter Von Leer
Woody	Virgil Frye
Bob	R. L. Armstrong
John Quinn	Dan Ades
Madame	Dorothy Newman
Freighter	Charles Wagenheim
Vern	Vern Chandler

Left: Marlon Brando, Jack Nicholson

Kathleen Lloyd, Jack Nicholson

Frederic Forrest, John Ryan, Harry Dean Stanton
Seated: Jack Nicholson, Randy Quaid

34

Jack Nicholson, Marlon Brando
Top: (L) Jack Nicholson, Kathleen Lloyd, (R) Marlon Brando

THE BINGO LONG TRAVELING ALL-STARS AND MOTOR KINGS

(UNIVERSAL) Executive Producer, Berry Gordy; Producer, Rob Cohen; Director, John Badham; Screenplay, Hal Barwood, Matthew Robbins; Based on novel by William Brashler; Photography, Bill Butler; Associate Producers, Michael Chinich, Janet Hubbard, Bennett Tramer; Editor, David Rawlins; Music, William Goldstein; Songs performed by Thelma Houston; Costumes, Bernard Johnson; Assistant Directors, Tom Joyner, L. Andrew Stone, Richard Wells; In Panavision and Technicolor; Rated PG; 110 minutes; May release

CAST

Bingo	Billy Dee Williams
Leon	James Earl Jones
Charlie Snow	Richard Pryor
Willie Lee	Rico Dawson
Louis	Sam "Birmingham" Brison
Champ Chambers	Jophery Brown
Fat Sam	Leon Wagner
Isaac	Tony Burton
Walter Murchman	John McCurry
Esquire Joe Calloway	Stan Shaw
Rainbow	DeWayne Jessie
Sallie Potter	Ted Ross
Bertha	Mabel King
Henry	Sam Laws
Horace	Alvin Childress
Honey	Ken Foree
Mack	Carl Gordon
Prostitute	Anna Capri
Mr. Holland	Joel Fluellen
Pearline	Sarina C. Grant

Jester Hairston (Furry), Emmett Ashford (Umpire), Ted Lehmann (Lars), Fred Covington (Auctioneer), Greg Oliver (Sheriff), John R. McKee (Stranger), Brooks Clift (Older Gentleman), Morgan Roberts, Marcia McBroom, Lidia Kristen, Steve Anderson, Dero Austin

Left: James Earl Jones

Jophrey Brown, Billy Dee Williams, John McCurry, Leon Wagner, Sam "Birmingham" Brison, James Earl Jones, Rico Dawson, Richard Pryor, Tony Burton, DeWayne Jessie, Stan Shaw

Stan Shaw, James Earl Jones, Billy Dee Williams
Top: James Earl Jones, Billy Dee Williams

THAT'S ENTERTAINMENT, PART 2

(UNITED ARTISTS) Producers, Saul Chaplin, Dan Melnick; New Sequences Directed by Gene Kelly; Narration, Leonard Gershe; Music, Nelson Riddle; Photography, George Folsey; Editors, Bud Friedgan, David Blewitt; In black and white and color; Rated G; 133 minutes; May release. An encore presentation of memorable moments from great MGM musicals, comedies and dramas of the past hosted by Fred Astaire and Gene Kelly

Robert Taylor, June Knight
in "Broadway Melody of 1936"

Doris Day, James Cagney
in "Love Me or Leave Me"

Greta Garbo, John Barrymore in "Grand Hotel"
Above: Fred Astaire, Gene Kelly

Spencer Tracy, Katharine Hepburn
in "Pat and Mike"

**Clark Gable, Joan Crawford
in "Strange Cargo"**

**Eleanor Powell
in "Born to Dance"**

**Judy Garland, Gene Kelly
in "For Me and My Gal"**

**Fernando Lamas, Lana Turner
in "The Merry Widow"**

**The Marx Brothers
in "A Night at the Opera"**

**Frank Sinatra, Grace Kelly
in "High Society"**

WON TON TON, THE DOG WHO SAVED HOLLYWOOD

(PARAMOUNT) Producers, David V. Picker, Arnold Schulman, Michael Winner; Director, Michael Winner; Screenplay, Arnold Schulman, Cy Howard; Photography, Richard H. Kline; Editor, Bernard Gribble; Music, Neal Hefty; Art Director, Ward Preston; Assistant Director, Charles Okun; In Technicolor; Rated PG; 92 minutes; May release.

CAST

Grayson Potchuck	Bruce Dern
Estie Del Ruth	Madeline Kahn
J. J. Fromberg	Art Carney
Murray Fromberg	Phil Silvers
Fluffy Peters	Teri Garr
Rudy Montague	Ron Leibman
Won Ton Ton	Augustus von Schumacher

Below: Madeline Kahn, Bruce Dern
Right: Gloria DeHaven, Art Carney, Phil Silvers, Bruce Dern Top: Madeline Kahn, Ron Leibman, Art Carney, Bruce Dern, Won Ton Ton

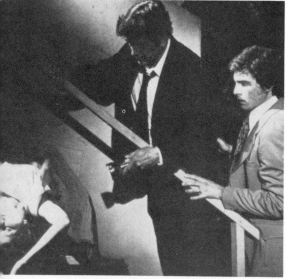

Barbara Carrera, Rock Hudson, John Elerick

EMBRYO

(CINE ARTISTS) Producers, Arnold H. Orgolini, Anita Doohan; Executive Producer, Sandy Howard; Director, Ralph Nelson; Screenplay, Anita Doohan, Jack W. Thomas, from a story by Jack W. Thomas; Photography, Fred Koenekamp; Editor, John Martinelli; Music, Gil Melle; Art Director, Joe Alves; Assistant Director, Michael S. Glick; In DeLuxe Color; Rated Pg; 106 minutes; May release

CAST

Dr. Paul Holliston	Rock Hudson
Martha	Diane Ladd
Victoria	Barbara Carrera
Riley	Roddy McDowall
Helen	Ann Schedeen
Gordon	John Elerick
Dr. Wiston	Jack Colvin
Collier	Vincent Bagetta
Trainer	Joyce Spitz
Forbes	Dick Winslowe
Janet Novak	Lina Raymond
Dr. Joyce Brothers	Herself

MOTHER, JUGS & SPEED

(20th CENTURY-FOX) Producers, Peter Yates, Tom Mankiewicz; Executive Producer, Joseph R. Barbera; Director, Peter Yates; Screenplay, Tom Mankiewicz; From story by Stephen Manes and Mankiewicz; Photography, Ralph Woolsey; Editor, Frank P. Keller; Design, Walter Scott Herndon; Assistant Director, Arthur Levinson; In DeLuxe Color; Rated PG; 95 minutes; May release

CAST

Jugs	Raquel Welch
Mother	Bill Cosby
Speed	Harvey Keitel
Harry Fishbine	Allen Garfield
Murdoch	Larry Hagman
Davey	L. Q. Jones
LeRoy	Bruce Davison
Rodeo	Dick Butkus
Barney	Milt Kamen
Miss Crocker	Barra Grant
Bliss	Allan Warnick
Naomi Fishbine	Valerie Curtin
Harvey	Ric Carrott
Moran	Severn Darden
Charles Taylor	Bill Henderson
Walker	Mike McManus
Addict	Toni Basil
Addict's Doctor	Edwin Mills
Massage Girl	Erica Hagen
Albert	Arnold Williams
Man with zipper	Charles Knapp
Pregnant Woman	Linda Geray

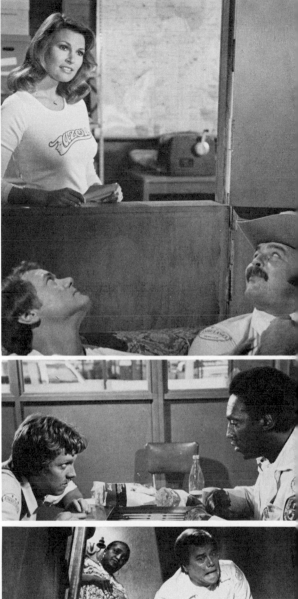

Right: Bruce Davison, Bill Cosby
Top: Raquel Welch, Larry Hagman, Dick Butkus

Alan Garfield, Harvey Keitel, Raquel Welch

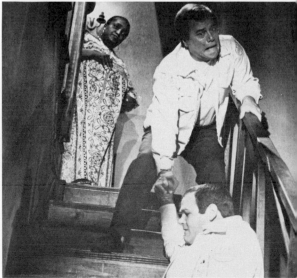

Larry Hagman, Mike McManus

THE TENANT

(PARAMOUNT) Producer, Andrew Braunsberg; Director, Roman Polanski; Screenplay, Roman Polanski, Gerard Brach, based on novel by Roland Topor; Photography, Sven Nykvist; Music, Philippe Sarde; Editor, Francoise Bonnot; Design, Pierre Guffray; In color; Rated R; 124 minutes; June release

CAST

Trelkovsky	Roman Polanski
Stella	Isabelle Adjani
Concierge	Shelley Winters
Mr. Zy	Melvyn Douglas
Mme. Dioz	Jo Van Fleet
Scope	Bernard Fresson
Mme. Gaderian	Lila Kedrova
Husband	Claude Dauphin
Neighbor	Claude Pieplu
Badar	Rufus
Simon	Romain Bouteille

and Jacques Monod, Patrice Alexsandre, Jean Pierre Bogot, Josiane Balasko, Michel Blanc, Florence Blot, Louba Chazel

Top: Shelly Winters, Roman Polanski
Below: Jo Van Fleet, Lila Kedrova

Roman Polanski, Isabelle Adjani Above: Melvyn Douglas, Polanski Top: Claude Dauphin, Roman Polanski, Louba Chazel

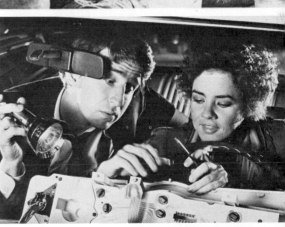

SWEET REVENGE

(UNITED ARTISTS) formerly "Dandy, The All American Girl"; Producer-Director, Jerry Schatzberg; Screenplay, B. J. Perla, Marilyn Goldin, from story by B. J. Perla; Photography, Vilmos Zsigmond; Editors, Evan Lottman, Richard Fetterman; Music, Paul Chihara; Art Director, Bill Kenney; Assistant Director, John Nicoletta; In Metrocolor; Rated PG; 89 minutes; June release

CAST

Dandy	Stockard Channing
LeClerq	Sam Waterston
John T	Norman Matlock
Andy	Richard Doughty
Edmund	Franklyn Ayayc
Greg	Ed E. Villa
Bailiff	Evan Lottman

Top: Stockard Channing Below: Sam Waterston, Norman Matlock, Stockard Channing

Sam Waterston, Stockard Channing, also above Top: Richard Doughty, Stockard Channing

HARRY AND WALTER GO TO NEW YORK

(COLUMBIA) Producers, Don Devlin, Harry Gittes; Executive Producer, Tony Bill; Director, Mark Rydell; Screenplay, John Byrum, Robert Kaufman; Story Don Devlin, John Byrum; Photography, Laszlo Kovacs; Music, David Shire; Lyrics, Alan and Marilyn Bergman; Designer, Harry Horner; Costumes, Theoni V. Aldredge; Associate Producer, Sheldon Shrager; Editors, David Bretherton, Don Guidice; Assistant Director, Jerry Ziesmer; Art Director, Richard Berger; In Panavision and color; Rated PG; 120 minutes; June release

CAST

Harry Dighby	James Caan
Walter Hill	Elliott Gould
Adam Worth	Michael Caine
Lissa Chestnut	Diane Keaton
Rufus T. Crisp	Charles Durning
Gloria Fontaine	Lesley Ann Warren
Chatsworth	Val Avery
Mischa	Jack Gilford
Lewis	Dennis Dugan
Florence	Carol Kane
Barbara	Kathryn Grody
Ben	David Proval
Billy Gallagher	Michael Conrad
Warden Durgom	Burt Young
Guard O'Meara	Bert Remsen
Leary	Ted Cassidy
Dan	Michael Greene
Barney	James DeCloss
Charley Bullard	Nicky Blair
Dutch Herman	George Greif
Ike Marsh	John Hackett
Officer O'Reilly	Phil Kenneally

and Jack Brodsky, Karlene Gallegly, Colin Hamilton, Roger Til, Tom Lawrence, Ben Davidson, Victor Romito, Alex Rodine, Selma Archerd, Elizabeth Summers, Louise DeCarlo, Michelle Breeze, Carmel Lougene, Suzanne Covington, Sig Frohlich, Christopher Rydell, Maureen Arthur, David Shire, Anthony Columbia, Danny Rees, Brion James, Read Morgan, Kim Lankford, Yolanda Mayer, George Gaynes, Robert Miller Driscoll, Geraldine Decker, Ginny Gagnon, Walter Willison, Harry Naughton, Carmine Coppola, Jay Thompson, Warren Berlinger, Jimmy Nickerson, Alex Sharpe, Eddy Donno, Seamon Glass, Charlie Murray, Don Ames, Ellen Blake, Lee Wolfberg, Sherry Moore, Emmett Brown, Evelyn Rydell, Ernie Mishko, Ellen Janes, Dee Hoty, Karen Powell

Right: Elliott Gould, Diane Keaton, James Caan
Top: James Caan, Elliot Gould

Dennis Dugan, Jack Gilford, James Caan,
Elliott Gould, David Proval, Diane Keaton

Michael Caine, Diane Keaton

ODE TO BILLY JOE

(**WARNER BROS.**) Producers, Max Baer, Roger Camras; Director, Max Baer; Story and Screenplay, Herman Raucher; Photography, Michel Hugo; Associate Producer, Mark Sussman; Music, Michel Legrand; Based on song and sung by Bobbie Gentry; Editor, Frank E. Morriss; Art Director, Philip Jefferies; Assistant Director, Anthony Brand; In Technicolor; Rated PG; 105 minutes; June release

CAST

Billy Joe McAllister	Robby Benson
Bobbie Lee Hartley	Glynnis O'Connor
Anna "Mama" Hartley	Joan Hotchkis
Glen "Papa" Hartley	Sandy McPeak
Dewey Barksdale	James Best
James Hartley	Terence Goodman
Becky Thompson	Becky Brown
Brother Taylor	Simpson Hemphill
Coleman Stroud	Ed Shelnut
Tom Hargitay	Eddie Talr
Dan McAllister	William Hallberg
Belinda Wiggs	Frannye Capelle
Mrs. Thompson	Rebecca Jernigan
Mrs. Hunicutt	Ann Martin
Trooper Bosh	Will Long
Trooper Ned	John Roper
Alabama Boys	Pat Purcell, Jim Westerfield
Alabama Driver	Jack Capelle
Master of Ceremonies	Al Scott

Right: Robby Benson, Glynnis O'Connor

Joan Hotchkis, Sandy McPeak, Glynnis O'Connor

THE OUTLAW JOSEY WALES

(WARNER BROS.) Producer, Robert Daley; Director, Clint Eastwood; Screenplay, Phil Kaufman, Sonia Chernus; From the novel "Gone to Texas" by Forrest Carter; Photography, Bruce Surtees; Associate Producers, Jim Fargo, John G. Wilson; Music, Jerry Fielding; Editor, Ferris Webster; Assistant Director, Jim Fargo; Designer, Tambi Larsen; In Panavision and DeLuxe Color; Rated PG; 135 minutes; June release

CAST

Josey Wales	Clint Eastwood
Lone Watie	Chief Dan George
Laura Lee	Sondra Locke
Terrill	Bill McKinney
Fletcher	John Vernon
Grandma Sarah	Paula Trueman
Jamie	Sam Bottoms
Little Moonlight	Geraldine Keams
Carpetbagger	Woodrow Parfrey

Left: Clint Eastwood

Clint Eastwood, Sondra Locke

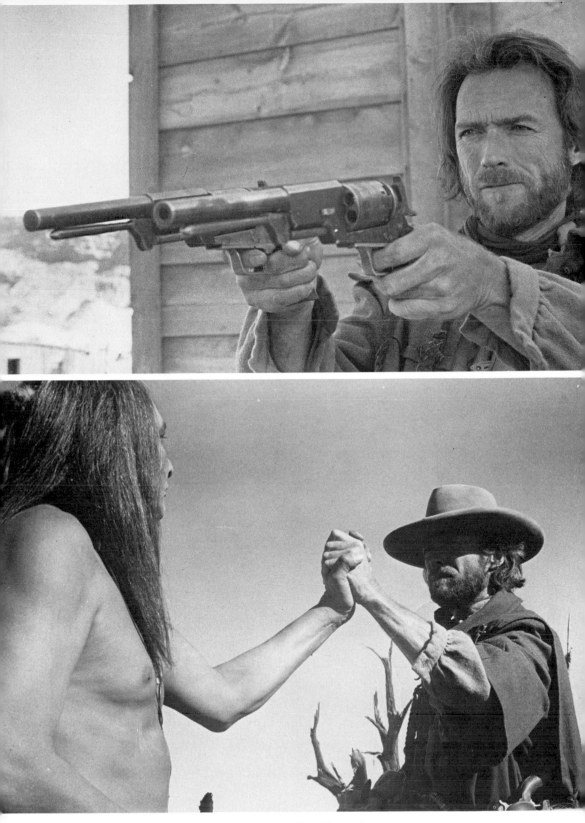

Will Sampson, Clint Eastwood
Top: Clint Eastwood

SILENT MOVIE

(20th CENTURY-FOX) Producer, Michael Hertzberg; Director, Mel Brooks; Screenplay, Mel Brooks, Ron Clark, Rudy DeLuca, Barry Levinson; Story Ron Clark; Music, John Morris; Photography, Paul Lonmann; Editors, John C. Howard, Stanford C. Allen; In DeLuxe Color; Rated PG; 86 minutes; June release

CAST

Mel Funn	Mel Brooks
Marty Eggs	Marty Feldman
Dom Bell	Dom DeLuise
Vilma Kaplan	Bernadette Peters
Studio Chief	Sid Caesar
Engulf	Harold Gould
Devour	Ron Carey
Pregnant Lady	Carol Arthur
News vendor	Lima Dunn
Maitre d'	Fritz Feld
Studio gate guard	Chuck McCann
Studio Chief's secretary	Yvonne Wilder
Intensive care nurse	Valerie Currin
Acupuncture man	Arnold Soboloff
Hotel bellhop	Patrick Campbell
Man in tailor shop	Harry Ritz
Blind man	Charlie Callas
Fly-in-soup man	Henny Youngman
British officer	Eddie Ryder

Mel Brooks Top: Marty Feldman, Dom DeLuise, Bernadette Peters

Top: Dom DeLuise, Mel Brooks, Marty Feldman
Below: Yvonne Wilder, Sid Caesar, Mel Brooks

Sid Caesar, Bernadette Peters, Marty Feldman
Above: Dom DeLuise, Mel Brooks, Bernadette Peters,
Marty Feldman Top: Harold Gould

Mel Brooks, Dom DeLuise, also
Top with Marty Feldman

MURDER BY DEATH

(COLUMBIA) Producer, Ray Stark; Director, Robert Moore; Screenplay, Neil Simon; Designer, Stephen Grimes; Music, Dave Grusin; Photography, David M. Walsh; Associate Producer, Roger M. Rothstein; Editor, Margaret Booth; Costumes, Ann Roth; Assistant Director, Fred T. Gallo; In Panavision and color; Rated PG; 94 minutes; June release

CAST

Tess Skeffington	Eileen Brennan
Lionel Twain	Truman Capote
Milo Perier	James Coco
Sam Diamond	Peter Falk
Bensonmum	Alec Guinness
Jessica Marbles	Elsa Lanchester
Dick Charleston	David Niven
Sidney Wang	Peter Sellers
Dora Charleston	Maggie Smith
Yetta	Nancy Walker
Miss Withers	Estelle Winwood
Marcel	James Cromwell
Willie Wang	Richard Narita

Left: Maggie Smith, David Niven, James Coco

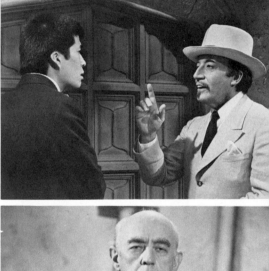

Eileen Brennan, Peter Falk

Alec Guinness, Nancy Walker
Above: Richard Narita, Peter Sellers

Peter Sellers, Peter Falk Above: Estelle Winwood,
Peter Falk, David Niven Top: James Coco, David Niven,
Elsa Lanchester, Peter Falk, Estelle Winwood

Eileen Brennan, Peter Falk
Top: Elsa Lanchester, Estelle Winwood

BUFFALO BILL AND THE INDIANS

(UNITED ARTISTS) Executive Producer, David Suskind; Producer-Director, Robert Altman; Screenplay, Alan Rudolph, Robert Altman; Based on play "Indians" by Arthur Koppit; Music, Richard Baskin; Photography, Paul Lohmann; Editors, Peter Appleton, Dennis Hill; Presented by Dino De Laurentiis; In color; Rated PG; 120 minutes; June release

CAST

Buffalo Bill	Paul Newman
Nate Salsbury	Joel Grey
Maj. John Burke	Kevin McCarthy
Col. Prentiss Ingraham	Allan Nicholls
Ed Goodman	Harvey Keitel
Jules Keen	Mike Kaplan
Crutch	Bert Remsen
Ned Buntline	Burt Lancaster
Annie Oakley	Geraldine Chaplin
Frank Butler	John Considine
Chief Sitting Bull	Frank Kaquitts
Interpreter	Will Sampson
Indian Agent McLaughlin	Denver Pyle
Grover Cleveland	Pat McCormick
Mrs. Cleveland	Shelly Duvall
Nina Cavalini	Evelyn Lear
Margaret	Bonnie Leaders
Lucille DuCharmes	Noelle Rogers
King of the Cowboys	Fred N. Larsen
Trick Riders	Jerri & Joy Duce
Old Soldier	Humphrey Gratz

Left: Paul Newman

Fran Kaquitts, Will Sampson, Paul Newman

John Considine, Geraldine Chaplin, Harvey Keitel, Joel Grey Above: Burt Lancaster, Paul Newman

Paul Newman, Joel Grey Above: Newman, Will Sampson
Top: Noelle Rogers, Newman Below: Newman, Harvey
Keitel, Geraldine Chaplin

Paul Newman
Top: Burt Lancaster

THE FOOD OF THE GODS

(AMERICAN INTERNATIONAL) Executive Producer, Samuel Z. Arkoff; Producer-Director, Screenplay, Bert I. Gordon; Based on novel by H. G. Wells; Music, Elliot Kaplan; Editor, Corky Ehlers; Photography, Reg Morris; Art Director, Graeme Murray; In Movielab Color; Rated PG; 88 minutes; June release

CAST

Morgan	Marjoe Gortner
Lorna Scott	Pamela Franklin
Bensington	Ralph Meeker
Mrs. Skinner	Ida Lupino
Brian	Jon Cypher
Rita	Belinda Balaski
Thomas	Tom Stovall

Top: Marjoe Gortner
Below: Marjoe Gortner, Chuck Courtney

Marjoe Gortner, Ralph Meeker
Above: Pamela Franklin Top: Ida Lupino

54

LIFEGUARD

(PARAMOUNT) Producer, Ron Silverman; Executive Producer, Ted Mann; Director, Daniel Petrie; Screenplay, Ron Koslow; Photography, Ralph Woolsey; Editor, Argyle Nelson, Jr.; Music, Dale Menten; Songs, Dale Menten, Paul Williams; In CFI Color; Rated PG; 96 minutes; June release

CAST

Rick Carlson	Sam Elliott
Cathy	Anne Archer
Larry	Stephen Young
Chris	Parker Stevenson
Wendy	Kathleen Quinlan
Machine Gun	Steve Burns
Tina	Sharon Weber

Top: Anne Archer, Sam Elliott
Below: Sam Elliott, Kathleen Quinlan

Sharon Weber, Sam Elliott Above: Scott Lichtig, Elliott, Parker Stevenson Top: Stephen Young, Sam Elliott

MIDWAY

(UNIVERSAL) Producer, Walter Mirisch; Director, Jack Smight; Screenplay, Donald S. Sanford; Photography, Harry Stradling, Jr.; Art Director, Walter Tyler; Editors, Robert Swink, Frank J. Urioste; Music, John Williams; Assistant Directors, Jerome Siegel, Richard Hashimoto; In Panavision and Technicolor; Rated PG; 132 minutes; June release

CAST

Capt. Matt Garth	Charlton Heston
Adm. Chester W. Nimitz	Henry Fonda
Capt. Vinton Maddox	James Coburn
Rear Adm. Raymond A. Spruance	Glenn Ford
Cmdr. Joseph Rochefort	Hal Holbrook
Adm. Isoroku Yamamoto	Toshiro Mifune
Adm. William F. Halsey	Robert Mitchum
Cmdr. Carl Jessop	Cliff Robertson
Lt. Cmdr. Ernest L. Blake	Robert Wagner
Rear Adm. Frank J. Fletcher	Robert Webber
Adm. Harry Pearson	Ed Nelson
Vice Adm. Chuichi Nagumo	James Shigeta
Haruko Sakura	Christina Kokubo
Cmdr. Max Leslie	Monte Markham
Capt. Miles Browning	Biff McGuire
Ens. George Gay	Kevin Dobson
Lt. Cmdr. C. Wade McClusky	Christopher George
Lt. Cmdr. John Waldron	Glenn Corbett
Capt. Elliott Buckmaster	Gregory Walcott
Lt. Tom Garth	Edward Albert

Left: Charlton Heston, Robert Webber

Henry Fonda, Kevin Dobson

Glenn Ford, Biff McGuire
Above: Seth Sakai, Toshiro Mifune,
Clyde Kusatsu, Bennett Ohta

Pat Morita, Lloyd Kino, James Shigeta, Robert
Ito Above: Henry Fonda, Robert Wagner Top:
Edward Albert, Charlton Heston

James Shigeta Above: Charlton Heston (also top),
Anthony Herrera

Michael York, Jenny Agutter, and
top with Richard Jordan

58

LOGAN'S RUN

(UNITED ARTISTS) Producer, Saul David; Director, Michael Anderson; Screenplay, David Zelag Goodman; Based on novel by William F. Nolan, George Clayton Johnson; Music, Jerry Goldsmith; Photography, Ernest Laszlo; Associate Producer, Hugh Benson; Editor, Bob Wyman; Designer, Dale Nennesy; Costumes, Bill Thomas; Assistant Director, David Silver; Presented by MGM; In Todd-AO and Metrocolor; Rated PG; 118 minutes; June release

CAST

Logan	Michael York
Jessica	Jenny Agutter
Francis	Richard Jordan
Box	Roscoe Lee Browne
Holly	Farrah Fawcett-Majors
Old Man	Peter Ustinov
Doc	Michael Anderson, Jr.
Billy	Gary Morgan
Runner #1	Denny Arnold
Runner #2	Glen Wilder
Woman Runner	Lara Lindsay
First Sanctuary Man	Bob Neil
Second Sanctuary Man	Randolph Roberts
Sanctuary Woman	Camilla Carr
Ambush Man	Greg Michaels
Daniel	Roger Borden
Mary Two	Michelle Stacy
Woman on Lastday	Ann Ford
New You Shop Customer	Laura Hippe

1976 Academy Award for Special Effects

Top: Michael Anderson, Jr., Michael York
Below: Peter Ustinov, Michael York, Jenny Agutter

Jenny Agutter, Farrah Fawcett-Majors Above: Roscoe
Lee Browne, Agutter, Michael York

Jenny Agutter, Michael York, (also top),
and above with Richard Jordan

59

THE OMEN

(20th CENTURY-FOX) Producer, Harvey Bernhard; Executive Producer, Mace Neufeld; Director, Richard Donner; Screenplay, David Seltzer; Photography, Gilbert Taylor; Editor, Stuart Baird; Music, Jerry Goldsmith; Art Director, Carmen Dillon; Assistant Director, David Tomblin; In DeLuxe Color; Rated R; 111 minutes; June release

CAST

Robert	Gregory Peck
Katherine Thorn	Lee Remick
Jennings	David Warner
Mrs. Baylock	Billie Whitelaw
Archaeologist	Leo McKern
Damien	Harvey Stevens
Father Brennan	Patrick Troughton
Father Spiletto	Martin Benson
Dr. Becker	Anthony Nicholls
Young Nanny	Holly Palance
Psychiatrist	John Stride
House Staff	Robert MacLeod, Sheila Raynor

1976 Academy Award for Best Original Score

Left: Harvey Stephens, Lee Remick, Gregory Peck

Lee Remick, Harvey Stephens

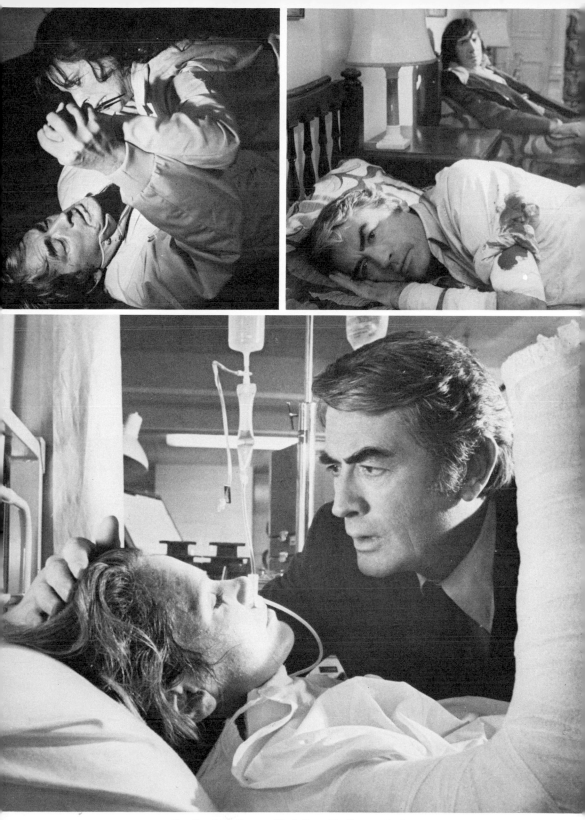

Lee Remick, Gregory Peck Top: (L) Gregory Peck,
Billie Whitelaw (R) Gregory Peck, David Warner

Top: Stockard Channing, John Beck Below: Larry Hagman,
Channing, Walter Brooke, Ned Beatty, Howard Hesseman
Top Right: Richard Mulligan, Bob Dishy, Sally Kellerman

THE BIG BUS

(PARAMOUNT) Produced and Written by Fred Freeman, Lawrence J. Cohen; Executive Producers, Michael and Julia Phillips;
Director, James Frawley; Photography, Harry Stradling, Jr.; Editor, Edward Warschilka; Music, Joel Schiller; Assistant Directors, Mel Efros, Chris Christenberry; In Movielab Color; Rated
PG; 88 minutes; June release

CAST

Dan Torrance	Joseph Bologna
Kitty Baxter	Stockard Channing
Shoulders O'Brien	John Beck
Father Kudos	Rene Auberjonois
Shorty Scotty	Ned Beatty
Dr. Kurtz	Bob Dishy
Ironman	Jose Ferrer
Old Lady	Ruth Gordon
Prof. Baxter	Harold Gould
Parking Lot Doctor	Larry Hagman
Sybil Crane	Sally Kellerman
Claude Crane	Richard Mulligan
Camille Levy	Lynn Redgrave
Emery Bush	Richard B. Shull
Alex	Stuart Margolin
Scotty's Aide Jack	Howard Hesseman
Mary Jane Beth Sue	Mary Wilcox
Mr. Ames	Walter Brooke
Goldie	Vic Tayback
Tommy Joyce	Murphy Dunne
Bus Bartender	James Jeter
Farm Family	Raymond Guth, Miriam Byrd-Nethery, Dennis Kort

Ruth Gordon, Bob Dishy, Murphy Dunne, Mary Wilcox,
Richard Shull, Lynn Redgrave, Rene Auberjonois,
Sally Kellerman, Richard Mulligan, (front) Joseph Bologna,
Stockard Channing, John Beck Above: Redgrave, Bologna

SPECIAL DELIVERY

(AMERICAN INTERNATIONAL) Producer, Richard Berg; Executive Producer, Charles A. Pratt; Director, Paul Wendkos; Screenplay, Don Gazzaniga; Photography, Harry Strading, Jr.; Editor, Houseley Stevenson; Music, Lalo Schifrin; Art Director, Jack Poplin; A Bing Crosby Productions film; In DeLuxe Color; Rated PG; 98 minutes; July release

CAST

Jack Murdock	Bo Svenson
Mary Jane	Cybill Shepherd
Zabelski	Tom Atkins
Bank Manager Zane	Sorrell Booke
Swivot	Gerrit Graham
Carl Graff	Michael C. Gwynne
Snake	Jeff Goldblum
Mr. Chu	Robert Ito
Marj	Lynnette Mettey
Artie	Richard Drout Miller
Barney	John Quade
Wyatt	Vic Tayback
Pierce	Edward Winter
Juliette	Kim Richards

Top: Bo Svenson Below: Cybill Shepherd

Bo Svenson, Cybill Shepherd

GUS

(BUENA VISTA) Producer, Ron Miller; Director, Vincent McEveety; Screenplay, Arthur Alsberg, Don Nelson; Based on story by Ted Key; Photography, Frank Phillips; Music, Robert F. Brunner; Associate Producer, Christopher Hibler; Art Directors, John B. Mansbridge, Al Roelofs; Editor, Robert Stafford; Assistant Director, Ronald R. Grow; Presented by Walt Disney Productions; In Technicolor; Rated G; 96 minutes; July release

CAST

Hank Cooper	Edward Asner
Coach Venner	Don Knotts
Andy Petrovic	Gary Grimes
Crankcase	Tim Conway
Debbie Kovac	Liberty Williams
Cal Wilson	Dick Van Patten
Joe Barnsdale	Ronnie Schell
Pepper	Bob Crane
Johnny Unitas	Himself
Rob Cargil	Dick Butkus
Charles Gwynn	Harold Gould
Spinner	Tom Bosley
Atoms Announcer	Dick Enberg
TV Interviewer	George Putnam
L. A. Sportscaster	Stu Nahan

Left: Liberty Williams, Gus, Gary Grimes

Edward Asner, Don Knotts

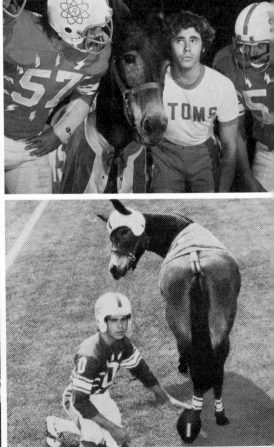

Gary Grimes, Gus Above: Dick Butkus, Gary Grimes

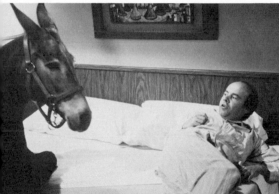

George Putnam, Gus, Gary Grimes
Above: Tim Conway Top: Tim
Conway, Tom Bosley

The Atomettes
Top: Edward Asner, Don Knotts

THE RETURN OF A MAN CALLED HORSE

(UNITED ARTISTS) Producer, Terry Morse, Jr.; Executive Producer, Sandy Howard; Director, Irvin Kershner; Screenplay, Jack DeWitt; Based on character from "A Man Called Horse" by Dorothy M. Johnson; Music, Laurence Resenthal; Photography, Owen Rolzman; Editor, Michael Kahn; In color; Rated PG; 125 minutes; July release

CAST

John Morgan	Richard Harris
Elk Woman	Gale Sondergaard
Zenas Morro	Geoffrey Lewis
Tom Gryce	Bill Lucking
Running Bull	Jorge Luke
Chemin d'Fer	Claudio Brook
Raven	Enrique Lucero
Blacksmith	Jorge Russek
Moonstar	Ana De Sade
Standing Bear	Pedro Damien
Thin Dog	Humberto Lopez-Pineda
Grey Thorn	Patricia Reyes
Lame Wolf	Regino Herrerra
Owl	Rigobert Rico
Red Cloud	Alberto Mariscal

Richard Harris Top: Jorge Russek, Richard Harris

Top: Gale Sondergaard Below: Richard Harris, Humberto Lopez-Pineda

Enrique Lucero, Richard Harris Above: Richard Harris, Gale Sondergaard Top: Richard Harris

Richard Harris Above: Ana DeSade Top: Pedro Damien, Richard Harris

SWASHBUCKLER

(**UNIVERSAL**) Executive Producer, Elliott Kastner; Producer, Jennings Lang; Associate Producer, William S. Gilmore, Jr.; Director, James Goldstone; Screenplay, Jeffrey Bloom; Story, Paul Wheeler; Photography, Philip Lathrop; Designer, John Lloyd; Editor, Edward A. Biery; Costumes, Burton Miller; Music, John Addison; Choreographer, Geoffrey Holder; Assistant Directors, Peter Bogart, Wayne Farlow; In Panavision and Technicolor; Rated R; 101 minutes; July release

CAST

Ned Lynch	Robert Shaw
Nick Debrett	James Earl Jones
Lord Durant	Peter Boyle
Jane Barnet	Genevieve Bujold
Major Folly	Beau Bridges
Cudjo	Geoffrey Holder
Polonski	Avery Schreiber
Mr. Moonbeam	Tom Clancy
Woman of Dark Visage	Anjelica Huston
Sir James Barnet	Bernard Behrens
Alice	Dorothy Tristan
Lute Player	Mark Baker
Willard Culverwell	Kip Niven
Corporal	Tom Fitzsimmons
Lady Barnet	Louisa Horton
Bald Pirate	Sid Haig
Bearded Pirate	Robert Ruth
Peglegged Pirate	Robert Morgan
Pirate Gun Captain	Jon Cedar
Landlady	Diana Chesney
Barnet Servant	Manuel DePina
Chaplain	Tom Lacy
Sailor	Alfie Wise
Banana Man	Harry Basch

Right: Robert Shaw, Beau Bridges, James Earl Jones Top: Robert Shaw, Genevieve Bujold

Geoffrey Holder, James Earl Jones

James Earl Jones, Genevieve Bujold, Robert Shaw

GATOR

(UNITED ARTISTS) Producers, Jules V. Levy, Arthur Gardner; Director, Burt Reynolds; Screenplay, William Norton; Songs sung by Jerry Reed, Bobby Goldsboro; Music, Charles Bernstein; Photography, William A. Fraker; Editor, Harold F. Kress; Art Director, Kirk Axtell; In color; Rated PG; 116 minutes; July release

CAST

Gator	Burt Reynolds
Irving Greenfield	Jack Weston
Aggie Maybank	Lauren Hutton
Bama McCall	Jerry Reed
Emmeline Cavanaugh	Alice Ghostley
Mayor Caffrey	Dub Taylor
Governor	Mike Douglas
Smiley	Burton Gilliam
Bones	William Engesser
Ned McKlusky	John Steadman
Suzie McKlusky	Lori Futch

Right: Lauren Hutton, Burt Reynolds

Mike Douglas, Burt Reynolds
Above: Jack Weston, Burt Reynolds

Lauren Hutton, Burt Reynolds
Above: Jerry Reed, Burt Reynolds

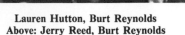

OBSESSION

(COLUMBIA) Producers, George Litto, Harry N. Blum; Executive Producer, Robert S. Bremson; Director, Brian DePalma; Screenplay, Paul Schrader; Photography, Vilmos Zsigmond; Editor, Paul Hirsch; Music, Bernard Herrmann; Art Director, Jack Senter; Assistant Directors, William Pool, Bob Bender; In Technicolor; Rated PG; 98 minutes; July release

CAST

Michael Courtland	Cliff Robertson
Elizabeth Courtland/Sandra Portinari	Genevieve Bujold
Robert LaSalle	John Lithgow
Maid	Sylvia Kuumba Williams
Amy Courtland	Wanda Blackman
Third Kidnapper	Patrick McNamara
Inspector Brie	Stanley J. Reyes
Farber	Nick Kreiger
Dr. Ellman	Stocker Fontelieu
Ferguson	Don Hood
D'Annunzio	Andrea Esterhazy

Left: Genevieve Bujold, Cliff Robertson

Cliff Robertson, Genevieve Bujold

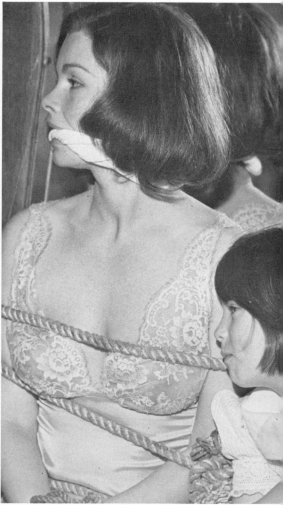

Genevieve Bujold, Wanda Blackman

70

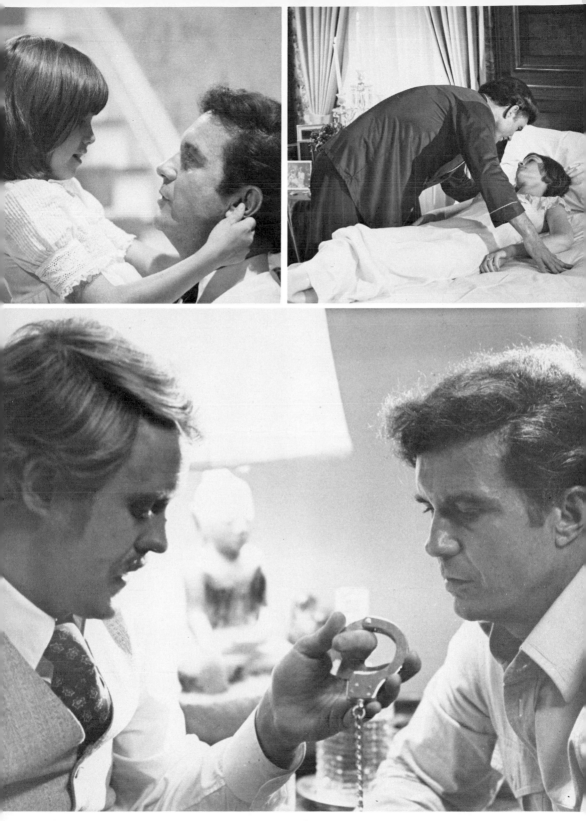

John Lithgow, Cliff Robertson Top: (L) Wanda Blackman,
Cliff Robertson (R) Cliff Robertson, Genevieve Bujold

THE SHOOTIST

(PARAMOUNT) Producers, M. J. Frankovich, William Self; Director, Don Siegel; Screenplay, Miles Hood Swarthout, Scott Hale; Based on novel by Glendon Swarthout; Music, Elmer Bernstein; Photography, Bruce Surtees; Editor, Douglas Stewart; Designer, Robert Boyle; Assistant Director, Joe Cavalier; Costumes, Moss Mabry, Luster Bayless, Edna Taylor; Presented by Dino DeLaurentiis; In Panavision and Technicolor; Rated PG; 99 minutes; August release

CAST

J. B. Books	John Wayne
Bond Rogers	Lauren Bacall
Gillom Rogers	Ron Howard
Dr. Hostetler	James Stewart
Sweeney	Richard Boone
Pulford	Hugh O'Brien
Cobb	Bill McKinney
Marshall Thibido	Harry Morgan
Beckum	John Carradine
Serepta	Sheree North
Dobkins	Richard Lenz
Moses	Scatman Crothers
Burly Man	Gregg Palmer
Barber	Alfred Dennis
Streetcar Driver	Dick Winslow
Girl on streetcar	Melody Thomas
School Teacher	Kathleen O'Malley

John Wayne

Top: John Wayne, James Stewart

John Wayne Top: Lauren Bacall, Ron Howard

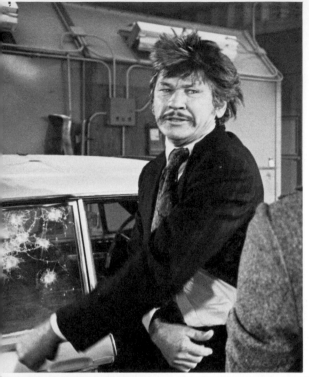

ST. IVES

(WARNER BROS.) Producers, Pancho Kohner, Stanley Canter; Director, J. Lee Thompson; Screenplay, Barry Beckerman; Photography, Lucien Ballard; Based on novel "The Procane Chronicle" by Oliver Bleeck; Editor, Michael F. Anderson; Music, Lalo Schifrin; Assistant Directors, Ronald L. Schwary, Ed Ledding; Designer, Philip M. Jefferies; In Technicolor; Rated PG; 93 minutes; August release

CAST

St. Ives	Charles Bronson
Procane	John Houseman
Deal	Harry Guardino
Oller	Harris Yulin
Charlie Blunt	Dana Elcar
Myron Green	Michael Lerner
Hesh	Dick O'Neill
Eddie	Elisha Cook
Finley	Val Bisoglio
Officer Frann	Burr DeBenning
Johnny Parisi	Daniel J. Travanti

and guest stars:

Constable	Maximilian Schell
Janet	Jacqueline Bisset

Left: Charles Bronson

Maximilian Schell, Jacqueline Bisset, Charles Bronson

Charles Bronson Top: Jacqueline Bisset

FROM NOON TILL THREE

(UNITED ARTISTS) Producers, M. J. Frankovich, William Self; Direction and Screenplay, Frank D. Gilroy; Based on novel by Mr. Gilroy; Photography, Lucien Ballard; Music, Elmer Bernstein; Designer, Robert Clatworthy; Art Director, Dick Lawrence; Costumes, Moss Mabry; Editor, Maury Winetrobe; Assistant Directors, Russ Saunders, Mike Kusley; In color; Rated PG; 98 minutes; August release

CAST

Graham Dorsey	Charles Bronson
Amanda Starbuck	Jill Ireland
Buck Bowers	Douglas V. Fowley
Ape	Stan Haze
Boy	Damon Douglas
Mexican	Hector Morales
Sheriff	Bert Williams
Rev. Cabot	William Lanteau
Edna	Betty Cole
Sam	Davis Roberts
Postmaster Hall	Fred Franklyn
Dr. Finger	Sonny Jones
Deke	Hoke Howell
Mr. Foster	Howard Brunner

Right: Charles Bronson, Jill Ireland

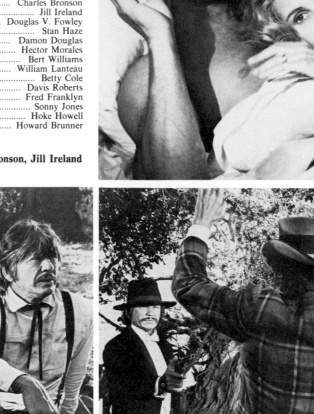

Jill Ireland, Charles Bronson
Above: Stan Haze, Charles Bronson

Damon Douglas, Charles Bronson, Hector Morales, Douglas V. Fowley, Stan Haze Above: Charles Bronson, Sonny Jones

76

NORMAN ... IS THAT YOU?

(UNITED ARTISTS) Producer-Director, George Schlatter; Screenplay, Ron Clark, Sam Bobrick, George Schlatter; Based on play of same title by Ron Clark and Sam Bobrick; Associate Producers, Albert J. Simon, S. Bryan Hickox; Music, William Goldstein; Photography, Gayne Rescher; Art Director, Stephen M. Berger; Editor, George Folsey, Jr.; Costumes, Michael Travis; Presented by MGM; In Metrocolor; Rated PG; 91 minutes; September release

CAST

Ben	Red Foxx
Beatrice	Pearl Bailey
Garson	Dennis Dugan
Norman	Michael Warren
Audrey	Tamara Dobson
Melody	Vernee Watson
Garson's Mother	Jayne Meadows
Bookstore Clerks	George Furth, Barbara Sharma
Desk Clerks	Sergio Aragones, Sosimo Hernandez
Larry	Wayland Flowers
Cab Driver	Allan Drake

Right: Pearl Bailey, Redd Foxx

Tamara Dobson, Redd Foxx Above: Jane Meadows, Dennis Dugan

Vernee Watson, Michael Warren Above: Wayland Flowers

THE RITZ

(WARNER BROS.) Producer, Denis O'Dell; Director, Richard Lester; Screenplay, Terrence McNally; Based on his play of same title; Photography, Paul Wilson; Designer, Phillip Harrison; Editor, John Bloom; Music, Ken Thorne; Songs sung by C. T. Wilkinson; Assistant Director, Dusty Symonds; Costumes, Vangie Harrison; In Technicolor; Rated PG; 90 minutes; August release

CAST

Gaetano Proclo	Jack Weston
Googie Gomez	Rita Moreno
Carmine Vespucci	Jerry Stiller
Vivian Proclo	Kaye Ballard
Chris	F. Murray Abraham
Claude	Paul B. Price
Michael Brick	Treat Williams
Tiger	John Everson
Duff	Christopher J. Brown
Abe	Dave King
Maurine	Bessie Love
Sheldon Farenthold	Tony DeSantis
Patron with bicycle	Ben Aris
Patron in chaps	Peter Butterworth
Small Patron	Ronnie Brody
Patron with cigar	Hal Gallili
Patrons	John Ratzenberger, Chris Harris
Old Man Vespucci	George Coulouris
Muscle-Bound Patron	Leon Greene
Disgruntled Patron	Freddie Earle
Disc Jockey	Hugh Fraser
Old Priest	Bart Allison
Gilda Proclo	Samantha Weysom
Pianist	Richard Holmes

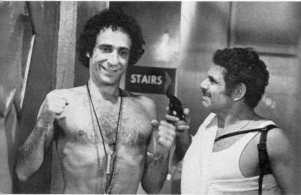

**Left: F. Murray Abraham, Jerry Stiller
Top: Rita Moreno, Jack Weston**

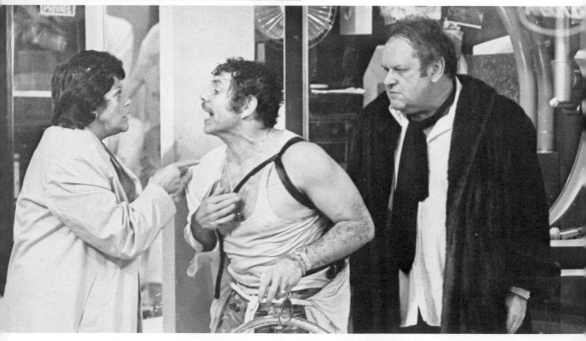

Kaye Ballard, Jerry Stiller, Jack Weston

Rita Moreno, Treat Williams
Top: Jerry Stiller, Rita Moreno, Jack
Weston, Kaye Ballard

Kaye Ballard, Jerry Stiller

FUTUREWORLD

(AMERICAN INTERNATIONAL) Executive Producer, Samuel Z. Arkoff; Producers, Paul N. Lazarus III, James T. Aubrey, Richard T. Heffron; Director, Richard T. Heffron; Screenplay, Mayo Simon, George Schenck; Photography, Howard Schwartz; Music, Fred Carlin; Editor, James Mitchell; Art Director, Trevor Williams; Costumes, Ann McCarthy; Assistant Director, Robert Koster; In Metrocolor; Rated PG; 107 minutes; August release

CAST

Chuck Browning	Peter Fonda
Tracy Ballard	Blythe Danner
Duffy	Arthur Hill
Gunslinger	Yul Brynner
Schneider	John Ryan
Harry	Stuart Margolin
Ron	Jim Antonio
Game Show MC	Allen Ludden
Mrs. Reed	Angela Greene
Mr. Reed	Robert Cornthwaite
Eric	Darrell Larson
Erica	Nancy Bell
Mr. Takaguchi	John Fujioka
His Aide	Dana Lee
Gen. Karnovski	Burt Conroy
Mrs. Karnovski	Dorothy Konrad
KGB Man	Alex Rodine
Maiden Fair	Joanna Hall

Left: Yul Brynner, Blythe Danner

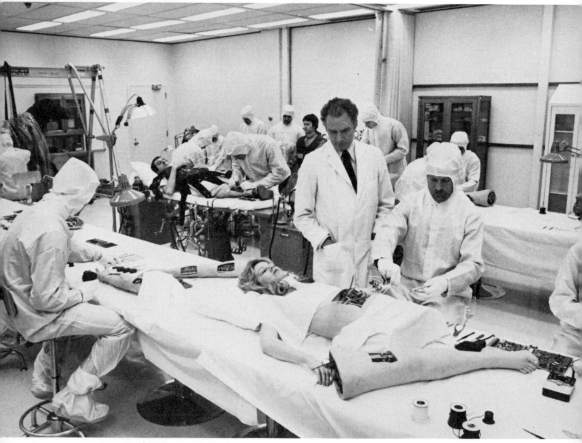

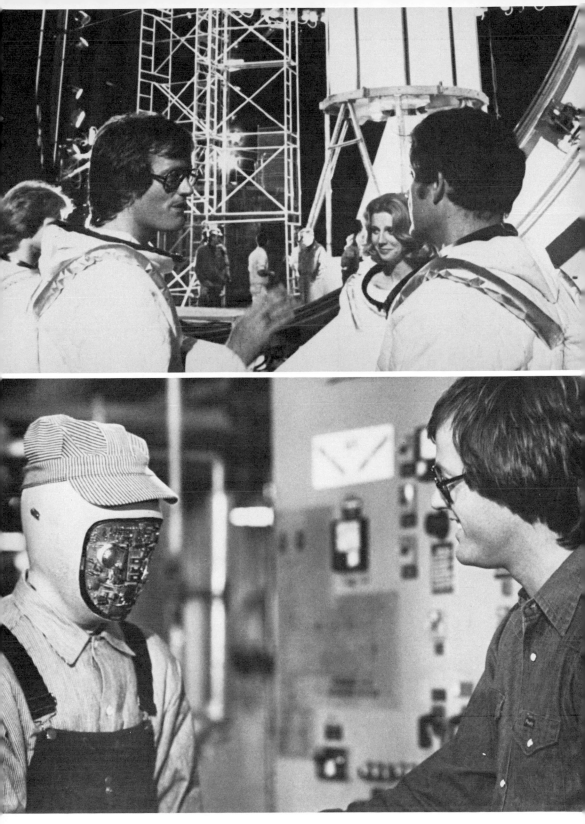

Peter Fonda (R) Top: Peter Fonda, Blythe Danner,

THE FRONT

(COLUMBIA) Executive Producer, Charles Joffe; Producer-Director, Martin Ritt; Screenplay, Walter Bernstein; Music, Dave Crusin; Photography, Michael Chapman; Art Director, Charles Bailey; Costumes, Ruth Morley; Editor, Sidney Levin; Associate Producer, Robert Greenhut; Assistant Directors, Peter Scoppa, Ralph Singleton; In Panavision and color; Rated PG; 94 minutes; September release

CAST

Howard Prince	Woody Allen
Hecky Brown	Zero Mostel
Phil Sussman	Herschel Bernardi
Alfred Miller	Michael Murphy
Florence Barrett	Andrea Marcovicci
Hennessey	Remak Ramsay
Myer Prince	Marvin Lichterman
Delaney	Lloyd Gough
Phelps	David Margulies
Sam	Joshua Shelley
Howard's Attorney	Norman Rose
Danny LaGattuta	Danny Aiello
Hampton	Scott McKay
Margo	Julie Garfield
Committee Counselor	Charles Kimbrough
Committee Chairman	M. Josef Sommer

and Georgann Johnson, David Clarke, I. W. Klein, John Bentley, Murray Moston, McIntyre Dixon, Rudolph Wilrich, Burt Britton, Albert M. Ottenheimer, William Bogert, Joey Faye, Marilyn Sokol, John J. Slater, Renee Paris, Gino Gennaro, Joan Porter, Andrew Bernstein, Jacob Bernstein, Matthew Tobin, Marilyn Persky, Sam McMurray, Joe Ramrog, Michael Miller, Lucy Lee Flippin, Jack Davidson, Donald Symington, Patrick McNamara

Woody Allen, Andrea Marcovicci
Top: Zero Mostel, Woody Allen

Michael Murphy, Woody Allen
Top: Woody Allen, Herschel Bernardi

83

BUGSY MALONE

(PARAMOUNT) Producer, Alan Marshall; Written and Directed by Alan Parker; Executive Producer, David Puttnam; Words and Music, Paul Williams; Choreographer, Gillian Gregory; Photography, Michael Seresin, Peter Biziou; Assistant Director, Ray Corbett; Editor, Gerry Hambling; Designer, Geoffrey Kirkland; Art Director, Malcolm Middleton; A Robert Stigwood Presentation; A Goodtimes Enterprises Production; In color; Rated G; 93 minutes; September release

CAST

Bugsy	Scott Baio
Blousey	Florrie Dugger
Tallulah	Jodie Foster
Fat Sam	John Cassisi
Dandy Dan	Martin Lev
LeRoy Smith	Paul Murphy
Knuckles	Sheridan Russell
Fizzy	Albin Jenkins
Smolsky	Paul Chirelstein
O'Dreary	Andrew Paul
Cagey Joe	Davidson Knight
Razamataz	Michael Jackson
Louis	Jeffrey Stevens
Ritzy	Peter Holder
Snake Eyes	Donald Waugh
Angelo	Michael Kirkby
Shoulders	Jon Zebrowski
Bronx Charlie	Jorge Valdez
Benny Lee	John Lee
Doodle	Ron Meleleu
Yonkers	Paul Besterman

and Kevin Reul, Brian Hardy, Dexter Fletcher, Bonita Langford, Mark Curry, Kathryn Apanowicz, Vivienne McKone, Helen Corran, Lynn Aulbaugh, Nick Amend, John Williams, Herbert Norville, Louise English, Kathy Spaulding

Left: Vivienne McKonne (C)
Top: Jodie Foster, John Cassisi

Martin Lev (center)

Florrie Dugger

Paul Murphy (L), Scott Baio (C)

CAR WASH

(UNIVERSAL) Producers, Art Linson, Gary Stromberg; Director, Michael Schultz; Screenplay, Joel Schumacher; Photography, Frank Stanley; Associate Producer, Don Phillips; Music, Norman Whitfield; Songs performed by Rose Royce; Art Director, Robert Clatworthy; Editor, Christopher Holmes; Costumes, Daniel Paredes; Assistant Directors, Phil Bowles, Richard Hashimoto, Dan Franklin; In Technicolor; 97 minutes; Rated PG; October release

CAST

T. C.	Franklyn Ajaye
Mr. B	Sully Boyar
Irwin	Richard Brestoff
Taxi Driver	George Carlin
Mad Bomber	Prof. Irwin Corey
Lonnie	Ivan Dixon
Duane	Bill Duke
Lindy	Antonio Fargas
Calvin	Michael Fennell
Charlie	Arthur French
Floyd	Darrow Igus
Earl	Leonard Jackson
Lloyd	DeWayne Jessie
Hooker	Lauren Jones
Scruggs	Jack Kehoe
Goody	Henry Kingi
Marsha	Melanie Mayron
Slide	Garrett Morris
Snapper	Clarence Muse
Justin	Leon Pinkney
Wilson Sisters	Pointer Sisters
Daddy Rich	Richard Pryor

and Lorraine Gary, Tracy Reed, Pepe Serna, James Spinks, Ray Vitte, Ren Woods, Carmine Caridi, Antonie Becker, Erin Blunt, Reginald Farmer, Ricky Fellen, Ben Fromer, Cynthia Hamowy, John Linson, Ed Metzger, Antar Mubarak, Derek Schultz, Mike Slaney, Al Stellone, Jackie Toles, Janine Williams, Otis Sistrunk, Timothy Thomerson, Jason Bernard, Jay Butler, Rod McGrew, J. J. Jackson, Sarina C. Grant, Billy Bass

**Top: Mona Tracy Reed, Franklyn Ajaye
Right: Arthur French, Ray Vitte, Antonio
Fargas, Pepe Serna Below: Ricky Fellen,
Loraine Gary, Pepe Serna**

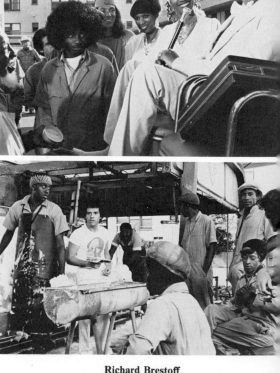

**Richard Brestoff
Above: Richard Pryor (R)**

THE MEMORY OF JUSTICE

(PARAMOUNT) Produced and Directed by Marcel Ophuls; A Hamilton Fish/Max Palevsky Production; Photography, Mike Davis; Editor, Inge Behrens; Associate Producer, Ana Carrigan; In black and white and color; Rated PG; 278 minutes; October release. Part One: Nuremberg and the Germans, Part Two: Nuremberg and Other Places.

A MATTER OF TIME

(AMERICAN INTERNATIONAL) Executive Producers, Samuel Z. Arkoff, Giulio Sbarigia; Producers, Jack H. Skirball, J. Edmund Grainger; Director, Vincente Minnelli; Screenplay, John Gay; Based on novel "Film of Memory" by Maurice Druon; Photography, Geoffrey Unsworth; Design, Veniero Colasanti, John Moore; Music, Nino Oliviero; Editor, Peter Taylor; In Movielab Color; Rated PG; 97 minutes; October release

CAST

Nina	Liza Minnelli
The Contessa	Ingrid Bergman
Count Sanziani	Charles Boyer
Mario Morello	Spiros Andros
Valentina	Tina Aumont
Jeanne Blasto	Anna Proclemer
Antonio Vicaria	Gabriele Ferzetti
Pavelli	Arnolda Foa
Gabriele D'Orazio	Orso Maria Guerrini
Charles Van Maar	Fernando Rey

Right: Liza Minnelli

Liza Minnelli

Fernando Rey, Liza Minnelli
Above: Charles Boyer, Ingrid Bergman

BITTERSWEET LOVE

(AVCO EMBASSY) Producers, Joseph Zappala, Gene Slott, Joel B. Michaels; Director, David Miller; Screenplay, Adrian Morrall, D. A. Kellogg; Music, Ken Wannberg; Photography, Stephen Katz; Editor, Bill Butler; Assistant Director, Ramiro Jaloma; Art Director, Vince Cresciman; In DeLuxe Color; Rated PG; 90 minutes; October release

CAST

Claire	Lana Turner
Howard	Robert Lansing
Marian	Celeste Holm
Ben	Robert Alda
Michael	Scott Hylands
Patricia	Meredith Baxter Birney
Roz	Gail Strickland
Alex	Richard Masur
Nurse Morrison	Denise DeMirjian
Josh	John Friedrich
Judy	Amanda Gavin
Psychiatrist	Jerome Guardino
Schoate	Jac Jozefson, Jr.
Dr. Green	Vince Milana
Minister	Erik Nelson
Joan	Elizabeth Rogers
Mara	Adriana Shaw
Blonde	Gretchen Sloate
Josie	Ann Sweeny
Martha	Patricia Tidy

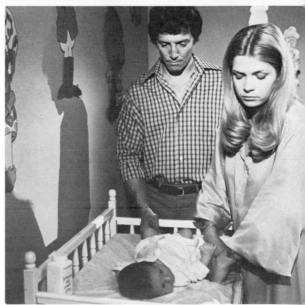

Top: Scott Hylands, Celeste Holm
Below: Scott Hylands, Celeste Holm, Meredith Baxter Birney

Scott Hylands, Meredith Baxter Birney
Above: Robert Lansing, Meredith Baxter Birney
Top: Lana Turner, Robert Alda

BURNT OFFERINGS

(UNITED ARTISTS) Producer-Director, Dan Curtis; Screenplay, William F. Nolan, Dan Curtis; Based on novel by Robert Marasco; Photography, Jacques Marquette, Stevan Larner; Music, Robert Cobert; Associate Producer, Robert Singer; Designer, Eugene Lourie; Presented by P.E.A. Films; In color; Rated PG; 116 minutes; October release.

CAST

Marian	Karen Black
Ben	Oliver Reed
Brother	Burgess Meredith
Roz	Eileen Heckart
David	Lee Montgomery
Walker	Dub Taylor
Aunt Elizabeth	Bette Davis
Chauffeur	Anthony James
Minister	Orin Cannon
Dr. Ross	James T. Myers
Young Ben	Todd Turquand
Ben's Father	Joseph Riley

Left: Karen Black, Lee Montgomery, Oliver Reed

Eileen Heckart, Burgess Meredith

Bette Davis, Karen Black
Above: Lee Montgomery

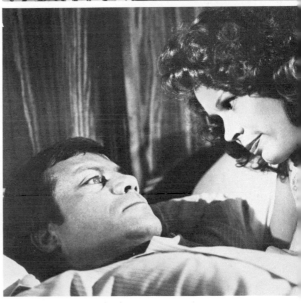

Karen Black, Lee Montgomery, also above with
Oliver Reed, Bette Davis
Top: Oliver Reed, Karen Black

Oliver Reed, Karen Black Above: Bette
Davis, Lee Montgomery Top: Anthony James

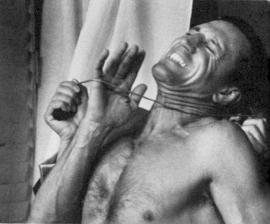

MARATHON MAN

(PARAMOUNT) Producers, Robert Evans, Sidney Beckerman; Director, John Schlesinger; Screenplay, William Goldman from his novel; Photography, Conrad Hall; Editor, Jim Clark; Music, Michael Small; Design, Richard MacDonald; Art Director, Jack DeShields; Assistant Directors, Howard W. Koch, Jr., Burtt Harris; In Metrocolor; Rated R; 125 minutes; October release

CAST

Babe Levy	Dustin Hoffman
Szell	Laurence Olivier
Doc Levy	Roy Scheider
Janeway	William Devane
Elsa	Marthe Keller
Professor	Fritz Weaver
Karl	Richard Bright
Erhard	Marc Lawrence
Mr. Levy	Allen Joseph
Melendez	Tito Goya
Szell's Brother	Ben Dova
Rosenbaum	Lou Gilbert
LeClerc	Jacques Marin
Chen	James Wing Woo
Nicole	Nicole Deslauriers
Old Lady in street	Lotta Andor-Palfi

Laurence Olivier
Top: Dustin Hoffman

Top: Dustin Hoffman, Marthe Keller
Below: Roy Schneider

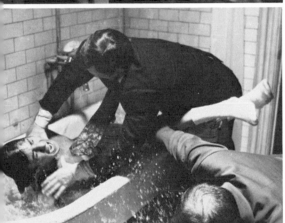

Dustin Hoffman, Marthe Keller Above: Dustin
Hoffman Top: William Devane

Dustin Hoffman, also above with Laurence
Olivier, and top

THE SEVEN-PER-CENT SOLUTION

(UNIVERSAL) Executive Producers, Alex Winitsky, Arlene Sellers; Producer-Director, Herbert Ross; Associate Producer, Stanley O'Toole; Screenplay, Nicholas Meyer, from his novel of same title; Photography, Oswald Morris; Design, Ken Adam; Music, John Addison; "The Madam's Song" by Stephen Sondheim; Costumes, Alan Barrett; Assistant Director, Scott Wodehouse; Editor, Chris Barnes; Art Director, Peter Lamont; In Panavision and color; Rated PG; 113 minutes; October release

CAST

Sigmund Freud	Alan Arkin
Lola Deveraux	Vanessa Redgrave
Dr. Watson	Robert Duvall
Sherlock Holmes	Nicol Williamson
Prof. Moriarty	Laurence Olivier
Lowenstein	Joel Grey
Mary Watson	Samantha Eggar
Baron von Leinsdorf	Jeremy Kemp
Mycroft Holmes	Charles Gray
Mrs. Freud	Georgia Brown
Madame	Regine
Freda	Anna Quayle
Mrs. Holmes	Jill Townsend
Berger	John Bird
Mrs. Hudson	Alison Leggatt
Marker	Frederick Jaeger
Butler	Erik Chitty
Dr. Schultz	Jack May
The Pasha	Gertan Klauber
Squire Holmes	Leon Greene
Young Freud	Ashley House
Nun	Sheila Shand Gibbs
Station Master	Erich Padalewsky
Train Engineer	John Hill

Left: Vanessa Redgrave

Alan Arkin

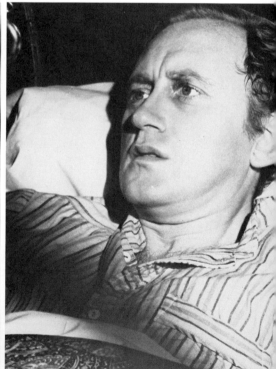

Nicol Williamson

Robert Duvall, Samantha Eggar Top: Nicol
Williamson, Alan Arkin, Robert Duvall

Joel Grey

ALEX & THE GYPSY

(20th CENTURY-FOX) formerly "Love and Other Crimes"; Producer, Richard Shepherd; Director, John Korty; Screenplay, Lawrence B. Marcus; Based on novella "The Bailbondsman" by Stanley Elkin; Photography, Bill Butler; Editor, Donn Cambern; Music, Henry Mancini; Design, Bill Malley; Assistant Director, Irby Smith; In DeLuxe Color; Rated R; 99 minutes; October release

CAST

Alexander Main	Jack Lemmon
Maritza	Genevieve Bujold
Crainpool	James Woods
The Golfer	Gino Ardito
Judge	Robert Emhardt
Morgan	Joseph X. Flaherty
Roy Blake	Todd Martin
Sanders	Victor Pinhiero

Right: Genevieve Bujold, Jack Lemmon

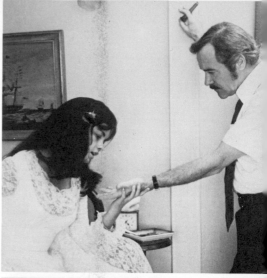

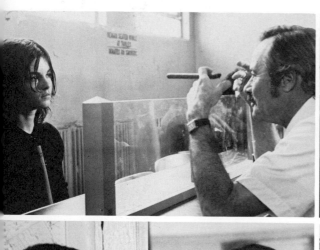

James Woods, Genevieve Bujold
Above: Genevieve Bujold, Jack Lemmon

Genevieve Bujold, Robert Miano
Above: James Woods, Jack Lemmon

THE NEXT MAN

(ALLIED ARTISTS) Producer, Martin Bregman; Director, Richard C. Sarafian; Co-Producer, Burtt Harris; Screenplay, Mort Fine, Alan Trustman, David M. Wolf, Richard C. Sarafian; Based on Story by Martin Bregman, Alan Trustman; Design, Gene Callahan; Photography, Michael Chapman; Design, Gene Callahan; Editors, Aram Avakian, Robert Lovett; Costumes, Anna Hill Johnstone; Music, Michael Kamen; Assistant Director, Allan Hopkins; Art Director, Stuart Wurtzel; In Technicolor; Rated R; 108 minutes; November release

CAST

Khalil Abdul-Muhsen	Sean Connery
Nicole Scott	Cornelia Sharpe
Hamid	Albert Paulsen
Al Sharif	Adolfo Celi
Justin	Marco St. John
Dedario	Ted Beniades
Fouad	Charles Cioffi
Ghassan Kaddara	Salem Ludwig
Hatim Othman	Tom Klunis
Rodriguez	Jaime Sanchez
Andy Hampses	Stephen D. Newman
TV Interviewer	Holland Taylor
Mrs. Scott	Peggy Feury
Mr. Scott	Patrick Bedford
Yassin	Roger Omar Serbagi
Abdel-Latif Khaldoun	Armand Dahan
Atif Abbas	Charles Randall
Devereaux	Ian Collier
Salazar	Michael Storm

and Maurice Copeland, George Pravda, Alex Jawdokimov, James Bulleit, Toru Nagai, Ryokei Kanokogi, Camille Yarbrough, Thomas Ruisinger, Edward Setrakian, Jack Davidson, Bill Snickowski, Lance Henrickson, John MacKay, Robert Levine, William Mooney, Robert Woolley, Alfred Bristol, Martin Bregman, Richard Sarafian, Burtt Harris, Bob Simmons, Tony Ellis, Jamila Massey, Jim Norris, Joe Zaloom, Richard Zakka, Jamie Ross, Jamal Shasad, David Kelly, Mela Hubert-Trimbal, Tony Carroll, Bill Golding, Mohammed Sedrihini, Diane Peterson

Right: Sean Connery Above: Marco St. John
Top: Sean Connery

Cornelia Sharpe, Sean Connery

Cornelia Sharpe, Adolfo Celi

CARRIE

(UNITED ARTISTS) Producer, Paul Monash; Director, Brian DePalma; Screenplay, Lawrence D. Cohen; Based on novel by Stephen King; Editor, Paul Hirsch; Associate Producer, Louis Stroller; Photography, Mario Tosi; Music, Pino Donaggio; Art Directors, William Kenny, Jack Fisk; Costumes, Rosanna Norton; Music, Michael Argiaga; In color; Rated R; 97 minutes; November release

CAST

Carrie	Sissy Spacek
Margaret White	Piper Laurie
Billy Nolan	John Travolta
Sue Snell	Amy Irving
Tommy Ross	William Katt
Chris Hargenson	Nancy Allen
Miss Collins	Betty Buckley
Norman Watson	P. J. Soles
Mr. Fromm	Sydney Lassick
Mr. Morton	Stefan Gierash
Mrs. Snell	Priscilla Pointer
Freddy	Michael Talbot
The Beak	Doug Cox
George	Harry Gold
Frieda	Noelle North
Cora	Cindy Daly
Thonda	Dierdre Berthron
Ernest	Anson Downes
Kenny	Rory Stevens
Helen	Edie McGlurg
Boy on bicycle	Cameron DePalma

Left: Sissy Spacek, William Katt

William Katt, Sissy Spacek

Piper Laurie, Sissy Spacek

Piper Laurie
Top: John Travolta, Nancy Allen

Sissy Spacek

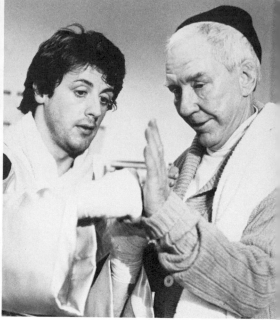

ROCKY

(UNITED ARTISTS) Producers, Irwin Winkler, Robert Chartoff; Director, John G. Avildsen; Screenplay, Sylvester Stallone; Executive Producer, Gene Kirkwood; Photography, James Crabe; Editor, Richard Halsey; Art Director, James H. Spencer; Music, Bill Conti; Performed by Valentine; Design, Bill Cassidy; Assistant Directors, Fred Gallo, Steve Perry; In color; Rated PG; 119 minutes; November release.

CAST

Rocky	Sylvester Stallone
Adrian	Talia Shire
Paulie	Burt Young
Apollo	Carl Weathers
Mickey	Burgess Meredith
Jergens	Thayer David
Gazzo	Joe Spinell
Mike	Jimmy Gambina
Fight Announcer	Bill Baldwin
Cut Man	Al Salvani
Ice Rink Attendant	George Memmoli
Marie	Jodi Letizia
TV Commentators	Diana Lewis, George O'Hanlon
TV Interviewer	Larry Carroll
Dipper	Stan Shaw
Special Guest Appearance	Joe Frazier
Bartender	Don Sherman
Owner of Pet Shop	Jane Marla Robbins
Fats	Jack Hollander
Club Fight Announcer	Billy Sands
Club Fighter	Pedro Lovell
Apollo's Corner	DeForest Covan
Club Corner Man	Simmy Bow
Apollo's Trainer	Tony Burton
Apollo's Cornerman	Hank Rolike
Secretary	Shirley O'Hara
Paulie's Date	Kathleen Parker
Timekeeper	Frank Stallone
Drunk	Lloyd Kaufman
Bodyguard	Joe Sorbello
Chiptooth	Christopher Avildsen
Club Fight Referee	Frankie Van
Championship Fight Announcer	Lou Fillipo
Street Corner Singers	Valentine: Frank Stallone, Jr.,

Robert L. Tangrea, Peter Glassberg,
William E. Ring, Joseph C. Giambelluca

*1976 Academy Awards for Best Picture,
Best Director, Best Editing*

Sylvester Stallone, Carl Weathers
100 **Above: Sylvester Stallone, Burt Young**

Top: Sylvester Stallone, Burgess Meredith
Left: Sylvester Stallone, Talia Shire

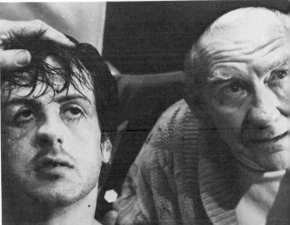

Burt Young, Sylvester Stallone, Talia Shire
Above: Diana Lewis, Sylvester Stallone
Top: Talia Shire, Sylvester Stallone

Sylvester Stallone, Burgess Meredith
Above: Stallone, Carl Weathers
Top: Sylvester Stallone

NETWORK

(UNITED ARTISTS) Producer, Howard Gottfried; Director, Sidney Lumet; Story and Screenplay, Paddy Chayefsky; Photography, Owen Roizman; Design, Philip Rosenberg; Costumes, Theoni V. Aldredge; Editor, Alan Heim; Associate Producer, Fred Caruso; Music, Elliot Lawrence; Assistant Directors, Jay Allan Hopkins, Ralph Singleton; In Panavision and Metrocolor; Rated R; 120 minutes; November release

CAST

Diana Christensen	Fay Dunaway
Max Schumacher	William Holden
Howard Beale	Peter Finch
Frank Hackett	Robert Duvall
Nelson Chaney	Wesley Addy
Arthur Jensen	Ned Beatty
Great Ahmed Kahn	Arthur Burghardt
TV Director	Bill Burrows
George Bosch	John Carpenter
Harry Hunter	Jordan Charney
Mary Ann Gifford	Kathy Cronkite
Joe Donnelly	Ed Crowley
Walter C. Amundsen	Jerome Dempsey
Barbara Schlesinger	Conchata Ferrell
Milton K. Steinman	Gene Gross
Jack Snowden	Stanley Grover
Caroline Schumacher	Cindy Grover
Bill Herron	Darryl Hickman
Arthur Zangwill	Mitchell Jason
TV Stage Manager	Paul Jenkins
Merrill Grant	Ken Kercheval
Associate Producer	Kenneth Kimmins
TV Production Assistant	Lynn Klugman
Max's Secretary	Carolyn Krigbaum
Audio Man	Zane Lasky
Tommy Pellegrino	Michael Lipton
Willie Stein	Michael Lombard
Herb Thackeray	Pirie MacDonald
TV Associate Director	Russ Petranto
Lou	Bernard Pollack
Sam Haywood	Roy Poole
Edward George Ruddy	William Prince
Helen Miggs	Sasha von Scherler
Robert McDonough	Lane Smith
Giannini	Theodore Sorel
Louise Schumacher	Beatrice Straight
Mosaic Figure	Fred Stuthman
TV Technical Director	Cameron Thomas
Laureen Hobbs	Marlene Warfield
Hunter's Secretary	Lydia Wilson
Narrator	Lee Richardson

1976 Academy Awards for Best Actor (Peter Finch), Best Actress (Faye Dunaway), Best Supporting Actress (Beatrice Straight), Best Original Screenplay

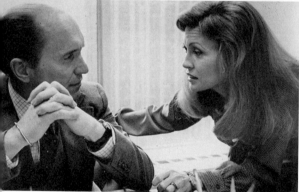

Robert Duvall, William Holden
Above: Duvall, Faye Dunaway

102

Faye Dunaway Top Left: William Holden,
Faye Dunaway Below: Peter Finch, Holden

Robert Duvall, Faye Dunaway, William Holden
Above: Peter Finch Top: Peter Finch, Robert
Duvall, Ned Beatty

Faye Dunaway Above: Beatrice Straight,
William Holden Top: Faye Dunaway,
Marlene Warfield

THE LAST TYCOON

(PARAMOUNT) Producer, Sam Spiegel; Director, Elia Kazan; Screenplay, Harold Pinter; Based on novel by F. Scott Fitzgerald; Photography, Victor Kemper; Music, Maurice Jarre; Design, Gene Callahan; Editor, Richard Marks; Costumes, Anna Hill Johnstone; Art Director, Jack Collis; Assistant Director, Danny McCauley; In Panavision and Technicolor; Rated PG; 122 minutes; November release

CAST

Monroe Stahr	Robert DeNiro
Rodriguez	Tony Curtis
Pat Brady	Robert Mitchum
Didi	Jeanne Moreau
Brimmer	Jack Nicholson
Boxley	Donald Pleasence
Kathleen Moore	Ingrid Boulting
Fleishacker	Ray Milland
Red Ridingwood	Dana Andrews
Cecilia Brady	Theresa Russell
Wylie	Peter Strauss
Popolos	Tige Andrews
Marcus	Morgan Farley
Guide	John Carradine
Doctor	Jeff Corey
Stahr's Secretary	Diane Shalet
Seal Trainer	Seymour Cassell
Edna	Angelica Huston
Brady's Secretary	Bonnie Bartlett, Sharon Masters
Norman	Eric Christmas
Mrs. Rodriguez	Leslie Curtis
Butler	Lloyd Kino
Assistant Editor	Brendan Burns
Lady in restaurant	Carrie Miller
Hairdresser	Peggy Feury
Lady Writer	Betsey Jones-Moreland
Girl on beach	Patricia Singer

Dana Andrews, Robert DeNiro
Top: Robert DeNiro

Top: Ingrid Boulting, Robert DeNiro
Below: Robert DeNiro, Theresa Russell

Ray Milland, Robert Mitchum, Jeanne Moreau, Robert DeNiro
Top Left: Robert DeNiro, Ingrid Boulting Below: Robert Mitchum
Top Right: Jeanne Moreau

PIPE DREAMS

(AVCO EMBASSY) Executive Producer, Barry Hankerson; Written, Produced and Directed by Stephen Verona; All songs performed by Gladys Knight and The Pips; Associate Producer, Jack Cummins; Assistant Directors, Jerry Lee Ballew, Cheryl Downey; Editor, Robert L. Estrin; Costumes, Glenda Ganis; In Panavision and color; Rated PG; 89 minutes; November release

CAST

Maria Wilson	Gladys Knight
Rob Wilson	Barry Hankerson
The Duke	Bruce French
Loretta	Sherry Bain
Mike Thompson	Wayne Tippit
Lydia	Altovise Davis
Sally	Sylvia Hayes
Moose	Frank McRae
Rosey Rottencrotch	Carol Ita White
Slimey Sue	Bobbi Shaw
Johnny Monday	Arnold Johnson
Mini-Guinea	Robert Corso
Two Street Betty	Sally Kirkland
Hollow Legs	Redmond Gleeson
Easy Money	David Byrd
Dave Anderson	Bruce Kimball
Franklin	John Mitchum
Palooka Joe	John Leoning
Dirty Diane	Kelly Britt
Maryalyce	Lisa Leslie
Big Red	Ben Bates
Burly Woman	Isabelle Horn
Old Lady	Margaret Wiley
Boat Captain	Charles Silverman

Top Left: Gladys Knight, Barry Hankerson
Below: Barry Hankerson, Gladys Knight, Bruce French

Arnold Johnson

Bobbi Shaw, Barry Hankerson, Gladys Knight

TWO-MINUTE WARNING

(UNIVERSAL) Producer, Edward S. Feldman; Director, Larry Peerce; Screenplay, Edward Hume; Based on novel by George LaFountaine; Photography, Gerald Hirschfeld; Art Director, Herman A. Blumenthal; Editor, Eve Newman, Walter Hannemann; Music, Charles Fox; Assistant Directors, Ken Swor, David O. Sosna; In Panavision and Technicolor; Rated R; 115 minutes; November release

CAST

Holly	Charlton Heston
Button	John Cassavetes
McKeever	Martin Balsam
Mike Ramsay	Beau Bridges
Lucy	Marilyn Hassett
Steve	David Janssen
Sandman	Jack Klugman
Janet	Gena Rowlands
Pickpocket	Walter Pidgeon
Paul	Brock Peters
Al	David Groh
Priest	Mitchell Ryan
Charlie Tyler	Joe Kapp
Peggy Ramsay	Pamela Bellwood
Jeffrey	Jon Korkes
Lt. Calloway	William Bryant
Mr. Green	Allan Miller
TV Director	Andy Sidaris
Assistant TV Directors	Ron Sheldon, Stanford Blum
Sniper	Warren Miller
Ted Shelley	Vincent Baggetta
Portman	Stewart Steinberg
Pickpocket's Accomplice	Juli Bridges
Tyler's Girl Friend	Brooke Mills
Ramsay Children	Brad Savage, Reed Diamond
Sandman's Girl Friend	Lina Raymond
Network Executive	Ross Durfee
Girl in TV Truck	Jenny Maybrook
Los Angeles Coach	Gerry Okuneff
Baltimore Coach	Tom Fears
Button's Wife	Sandy Johnson

and Buck Young, Jess Nadelman, Allan Eisenman, Fred Hice, Richard Feldman, Lisa Lyke, Dick Winslow, Jack Brodsky, Arnold Carr, Shelley Siverstein, J. A. Preston, James Parkes, Garry Waldberg, Kate Archer, Colin Hamilton, Gracia Lee, Robert Ginty, Richard Hinz, Forrest Wood, Terry Hinz, Boris Aplon, Edward McNally, Ray Nadeau, John Ramsay, Tom Huff, Patty Elder, Christine Nelson, Holly Irving, Eugene Daniels, Henry Deas, Sander Peerce, Glen Wilder, David Cass, Karl Lukas, Hanna Hertelendy, John West, Sharri Zak, Howard Cosell, Frank Gifford, Dick Enberg

Top: John Cassavetes, Charlton Heston
Right: David Janssen, Gena Rowlands

Marilyn Hassett, David Groh
Above: John Cassavetes

THE ENFORCER

(WARNER BROS.) Producer, Robert Daley; Director, James
Fargo; Screenplay, Stirling Silliphant, Dean Reisner; Story, Gail
Morgan Hickman, S. W. Schurr; Based on characters created by
Harry Julian Fink, R. M. Fink; Art Director, Allen E. Smith;
Editors, Ferris Webster, Joel Cox; Music, Jerry Fielding; Photog-
raphy, Charles W. Short; Assistant Directors, Joe Cavalier, Joe
Florence, Billy Ray Smith; In Panavision and DeLuxe Color; A
Malpaso Co. film; Rated R; 96 minutes; December release

CAST

Harry Callahan	Clint Eastwood
Lt. Bressler	Harry Guardino
Capt. McKay	Bradford Dillman
Kate Moore	Tyne Daly
DiGeorgio	John Mitchum
Bobby Maxwell	DeVeren Bookwalter
The Mayor	John Crawford

Clint Eastwood

Top: Tyne Daly, Clint Eastwood

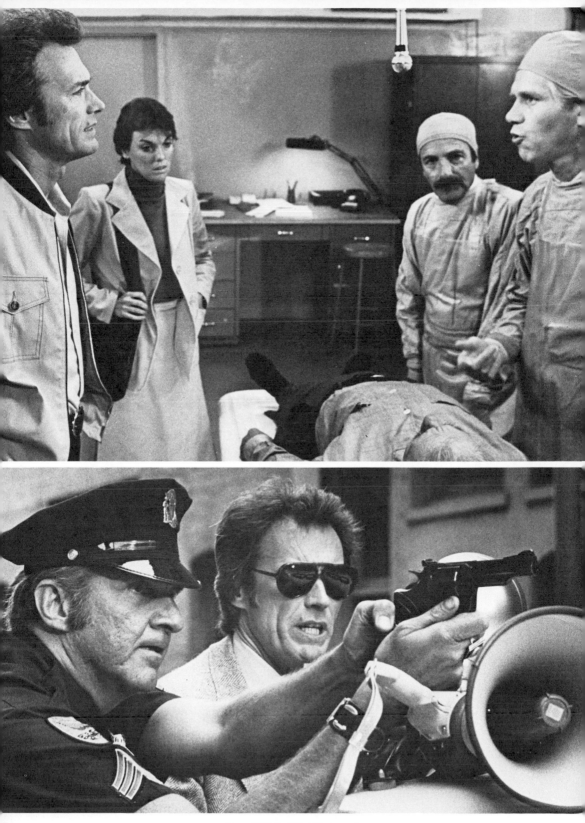

Tom O'Neil, Clint Eastwood
Top: Clint Eastwood, Tyne Daly, Robert Behling

A STAR IS BORN

(WARNER BROS.) Producer, Jon Peters; Director, Frank Pierson; Executive Producer, Barbra Streisand; Screenplay, John Gregory Dunne, Joan Didion, Frank Pierson; Based on story by William Wellman, Robert Carson; Photography, Robert Surtees; Editor, Peter Zinner; Design, Polly Platt; Assistant Directors, Stu Fleming, Michele Ader, Ed Ledding; Art Director, William Hiney; Choreography, David Winters; In Panavision and Metrocolor; Rated R; 140 minutes; December release

CAST

Esther Hoffman	Barbra Streisand
John Norman Howard	Kris Kristofferson
Bobby Ritchie	Gary Busey
Gary Danziger	Oliver Clark
Oreos	Vanetta Fields, Clydie King
Quentin	Marta Heflin
Bebe Jesus	M. G. Kelly
Photography	Sally Kirkland
Freddie	Joanne Linville
Mo	Uncle Rudy
Brian	Paul Mazursky

1976 Academy Award for Best Song ("Evergreen")

Left: Barbra Streisand

The Oreos, Barbra Streisand (C)

Tony Orlando, Kris Kristofferson, Barbra Streisand
Top: (L) Kris Kristofferson, Barbra Streisand (R) Kris Kristofferson

SILVER STREAK

(20th CENTURY-FOX) Executive Producers, Frank Yablans, Martin Ransohoff; Producers, Edward K. Milkis, Thomas L. Miller; Director, Arthur Hiller; Screenplay, Colin Higgins; Music, Henry Mancini; Photography, David M. Walsh; Editor, David Bretherton; Design, Alfred Sweeney; Assistant Directors, Jack Roe, Lively Andrew Stone; In DeLuxe Color; Rated PG; 113 minutes; December release

CAST

George Caldwell	Gene Wilder
Hilly Burns	Jill Clayburgh
Grover Muldoon	Richard Pryor
Roger Devereau	Patrick McGoohan
Sweet	Ned Beatty
Sheriff Chauncey	Clifton James
Mr. Whiney	Ray Walston
Johnson (Prof. Schreiner)	Stefan Gierasch
Chief	Len Birman
Plain Jane	Valerie Curtin
Reace (Goldtooth)	Richard Kiel
Rita Babtree	Lucille Benson
Ralston	Scatman Crothers
Jerry Jarvis	Fred Willard
Burt	Delos Smith
Blue-haired Lady	Matilda Calnan
Shoeshiner	Nick Stewart
Mexican Mama San	Margarita Garcia
Conductor	Jack Mather
Porter	Lloyd White
Benny	Ed McNamara
Night Watchman	Ray Goth
Engineer	John Day
Cab Driver	Tom Erhart
Moose	Gordon Hurst
Fat Men	Jack O'Leary, Lee McLaughlin
Conventioneers	Henry Beckman, Steve Weston, Harvey Atkin

Scatman Crothers, Richard Pryor, Gene Wilder, Jill Clayburgh

Top: Richard Pryor, Gene Wilder, Jill Clayburgh, Patrick McGoohan, Ray Walston

Richard Pryor, Gene Wilder Above: **Gene Wilder,
Jill Clayburgh** Top: **Ned Beatty, Gene Wilder**

Richard Pryor, Gene Wilder, Jill Clayburgh
Top: **Patrick McGoohan, Richard Pryor**

NICKELODEON

(COLUMBIA) Producers, Irwin Winkler, Robert Chartoff; Director, Peter Bogdanovich; Screenplay, W. D. Richter, Peter Bogdanovich; Associate Producer, Frank Marshall; Photography, Laszlo Kovacs; Art Director, Richard Berger; Costumes, Theadora Van Runkle; Editor, William Carruth; Assistant Director, Jack Sanders, Choreographer, Rita Abrams; In Panavision and Metrocolor; Rated PG; 121 minutes; December release

CAST

Leo Harrigan	Ryan O'Neal
Buck Greenway	Burt Reynolds
Alice Forsyte	Tatum O'Neal
H. H. Cobb	Brian Keith
Marty Reeves	Stella Stevens
Franklin Frank	John Ritter
Kathleen Cooke	Jane Hitchcock
Dobie	Harry Carey, Jr.
Jim	James Best
Reginald Kingsley	George Gaynes
Logan	M. Emmet Walsh

and Jack Perkins, Brion James, Sidney Armus, Joe Warfield, Tamar Cooper, Alan Gibbs, Mathew Anden, Lorenzo Music, Arnold Soboloff, Jeffrey Byron, Priscilla Pointer, Don Calfa, Philip Bruns, Edward Marshall, John Blackwell, E. J. Andre, Christa Lang, Maurice Manson, Louis Guss, Frank Marshall, Andrew Winner, Matilda Calnan, Gustar Unger, Bertil Unger, James O'-Connell, Ric Mancini, Mark Dennis, E. Hampton Beagle, Hedgemon Lewis, Bill Riddle, Dino Judd, Jack Verbois, John Chappell, Carleton Ripple, Rita Abrams, Sara Jane Gould, Mary Beth Bell, Miriam Byrd Nethery, Rusty Blitz, Les Josephson, Tom Erhart, Griffin O'Neal, Patricia O'Neal, Morgan Farley, Anna Thea, Elaine Partnow, Joseph G. Medalis, Billy Beck, Roger Hampton, Gordon Hurst, Charles Thomas Murphy, Hamilton Camp, Ted Gehring, Stanley Brock, Vincent Milana, Lee Gordon Moore, John Finnegan, Christian Grey, Robert E. Ball, Chief Elmer Tugsmith, Rude Frimel, Hal Needham, Julie Ann Johnson, Joe Amsler, Ron Stein, Charles Tamburro

Left: Ryan O'Neal

Jane Hitchcock, Ryan O'Neal, Burt Reynolds

Tatum O'Neal

Stella Stevens Above: Burt Reynolds, Jane Hitchcock, Ryan O'Neal, Stella Stevens

Burt Reynolds, Jane Hitchcock, Ryan O'Neal Above: Burt Reynolds, Tatum O'Neal Top: Ryan O'Neal, Brian Keith, John Ritter, Reynolds

KING KONG

(PARAMOUNT) Producer, Dino De Laurentiis; Director, John Guillermin; Screenplay, Lorenzo Semple, Jr.; Executive Producers, Federico De Laurentiis, Christian Ferry; Photography, Richard H. Kline; Music, John Barry; Editor, Ralph E. Winters; Design, Mario Chiari, Dale Hennesy; Assistant Directors, David McGiffert, Kurt Neumann, Pat Kehoe; Costumes, Moss Mabry; Choreography, Claude Thompson; In Panavision and color; Rated PG; 134 minutes; December release

CAST

Jack Prescott	Jeff Bridges
Fred Wilson	Charles Grodin
Dwan	Jessica Lange
Captain Ross	John Randolph
Bagley	Rene Auberjonois
Boan	Julius Harris
Joe Perko	Jack O'Halloran
Sunfish	Dennis Fimple
Carnahan	Ed Lauter
Garcia	Jorge Moreno
Timmons	Mario Gallo
Chinese Cook	John Lone
Army General	Garry Halberg
City Official	John Agar
Petrox Chairman	Sid Conrad
Army Helicopter Pilot	George Whiteman
Air Force Colonel	Wayne Heffley
Ape Masked Man	Keny Long

Kong, and top with Jessica Lange

1976 Academy Award for Special Effects

Jessica Lange, Jeff Bridges

THE SHAGGY D.A.

(BUENA VISTA) Executive Producer, Ron Miller; Producer, Bill Anderson; Director, Robert Stevenson; Screenplay, Don Tait; Suggested by "The Hound of Florence" by Felix Salten; Photography, Frank Phillips; Music, Buddy Baker; Title song sung by Dean Jones; Art Directors, John B. Mansbridge, Perry Ferguson; Editors, Bob Bring, Norman Palmer; Assistant Director, Christopher Seiter; A Walt Disney Production in Technicolor; Rated G; 91 minutes; December release

CAST

Wilby Daniels	Dean Jones
Betty Daniels	Suzanne Pleshette
Tim	Tim Conway
John Slade	Keenan Wynn
Katrinka Muggelberg	Jo Anne Worley
Raymond	Dick Van Patten
Brian Daniels	Shane Sinutko
Eddie Roschak	Vic Tayback
Admiral Brenner	John Myhers
Freddie	Dick Bakalyan
Dip	Warren Berlinger
T. V. Director	Ronnie Schell
TV Interviewer	Jonathan Daly
Howie Clemmings	John Fiedler
Prof. Whatley	Hans Conried
Sheldon	Michael McGreevey
Desk Sergeant	Richard O'Brien
Roller Rink Announcer	Dick Lane
Waiter	Benny Rubin
Song Chairman	Ruth Gillette
Policeman	Hank Jones
Manageress	Iris Adrian
Bartender	Pat McCormick

and Henry Slate, Milton Frome, Walt Davis, Albert Able, Mary Ann Gibson, Helene Winston, Joan Crosby, Sarah Fankboner, Danny Wells, Herb Vigran, Olan Soule, Vern Rowe, Karl Lukas, John Hayes, Christina Anderson, George Kirby (canine character voices)

**Left: Dean Jones, Shane Sinutko,
Suzanne Pleshette**

Tim Conway, Jo Anne Worley

Pat McCormick, Tim Conway

**Shane Sinutko, Tim Conway, Dean Jones
Above: Dean Jones Top: Suzanne Pleshette,
Dean Jones, Keenan Wynn**

**Keenan Wynn, Dean Jones Above: Jones, Tim
Conway, Pat McCormick Top: Dean Jones,
Suzanne Pleshette**

John Cassavetes

MIKEY & NICKY

(PARAMOUNT) Executive Producer, Bud Austin; Produce[r]
Michael Hausman; Direction and Screenplay, Elaine May; Ph[o]-
tography, Victor J. Kemper; Editor, John Carter; Music, Joh[n]
Strauss; Designer, Paul Sylbert; Assistant Directors, Pet[e]
Scoppa, Michele Adler; Editor, Sheldon Kahn; In Panavision an[d]
Movielab Color; Rated R; 119 minutes; December release

CAST

Mikey	Peter Fal[k]
Nicky	John Cassavete[s]
Kinney	Ned Beat[ty]
Annie	Rose Arric[k]
Nell	Carol Grac[e]
Sid Fine	William Hicke[y]
Dave Resnick	Sanford Meisn[er]
Jan	Joyce Van Patte[n]
Bus Driver	M. Emmet Wals[h]
Hotel Clerk	Sy Trave[rs]
Counter Man	Peter Scopp[a]
Jan's Mother	Virginia Smi[th]
Lady on bus	Jean Shevl[in]
Harry	Danny Kle[in]
Candy Store Man	Martin Wolfso[n]
Mel	Eugene Hobgo[od]
Bar Patron	David Pendleto[n]
Bartender	William Gi[?]
Shirley	Marilyn Randa[ll]
Franklyn	Reuben Gree[n]

Top: John Cassavetes, Peter Falk

John Cassavetes, Marilyn Randall
Top: John Cassavetes, Peter Falk

Peter Falk, John Cassavetes

BOUND FOR GLORY

(UNITED ARTISTS) Producers, Robert F. Blumofe, Harold Leventhal; Director, Hal Ashby; Screenplay, Robert Getchell; Based on autobiography by Woody Guthrie; Photography, Haskell Wexler; Editors, Robert Jones, Pembroke J. Herring; Design, Michael Haller; Art Director, William Sully, James H. Spencer; Assistant Director, Charles A. Myers; In DeLuxe Color; Rated PG; 147 minutes; December release

CAST

Woody Guthrie	David Carradine
Ozark Bule	Ronny Cox
Mary Guthrie	Melinda Dillon
Pauline	Gail Strickland
Locke	John Lehne
Slim Snedeger	Ji-Tu Cumbuka
Luther Johnson	Randy Quaid
Liz Johnson	Elizabeth Macey
Agent	Allan Miller

1976 Academy Awards for Best Cinematography, Best Scoring

Left: David Carradine

Ji-Tu Cumbaka, David Carradine
Above: David Carradine, Melinda Dillon

James Jeter, David Carradine, Ti-Ju Cumbaka
Above: David Carradine (L)

David Carradine, Ronny Cox Above: Carradine,
Betty Mazik, Randy Quaid Top: Carradine,
Melinda Dillon

David Carradine
Top: Gail Strickland, David Carradine

VOYAGE OF THE DAMNED

(AVCO EMBASSY) Producer, Robert Fryer; Director, Stuart Rosenberg; Associate Producer, Bill Hill; Photography, Billy Williams; Screenplay, Steve Shagan, David Butler; Design, Phyllis Dalton; Art Director, Jack Stephens; Music, Lalo Schifrin; Assistant Director, David Tringham; Editor, Tom Priestly; In Eastmancolor and Panavision; Rated PG; 155 minutes; December release

CAST

Denise Kreisler	Faye Dunaway
Captain Gustav Schroeder	Max Von Sydow
Dr. Egon Kreisler	Oskar Werner
Max Gunter	Malcolm McDowell
Estedes	Orson Welles
Remos	James Mason
Lilian Rosen	Lee Grant
Morris Troper	Ben Gazzara
Mira Hauser	Katharine Ross
Professor Weiler	Luther Adler
Clasing	Michael Constantine
Admiral Canaris	Denholm Elliott
Miguel Benitez	Jose Ferrer
Anna Rosen	Lynne Frederick
Otto Schiendick	Helmut Griem
Alice Feinchild	Julie Harris
Rebecca Weiler	Wendy Hiller
Dr. Hans Glauner	Donald Houston
Aaron Pozner	Paul Koslo
Mr. Hauser	Nehemiah Persoff
President Bru	Fernando Rey
Commander	Leonard Rossiter
Mrs. Hauser	Maria Schell
Dr. Max Strauss	Victor Spinetti
Leni Strauss	Janet Suzman
Carl Rosen	Sam Wanamaker
Joseph Manasse	Jonathan Pryce

and Keith Barron, Ian Cullen, David Daker, Constantin de Goguel, David De Keyser, Carl Duering, Brian Gilbert, Georgina Hale, Don Henderson, Bernard Hepton, Anthony Higgins, Frederick Jaeger, Della McDermott, Garry McDermott, Gunter Meisner, Roy Pattison, Toby Salaman, Milo Sperber, Adele Strong, Genevieve West, Ben Aris, George Batalla, Giorgio Bosso, Chris Carbis, Robert Case, Stephen Churchett, Luis Citges, Gerry Crampton, Michael Damian, Jan Denyer, Joe Dunne, Laura Gemser, Henry Hackett, Robin Halstead, Paul Humpoletz, Chris Jenkinson, Bernard Kaye, Robin Marchal, Elmer Modlin, Juan Moreno, Douglas Nottage, Brian Ralph, Vikki Richards, Marika Rivera, Ina Shriver, Philip Stone, Ana Viera, Florilyn Waddell

Left: Nehemiah Persoff, Maria Schell
Above: Jonathan Pryce, Max von Sydow
Top: Max von Sydow

Wendy Hiller, Luther Adler

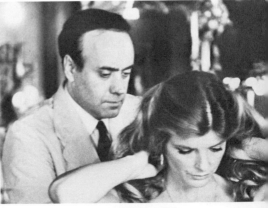

Victor Spinetti, Katharine Ross

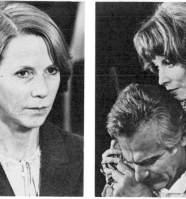

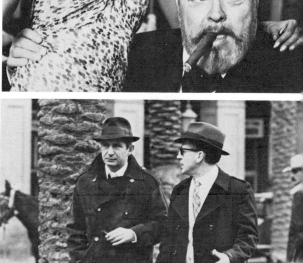

**Oskar Werner, Faye Dunaway Above: Julie Harris,
Sam Wanamaker, Lee Grant Top: Malcolm McDowell,
Lynne Frederick Below: Jonathan Pryce, Paul Koslo**

**Ben Gazzara, Bernard Hepton Above: Laura
Gemser, Orson Welles Top: Faye Dunaway,
Oskar Werner**

"The Divine Obsession"

Richard Pryor, Fred Williamson
in "Adios Amigo"

THE DIVINE OBSESSION (Melody Films) Producers, Louis Su (Lloyd Kaufman), David Wynn; Director, Louis Su; Photography, Frank Murdock; Editor, Louis Su; In color; Rated X; 95 minutes; January release. CAST: Julia Franklin (Julia), Bree Anthony (Patty), National Velvet (Peaches), Tony Dester (Peter), Alan Marlo (Ted) Levi Richards (Oswald) Eric Edwards (Frank), Roderick Ghyka(1st Producer), Phil Esposito (Sidney), Don Veril (Harold), and Carl Ash, Horace Moon, Robert Worker, Lottie Hallsey, Roberta Woods, Steven Long, Rosie O'Hare, Bill Brent

ADIOS AMIGO (Atlas Films) Produced, Directed and Written by Fred Williamson; Executive Producer, Lee B. Winkler; Music, Luici de Jesus, William M. Stevenson; In Panavision and Eastmancolor; Rated PG; 87 minutes; January release. CAST: Fred Williamson (Ben), Richard Pryor (Sam), Thalmus Rasulala (Noah), and James Brown, Robert Phillips, Mike Henry, Suhaila Farhat, Victoria Jee, Lynne Jackson, Heidi Dobbs, Liz Treadwell, Joy Lober

CARNAL HAVEN Produced, Directed, Written, Photographed and Edited by Troy Beny; Assistant Producer, Sharon Thorpe; Assistant Cameraman, Fernando Fortes; Music, Carl Esser; In color; Rated X; January release. CAST: Sharon Thorpe, Leslie Bovee, John L. Dupre, Annette Haven, Miguel Jones, Pat Lee, Bonnie Holiday, Bob Migliano

PEEPER (20th Century-Fox) Producers, Irwin Winkler, Robert Chartoff; Director, Peter Hyams; Screenplay, W. D. Richter from novel "Deadfall" by Keith Laumer; Photography, Earl Rath; Editor, James Mitchell; Music, Richard Clements; Design, Albert Brenner; Decoration, Marvin March; Assistant Director, Hal Needham; In DeLuxe Color; Rated PG; 87 minutes; January release. CAST: Michael Caine (Tucker), Natalie Wood (Ellen), Kitty Winn (Mianne) Thayer David (Frank), Liam Dunn (Billy), Dorothy Adams (Mrs. Prendergast), Timothy Agoglia Carey (Sid), Don Calfa (Rosie), Michael Constantine (Anglich), Liz Renay (Dancer), Snag Werris (Comic), Guy Marks (Man in Alley), Margo Winkler (Lady with luggage)

SHERLICK HOLMES (Webster) Producer, Ralph Ell; Director, Tim McCoy; In color; Rated X; January release. CAST: Harry Reems, Zebedy Colt, Bobby Astyr, Elvera, Candy Love, Annie Sprinkle

NIGHT PLEASURES (San Fran 1) Producer, William Dancer; Director, Hans Christian; In color; Rated X; January release. CAST: Melba Raye, John Leslie Dupre, John Seeman, Alice Fairchild, Joan Manning, Ken Cotten, Turk Lyon, P. L. Mann, Pat Desado

THE LEGEND OF BIGFOOT (Palladium Pictures) Producer, Stephen Houston Smith; Director, Harry S. Winer; Executive Producers, Ivan Marx, Don Reese; Screenplay, Harry S. Winer, Paula Labrot; Music, Don Peake; Editor, Paula Labrot; Color by CFI; Rated G; 76 minutes; January release. A documentary about the missing link.

HELP ME. . . . I'M POSSESSED (Riviera) Directed by Charles Nizet; Rated PG; In Eastmancolor; January release. CAST: Bill Greer, Deedy Peters

WHITE SLAVERY IN NEW YORK (Independent) No credits available. Rated X; In color; January release. CAST: Kim Pope (Jackie), Don Millo (Editor), Ty Windsor (Rocco), Stephanie (Suzy), Brenda Gill (Lauri)

LITTLE ANGEL PUSS (DeNeuve Sisters) Director, Danielle de Neuve; In color; Rated X; January release. CAST: Giovanina, Susan Catharine, Sharon Thorpe, Dave Brooks, Pharaoh Amos, Ric Lutze

TARZ & JANE & BOY & CHEETA (Fine Brothers) (Ded Films) Producer-Director, Hans Johnson; In color; Rated X; 80 minutes; January release. CAST: Jennifer Welles (Cynthia), Sammy Teen (Kevin), Serena (Student), Sharon Thorpe (Teacher), Terri Hall (Molly), Seymour Ashley (Jeff), Eric Von Shrokehardt (Clem), Mary Stuart (Jessica), Marc Anthony (Mel), Bree Anthony (Lisa), Al Goldstein (Al), Arlana Blue (Lois), Bobby Astyr (Dick)

Michael Caine, Natalie Wood, Thayer David
in "Peeper"

"Carnal Haven"

Elliott Gould, Fred Williamson
in "Mean Johnny Barrows"

"Hugo the Hippo"

STARBIRD AND SWEET WILLIAM (Howco International) Producer, Dick Alexander; Director, Jack B. Hivley; Screenplay, Axel Gruenberg; Music, A. Martinez; In Eastmancolor; Rated G; 90 minutes; January release. CAST: A. Martinez, Louise Fitch, Dan Haggerty, Ancil Cook, Skip Homier, Skeeter Vaughn, Monika Ramirez

CARNIVAL OF BLOOD (Monarch) Produced and Directed by Leonard Kirtman: In color; Rated PG; January release. CAST: Earle Edgerton, Judith Resnick

THE CHARITY BALL (No credits available) Rated X; In color; January release. CAST: Andrea True, Marc Stevens, Cindy West

MEAN JOHNNY BARROWS (Atlas) Executive Producer, Lee Winkler; Director, Fred Williamson; A Ramana Production; In Panavision and Movielab Color; Rated R; 90 minutes; January release. CAST: Fred Williamson (Johnny), Roddy McDowall (Tony), Stuart Whitman (Maurio), Jenny Sherman (Nancy), Luher Adler (Don Riconi), Tony Caruso (Don DaVince), Mike Henry (Carlo), R. G. Armstrong (Richard), Elliott Gould (Professor), Bob Phillips, Aaron Banks, James Brown

HUGO THE HIPPO (20th Century-Fox) Executive Producer, George Barrie; Producer, Robert Halmi; Director, Bill Feigenbaum; Screenplay, Tom Baum; Design, Graham Percy; Music and Lyrics, Robert Larimer; Score, Burt Keyes; In color; Rated G; 78 minutes; January release. Animated feature using the voices of Robert Morley, Paul Lynde, Jesse Emmet, Lance Taylor, Sr., Ronnie Cox, Len Maxwell, Percy Rodriguez, Burl Ives, Marie and Jimmy Osmond

HONEYPIE (Ded Films) Producer-Director, Hans Johnson; In color; Rated X; 80 minutes; January release. CAST: Jennifer Welles (Cynthia), Sammy Teen (Kevin), Serena (Student), Sharon Thorpe (Teacher), Terri Hall (Molly), Seymour Ashley (Jeff), Eric Von Shrokehardt (Clem), Mary Stuart (Jessica), Mac Anthony (Mel), Bree Anthony (Lisa), Al Goldstein (Al), Arlana Blue (Lois), Bobby Astyr (Dick)

THE COMMITMENT (Borden) Producer, Elliott Brandes; Director, Richard Grand, Louis A. Shaffner; Screenplay, Andrew Laskos, Louis A. Shaffner, Richard Grand; From story by Barbara Grand; Photography, Louis A. Shaffner; Editor, Elen Orson; Music, Dobie Gray, John D'Andrea; Songs sung by Dobie Gray; Art Director, Karen Shaffner, Janice Orson; In color; Rated PG; 88 minutes: January release. CAST: Richard Grand (Steve), Barbara Graham (Amie), Joseph Turkel (Jules), Diane Vincent (Terri), Jon Ian Jacobs (Bill), Tom Bower (Abe), Bruce Kirby (Simon), Richard Adams, Frank Arata, Mimi Davis, Cal Haynes, Esther Sutherland, Jeremiah Gorwitz, Syl Words, Peg Shirley, John Kirby, Joe Valino, Carol McGinnis, Allen Garfield

DR. BLACK MR. HYDE (Dimension) Producer, Charles Walker; Director, William Crain; Screenplay, Larry LeBron; Photography, Tak Fujimoto; Music, Johnny Pate; Editor, Jack Horger; In Metrocolor; Rated R; 87 minutes; January release. CAST: Bernie Casey (Dr. Pride/Hyde), Rosalind Cash, Marie O'Henry, Ji-Tu Cumbuka, Milt Kogan, Stu Gilliam

LAS VEGAS LADY (Crown International) Producers, Joseph Zappala, Gene Slott; Director, Noel Nosseck; Screenplay, Walter Dallenbach; Photography, Stephen Katz; Editor, Robert Gordon; Music, Alan Silverstri; In color; Rated PG; 87 minutes; January release. CAST: Stella Stevens (Lucky), Stuart Whitman (Vic), George DiCenzo (Eversull), Lynne Moody (Carole), Linda Scruggs (Lisa), Joseph della Sorte (A.C.), Jesse White (Big Jake), Hank Robinson, Karl Lukas, Emilia Dallenback, Max Starkey, Andrew Stevens, Frank Bonner, Walter Smith, Jack Gordon, Stephanie Faulkner, Ava Readdy, Gene Slott, Tony Bill

BARN OF THE NAKED DEAD (Twin World) Produced and Written by Gerald Cormier; Director, Alan Rudolf; In color; Rated R; 86 minutes; February release. CAST: Andrew Prine, Manuella Theiss, Sherry Alberoni, Gyl Roland, Al Cormier

JACK AND THE BEANSTALK (Columbia) Direction and Screenplay, Peter J. Solmo; In color; Rated G; 92 minutes; February release. An animated feature.

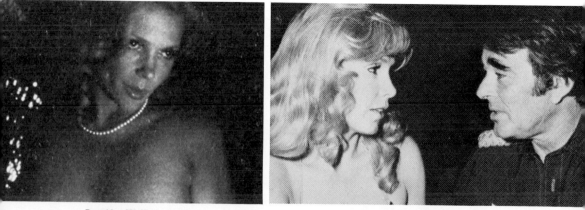

Jennifer Welles
in "Honeypie"

Stella Stevens, Stuart Whitman
in "Las Vegas Lady"

**Sharon Thorpe
in "3 A.M."**

**Al Poe
in "Tongue"**

SHRIEK OF THE MUTILATED (Film Brokers Ltd) Producer, Ed Adlum; Director, Michael Findlay; Screenplay, Ed Kelleher, Ed Adlum; In color; Rated R; February release. CAST: Alan Brock, Tawm Mellis, Jennifer Stock, Michael Harris, Darcy Brown

DIXIE Producer-Director, Steve Brown; In color; Rated X; February release. CAST: Abigail Clayton, Candy Redding, Turk Lyon

3 A. M. (Westwood) Producer-Director, Robert McCallum; Screenplay, Tony Trelos; Music, Peter Van Den Beemt; In color; Rated X; February release. CAST: Georgina Spelvin (Kate), Rhonda Gallard (Mother), Charles Hooper (Ronny), Claire Dia (Stacy), Sharon Thorpe (neighbor), Frank Mauro (Father), Judith Hamilton (Stranger)

CHRISTY (Independent) Music, Sleepy Hollow; In color; Rated X; February release. CAST: Andrea True, Marc Stevens, Anne Christian, Harry Reems, Cindy West

RENDEZVOUS WITH ANNE (Leo Productions) Produced, Directed and Written by Lowell Pickett; In color; Rated X; February release. CAST: Lisa Troy, Keri Carpenter, Cazander Zim, Art Kane, James Brooks, Steve Gibson, Jeff Darwin

NORTH OF THE SUN (American Cinema) Producer-Director, Gordon Eastman; In Technicolor; Rated G; 84 minutes; February release. A documentary about an Eskimo community.

THE WITCH WHO CAME FROM THE SEA (Moonstone) Producer-Director, Matt Cimber; Screenplay, Robert Thom; Music, Herschell Burke Gilbert; In Todd-AO and Movielab Color; Rating R; February release. CAST: Millie Perkins, Lonny Chapman, Vanessa Brown, Peggy Feury, Rick Jason, Jean Pierre Camps, Mark Livingston

TONGUE (J & A Productions) Director, K. B.; Associate Producer, Niva Ruschell; Music, Roger Hamilton Spotts; Title Song sung by Caprice Clarke; In color; Rated X; 80 minutes; February release. CAST: Al Poe (Quasi) Brigitte Maier (Cherry), Margoh (Nancy)

FEAR OR FANTASY Produced, Directed and Written by Bob Mason; In color; Rated X; February release. CAST: Andrea True, Jennifer Jordan, Jamie Gillis, Ed Marshall

NIGHT CALLER (Essex) Director, Wes Brown; Screenplay, Dean Rogers; In color; Rated X; February release. CAST: David Book, Monique Starr, Stuart Hemple, Fran Lane, Linda Brooks, Cary Corman, Laura Bond

THE IMAGE (Audubon) Producers, Marty Richards, Gill Champion; Director, Radley Metzger; Screenplay, Jake Barnes; Photography, Rene Lefevre; Adapted from novel "L'Image" by Jean de Berg; In color; Rated X; 89 minutes; February release. CAST: Mary Mendum (Anne), Marilyn Roberts (Claire), Carl Parker (Jean)

GABLE AND LOMBARD (Universal) Producer, Harry Korshak; Director, Sidney J. Furie; Screenplay, Barry Sandler; Photography, Jordan S. Cronenweth; Designer, Edward C. Carfagno; Editor, Argyle Nelson; Costumes, Edith Head; Music, Michel Legrand; Assistant Directors, James A. Westman, Mike Messinger, Jon Triesault; In Technicolor; Rated R; 131 minutes; February release CAST: James Brolin (Gable), Jill Clayburgh (Lombard), Allen Garfield (Mayer), Red Buttons (Cooper), Joanne Linville (Ria), Melanie Mayron (Dixie), Carol McGinnis (Noreen), Noah Keen (Broderick), Alan D. Dexter (Sheriff), S. John Launer (Judge), William Bryant (Colonel), Alice Backes (Hedda), John Lehne (Kramer), Karnes (Gables' Director), Ross Elliott (Lombard's Director), Morgan Brittany (Vivien Leigh), Aron Kincaid (Guest), Betsy Jones-Moreland, Jodean Russo, Drew Michaels, Richard Gittings, Sally Kemp, Army Archerd, Frank Stell, Jack Griffin, Andy Albin, Ivan Bonar

"The Image"

**James Brolin, Jill Clayburgh
in "Gable and Lombard"**

**Ben Gazzara
in "The Killing of a Chinese Bookie"**

**Edward Bell, Sharon Farrell
in "The Premonition"**

THE KILLING OF A CHINESE BOOKIE (Faces) Producer, Al Ruban; Direction and Screenplay, John Cassavetes; Design, Sam Shaw; Art Director, Phedon Papamichael; Editor, Tom Cornwell; Music, Bo Harwood; Associate Producer, Phil Burton; In color; Rated R; 135 minutes; February release. CAST: Ben Gazzara (Cosmo Vitelli), Timothy Agoglia Carey (Flo), Seymour Cassel (Mort), Robert Phillips (Phil), Morgan Woodward (John), John Red Kullers (Eddie-Red), Al Ruban (Marty), Azizi Johari (Rachel), Virginia Carrington (Betty), Meade Roberts (Mr. Sophistication), Alice Friedland (Sherry), Donna Gordon (Margo), Haji (Haji), Carol Warren (Carol), Derna Wong Davis (Derna), Kathalina Veniero (Annie), Yvette Morris (Yvette), Jack Ackerman (Musical Director), David Rowlands, Trisha Pelham, Eddie Ike Shaw, Salvatore Aprile, Gene Darcy, Benny Marino, Arlene Allison, Vince Barbi, Val Avery, Elizabeth Deering, Soto Joe Hugh, Catherine Wong, John Finnegan, Miles Ciletti, Mike Skloot, Frank Buchanan, Jason Kincaid, Frank Thomas, Jack Krupnick

JIM—THE WORLD'S GREATEST (Universal) Producer, Don Coscarelli; Direction and Screenplay, Don Coscarelli, Craig Mitchell; Executive Producers, D. A. Coscarelli, S. T. Coscarelli; Photography, Rex Metz, Don Coscarelli, Craig Mitchell; Music, Fred Myrow; Art Directors, Phil Barber, Phil Neel, E. G. Culman, James Catti; Editors, J. Terry Williams, Don Coscarelli, Craig Mitchell; Assistant Directors, Phil Bowles, Paul Pepperman, Richard Hashimoto; A Newbreeds Production in Technicolor; Rated PG; 94 minutes; February release. CAST: Gregory Harrison (Jim), Robbie Wolcott (Kelly), Rory Guy (Father), Marla Pennington (Jan), Karen McLain (Lisa), David Lloyd (Brian), Larry Gabriel (Counselor), Tony Lucatorto (Quarterback), Ralph Richmond (Coach), Tim Simmons (Kid), Reggie Bannister (Silengsly), Larry Southwick (Southwick), David Pollock (Young Jim), Larry Pollock (Principal), Shirley Coscarelli (Receptionist), Ernie Morrison (Teacher), Charlotte Mitchell (Secretary), George M. Singer, Jr. (Rowdy), Walter Inman (Terry), Mark Annerl (Guy), Steve Goldman, Cyndie Coscarelli, Keith Mitchell, D. A. Coscarelli, J. D. Sarver, Richard Byers

TANYA (Boxoffice International) Producer-Director, Nate Rogers; A Harry Novak Presentation; In color by Movielab; February release. CAST: Marie Andrews, Sasha Gibson, Suzi Adams

REFLECTIONS FROM A BRASS BED (Hemisphere) Direction and Screenplay by Richard Clausen; In Eastmancolor; Rated R; February release. CAST: Carl John, Betty Nielsen

MARRIAGE AND OTHER FOUR LETTER WORDS Executive Producer, Robert Raymond Peterson; Director, Rick Jr.; Screenplay, J. W. Mitchel; In color; Rated X; February release. CAST: Rainbow Robbins, Tom Cantrell, Brigitte

THE PREMONITION (AVCO Embassy) Executive Producer, M. Wayne Fuller; Producer-Director, Robert Allen Schnitzer; Screenplay, Anthony Mahon, Robert A. Schnitzer, Louis Pastore; Photography, Victor C. Milt; Editor, Sidney Katz; Music, Henry Mollicone, Pril Smiley; Vocals, Ellen Barber; Art Director, John Lawless; Assistant Director, Norman C. Berns; In TVC Color; Rated PG; 90 minutes; February release. CAST: Sharon Farrell (Sheri), Richard Lynch (Jude), Jeff Corey (Det. Denver), Ellen Barber (Andrea), Edward Bell (Miles), Chiitra Neogy, Danielle Brisebois, Rosemary McNamara, Thomas Williams, Margaret Graham, Roy White, Wilmuth Cooper, Robert Harper

PATTY (Trans World) Producer-Director, Robert L. Roberts; Screenplay, Joyce Richards, Robert Roberts; Photography, Henry Smafwitz; Score, Al Goodman, Sammy Lowe; In color; Rated X; 90 minutes; February release. CAST: Sarah Nicholson, Turk Turpin, Lenny Montana, Frank Sciocia, Rene Granville, Howard Don Smolen, Jamie Gillis

BLACK STREETFIGHTER (New Line) A Centaur Film; Producers, Peter S. Traynor, William D. Sklar; Director, Timothy Galfas; Executive Producer, Peter S. Traynor; Screenplay, Tim Kelly, Melvyn Frohman; In color; February release. CAST: Richard Lawson, Annazette Chase, Robert Burr

**Marlo Pennington, Gregory Harrison
in "Story of a Teenager"**

"The Black Street Fighter"

Richard Dreyfuss
in "Inserts"

Warren Berlinger, Victoria Principal, Diane Keaton,
Elliott Gould in "I Will, I Will . . . for Now"

INSERTS (United Artists) Producers, Davina Belling, Clive Parsons; Direction and Screenplay John Byrum; Associate Producer, Harry Benn; Editor, Mike Bradsell; Costumes, Shirley Russell; Art Director, John Clark; Photography, Denys Coop, John Harris; In color; Rated X; 117 minutes; February release. CAST: Richard Dreyfuss (Boy Wonder), Jessica Harper (Cathy), Stephen Davies (Rex), Veronica Cartwright (Harlene), Bob Hoskins (Big Mac)

I WILL, I WILL . . . FOR NOW (20th Century-Fox) Producer, George Barrie; Director, Norman Panama; Screenplay, Norman Panama, Albert E. Lewin; Photography, John A. Alonzo; A Brut Production; In color; Rated R; 107 minutes; February release. CAST: Elliott Gould (Les), Diane Keaton (Katie), Paul Sorvino (Lou), Victoria Principal (Jackie), Robert Alda (Dr. Magnus), Warren Berlinger (Steve), Madge Sinclair (Dr. Williams), Candy Clark (Sally), Carmen Zapata (Maria), George Tyne (Counsellor)

GREY GARDENS (Portrait Films) Produced and Directed by David Maysles and Albert Maysles; Associate Producer, Susan Froemke; Photography, Maysles Brothers; In EFX Color; Rated PG; 95 minutes; February release. Documentary on Edith Beale and her mother.

INSIDE MARILYN CHAMBERS (Mitchell Brothers) In color; rated X; 78 minutes; February release. No other credits provided. Documentary on the life of pornography star with Marilyn Chambers, Jim Mitchell, Art Mitchell, Johnny Keyes, George S.

GOODBYE, NORMA JEAN (Stirling Gold) Producer-Director, Larry Buchanan; Screenplay, Lynn Hubert, Larry Buchanan; Executive Producer, Amadeo Curcio; Photography, Bob Sherry; Music, Joe Beck; In color; Rated R; 95 minutes; February release. CAST: Misty Rowe (Norma Jean), Terence Locke (Ralph), Patch Mackenzie (Ruth), Preston Hanson (Hal), Marty Zagon (Irving), Andre Philippe, Ivey Bethune, Steve Brown, Adele Claire, Frank Curcio, Jean Sarah Frost, Stuart Lancaster, Lilyan McBride, Burr Middleton, Paula Mitchell, Garth Pillsbury

EXPOSE ME LOVELY (Mature) Produced, Directed, Edited and Written by Armand Weston; Photography, Harry Flecks; Executive Producer, Vahagn Hovannes; In color; Rated X; 96 minutes; February release. CAST: Jennifer Welles, Raf Kean, Eve Adams, Cary Lacy, Jody Maxwell

BENEATH THE MERMAIDS (Sirens) Produced and Directed by Frank Renfroe; Screenplay, Ned Weston, Frank Renfroe; Music, Peggy Reed; In color; Rated X; March release. CAST: Julia Franklin, Kim Pope, Erica Reed, Mike Shea, Diane Black, Cynthia Prescot, Darby Lloyd Rains, Arlana Blue

INVASION OF THE BLOOD FARMERS (NMD) Produced and Directed by Ed Adlum; Screenplay, Ed Kelleher, Ed Adlum; In color; Rated PG; March release. CAST: Cynthia Fleming (Onhorrid), Norman Kelly (Roy), Tanna Hunter (Jenny), Bruce Detrick (Don), Frank Iovieno (Chief)

THE PRESIDENTIAL PEEPERS (Independent) No credits available; In color; Rated X; March release. CAST: Richard M. Dixon, Tina Russell

HIGHWAY HOOKERS (Hudson) Director, Carter Stevens; In color; Rated X; March release. CAST: Linda Lovemore, Angel Barrett, Lorraine Alraune, Bree Anthony, Mike Jefferson, Eric Edwards, Leo Lovelace, Cheryl Ann White, Ruth Morgan

THE NORTHVILLE CEMETERY MASSACRE (Cannon) Produced, Directed and Photographed by William Dear and Thomas L. Dyke; In Technicolor; Rated R; March Release. CAST: David Hyry, Carson Jackson, Jan Sisk, J. Craig Collicut

TEENAGE SEX THERAPY (Art Mart) Director, Buzz Richards; In color; Rated X; March release. CAST: Annette Haven, Ann-May Tomkins, Robert Matsumoto, Ken Scutter

THE AGONY AND ECSTASY OF MICHAEL, ANGELO AND DAVID No credits available; Rated X; In color; March release. CAST: Marc Stevens, David Savage, Brian Haines

Misty Rowe
in "Goodbye, Norma Jean"

Dyanne Thorne in "Ilsa, Harem Keeper
of the Oil Sheiks"

**Glenn Corbett, Monica Gayle
in "Nashville Girl"**

**Bruce Kimmel, Cindy Williams, Stephen Nathan
in "The First Nudie Musical"**

NASHVILLE GIRL (New World) Produced and Written by Peer J. Oppenheimer; Director, Gus Trikonis; Score, Kim Richmond; Songs, Rory Bourke, Johnny Wilson, Gene Dobbins, John Wills, Bob Wills; Photography, Irv Goodnoff; In Metrocolor; Rated R; 90 minutes; March release. CAST: Monica Gayle (Jamie) Glenn Corbett (Jeb) Roger Davis (Kelly) Johnny Rodriguez (Himself), Jesse White (C. Y.), Marcie Barkin (Alice), Shirley Jo Finney (Frisky), Judith Roberts (Fran), Mary S. Harkey (Lois), Jackie Wright (Beauty), Leo Gordon (Burt)

THE CREATURE FROM BLACK LAKE (Howco International) Producer, Jim McCullough; Executive Producer, W. Lewis Ryder; Director, Joy Houck, Jr.; Screenplay, Jim McCullough, Jr; Music, Jaime Mendoza-Nava; In Todd-AO and Eastmancolor; Rating PG; 95 minutes; March release. CAST: Jack Elam, Dub Taylor, Dennis Fimple, John David Carson, Bill Thurman

SELF-SERVICE SCHOOLGIRLS (Hemisphere) A JSM Associates film in Eastmancolor; Rated R; March release. CAST: Georgette Pope, Margo Younger

BEYOND FULFILLMENT (Essex) Producer-Director, Billy Thornberg; In color; Rated X; March release. CAST: John C. Holmes, Claudine Grayson, Barbara Barton, Penni Walters, Sally Andrews

SUMMER OF LAURA (Stu Segall) Producer, Y. B. Wellington; Director, David Davidson; In color; Rated X; March release. CAST: Marsha Moon, David Hunter, Eric Edwards, Wade Nichols, Kim Pope, Helen Madigan

MUSTANG COUNTRY (Universal) Produced, Directed and Written by John Champion; Photography, J. Barry Herron; Editor, Douglas Robertson; Music, Lee Holdridge; "Follow Your Restless Dreams" sung by Denny Brooks; Assistant Directors, Frank Arrigo, Donald Granberry; In Technicolor; Rated G; 79 minutes; March release. CAST: Joel McCrea (Dan), Robert Fuller (Griff), Patrick Wayne (Tee Jay), Nika Mina (Nika)

THE FIRST NUDIE MUSICAL (Paramount) Producer, Jack Reeves; Directors, Mark Haggard, Bruce Kimmel; Screenplay, Music and Lyrics, Bruce Kimmel; Photography, Douglas Knapp; Art Director, Thomas Rasmussen; Executive Producers, Stuart W. Phelps, Peter S. Brown; A Hal Landers-Bobby Roberts-Jerry Bick presentation; In color; Rated R; 97 minutes; March release. CAST: Stephen Nathan (Harry), Cindy Williams (Rosie), Bruce Kimmel (John), Leslie Ackerman (Susie), Alan Abelew (George), Diana Canova (Juanita), Alexandra Morgan (Mary), Frank Doubleday (Arvin), Kathleen Hietala (Eunice), Art Marino (Eddie), Hy Pyke (Benny), Greg Finley (Jimmy), Herb Graham (Frankie), Rene Hall (Dick), Susan Stewart (Joy Full), Artie Shafter, Jerry Hoffman, Wade Crookham, Nancy Chadwick, John Kirby, Vern Joyce, Ian Praise, Eileen Ramsey, Jane Ralston, Claude Spence, Chris Corso, Alison Cohen, Susan Gelb, Nancy Bleier, Susan Buckner, Joel Blum, Kathryn Kimmel

ILSA, HAREM KEEPER OF THE OIL SHEIKS (Cambist) Producer, William J. Brody; Director, Don Edmonds; Screenplay, Langton Stafford; In color; Rated R; 89 minutes; March release. CAST: Dyanne Thorne (Ilsa), Michael Thayer (Adam), Victor Alexander (El Sharif), Tanya Boyd (Satin), Marilyn Joy (Velvet), Wolfgang Roehm (Kaiser), Sharon Kelly, Haji Cat

SKY RIDERS (20th Century-Fox) Producer, Terry Morse, Jr.; Executive Producer, Sandy Howard; Director, Douglas Hickox; Screenplay, Jack Dewitt, Stanley Mann, Garry Michael White; In color; Rated PG; 91 minutes; March release. CAST: James Coburn (McCabe), Susannah York, Robert Culp, Charles Aznavour (Police Chief), Werner Pochath, Zou Zou, Kenneth Griffith, Harry Andrews, Simon Harrison, Stephanie Matthews, John Beck, Barbara Trentham, Cherie Latimer, Ernie Orsatti, Henry Brown, Steven Keats

MORNING, NOON AND NIGHT (Marathon) Producer, Taylor Benson; Written, Directed and Photographed by Nick Eliot; Editor, Cal Davis; Assistant Director, Glen Nathan; In color; Rated X; March release. CAST: Dave Daniel (Jim), Greg Miers (Matt), Scott Heath (Morning), Tony Lee (Noon), Joe Gage (Night)

**Patrick Wayne
in "Mustang Country"**

**Robert Culp, Charles Aznavour
in "Sky Riders"**

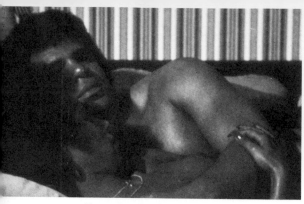

**Tanya Boyd, John DAniels
in "Black Shampoo"**

"All Night Long"

RATTLERS (Boxoffice International) Producer-Director, John McCauley; Executive Producer, Harry Novak; Story, Jerry Golding; Movielab Color; Rated PG; 82 minutes; April release. CAST: Sam Chew, Elizabeth Chauvet, Dan Priest, Ron Gold, Tony Ballen

BLACK SHAMPOO (Dimension) Producer, Alvin L. Fast; Director, Greydon Clark; Screenplay, Alvin L. Fast, Greydon Clark; Music, Gerald Lee; Editor, Earl Watson, Jr.; Color by Movielab; Rated R; 83 minutes; April release. CAST: John Daniels (Jonathan), Tanya Boyd (Brenda), Joe Ortiz (Wilson), Skip Lowe (Arnie), Gary Allen (Richard), Jack Mehoff (Maddox), Bruce Kerley (Jackson), Diana St. Clair (Mrs. Simpson)

SUPER SEAL (Epoh) Producer, Victor Lundin; Director, Michael Dugan; Screenplay, Victor Lundin, Joshua Smith; DeLuxe Color; Rated G; 86 minutes; April release. CAST: Foster Brooks, Sterling Holloway, Sarah Brown, Bob Sheperd, Nada Rowand, Larry Edsley

SECRET OF NAVAJO CAVE (Epoh) Producer-Director, James T. Flocker; Narrator, Rex Allen; Photography, David E. Jackson; In Eastmancolor; Rated G; 87 minutes; April release. CAST: Rex Allen, Holger Kasper, Steven Benally, Jr.

DEATH IS NOT THE END (Libert Films International) Producer, Elroy Schwartz; Director, Richard Michaels; Music, Mort Garsin; Photography, Alan Stensvold; In Eastmancolor; Rated G; April release. A documentary about reincarnation and procarnation.

SANDSTONE (Don Henderson) Producers, Jonathan Dana, Bunny Dana; Color by CFI; Rated X; 80 minutes; April release. A documentary about open sexuality at the Sandstone retreat in California.

LAST STOP ON THE NIGHT TRAIN (Bryanston) Producer-Director, Evans Isle; In Technicolor; Rated R; 85 minutes; April release. CAST: Kay Beal, Patty Edwards, Norma Knight, Delbert Moss, Richard Davis

THE INFIDEL (Freeway) Directed and Written by Charles Bodine; Producer, Michael James; In color; Rated X; April release. CAST: Sharon Thorpe, Rick Lutz, Ken Scudder, Melody West

SIP THE WINE (Liberty Street) Director, Dan Caldwell; Music, Geodopoulis; In Eastmancolor; Rated X; 89 minutes; April release. CAST: Anni Long (Virginia), Erica Hart (Lisa), James Whalen (Michael), Colin Phillips (Jeremy), Marion Eaton (Alameda), Diane Montgomery (Honey), George S. McDonald (Hugo)

DOMINATRIX WITHOUT MERCY Producer, Jason Russell; In color; Rated X; April release. CAST: Marlene Willoughby, Terri Hall, John Leslie Dupre, C. J. Laing, Grover Griffith, Marc Anthony, Vanessa Del Rio, Fred Lincoln, Ultra Max, Marc Stevens, Jamie Gillis

ALL NIGHT LONG (Essex) Producer-Director, Alan B. Colberg; Executive Producer, Billy Thornberg; Title Song-Original Score, Roberto Verano; Photography, Franklin DeCeco; In Eastmancolor; Rated X; April release. CAST: John Holmes, Ric Lutze, Sharon Thorpe, Rikki Gambino, Patricia Lee, Esther Walker, Kevin Goodrum

C. B. MAMAS (Mitchell Brothers) Directed by James Mitchell, Artie Mitchell; In color; Rated X; April release. CAST: Leslie Bovee, Sally Foremost, Rushka, Melissa Cooke, Paul Thomas, Joey Severa, Pat Lee

THE AMOROUS ADVENTURES OF DON QUIXOTE AND SANCHO PANZA (Burbank International) Producer-Director, Raphael Nussbaum; Executive Producer, Roberta Reeves; Screenplay, Raphael Nussbaum, Ed Woodworth, Al Bukzin; Photography, Bill de Diego; Editor, Dick Brummer; Music, Don Great; Art Director, Joel Leonard; Assistant Director, Henning Schellerup; In CFI Color; Rated R; 127 minutes; April release. CAST: Corey John Fischer (Don Quixote), Hy Pyke (Sancho), Maria Aronoff, Olivia Enke, Haji, Glenda Crabtree

"Sandstone"

**Jim Kelly, Judith Brown, Geoffrey Binney
in "Hot Potato"**

El Gran Combo
in "Salsa"

Marjoe Gortner, Lynda Carter
in "Bobbie Jo and the Outlaw"

SALSA (Fania) Producer, Jerry Masucci, Leon Gast, Jeff Cahn; Photography, Kevin Keating; Dialogue, Geraldo Rivera; In color; Rated G; 80 minutes; April release. CAST: Fania All Stars, and special guests Geraldo Rivera, El Gran Combo, Desi Arnaz, DeCastro Sisters, Delores Del Rio, Billy Cobham, Manu Dibango, Jorge "Malo" Santana

HOT POTATO (Warner Bros) Producers, Fred Weintraub, Paul Heller; Direction and Screenplay, Oscar Williams; Photography, Ronald Garcia; Music, Christopher Trussell; Editor, Peter Berger; Associate Producer, T. C. Wang; Based on character created by Alex Rose and Fred Weintraub; Art Director, Urai Sirisombat; Assistant Directors, Terry Marcel, Anuson Kayoonwong; Costumes, Sherry Chen; In color; Rated PG; 87 minutes; April release. CAST: Jim Kelly (Jones), George Memmoli (Rhino), Geoffrey Binney (Chicago), Irene Tsu (Pam), Judith Brown (Leslie/June), Sam Hiona (Rangoon), Ron Prince (General), Hardy Stockmann (Krugman), Metta Rungrat (Rhino's Lady), Supakorn Songsermvorakul (Boy), Somcjai Meekunsut (Pujo), Veerapol Pitavan (Longkat), Punchong Nakaraj (Hoss), Kachain Onching (Little Joe)

JACKSON COUNTY JAIL (New World) Producer, Jeff Begun; Director, Michael Miller; Executive Producer, Roger Corman; Screenplay, Donald Stewart; Photography, Bruce Logan; Editor, Caroline Ferriol; Music, Loren Newkirk; Associate Producer, Paul Gonsky; Assistant Directors, Richard Schor, Gary Dorf; Art Director, Michael McCloskey; Costumes, Cornelia McNamara; In Metrocolor; Rated R; 85 minutes; April release. CAST: Yvette Mimieux (Dinah), Tommy Lee Jones (Coley), Robert Carradine (Bobby), Frederic Cook (Hobie),· Severn Darden (Sheriff), Nan Martin (Allison), Mary Woronov (Pearl), Howard Hesseman (David), John Lawlor, Britt Leach, Nancy Noble, Lisa Copeland, Clifford Emmich, Michael Ashe, Edward Marshall, Marcie Drake, Betty Thomas, Ken Lawrence, Arthur Wong, Marci Barkin, Michael Hilkene, Roy David Hagle, William Molloy, Ira Miller, Jackie Robin, Gus Peters, Patrice Rohmer, Amparo Mimieux, Richard Lockmiller, Jack O'Leary, Duffy Hambleton, Mark Carlton, Don Hinz, James Arnett, Norma Moye, Hal Needham

BOBBIE JO AND THE OUTLAW (American International) Producer-Director, Mark L. Lester; Screenplay, Vernon Zimmerman; Co-Producers, Lynn Ross, Steve Brodie; Music, Barry DeVorzon; Photography, Stanley Wright; Editor, Michael Luciano; Assistant Director, Dennis Jones; Costumes, Connie McNamara; Art Director, Mike Levesque; "Those City Lights" sung by Bobby Bare; In Movielab Color; Rated R; 89 minutes; April release. CAST: Marjoe Gortner (Lyle), Lynda Carter (Bobbie Jo), Jesse Vint (Slick), Merrie Lynn Ross (Pearl), Belinda Balaski (Essic), Gene Drew (Sheriff), Peggy Stewart (Hattie), Gerrit Graham, John Durren, Virgil Frye, James Gammon, Howard Kirk, Aly Yoder, Joe Kurtzo, Jr., Chuck Russell, Richard Breeding, Jesse Price, Kip Allen, Jose Toldeo, Robert Fleming

SPARKLE (Warner Bros.) Producer, Howard Rosenman; Director, Sam O'Steen; Screenplay, Joel Schumacher; Story, Joel Schumacher, Howard Rosenman; Executive Producers, Beryl Vertue, Peter Brown; Photography, Bruce Surtees; Editor, Gordon Scott; Music, Curtis Mayfield; Choreography, Lester Wilson; Art Director, Peter Wooley; Assistant Directors, Ken Swor, Victor Hsu; A Robert Stigwood production; In Technicolor; Rated PG; 99 minutes; April release. CAST: Philip M. Thomas (Stix), Irene Cara (Sparkle), Lonette McKee (Sister), Dwan Smith (Dolores), Mary Alice (Effie), Dorian Harewood (Levi), Tony King (Satin), Beatrice Winde (Mrs. Waters), Paul Lambert (Moe), Joyce Easton (Lee), DeWayne Jessie (Ham), Norma Miller (Doreen), Talya Ferro, Robert W. Delegall, Armelia McQueen, Don Bexley, Timmie Rogers, Ken Renard, John Hawker

ASSAULT ON AGATHON (Nine Network) Producer, Nico Minardos; Director, Lasic Benedek; Screenplay, Alan Caillou, based on his novel of same title; Co-Producers, Igo Kanter, Kjell Qvale; Photography, George Arvanitis, Aris Stavrou; Music, Ken Thorne; In color; 96 minutes; April release. CAST: Nico Minardos (Cabot), Nina Van Pallandt (Maria), John Woodvine (Inspector), Marianne Faithfull (Helen), Kostas Baladimas, George Moussou, Dimitri Aronis, Takis Nevouras, Tina Spathi

Tom Lee Jones
in "Jackson County Jail"

Philip Thomas, Irene Cara
in "Sparkle"

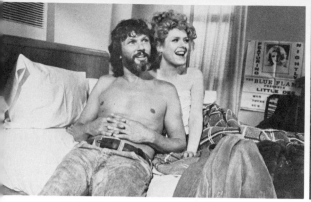

**Kris Kristofferson, Bernadette Peters
in "Vigilante Force"**

**Jodie Foster, Richard Harris, Lois Nettleton
in "Echoes of a Summer"**

VIGILANTE FORCE (United Artists) Producer, Gene Corman; Direction and Screenplay, George Armitage; Photography, William Cronjager; Music, Gerald Fried; Art Director, Jack Fisk; Editor, Morton Tubor; In color; Rated PG; 89 minutes; April release. CAST: Kris Kristofferson (Aaron), Jan-Michael Vincent (Ben), Victoria Principal (Linda), Bernadette Peters (Little Dee), Brad Dexter (Mayor), Judson Pratt (Harry), David Doyle (Homer), Antony Carbone (Freddie), Andrew Stevens (Paul), Sheely Novack (D. O.), Paul X. Gleason (Michael), John Steadman (Shakey), Lilyan McBride (Boots), James Lydon (Tom), Peter Coe (Lu), Debbie Lytton (Molly), Charles Cybbers (Perry), Carmen Argenziano (Brian), Don Pulford (Davd), Suzanne Horton (Sally)

TRACKDOWN (United Artists) Producer, Bernard Schwartz; Director, Richard T. Heffron; Screenplay, Paul Edwards; Story, Ivan Nagy; Photography, Gene Polito; Music, Charles Bernstein; Editor, Anthony De Marco; An Essaness Pictures production; Rated R; 98 minutes; April release. CAST: Jim Mitchum (Jim), Karen Lamm (Betsy), Anne Archer (Barbara), Erik Estrada (Chucho), Cathy Lee Crosby (Lynn), Vince Cannon (Johnny), John Kerry (Sgt.), Robert Rodriguez (Feo), Ernie Wheelwright (Rosey), Zitto Kazann (Curtain), Elisabeth Chauvet (Billie), Rafael Lopez, Gilbert De La Pena, Joe La Due, Ray Sharkey, James R. Parkes, Frederick Rule, Don Reed, Tony Burton, Lanny Gustavson, Leslie Simms, Jim Stathis, Larry Gabriel, Robert Forward, Simmy Bow

LEGACY (Kino International) Director, Karen Arthur; Screenplay, Joan Hotchkis; Photography, John Bailey; Editor, Caro Littleton; Music, Roger Kellaway; In color; Rated R; 90 minutes; April release. CAST: Joan Hotchkis (Woman), George McDaniel (Husband), Sean Allan (Lover), Dixie Lee (Mother)

MIDNIGHT DESIRES (Ambar) Producer, Warren Evans; Written and Directed by Amanda Barton; Photography, David Measless; Editor, Joseph Masolini; In color; Rated X; 74 minutes; April release. CAST: Karen Regis, Jaimie Gillis, C. J. Laing, Eric Edwards, Ursula Pasarell, Linda Lovemore, Ray Jeffries

ANGELS (Boxoffice International) Producer, Denis Rubin; Director, Spencer Compton; Screenplay, Drew Abrams, Richard Power, Spencer Compton, Ed Margulies; Photography, Rob Hahn, Michael Parker; Editor, Gary Gasgarth; Music, Olubji Adetoye; In color; Rated R; 90 minutes; April release. CAST: Vincent Schiavelli, Keith Berger, Marquita Callwood, David Bryant, Mark Suben, Dan McCarthy

ECHOES OF A SUMMER (Cine Artists) formerly "The Last Castle"; Producer, Robert L. Joseph; Executive Producers, Sandy Howard, Richard Harris; Director, Don Taylor; Screenplay, Robert L. Joseph; Photography, John Coquillon; Editor, Michael F. Anderson; Music, Terry James; Art Director, Jack McAdams; In Eastmancolor; Rated PG; 99 minutes; April release. CAST: Richard Harris (Eugene), Lois Nettleton (Ruth), Geraldine Fitzgerald (Sara), William Windom (Dr. Hallett), Brad Savage (Philip), Jodie Foster (Deirdre)

IT'S SHOWTIME (United Artists) Producers, Fred Weintraub, Paul Heller; Screenplay, Alan Myerson; Music, Artie Butler; Editors, Alan Holzman, Peter E. Berger; In color, black and white; Rated G; 86 minutes. April release. Compilation of film clips of nearly every great animal actor from past to present.

THE RIVER NIGER (Cine Artists) Producers, Sidney Beckerman, Isaac L. Jones; Director, Krishna Shah; Screenplay, Joseph A. Walker from his play of same title; Photography, Michael Margulies; Editor, Irving Lerner; Music, War; Design, Seymour Klate; Assistant Director, Tony Brand; In Movielab Color; Rated R; 105 minutes; April release. CAST: Cicely Tyson (Mattie), James Earl Jones (John), Lou Gossett (Stanton), Glynn Turman (Jeff), Roger E. Mosley (Big Moe), Jonelle Allen (Ann), Hilda Haynes (Grandma), Theodore Wilson (Chips), Charles Weldon (Skeeter), Ralph Wilcox (Al), Shirley Joe Finney (Gail)

**Cathy Lee Crosby, James Mitchum, Erik Estrada
in "Trackdown"**

**Myrna Loy, William Powell in "Song of the
Thin Man" from "It's Showtime"**

Christopher Norris, Ron Howard
in "Eat My Dust"

"One of a Kind"

DEEP JAWS (Manuel S. Conde) Executive Producer, Charles Teitel; Director, Perry Dell; Screenplay, Walt Davis; Story, Charles Teitel; Photography, Manuel S. Conde; Editor, Andrew Herbert; Music and Vocals, Jack Millman; In color; Rated X; 89 minutes; April release. CAST: David Kelly, Anne Gaybis, Gordon Herigstadt, Candy Samples, Sandra Casey, Rhiannon Vaughan, Richard Nathan, Byron Cole, Gordon Freed, Adrianna Bijou, Mickel Van Scott, Earl Karpen, Lady Diana, Suzanne Delor, Wilma Shock

COUNTDOWN AT KUSINI (Columbia) Producer, Ladi Ladebo; Director, Ossie Davis; Screenplay, Ossie Davis, Ladi Ladebo, Al Freeman, Jr.; Story, John Storm Roberts; Photography, Andrew Laszlo; Music, Manu Dibango; Assistant Directors, Dwight Williams, Joseph Ray Johnson; In Metrocolor; Rated PG; 99 minutes; April release. CAST: Ruby Dee (Leah), Ossie Davis (Ernest), Greg Morris (Red), Tom Aldredge (Ben), Michael Ebert (Charles), Thomas Baptiste (John), Jab Adu (Juma), Elsie Olusola (Mamouda), Funso Adeolu (Marni)

EAT MY DUST! (New World) Producer, Roger Corman; Direction and Screenplay, Charles B. Griffith; Photography, Eric Saarinen; Editor, Tina Hirsh; Music, David Grisman; Assistant Directors, Barbara Peeters, Nicole Scott; Art Director, Peter Jamison; In Metrocolor; Rated PG; 89 minutes; May release. CAST: Ron Howard (Hoover), Christopher Norris (Darlene), Warren Kemmerling, Dave Madden, Robert Broyles, Evelyn Russel, Rance Howard, Jessica Potter, Charles Howerton, Kathy O'Dare, Brad David, Clint Howard, Kedric Wolfe, John Thompson, Don Brodie, Harry Frazier, Mickey Fox, Pete Isacksen, W. L. Luckey, Paul Bartel, Lynn Brown, Margaret Fairchild, John J. Fox, John Kramer

ONE OF A KIND (Hollywood International) Executive Producer, Mike Merino; Produced, Directed, Photographed and Edited by Troy Benny; Screenplay, Michelangelo Gianini; In Eastmancolor; Rated X; 85 minutes; May release. CAST: Joey Severa, Bob Migleano, Leslie Bovee, Annette Haven, Laura Vereneti, Sharon Thorpe, Bonnie Holiday, Stacy Holmes

JESSIE'S GIRLS (Manson) Producers, Michael F. Goldman, Al Adamson; Director, Al Adamson; Screenplay, Budd Donnelly; In color; Rated R; 86 minutes; May release. CAST: Sondra Currie, Geoffrey Land, Ben Frank, Regina Carrol, Jenifer Bishop, John Durren, Rod Cameron

MARK TWAIN, AMERICAN (Emerson) Producers, Steve Verderame, Al Schriver; Executive Producer, Rudy Rutkin; Director, Robert Wilbor; Adapted for the screen by Ed Trostle; A Prelude Production in DeLuxe Color; Rated G; May release. CAST: Ed Trostle (Mark Twain)

KISS OF THE TARANTULA (Omni) Producer, Daniel B. Cady; Director, Chris Munger; Screenplay, Warren Hamilton, Jr.; Story, Daniel B. Cady; Music, Phillan Bishop; Executive Producers, Curt Drady, John Holokan; Photography, Henning Schellerup; In Eastmancolor; A Cinema-Vu Production; Rated PG; 85 minutes; May release. CAST: Eric Mason, Suzanne Ling, Herman Wallner, Patricia Landon, Beverly Eddins, Jay Scott, Rita French, Rebecca Eddins, Linda Spatz

THE FLASHER (Vincent) Produced and Directed by Barry Kerr; In color; Rated X; May release. CAST: Harry Reems

WINTER HEAT Produced and Directed by Claude Goddard; In Technicolor; Rated X; May release. CAST: Sue Rowan, Helen Madigan, Lisa Young, Jamie Gillis, Bob Tucker

HOT AND HEAVY Directed by Joseph Davian; In color; Rated X; May release. CAST: Marc Stevens, Stan Eleven

GRIZZLY (Film Ventures International) Produced and Written by David Sheldon, Harvey Flaxman; Director, William Girdler; Music, Robert O. Ragland; Executive Producer, Edward L. Montoro; Photography, William Anderson; Special Effects, Phil Corey; In Todd-AO 35 and Movielab Color; Rated PG; 90 minutes; May release. CAST: Christopher George (Kelly), Andrew Prine (Don), Richard Jaeckel (Scott), Joan McCall (Allison), Joe Dorsey (Kittridge), Maryann Hearn (1st victim), Charles Kissinger (Doctor), Kermit Echols (Corwin)

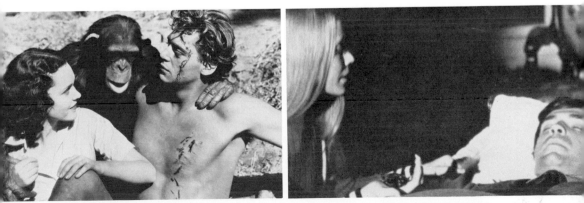

Maureen O'Sullivan, Johnny Weissmuller
in "Tarzan" from "It's Showtime"

"Kiss of the Tarantula"

Fred Williamson
in "Death Journey"

"The Student Body"

M*A*S*H*D (Hudson) Produced, Directed and Written by Emton Smith; In color; Rated X; 75 minutes; May release. CAST: Annie Sprinkle, Mike Jefferson, Andrea True, J. J. Jones, Herschel Richard, George Arthur, Justin Case, Ed Marshall

LIBERTY Directed by James Wilson; A Thomas Lynch, Jr. Production; Screenplay, Jacob Hart; In color; Rated X; May release. CAST: Tom Stone, Roshell Rush, Sondra Hayward, Liz Ross

DEATH JOURNEY (Atlas) Director, Fred Williamson; Story and Screenplay, Abel Jones; Music, Anthony Shinault; In Panavision and DeLuxe Color; A Po' Boy Production; Rated R; May release. CAST: Fred Williamson (Crowder), Bernard Kuby (Finley), D'Urville Martin (Attendant), Heidi Dobbs, Stephanie Faulkner, Alexis Tramunti

THE STUDENT BODY (Surrogate) Executive Producer, John Shipp; Producer, Ed Carlin; Director, Gus Trikonis; Photography, Gary Graver; Editor, Jerry Cohen; Music, Don Bagley, Steve Michaels; Screenplay, Hubert Smith; Art Director, Mike Bennett; In CFI Color; A Brandywine Production; Rated R; 84 minutes; May release. CAST: Warren Stevens (Dr. Blalock), Jillian Kesner (Carrie), Janice Heiden (Chicago), June Fairchild (Mitzi), Peter Hooten (Carter), Alan McRae (John), David Ankrum (LeRoy), Judith Roberts (Mrs. Blalock), Vic Jolley (Vernon), Faith Barnhardt (Sharon), Holmes Osborne (Joe), Sanford Lee (Pjil), Gary Gitchell, Joseph Kanter, Henry Effertz, Cindy Jaco, Debora Layman, Jack Poessiger, Robert Elliot

THE ALL-AMERICAN WOMAN (Manuel S. Conde) Direction and Screenplay, Mark Haggard; Executive Producer, M. D. Maury; Photography, Manuel S. Conde; Music, Bruce Kimmel; Editor, Mark Haggard; In color; Rated X; 80 minutes; May release. CAST: Marilyn James (Jean), Steven Bennett (Frank), Robbie Mayhew (Debbie), Ward Egan (Raff), Linda Weeks (Mrs. Sullivan), Robert Prestwood (Gary), Roger Vaughn, Richard Moyer

VIRGIN SNOW (Snow Ball) Produced and Directed by Dexter Eagle; Rated X; In color; May release. CAST: Jean Jensen, Laura Hunt, Hope Stockton, Roger Caine, Ursula Pasarell, Eric Edwards, Sonny Landham, Vanessa Del Rio, Trevor Manmak, Jeffrey Hurst

PLEASURE CRUISE (No credits available) In color; Rated X; May release. CAST: Andrea True, Harry Reems

FANTASEX (Command Cinema) Producer, Bud Green; Directed and Written by Howar Winters, Robert Norman; In color; Rated X; 80 minutes; May release. CAST: Terri Hall (Jane), Jeffrey Hurst (Bernard), Lundee Mitchell (Momma), Jennifer Jordan (Laverne), Juliet Graham (Dolly), Melody Gerdon (Blond), Michael Jeffries (Crotchmeyer)

DIXIE DYNAMITE (Dimension) Producer, Wes Bishop; Director, Lee Frost; Screenplay, Lee Frost, Wes Bishop; Music, Styner & Jordan; Performed by Duane Eddy, Mike Curb Congregation, Dorsey Burnette; Color by CFI; Rated PG; 90 minutes; May release. CAST: Warren Oates, Christopher George, Jane Anne Johnstone, Kathy McHaley, R. G. Armstrong, Stanley Adams

DRIVE-IN (Columbia) Producers, Alex Rose, Tamara Asseyev; Director, Rod Amateau; Executive Producer, George Litto; Associate Producers, Robert S. Bremson, Harry N. Blum; Screenplay, Bob Peete; Photography, Robert Jessup; Editors, Bernard F. Caputo, Guy Scarpitta; Assistant Directors, Robert Greene, Terrance Croghan; In Panavision and color; Rated PG; 96 minutes; May release. CAST: Lisa Lemole (Glowie), Glenn Morshower (Orville), Gary Cavagnaro (Little Bit), Billy Milliken (Enoch), Lee Newsom (Alabam), Regan Kee (Spoon), Andy Parks (Backwoods), Trey Wilson (Gifford), Gordon Hurst (Will), Kent Perkins (Bill), Ashley Cox (Mary Louise), Louis Zito, Linda Larimer, Barry Gremillion, David Roberts, Phil Ferrell, Joe Flower, Carla Palmer, Carrie Jessup, Bill McGhee, Gloria Shaw, Jessie Lee Fulton, Robert Valgova, Michelle Franks, Jack Isbell, Dejah Moore, Curtis Posey, Billy Vance White, Hank Stohl

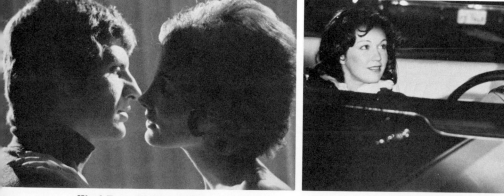

Ward Egan, Marilyn James
in "The All-American Woman"

Lisa Lemole, Glenn Morshower
in "Drive-In"

**Jan-Michael Vincent, Glynnis O'Connor
in "Baby Blue Marine"**

**Fred Williamson
in "No Way Out"**

BABY BLUE MARINE (Columbia) Producers, Aaron Spelling, Leonard Goldberg; Director, John Hancock; Screenplay, Stanford Whitmore; Music, Fred Karlin; Photography, Laszlo Kovacs; Editor, Marion Rothman; Designer, Walter Scott Herndon; Associate Producer, Robert LaVigne; Assistant Director, Michael Daves; "I'll Be Seeing You" sung by Fred Karlin; In Panavision and Color; Rated PG; 90 minutes; May release. CAST: Jan-Michael Vincent (Marion), Glynnis O'Connor (Rose), Katherine Helmond (Mrs. Hudkins), Dana Elcar (Sheriff), Bert Remsen, B. Kirby, Jr., Richard Gere, Art Lund, Michael Conrad, Allan Miller, Michael LeClair, Will Seltzer, Ken Tobey, Lelia Goldoni, Marshall Efron, Barton Heyman, Adam Arkin, Damon Douglas, Barry Greenberg, John Blythe Barrymore, John Calvin, Richard Narita, Evan Kim, Keone Young, Phyllis Glick, William Martel, Warren Burton, Abraham Alvarez, Bill Sorrells, Carole Ita White, Duncan Gamble, Lanie O'Grady, Tita Bell, Barbara Dodd, Tomm Lee McFadden, James Lough

REVENGE OF THE CHEERLEADERS (Monarch) Producers, Richard Lerner, Nathaniel Dorsky; Director, Richard Lerner; Screenplay, Ted Greenwald, Ace Baandage, Nathaniel Dorsky; Photography, Nathaniel Dorsky; Editors, Richard S. Brummer, Joseph Ancore, Jr.; Music, John Sterling; Choreography, Xavier Chatman; In color; Rated R; 88 minutes; May release. CAST: Jeril Woods, Rainbeaux Smith, Helen Lang, Patrice Rohmer, Susie Elene, Eddra Gale, William Bramley, Norman Thomas Marshall, Regina Gleason, Carl Ballantine, Fred Gray, Carrie Dietrich, Sheri Myers, Lillian McBride, Bert Conroy, Gary Walberg, Mike Steele, David Hasselhoff, David Robinson, Patrick Wright, Ivanna Moore

SMILE ORANGE (Knuts) Producer, Edward Knight; Executive Producer, Milton Verley; Director, Trevor D. Rhone; Screenplay, Trevor Rhone, David Ogden from play by Trevor Rhone; Photography, David McDonald; Editor, Mike Gilligan; Music, Melba Liston; In color; Rated PG; 86 minutes; May release. CAST: Carl Bradshaw (Ringo), Glenn Morrison (Bus Boy), Stanley Irons (Joe), Vaughn Crosskill (Assistant Manager)

CRY FOR CINDY (Cindy) Producer, Henry Locke; Director, Wendy Lions; Screenplay, Dean Rogers; Photography, Casey Maxwell; In color; Rated X; 90 minutes; May release. CAST: Amber Hunt (Anna/Cindy), Maryanne Fisher (Yvonne), Mitzi Fraser (Nora), Fred James (Dennis), Mark McGuire (Ben), John Leslie Dupre, Kenny Cotten

FEMMES DE SADE (Variety) Produced, Directed and Written by Alex de Renzy; In color; Rated X; 80 minutes; May release. CAST: Ken Turner (Rocky), Joe Nassivera (Joey), Gail Lawrence (Alice), John Leslie (Johnny), Monique Star (Royce), Mimi Morgan, Melba Bruce, Linda Wong, Kyoko Shoji, Leslie Bovee, Annette Haven, Sharon Thorpe, Johnny Keyes

NO WAY BACK (Atlas) Written, Produced and Directed by Fred Williamson; Executive Producer, Jeff Williamson; Photography, Robert Hopkins; Editor, James E. Nownes; Assistant Director, Phillip Browning; In CFI Color; Rated R; 91 minutes; May release. CAST: Fred Williamson (Jess), Charles Woolf (Pickens), Tracy Reed (Candy), Virginia Gregg (Mrs. Pickens), Stack Pierce (Bernie), Argy Allen (Pickens' Brother), Paula Sills (Secretary), Don Cornelius

THE OPENING OF MISTY BEETHOVEN (Catalyst) Producer, L. Sultana; Director, Henry Paris (Radley Metzger); Screenplay, Jake Barnes; Photography, Robert Rochester; Editor, Bonnie Karrin; Music, George Craig; Art Director, Anton Stone; In color; Rated X; 87 minutes; May release. CAST: Constance Money, Jamie Gillis, Jaqueline Beaudant, Terri Hall, Gloria Leonard, Casey Donovan, Ras Kean

UNDERGROUND (New Yorker) Producers, Photographers and Editors, Emile DeAntonio, Mary Lampson, Haskell Wexler; In color; 88 minutes; May release. A documentary about Weather Underground fugitives Billy Ayers, Kathy Bouldin, Bernardine Dohrn, Jeff Jones, Cathy Wilkerson

THE MONEY (Coliseum) Produced, Directed and Written by Carl Workman; In color; Rated R; June release. CAST: Laurence Luckinbill, Graham Beckel, Sam Levene

**Terri Hall, Jamie Gillis
in "The Opening of Misty Beethoven"**

**Laurence Luckinbill, Elizabeth Richards
in "The Money"**

**Kristine DeBell
in "Alice in Wonderland"**

"Hollywood She-Wolves"

EBONY IVORY AND JADE (Dimension) Producers, Robert E. Waters, Cirio H. Santiago; Story and Screenplay, Henry Barnes; Music, Eddie Nova; In color; Rated PG; June release. CAST: Rosanne Katon, Colleen Camp, Sylvia Anderson, Ken Washington, Christie Mayuga, Leo Martinez, Ken Metcalfe

CONFESSIONS OF A YOUNG AMERICAN HOUSEWIFE (Associated) Direction and Screenplay, Joe Sarno; Music, Jack Justis; Movielab Color; June release. CAST: Jennifer Welles, Rebecca Brooke, Chris Jordan, Eric Edwards

THE MANICURIST (Clover) Produced and Written by Harold Perkins; Director, John Hayes; Photography, Paul Hipp; In color; June release. CAST: Pennie Walter, Lola French, Flame Fontaine, Alberta Steinberg, Frances Buchanan

IN SEARCH OF BIGFOOT (Atlantic) Produced and Directed by Lawrence P. Crowley, William F. Miller; Photography, Lawrence P. Crowley; Screenplay, William F. Miller; Editor, J. H. Moss; Narrator, Phil Tonkin; A Bostonia Films Production; In color; Rated G; 75 minutes; June release. A documentary featuring Robert W. Morgan of the American Anthropological Foundation

VELVET SMOOTH (Howard Mahler) Producers, Marvin Schild, Joel Schild, Michael Fink; Director, Michael Fink; Music, Media Counterpoint; A Neshobe Films Production in association with Stygian Productions; In color; Rated R; June release. CAST: Johnnie Hill, Owen Watson, Rene Van Clief, Elsie Roman, Frank Ruiz, Moses Iyllia, Emerson Boozer

DEAR PAM Director, Harold Hindgrind; Music, Slim Pickins; In color; Rated X; June release. CAST: Crystal Sync (Pam), Eric Edwards (Harry), C. J. Laing (Gladys), Tony Perez (Barton), John C. Holmes (Richard), Jennifer Jordan, Lorraine Alraune

KISS TODAY GOODBYE Producer-Director, Francis Ellie; In color; Rated X; June release. CAST: George Payne, Lew Seager, David Savage

ALICE IN WONDERLAND (General National Enterprises) Producer, William Osco; Director, Bud Townsend; Screenplay, B. Anthony Fredricks; Based on same title by Lewis Carroll; Executive Producer, Roy Cruiser; Music and Lyrics, Bucky Searles; Photography, Joseph Bardo; Editor, Shaun Walsh; Choreography, Noah; In color; Rated X; 88 minutes; June release. CAST: Kristine De Bell (Alice), Larry Gelman (Rabbit), Allan Novak (Mad Hatter), Tony Tsengoles (Tweedle Dee), Sue Tsengoles (Tweedle Dum) J. P. Parradine (Scrugg), Bradford Armdexter (Humpty Dumpty), Ron Nelson (William), Kristen Steen (Oogaloo), Nancy Dore, Terry Hall (Nurses), John Laurence (King), Juliet Graham (Queen), Astrid Hayase (Tart), Bruce Finklestein (Black Knight), Jason Williams (White Knight), and Ed Marshall, Angel Barrett, Marcia Raven, Melvina Peoples

HOLLYWOOD SHE-WOLVES (Belladonna) Produced and Directed by Peter Balachoff; Executive Producer, Alberto Fasana; Screenplay, Pierre LaPouf; Photography, Roy Snowy; Art Director, Belinda Gayles; In color; Rated X; 93 minutes; June release. CAST: June Webster (Jane), Jim Boland (Mickey), Brandi Saunders (Suzie), William Margold (Director), Hillary Scott (Louise), Mona Hebert (Alice), Kevin Jamieson (Jim), Myra Boston (Cynthia), Roger Roy (Actor), Collette Antoinesse (Lola), Titus Moody (Photographer)

THE POM POM GIRLS (Crown International) Executive Producer, Marilyn J. Tenser; Produced, Directed and Written by Joseph Ruben; Associate Producer, Cal Naylor; Photography, Stephen M. Katz; Music, Michael Lloyd; Editor, George Bowers; Assistant Director, Cal Naylor; In DeLuxe Color; Rated PG; 90 minutes; June release. CAST: Robert Carradine (Johnnie), Jennifer Ashley (Laurie), Michael Mullins (Jesse), Lisa Reeves (Salley), Bill Adler (Duane), James Gammon (Coach), Susan Player (Sue Ann), Rainbeaux Smith (Roxanne), Diane Lee Hart (Judy), Lou Pant (Principal), John Lawrence (Sheriff), Sandra Lowell (Miss Pritchett), Faith Christopher, John Sebastian, Jim Kester, Cooper Huckabee

**John C. Holmes, Crystal Sync
in "Dear Pam"**

**Jennifer Ashley, Robert Carradine, Lisa Reeves,
Michael Mullins in "The Pom Pom Girls"**

**Elizabeth Ashley, Kay Lenz, Lee Marvin
in "The Great Scout and Cathouse Thursday"**

**Oliver Reed, Robert Culp
in "the Great Scout and Cathouse Thursday"**

THE WINDS OF AUTUMN (Howco International) Producer-Director, Charles B. Pierce; Screenplay, Earl E. Smith; Music, Jaime Mendoza-Nava; In Technicolor and Panavision; Rated PG; June release. CAST: Jack Elam, Jeanette Nolan, Andrew Prine, Earl E. Smith, Chuck Pierce, Jr., Dub Taylor.

THE ULTIMATE WARRIOR (Warner Bros.) Producers, Fred Weintraub, Paul Heller; Direction and Screenplay, Robert Clouse; In Technicolor; Rated R; 92 minutes; June release. CAST: Yul Brynner, Max Von Sydow, Joanna Miles, William Smith, Richard Kelton.

HE IS MY BROTHER (Atlantic) Producer, James Polakof; Director, Edward Dmytryk; In Metrocolor; Rated G; June release. CAST: Bobby Sherman, Kathy Paulo, Keenan Wynn, Robbie Rist, Joaquin Martinez, Benson Fong.

SECRETS OF THE GODS (Film Ventures International) Producer, Donn Davison; Director, William Sachs; Written by Donn Davison, William Sachs; Presented by Edward L. Montoro; In Movielab Color; June release.

DEATH MACHINES (Crown International) Producer, Ron Marchini; Director, Paul Kyriazi; Screenplay, Joe Walders, Paul Kyriazi; Story, Joe Walders; Photography, Donald Rust; Editor, Mark Krigbaum; Art Director, Roy Cox; Music, Don Hulette; In Techniscope and Metrocolor; Rated R; 90 minutes; June release. CAST: Ron Marchini, Michael Chong, Joshua Johnson, Mari Honjo, Ron Ackerman, John Lowe, Mary Carole Frederickson, Edward Blair, Chuch Karzakian, Rick Gau-uan, Felix McGill, George Neal, Eugene Wisenor, Bob Cori, Phillip DeAngelo, Ray Rustigian, Colleen Kinsley, Frank Wilbur, Gerard Hurley, Glenn Pierson, John Rasback, Emmett Littleton, Gene Cannon, Sonja Wyatt, John Jutt, Thomas Kernan, Robert Sapp, Jerrie Kyriazi, Eric Lee, Steve Labounty, Ralph Castellanos, Tony Saenz, Quin Fraizer, Bob Tumelty, John Lawton, Dianne Wynn, Karen Tumelty, Mike Marchini, Julie Sutherlan, Nancy Marlow, Melissa Pritchett, Tony Travino, Harry Nagy, Bob Rodriguez, Sid Campbell.

THE GREAT SCOUT AND CATHOUSE THURSDAY (American International) Executive Producer, Samuel Z. Arkoff; Producers, Jules Buck, David Korda; Director, Don Taylor; Screenplay, Richard Shapiro; Music, John Cameron; Photography, Alex Phillips, Jr; Designer, Jack Martin Smith; Editor, Sheldon Kahn; Assistant Director, Brad Aronson; Costumes, Rene Conley; Music, Ken Johnson; In Technicolor; Rated PG; 102 minutes; June release. CAST: Lee Marvin (Sam), Oliver Reed (Joe), Robert Culp (Jack), Elizabeth Ashley (Nancy), Strother Martin (Billy), Sylvia Miles (Mike), Kay Lenz (Thursday), Howard Platt (Vishniac), Jac Zacha (Trainer), Phaedra (Friday), Leticia Robles (Saturday), Luz Maria Pena (Holidays), Erika Carlson (Monday), C. C. Charity (Tuesday), Ana Verdugo (Wednesday).

THE FAKING OF THE PRESIDENT (Spencer) Produced, Written and Directed by Jeanne and Alan Abel; Associate Producer, Alan J. Barinholtz; In color; 80 minutes; June release. CAST: Marshall Efron (Donald Segretti), Alan Barinholtz (Ronald Ziegler), Robert Staats (G. Gordon Liddy), William Daprato (Abraham Lincoln), Richard Dixon (Richard Nixon).

THE CARS THAT EAT PEOPLE (New Line) Producers, Hal McElroy, Jim McElroy; Director, Peter Weir; Music, Bruce Smeaton; In Panavision and Eastmancolor; Rated PG; 90 minutes; June release. CAST: Terry Camilleri (Arthur), John Meillon (Mayor), Melissa Jaffa (Beth), Kevin Miles (Dr. Midland), Max Gillies (Metcalf), Peter Armstrong (Gorman), Edward Howell (Tringham), Bruce Spence (Charlie), Derek Barnes (Al), Charlie Metcalfe (Clive), Chris Heywood (Daryl), Tim Robertson (Les), Max Phipps (Rev. Mowbray), Frank Saba (Con).

A BOY AND HIS DOG (Marvin) Producer, Alvy Moore; Written and Directed by L. Q. Jones; Based on novella by Harlan Ellison; Photography, John Arthur Morrill; Music, Tim McIntire; In color; Rated R; 89 minutes; June release. CAST: Don Johnson (Vic), Susanne Benton (Quilla June), Jason Robards (Lew), Ron Feinberg (Fellini), Tim McIntire (Voice of Blood).

"Death Machines"

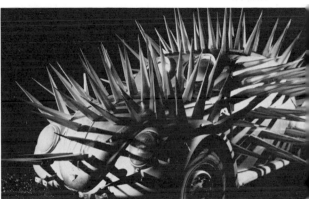

"The Cars That Eat People"

**David Kyle, Steve Bond
in "Cat Murkil and the Silks"**

**Robert Bettles
in "Ride a Wild Pony"**

THE LONG NIGHT (Howard Mahler) Producers, Woodie King, St. Clair Bourne; Director, Woodie King; Screenplay, Julian Mayfield, Woodie King; Based on novel by Julian Mayfield; Music, William Daniels, Michael Felder; Associate Producer, Ed Pitt; In color; Rated PG; 85 minutes; June release. CAST: W. Geoffrey King (Steely), Dick Anthony Williams (Paul), Peggy Kirkpatrick (Mae)

CONFESSIONS OF A TEENAGE PEANUT BUTTER FREAK (Freeway) Director, Gerald Graystone; Screenplay, Zachary Youngblood, Gerald Graystone; In color; Rated X; June release. CAST: John C. Holmes, Jennifer Mason, Rex Roman, Jacque Hanson

DOMINATION BLUE Director Joe Davian; In color; Rated X; June release. CAST: Sharon Mitchell, Vanessa Del Rio, Red Baron, Paula Morton

BLACK HEAT (Independent International) Director, Al Adamson; In Movielab Color; Rated R; June release. CAST: Timothy Brown, Russ Tamblyn, Jana Bellan, Geoffrey Land, Regina Carrol, Al Richardson, Darlene Anders, Tanya Boyd, J. C. Wells

POOR WHITE TRASH: PART 2 (Dimension) formerly "Scum of the Earth"; Producer-Director, S. F. Brownrigg; Screenplay, Mary Davis, Gene Ross; Music, Robert Farrar; Associate Producer, M. A. Ripps; In color; Rated R; 83 minutes; June release. CAST: Norma Moore, Gene Ross, Ann Stafford, Charlie Dell, Camilla Carr, Joel Cole

THREE SHADES OF FLESH (Today) Director, Hans Christian; In color; Rated X; July release. CAST: Leslie Alroe, Karen Baldwin, Helen Carrol, T. J. Youngblood, John Seeman, John Leslie, Ken Scudder

NEVER TOO YOUNG TO ROCK (Libert International) Producers, Greg Smith, Ron Inkpen; Director, Dennis Abey; Screenplay, Ron Inkpen, Dennis Abey; A GTO presentation; In color; Rated G; July release. CAST: Mud, The Rubettes, The Glitter Band, Freddie Jones, Peter Denyer

RIDE A WILD PONY (Buena Vista) Executive Producer, Ron Miller; Producer, Jerome Courtland; Director, Don Chaffey; Photography, Jack Cardiff; Music, John Addison; Art Director, Robert Hilditch; Editor, Mike Campbell; Costumes, Judith Dorsman; Assistant Director, Mark Egerton; Screenplay, Rosemary Anne Sisson; From novel "A Sporting Proposition" by James Aldridge; In Technicolor; Rated G; 91 minutes; July release. CAST: Michael Craig (James), John Meillon (Quayle), Robert Bettles (Scott), Eva Griffith (Josie), Graham Rouse (Bluey), Alfred Bell (Angus), John Meillon, Jr. (Kit), Roy Haddrick (J. C.), Peter Gwynne (Sgt. Collins), Melissa Jaffer (Angus' wife), Lorraine Bayly (James' wife), Wendy Playfair

CAT MURKIL AND THE SILKS (Gamma III) Produced and Written by William C. Thomas; Director, John Bushelman; Music, Bernie Kaailewis; Photography, Bruce Logan; Editor, Jeff Bushelman; A Pine-Thomas Production; In Movielab Color; "Slow Down Baby" sung by Hollingsworth; Rated R; 102 minutes; July release. CAST: David Kyle (Cat), Steve Bond (Joey), Kelly Yaegermann (Claudine), Rhodes Reason (Det. Harder), Meegan King (Marble), Don Carter (Bumps), Derrel Maury (Punch), Joe Reteria (Carlos), Ruth Manning (Mrs. Murkil)

DEATH RIDERS (Crown International) Producers, Dave Adams, Phil Tucker; Director, James Wilson; Photography, Vilmos Zsigmond, James Wilson; Music, Styner and Jordan; A Hallmark Picture; In DeLuxe Color; Rated PG; 88 minutes; July release. CAST: Floyd Reed, Sr., Rusty Smith, Jim Cates, Joe Byars, Larry Mann, Danny Reed, Henry Trumplay, Bob Speare, Jim Moreau, Floyd Reed, Jr., Bub Baerma, Ron Cheesman

HUSTLER SQUAD (Crown International) Producers, Cirio Santiago, Bob Waters; Director, Cesar Gallardo; In Metrocolor; Rated R; 98 minutes; July release. CAST: John Ericson (Maj. Stonewall), Karen Ericson (Lt. West), Lynda Sinclaire (Cindy), Nory Wright (Rose), Ramon Revilia (Paco), Johanna Raunio (Anna), Liza Lorena (Sonya)

"Death Riders"   **"Hustler Squad"**

"Rollerbabies"

Patricia Pearcy, Peter McLean, Don Scardino
in "Squirm"

IN SEARCH OF NOAH'S ARK (Sun Classic) Producer, Charles L. Sellier, Jr.; Director, James L. Conway; Executive Producer, Raylan Jensen; Narrator, Brad Crandall; In Technicolor; Rated G; 95 minutes; July release. A documentary examining the story of Noah.

THE TRAP OF COUGAR MOUNTAIN (Manson) No credits available; In Technicolor; Rated G; 94 minutes; July release. CAST: Keith Larsen, Karen Steele

ROLLERBABIES (Classic) Producer-Director, Carter Stevens; Screenplay, Wesson Smith; In Eastmancolor; Rated X; 84 minutes; July release. CAST: Robert Random, Suzanne McBain, Yolanda Savalas, Terri Hall, A. Chameleon, Phillip DeHat, Jerry Schneiderman

ANGEL ON FIRE (Essex) Director, Roberta Findley; A Volcano Films presentation; Rated X; In color; July release. CAST: Darby Lloyd Rains, Jamie Gillis, Marc Stevens, Jennifer Jordan

THE JAWS OF DEATH (Cannon) Producer-Director, William Grefe; Screenplay, Robert Madaris; In color; Rated PG; July release. CAST: Richard Jaeckel, Jenifer Bishop, Harold Sakata, John Chandler, Buffy Dee, Ben Kronen, Paul Preston, Milton Smith, Robert Gordon, Jerry Albert, Luke Halpin, Marcie Knight

TENDER FLESH (Brut) Former "Welcome to Arrow Beach"; Director, Laurence Harvey; Screenplay, Wallace C. Bennett; In color; Rated R; 85 minutes; July release. CAST: Laurence Harvey, Joanna Pettet, Meg Foster, Stuart Whitman, John Ireland, Gloria LeRoy, David Macklin

THEY CAME FROM WITHIN (Trans-America) Producer, Ivan Reitman; Direction and Screenplay, David Cronenberg; Executive Producers, John Dunning, Andre Link, Alfred Pariser; Photography, Robert Saad; In Movielab Color; Rated R; 88 minutes; July release. CAST: Paul Hampton (Roger), Joe Silver (Rollo), Lynn Lowry (Forsythe), Alan Migicovsky (Nicholas), Susan Petrie (Janine), Barbara Steele (Betts), Ronald Mlodzik Merrick)

SQUIRM (American International) Executive Producers, Edgar Lansbury, Joseph Beruh; Producer, George Manasse; Direction and Screenplay, Jeff Lieberman; Photography, Joseph Mangine; Editor, Brian Smedley-Aston; Costumes, Dianne Finn Chapman; Music, Robert Prince; In Movielab Color; Rated R; 92 minutes; July release. CAST: Don Scardino (Mick), Patricia Pearcy (Geri), R. A. Dow (Roger), Jean Sullivan (Naomi), Peter MacLean (Sheriff), Fran Higgins (Alma), William Newman (Quigley), Barbara Quinn (Sheriff's Girl), Carl Dagenhart (Willie), Angel Sande (Millie), Carol Jean Owens (Bonnie), Kim Iocouvozzi (Hank), Walter Dimmick (Danny), Julia Klopp (Mrs. Klopp)

J. D.'S REVENGE (American International) Producer-Director, Arthur Marks; Screenplay, Jaison Starkes; Music, Robert Prince; Assistant Director, Lee Rafner; Photography, Harry May; Editor, George Folsey, Jr.; In Movielab Color; Rated R; 95 minutes; July release. CAST: Glynn Turman (Ike), Lou Gossett (Rev. Bliss), Joan Pringle (Christella), Carl Crudup (Tony), James Louis Watkins (Carl), Alice Jubert (Roberta), Stephanie Faulkner (Phyllis), Fred Pinkard (Theotis), Fuddle Bagley (Enoch), Jo Anne Meredith (Sarah), David McKnight (J. D.)

TREASURE OF MATECUMBE (Buena Vista) Executive Producer, Ron Miller; Producer, Bill Anderson; Director, Vincent McEveety; Screenplay, Don Tait; Based on "A Journey to Matecumbe" by Robert Lewis Taylor; Photography, Frank Phillips; Music, Buddy Baker; Editor, Cotton Warburton; Designer, Robert Clatworthy; Art Director, John B. Mansbridge; Costumes, Shelby Anderson; Assistant Directors, Paul Nichols, Bud Grace; Choreographer, Burch Mann; In Technicolor; Rated G; 117 minutes; July release. CAST: Robert Foxworth (Jim), Joan Hackett (Lauriette), Peter Ustinov (Dr. Snodgrass), Vic Morrow (Spangler), Johnny Doran (David), Billy Attmore (Thad), Jane Wyatt (Aunt Effie), Robert DoQui (Ben), Mills Watson (Catrell), Val De Vargas (Charlie), Virginia Vincent (Aunt Lou), Don Knight (Skaggs), Dub Taylor (Sheriff), Dick Van Patten (Gambler)

**Paul Hampton, Lynn Lowry
in "They Came from Within"**

**Billy Attmore, Robert Foxworth, Johnny Doran, Peter
Ustinov, Joan Hackett in "Treasure of Matecumbe"**

141

**Peter Graves, Peter Hurkos
in "the Mysterious Monsters"**

**David Carradine, Veronica Hamel
in "Cannonball"**

WILDCAT WOMEN (Parliament) No credits available; In color and 3-D; Rated R; July release. CAST: Serena

COUPLES (Sombrero) Producer, Rod Whipple; Director, Claude Goddard; In color; Rated X; July release. CAST: Angel Barrett, Jeffrey Hurst, Jamie Gillis, Gloria Haddit

THE MYSTERIOUS MONSTERS (Sun Classic) Formerly "Bigfoot: The Mysterious Monster"; Executive Producer, Raylan Jensen; Producer, Charles E. Sellier, Jr.; Co-Producer, Director, Screenplay, Robert Guenette; Photography, David Myers, Eric Daarstadt, Tony Coggans; Associate Producer, James L. Conway; Composer, Rudy Raksin; Editors, Earle Herdan, Robert Lambert; Narrator, Peter Graves; In color; Rated G; 86 minutes; July release.

CANNONBALL (New World) Executive Producers, Run Run Shaw, Gustave Berne; Producer, Samuel W. Gelfman; Director, Paul Bartel; Screenplay, Paul Bartel, Donald C. Simpson; Photography, Tak Fujimoto; Editor, Morton Tubor; Associate Producer, Peter Cornberg; Assistant Directors, Cathy McCabe, Jan Lloyd; Art Director, Michel Levesque; Music, David A. Axelrod; A Cross-Country Production in Metrocolor; Rated PG; 93 minutes; July release. CAST: David Carradine (Coy "Cannonball" Buckman), Bill McKinney (Cade), Veronica Hamel (Linda), Gerri Graham (Perman), Robert Carradine (Jim), Belinda Balaski (Maryann), Judy Canova (Sharma), Carl Gottlieb (Terry), Mary Woronov (Sandy), Aron Kincaid (David), Archie Hahn, David Arkin, John Herzfeld, James Keach, Dick Miller, Louisa Mortiz, Patrick Wright, Stanley Clay, John Alderman, Deirdre Ardell, Gretchen Ardell, Allan Arkush, Gary Austin, Wendy Bartel, Linda Civitello, Jim Conners, Roger Corman, Peter Cornberg, Joe Dante, Miller Drake, Mike Finnell, Samuel W. Gelfman, Paul Glickler, David Gottlieb, Lea Gould, Diane Lee Hart, Glen Johnson, Jonathan Kaplan, Saul Krugman, James Lashly, Joe McBride, Todd McCarthy, Keith Michl, Read Morgan, Mary-Robin Redd, Glynn Rubin, Martin Scorsese, Donald Simpson, George Wagner, Joe Wong, Paul Bartel

LACEY BODINE (De Neuve Sisters) Producers, Danielle and Renee de Neuve; In color; Rated X; July release. CAST: Joanie Jackson, Ken Scutter, Johnnie Keyes

TERROR HOUSE (Intercontinental) Producer, Michael Macready; Director, Bud Townsend; Screenplay, Allen J. Actors; In color; Rated PG; July release. CAST: Linda Gillin, Arthur Space, John Neilson, Mary Jackson, Michael Macready, Earl Parker, Janet Wood, Margaret Avery

LIQUID LIPS (Freeway) Producer, Damon Christian; Director, Bob Chinn; Screenplay, Robert Mathews; In color; Rated X; July release. CAST: John C. Holmes, Monique Starr, Enjil Von Bergdorfe, Melba Bruce, Mike Weldon, Phadre, Candice Chambers, John Seeman, Jerry Mills

MY EROTIC FANTASIES (William Mishkin) Credits not available; In color; Rated X; July release. CAST: Marc Stevens, Bree Anthony, Annie Sprinkle, Big Sally Stroke

HEADMASTER Producer, Jason Russell; In color; Rated X; July release. CAST: Jamie Gillis

THE DAY THE LORD GOT BUSTED (American Films) Produced, Directed and Written by Burt Topper; Associate Producer, Byron Roberts; Photography, Alan Stensvold; Editor, Kenneth Crane; Art Director, Donald S. Ament; Music, Harley Hatcher; In DeLuxe Color; Rated PG; 81 minutes; July release. CAST: Fabian Forte (Mathew), Nai Bonet (Helena), Tony Russel (Rev. Calder), Larry Bishop (Brian), Casey Kasem (Bernie), Marshall Reed (Rev. Billy), William Bonner (Ira), Kitty Vallacher (Julie), Larry Easley (Kelly), Robert Swan (Sheriff), Lionel Ames (Dan), Tracy Morgan (Annie), Carolyn Payne (Ciel)

GO FOR IT (World Entertainment) Producers, Paul Rapp, Richard Rosenthal; Executive Producer, Wilt Chamberlain; Director, Paul Rapp; Screenplay, Nell Rapp; Photography, Rick Robertson; Editor, John O'Connor; Music, Dennis Dragon; In CFI Color; Rated PG; 96 minutes; July release. A youth sports documentary

**Martin Scorsese, Paul Bartel, Sylvester Stallone
in "Cannonball"**

**Fabian Forte, Larry Bishop
in "The Day the Lord Got Busted"**

**Isela Vega, Warren Oates, Fiona Lewis
in "Drum"**

**Susan George
in "A Small Town in Texas"**

TUNNELVISION (World Wide Films) Executive Producer, Neil Israel; Producer, Joe Roth; Directors, Brad Swirnoff, Neil Israel; Screenplay, Neil Israel, Michael Mislove; Music, Dennis Lambert, Brian Potter; Art Director, C. D. Taylor; Photography, Don Knight, Editors, Roger Parker, Dayle Mustain; Associate Producer, Michael Mislove; Assistant Director, Edward Markley; In color; Rated R; 75 minutes; July release. CAST: Chevy Chase, Phil Proctor (Christian Broder), Rick Hurst (Father Phaser Gun), Larraine Newman (Sonja), Howard Hesseman (Sen. McMannus), Roger Bowen (Kissinger), Ernie Anderson, Edwina Anderson, James Bacon, Ron Silver, Roberta Kent, Lorry Goldman, Lynn Marie Stewart, Gerrit Graham, Pamela Toll, Sam Riddle, Betty Thomas, Joe O'Flaherty, Bart Williams, Roger Bowen, Ron Prince, Nellie Bellflower, Tom Davis, Al Franken, Frank Von Zerneck, Doug Steckley, Wayne Satz, Michael Overly Band, Elizabeth Edwards, Bill Schallert, Frank Alesia, Howard Storm, Julie Mannix, Michael Mislove, Ira Miller, Bill Saluga, Terri Seigel, Neil Israel, Mary McCuster, Jimmy Martinez, Rod Gist, Jose Kent, Michael Popovich, Bo Kaprall, Larry Gelman, Barry Michlin, Danny Dark, Kurt Taylor, Joe Roth, C. D. Taylor, Bob McClurg, Cary Hoffman, Dody Dorn

DRUM (United Artists) Producer, Ralph Serpe; Director, Steve Carver; Screenplay, Norman Wexler; Based on novel by Kyle Onstott; Photography, Lucien Ballard; Music, Charlie Smalls; Designer, Stan Jolley; Costumes, Ann Roth; Editor, Carl Kress; Art Director, Bill Kenney; In color; Rated R; 102 minutes; July release. CAST: Warren Oates (Hammond), Isela Vega (Marianna), Ken Norton (Drum), Pam Grier (Regine), Yaphet Kotto (Blaise), John Colicos (Bernard), Fiona Lewis (Augusta), Paula Kelly (Rachel), Royal Dano (Zeke), Lillian Hayman (Lucretia), Rainbeaux Smith (Sophie), Alain Patrick, Brenda Sykes, Clay Tanner, Lila Finn, Henry Wills, Donna Garrett, Harvey Parry, May Boss

JUDGEMENT DAY (Playtime) Producer, Bella Maria; Director, Jon Cutaia; In color; Rated X; July Release. CAST: P. J. Whigham, Morning Star, John Leslie, T. J. Youngblood, Turk Lyon, Melba Peach

A SMALL TOWN IN TEXAS (American International) Producer, Joe Solomon; Executive Producer, Louis S. Arkoff; Director, Jack Starrett; Screenplay, William Norton; Photography, Bob Jessup; Editors, John C. Horger, Larry L. Mills, Jodie Copelan; Music, Charles Bernstein; Art Director, Elayne Cedar; Assistant Director, Thomas B. McCrory; In Movielab Color; Rated PG; 95 minutes; July release. CAST: Timothy Bottoms (Poke), Susan George (Mary Lee), Bo Hopkins (Duke), Art Hindle (Boogie), John Karlen (Lenny), Morgan Woodward (C. J.), Patrice Rohmer (Trudy), Hank Rolike (Cleotus), Buck Fowler (Bull), Clay Tanner (Junior)

MOVING VIOLATION (20th Century-Fox) Producer, Julie Corman; Executive Producer, Roger Corman; Director, Charles S. Dubin; Screenplay, David R. Osterhout, William Norton, from story by David R. Osterhout; Photography, Charles Correll; Editors, Richard Sprague, Howard Terrell; Music, Don Peake; Art Director, Sherman Loudermilk; In DeLuxe Color; Rated PG; 91 minutes; July release. CAST: Stephen McHattie (Eddie), Kay Lenz (Cam), Eddie Albert (Alex), Lonny Chapman (Sheriff), Will Geer (Rockfield), Jack Murdock (Bubba), John S. Ragin (Shank), Dennis Redfield (Tylor), Michael Ross (Verona Harvey) Francis de Sales (Lawyer), Dick Miller (Mack)

THE GUMBALL RALLY (Warner Bros.) Producer-Director, Chuck Bail; Screenplay, Leon Capetanos; Story, Chuck Bail, Leon Capetanos; Photography, Richard C. Glouner; Editors, Gordon Scott, Stuart H. Pappe, Maury Winetrobe; Music, Dominic Frontiere; Associate Producer, Leon Capetanos; Assistant Director, Frank Beetson; Art Director, Walter Simonds; In Panavision and Technicolor; A First Artists Production; Rated PG; 106 minutes; August release. CAST: Michael Sarrazin (Michael), Norman Burton (Roscoe), Gary Busey (Gibson), John Durren (Preston), Susan Flannery (Alice), Harvey Jason (Lapchick), Steven Keats (Kandinsky), Tim McIntire (Smith), Joanne Nail (Jane), J. Pat O'Malley (Barney), Tricia O'Neil (Angie), Lazaro Perez (Jose), Nicholas Pryor (Graves), Vaughn Taylor (Andy), Wally Taylor (Avila), Raul Julia (Franco)

**Ken Norton, Brenda Sykes, John Colicos
in "Drum"**

**Raul Julia, Michael Sarrazin
in "The Gumball Rally"**

**Karen Leslie
in "Death Play"**

THE GREAT TEXAS DYNAMITE CHASE (New World) Producer, David Irving; Executive Producers, Marshall Backlar, Marshall Whitfield, Karen Whitfield; Director, Michael Pressman; Screenplay, David Kirkpatrick; Based on story by Mark Rosin; Photography, Jamie Anderson; Editor, Millie Moore; Music, Craig Safan; Design, Russel Smith; Assistant Director, Sean Daniel; In Metrocolor; Rated R; 90 minutes; August release. CAST: Claudia Jennings (Candy), Jocelyn Jones (Ellie), Johnny Crawford (Slim), Chris Pennock (Jake), Tara Strohmeier (Pam), Miles Watkins, Bart Braverman, Nancy Bleier, Buddy Kling

THE MANSON MASSACRE (Newport) Director, Kentucky Jones; Rated R; 65 minutes; August release. CAST: Blaidsell Makee, Debbie Osborne, Sean Kenney, Candice Roman

HOT SUMMER IN THE CITY (Imperial) Director, The Hare; Screenplay, P. James Write; In Eastmancolor; Rated X. August release. CAST: Lisa Baker, Duke Johnson, Shorty Roberts, Stitch Umbas, Coke Chain, Black Orchid

THE THURSDAY MORNING MURDERS (Aurora International) Produced, Directed and Written by Michael Nahay; An Associated Artists Production; In CFI Color; Rated R; August release. CAST: Michael Nahay, Gordon Austin, Lyle S. Wall, J. B. Young, Lawrence Harris, Jean Rapstead

LOVE SLAVES (Savant) Producer, David Goldstein; Director, Robert Husong; In color; Rated X; August release. CAST: John Leslie, Pat Lee, Enjil Von Bergdorfe, Laura Bourbon, Alexandra Lyon, Sharon Thorpe

BIG ABNER (Evart Industries) No credits available; In color; Rated X; August release. CAST: John C. Holmes, Jim Cassidy

EVIL IN THE DEEP (Golden) Producers, Virginia Stone, J. A. S. McCombie; Director, Virginia Stone; Music, Christopher Stone; A D&R Film Project; In Todd-AO and DeLuxe Color; A Producers Group Production; Rated PG; August release. CAST: Stephen Boyd, Rosey Grier, David Ladd, Cheryl Stoppelmoor, Chuck Wooley

ONCE UPON A GIRL (PRO International) Producer, Joel Seibel; Director, Don Jurwich; Executive Producers, William B. Silberkleit, David Winters; Associate Producer, Murray M. Kaplan; Music, Martin Slavin; In color; Rated X; 77 minutes; August release. An animated feature with live sequences featuring Richmond Johnson, Carol Piacente, Kelly Gordon

MY NAME IS LEGEND (SR) Produced and Directed by Duke Kelly; In color; Rated G; August release. CAST: Duke Kelly, Tommy Kirk, Rand Porter, Stan Foster, Scott Kelly, Roberta Eaton, Kerry Smith

THE WACKIEST WAGON TRAIN IN THE WEST (Topar) Presented by Tom Parker and Morrie Parker; In color; Rated G; August release. CAST: Forrest Tucker, Bob Denver

SWEET CAKES (SFC) Producer-Director, Hans Johnson; In color; Rated X; August release. CAST: Jennifer Welles, Linda Wong, Serena, Pat Lee, Ras Kean, Brooke Young, Taylor Young, Jeanine Dalton

HIGH SCHOOL HONIES (Beehive) Producer-Director, Tom Gordon; Screenplay, Lem Lary; In color; Rated X; August release. CAST: William Margold, Diana St. Clair

LOLLIPOP PALACE (Lollipix) Producer-Director, Kirdy Stevens; Rated X; In Eastmancolor; August release. CAST: John C. Holmes, Bunny Savage, Laura Bacalle, Suzanne Catharine, Cynthia Sweet, Bob Lash, Bobby Stewart, Rick Lutz, Frenchie Dior

DEATH PLAY (New Line) Executive Producer, Joseph Lyttle; Producer, Norman I. Cohen; Director, Arthur Storch; Screenplay, Jeff Tambornino; Photography, Gerald Cotts; Associate Producers, Milt Felsen, Ron Breeding; Editor, Arthur Williams; Music, Rupert Holmes; Theme Song sung by Joanne Beretta; Costumes, Francine Tint; In color; Rated PG; 86 minutes; August release. CAST: Karen Leslie (Karen), Michael Higgins (Sam), James Keach (Steve), Hy Anzel (Harry), James Catusi (Ernie), Elizabeth Farley (Linda), Don Fellows (Arthur), Jack Hollander (Frank), Robert Jackson (Don), Zina Jasper (Nancy), Virginia Kiser (Laura), James Noble (Norman), Nancy R. Pollock (Esther), Stephen Strimpell (Jerry)

EVERYDAY (American Films) Producers, Greg Britton, Aaron Mann; Associate Producer, Phyllis Denny; Director, George B. Britton; Story, Aaron Mann; Screenplay, Aaron Mann, Murray Kalis, Rebecca Hillman; Photography, Jeffrey Smith; Music, Ken A. Little; Editor, Christopher Arnold; Theme performed by Major Cornell, Jim Townsend; In color; Rated R; 84 minutes; August release. CAST: David E. Michaels (Jasper), Anthony Gulassa (Ray), Stephen McGuire (Phil), Maury Espelin (Yon), Barbara Freeman (Diane), Jean Sarah Frost (Mme. Pissoire), Denise Denny (Everyone), Elana Casey (Sue), and Phyllis Denny, Stephanie Gates, Laurie Pickering, Karrin Gidekel, Elaine Kleinberg, Robin Murphy, Bobbi Sisney, Chuck Thornton, William Kaye, Elizabeth Brandun, Leonard Denny, Bob Koon, Bob Woods, Chris Richardson, Robert Gage, Judith Spevack, Jennifer Rowen, Angela Field, Sheryl Cline, Norman Cannon, Alan Gifford, Kathy Hilton, Gino Dentie, Ron Letterman, Christine Abbott

NAUGHTY SCHOOL GIRLS (NMD) Producer, John Wheeler; Director, Jean Paul Scardino; Screenplay, Alonzo Pye; A Blazer Co. Production; In Movielab Color; Rated R; 86 minutes; September release. CAST: Rebecca Brooke, Sandra Gartner, Judy Rauch, Kim Schachel, Claire Waugh, Dan Stone, Jeff Kohlberg

FEMALE CHAUVINISTS produced and Director by Jay Jackson; Screenplay, Jack Holtzman; In color; Rated X; 89 minutes; September release. CAST: Roxanne Brewer, Rick Dillon, Uschi Digart, Ludmila, Debora McGuire, Fillip Holiday, Sue Kaftel, Ronnie Summers, Larry Justin, Jim Habif, Wayne Chapman, Wendell Hamburg

MASSACRE AT CENTRAL HIGH (Brian) Direction and Screenplay, Renee Daalder; Producer, Harold Sobel; Music, Tony Leonetti; In color; Rated R; 85 minutes; September release. CAST: Derrel Maury (David), Andrew Stevens (Mark), Kimberly Beck (Theresa), Robert Carradine (Spoony), Ray Underwood (Bruce), Rainbeaux Smith (Mary) Lani O'Grady (Jane), Steve Bond (Craig), Dennis Kort (Arthur), Steve Sikes (Rodney), Damon Douglas, Jeffrey Winner

**Roosevelt Grier
in "Evil in the Deep"**

BROTHERHOOD OF DEATH (Downtown) Producers, Richard Barker, Bill Berry; Direction and Screenplay, Bill Berry; Story, Ronald K. Goldman; Rated R; September release. CAST: Roy Jefferson, Mike Thomas, Larry Jones, Frank Grant, Mike Bass, Dennis Johnson, Le Tari, Haskell V. Anderson III, Reggie Rucker, Felix Lobdell

WOMAN IN THE RAIN (Boxoffice International) Producer, Michael Bennett; Director, Paul Hunt; Executive Producer, Phil Yankowitz; In Movielab Color; Rated PG; September release. CAST: Barbara Luna, Alex Nicol, Ron Masak, Mary Frann, Stanley Adams, Kyle Johnson

SAMMY SOMEBODY (Athena) Producer, William A. Zeitler; Director, Joseph Adler; A Screen Arts International presentation; A Crismar Associates Production in color; Rated R; September release. CAST: Zalman King, Susan Strasberg, Sarah Kennedy, Jan Sterling

THE BOOBY HATCH (Constellation) Producers, John Russo, Russell W. Streiner; Direction and Screenplay, Rudy Ricci, John Russo; A New American Film in Eastmancolor; Rated X; 86 minutes; September release. CAST: Sharon Joy Miller, Rudy Ricci, Doug Sortino, N. Detroit, Herb Elliotte, Mike Waterkotte, David Emge, Alan Harris, John Upson, Dana Christian

FLASH AND FIRECAT (Sebastian) Produced, Directed and Written by Ferd and Beverly Sebastian; In Movielab Color; Rated PG; 89 minutes; September release. CAST: Roger Davis (Firecat), Tricia Sembera (Flash), Dub Taylor (Sheriff), Richard Kiel (Investigator), Joan Shawlee (Rose), Philip Burns, Tracy Sebastian

MISS NUDE AMERICA (Eroica Enterprises) Produced-Director, James P. Blake; Music and Editing, Michael Karp; In color; Rated R; 74 minutes; September release. A documentary about Naked City, IN.

THE CLIMAX OF BLUE POWER Producer-Director, F. C. Perl; Rated X; In color; September release. CAST: Jason Karns, Linda Harris, Betty Childs, Mary Tomkins, Sally Martin, Gloria Jane Medford

SURFER GIRLS (Essex) Director, Boots McCoy; Music, Reep Dagle; In color; Rated X; September release. CAST: Melba May, Lance Stringer, Stephanie Young, Joe Severa, Valerie Franklin

THE AMAZING DR. JEKYLL (Webster) Producer, Ralph Ell; Director, Tim McCoy; In color; Rated X; September release. CAST: Harry Reems, Bobby Astyr, C. J.Laing, Susan Sparkle, Sue Rowan, Zebedy Colt, Terri Hall

CHEESE title changed to "Hot Shots"; Producer, Ward Summers; Director, Alan West; Photography, Todd East; In color; Rated X; September release. CAST: Sonny Landham, Sarah Lee Jens, Helen Willis, Eve Hull

SLUMBER PARTY '57 (Cannon) Producer, John Ireland, Jr.; Director, William A. Levey; Screenplay, Frank Farmer; In color; Rated R; 95 minutes; September release. CAST: Janet Wood, Debra Winger, Rainbeaux Smith, Bridget Holloman, Noelle North, Mary Ann Appleseth, R. G. Armstrong, Rafael Campos, Larry Gelman, Will Hutchins, Joyce Jillson, Victor Rogers, Joe E. Ross, Bill Thurman

THE AUTOBIOGRAPHY OF A FLEA (Mitchell Bros.) Producers, James and Artie Mitchell; Director, Sharon McNight; Based on novel of same name; In color; Rated X; 90 minutes; September release. CAST: Jean Jennings (Belle), John Holmes (Father Clement), Paul Thomas (Father Ambrose), Annette Haven (Mme. Verbouc), Dale Meador (Verbouc), Joanna Hilden (Julia), John Leslie, Mitch Mandell

THE CALIFORNIA REICH (Intercontinental) Produced, Directed, Photographed, Edited by Walter Parkes and Keith Critchlow; Executive Producers, Marshall C. Whitfield, Karen J. Whitfield; Music, Craig Safan; Rated PG; In color; September release. A documentary about the Nazi Party in America

THE MISLAID GENIE (Cineclub 24) Produced and Directed by Eric and Shelley Haims; Screenplay Thomas Earl, Shelley Haims; In color; Rated X; 91 minutes; September release. CAST: Frank Anthony, Howard Mayo, Jeanne Steele, Diana Hardy, Mary Steely, Rene Bond, Anne Ali

**Jean Jennings
in "The Autobiography of a Flea"**

ONE CHANCE TO WIN (Pan American) A Zephyr Films Production; In color; Rated G; September release. CAST: Tony DiStefano, Pierre Karsmakers, Brad Lackey, Marty Smith, Jim Weinert

THROUGH THE LOOKING GLASS (Mature) Producer-Director, Jonas Middleton; Screenplay, Ronald Wertheim; Photography, Harry Flecks; Editor, Maurizio Zaubmann, James Macreading; Design, Tyrone Browne; Music, Arlon Ober; In color; Rated X; 91 minutes; September release. CAST: Catharine Burgess, Douglas Wood, Jamie Gillis, Laura Nicholson, Marie Taylor, Al Letivsky, Terri Hall, Jeffrey Hurst, Ultramax, Kim Pope, Eve Every, Jacob Pomerantz, Susan Swanson

THE DOUBLE EXPOSURE OF HOLLY (Scope) Producers, Ronan O'Casey, Bernard Stone; Director, Bob Gill; Screenplay, Ronan O'Casey; Score, Stan Free; In color; Rated X; 77 minutes; September release. CAST: Catherine Earnshaw, Ronan O'Casey, Terri Hall, Jamie Gillis, Con Peterson, Robert Maroff, Annie Sprinkle, Bree Anthony, Tony Blue, Bobby Astyr, Sol Weiner, Tina Mira, Steve Lincoln, Cecilia Gardner, Darryl Speer, Ed Dowling, Turk Turpin, Roy Palladino

THE LAST AFFAIR (Chelex) Written, Produced, Directed and Edited by Henri Charbakshi; Executive Producer, Alexander Boas; Photography, Robin Rutledge; Music, Sooren Alexander; In color; Rated R; 80 minutes; September release. CAST: Jack Wallace, Ron Dean, Del Close, Betty Thomas, Marigray Jobes, Debbie Dan, William Norris, Jack Hafferkamp

STREET PEOPLE (American International) Director, Maurice Lucidi; Screenplay, Ernest Tidyman, Randall Kleiser; Music, Luis Enriquez; Art Director, Gastogne Carsetti; In Movielab Color; Rated R; 92 minutes; September release. CAST: Roger Moore (Ulysses), Stacy Keach (Phil), Ivo Garrani (Salvatore), Entore Manni (Bishop), Ennio Balbo (Continenza), Fausto Tozzi (Nicoletta) Pietro Martellanz (Pano), Ramon Puppo (Fortunate)

**Stacy Keach, Roger Moore
in "Street People"**

Margaret Leighton, John Mills
in "Dirty Knights' Work"

Nancy Kwan
in "Project: Kill"

EASY ALICE (California Continental Cinema) Producer-Director, Tom Hoffman; In color; Rated X; September release. CAST: Linda Wong, Joey Severa, Leslie Bovee, Annette Haven, Bob Migliette, Paul Scarif

AMERICA AT THE MOVIES (Cinema V) Producer, American Film Institute, George Stevens, Jr.; Associate Producer, Harrison Engle; Narration written by Theodore Strauss; Narrated by Charlton Heston; Editor, David Saxton; Music arranged by Nelson Riddle; Designer, Ivan Chermayeff; In color, black and white; Rated PG; 116 minutes; September release. A feature length compilation of scenes from 83 films, divided into 5 segments: The Land, The Cities, The Families, The Wars, The Spirit

DIRTY KNIGHTS' WORK (Gamma III) Producers, Fred Weintraub, Paul Heller; Director, Kevin Connor; Screenplay, Julian Bond, Steven Rossen, Mitchell Smith; Story, Fred Weintraub, Paul Heller; Photography, Alan Hume; Designer, Edward Marshall; Music, Frank Cordell; Editor, Willy Kemplen; In Movielab Color; Rated PG; 88 minutes; September release. CAST: John Mills (Bertie), Donald Pleasence (Sir Giles), Barbara Hershey (Marion), David Birney (Sir John), Margaret Leighton (Ma Gore), Peter Cushing (Sir Edward), Brian Glover, John Savident, John Hallam, Keith Buckley, Neil McCarthy, Thomas Heathcote, Bernard Hill, Alexander John, Diane Langton, Roy Holder, Una Brandon-Jones, Brian Hall, Peter Childs, John Bindon, Brian Coburn, Kevin Lloyd, Max Faulkner, Bill Weston, Mike Horsburgh, Marc Harrison

MANSION OF THE DOOMED (Group 1) Producer, Charles Band; Director, Michael Pataki; Screenplay, Frank Ray Perilli; Music, Robert O. Ragland; Photography, Andrew Davis; In DeLuxe Color; Rated R; 89 minutes; October release. CAST: Richard Basehart (Dr. Chaney), Gloria Grahame (Katherine), Trish Stewart (Nancy), Lance Henriksen (Dr. Bryan), Libbie Chase (Girl), Vic Tayback (Detective)

PROJECT: KILL (Stirling Gold) Producer, David Sheldon; Director, William Girdler; Screenplay Donald G. Thompson; Story, David Sheldon, Donald G. Thompson; Executive Producer, Fred Soriano, Jr.; Music, Robert O. Ragland; Rated R; 90 minutes; October release. CAST: Leslie Nielsen, Gary Lockwood, Nancy Kwan, Vic Silayan, Vic Diaz, Galen Thompson, Pamela Parsons, Maurice Down, Carlos Salazar

POSSE FROM HEAVEN (P.M.) Produced and Written by Ward Wood and Phillip Pine; Director, Phillip Pine; In Eastmancolor; Rated R; 87 minutes; October release. CAST: Fanne Foxe (Angel), Todd Compton (Appletime), Sherry Bain (Lola), Ward Wood (Gabriel), Rod Roddy (Diety), Dick Burch (Buffalo), Robert Perkin

THE SWINGING COEDS (Omni) Producer, Will Hartig; Director, Ross Meyers; Screenplay, Candy Clifford Diehl; In color; Rated R; October release. CAST: Susan Justice, Judy Marlow, Mandy Chandler, Bianca Herr, Astrid Blythe

SATURDAY NIGHT SPECIAL (MSW) Producer, Robert Petroff; Director, Sam Bloch; Screenplay, Joel Seigal; In color; Rated X; October release. CAST: Georgette Jennings, Jamie Gillis, Jeffrey Hurst

TEENAGE TWINS (MSW) Director, Carter Stevens; Screenplay, Al Hazard; In color; Rated X; October release. CAST: Brooke Young, Taylor Young, Tia Von-Davis, Eric Edwards

UP (RHM) Produced, Directed, Photographed, Edited by Russ Meyer; Screenplay, B. Callum; Art Director, Michele Levesque; Music, William Loose, Paul Ruhland; In color; Rated X; 80 minutes; October release. CAST: Robert McLane (Paul), Edward Schaaf (Adolph), Mary Gavin, Elaine Collins, Su Ling, Janet Wood, Linda Sue Ragsdale, Harry, Monte Bane, Raven De La Croix, Larry Dean, Marianne Marks, Bob Schott, Foxy Lae, Fred Owens, Wilburn Kluck, Ray Reinhardt, Francesca Natividad

Donald Pleasence, John Mills, David Birney
in "Dirty Knights' Work"

"Swinging Teacher"

**Nick Dimitri, Connie Stevens
in "Scorchy"**

**Marlene Schmidt, Greg Evigan, Connie Stevens,
Cesare Danova in "Scorchy"**

A*P*E* (Worldwide Entertainment) Producers, Paul Leder, K. M. Yeung; Director, Paul Leder; Screenplay, Paul Leder, Reuben Leder; Music, Bruce MacRae; Presented by Jack H. Harris; In color and 3-D; Rated PG; 87 minutes; October release. CAST: Rod Arrants, Joanna DeVarona, Alex Nicol

TELL THEM JOHNNY WADD IS HERE (Freeway) Producer, Damon Christian; Director, Bob Chinn; Screenplay, Robert Mathews; In color; Rated X; October release. CAST: John C. Holmes, Felicia Sanda, Veronica Taylor, Joan Devlon, Annette Haven, Carlos Tobalina, Paul Stifflerin, Michelle Scherr, Candice Chambers

THE DESTROYING ANGEL (Hand-in-Hand) Director, Peter DeRome; In color; Rated X; October release. CAST: Tim Kent, Philip Darden, Bill Eld Young

HOT NASTIES (Troma) Produced and Directed by Alexander Newman; In color; Rated X; October release. CAST: Heather Leigh, Julia Marlino, Susan Catharine, Trevor Saunders

SWINGING TEACHER (Worldwide Entertainment) Producer, Michael Montgomery; Director, David Feldshuh; Screenplay, Kathy Fehn; Photography, Gene Borman; Editor, Ken Robinson; Music, Dale Menten; Associate Producer, Paul Wesman; In color; Rated R; Presented by Jack H. Harris; 95 minutes; October release. CAST: Michael Montgomery (Mitchell), Lynn Baker (Kathy), Charlie McCarty (Frank), Marjorie D'Aquila (Mary), Nancy Nelson (Carol), John Pike, Jr. (Billy), Fred Tiemens (Guy), Chuck Walter (Joey), Peter Goetz (Store Owner), Ann Zaleski (Agent), Joe Giannetti (Cabbie), Mary Sumner (Grandmother)

THE BAD BUNCH (Dimension) Executive Producers, Mardi Rustam, Robert Brown; Producer, Alvin L. Fast; Director, Greydon Clark; Screenplay, Greydon Clark, Alvin L. Fast; In Eastmancolor; Rated R; October release. CAST: Greydon Clark (Jim), Tom Johnigarn (Markimba), Aldo Ray (Stans), Jock Mahoney (Berry), Pamela Corbett, Jacqulin Cole

THE HUMAN TORNADO (Dimension) A Comedian International Picture; Produced by Rudy Ray Moore in association with Theadore Toney; Director, Cliff Roquemore; Screenplay, Jerry Jones; Music, Arthur Wright; In color; 98 minutes; Rated R; October release. CAST: Rudy Ray Moore (Dolemite), Lady Reed (Queen Bee), Glorya de Lani (Hurricane Annie), Jimmy Lynch (Mr. Motion), Jerry Jones (Pistol Pete)

SCORCHY (American International) Executive Producer, Marlene Schmidt; Produced, Directed and Written by Hikmet Avedis; Photography, Laszlo Pal; Editor, Michael Luciano; Associate Producers, Laszle Pal, Sam Chebeir; Music, Igo Kantor; Assistant Director, Bruce Wilson; In Movielab Color; Rated R; 97 minutes; October release. CAST: Connie Stevens (Jackie), Cesare Danova (Philip), Marlene Schmidt (Claudia), William Smith (Carl), Normann Burton (Chief O'Brien), John David Chandler (Nicky), Joyce Jameson (Mary), Greg Evigan (Alan), Nick Dimitri (Steve), Nate Long (Charlie), Ingrid Cedergren (Suzi), Ellen Thurston (Maria), Ray Sebastian (Counterman), Mike Esky (Dimitri), Gene White (Big Boy)

PART 2 SOUNDER (Gamma III) Executive Producer, Robert B. Radnitz; Producer, Terry Nelson; Director, William A. Graham; Music, Taj Mahal; Screenplay, Lonne Elder III; Based on novel by William H. Armstrong; Photography, Urs B. Furrer; Designer, Walter Scott Herndon; Editor, Sid Levin; In color; Rated G; 98 minutes; October release. CAST: Harold Sylvester (Nathan), Ebony Wright (Rebecca), Taj Mahal (Ike), Annazette Chase (Camille), Darryl Young (David), Ericka Young (Josie), Ronald Bolden (Earl), Barbara Chaney (Mrs. Boatwright), Kuumba (Harriet), Ted Airhart (Perkins), Walter Breaux (Stranger), Irene Nofles (Mrs. Roberts), Harry Franklin, Sr. (Rev.), and Carol Sutton, Warren Kenner, Emanual Jarrell, Don Bynum, Earl Billings, Raymond Armelino

THE BOD SQUAD (Film Ventures International) Presented by Edward L. Montoro; In color; Rated R; 99 minutes; October release. CAST: Tamara Elliot, Sonja Jeanine, Diana Drube, Debra Ralls, Gillian Bray

"The Bad Bunch"

"Part 2 Sounder"

Denver Pyle, Dan Haggerty
in "The Adventures of Frontier Fremont"

MISTY (Cineworld) Directed and Written by Joe Sarno; Music, Jack Justis; In color; 100 minutes; October release. CAST: Rebecca Brooke, Eric Edwards, Sarah Nicholson, Jennifer Welles, Jamie Gillis, Chris Jordan, Carol Adams, Doug Wood, Julia Sorel, Fred Lincoln, Jennifer Mason.

CALL ME ANGEL SIR! (Jill Ross) Director, Kiki Young; Screenplay, E. Von Eaton; Music, Ron Frangipane; Photography, Bruce Jeffreys; In Eastmancolor; Rated X; 73 minutes; October release CAST: Diane Dalton, Jeff Hurst, Ultra Maxine, Annie Sprinkle, Short Stud, Bambi Deer, Wade Nichols

NAKED AFTERNOON (Westwood) Producer-Director, Alan B. Goldberg; Story and Screenplay, Utah Green; Photography, Franklin DeCeco; Executive Producer, Chelsea Lake; Music, Robert Summers, Steve Grossman; In color; Rated X; 86 minutes; October release. CAST: Abigail Clayton, John Leslie Dupre, Annette Haven, Kenny Cotten, Sarah Mills, Mark McIntire, Claire Dia, Joe Civera, Turk Lyon, Al Nulli

THAT LADY FROM RIO (Carioca) Written, Produced and Directed by Amanda Barton; In color; Rated X; October release. CAST: Vanessa Del Rio, Bobby Astyr, Marlene Willoughby, Jamie Gillis, Roger Caine, Joanna Hau

TOO HOT TO HANDLE (L. Kirtman) Director, James Beckley; Music, The Crews; In color; Rated X; October release. CAST: Kim Garling, Archie Flyn, Neil Gallo, Ella Butler, Candy Karen

DEATH COLLECTOR (Epoh) Producer, William N. Panzer; Directed and Written by Ralph DeVito; Executive Producer, Peter S. Davis; A John B. Kelly film; In color; Rated R; October release. CAST: Joseph Cortese, Lou Criscuola, Joseph Pesci, Anne Johns, Keith Davis, Bobby Alto, Frank Vincent

SEX WISH (Bonefide) A Taurus Production in Eastmancolor; Rated X; October release. CAST: Harry Reems, C. J. Laing, Zebedy Colt, Terri Hall, Dennea Benfante, Tony Rome, Candy Love, Joaquin La Habana, Nancy Dare

ASSAULT ON PRECINCT 13 (Turtle Releasing Org.) Presented by CKK Corp.; Executive Producer, Joseph Kaufman; Producer, J. S. Kaplan; Written and Directed by John Carpenter; Music, John Carpenter; Assistant Director, James Nichols; Photography, Douglas Knapp; Editor, John T. Chance; Art Director, Tommy Wallace; In Panavision and Metrocolor; Rated R; 91 minutes; October release. CAST: Austin Stoker (Bishop), Darwin Joston (Wilson), Laurie Zimmer (Leigh), Martin West (Lawson), Tony Burton (Wells), Charles Cyphers (Starker), Nancy Loomis (Julie), Peter Bruni (Ice Cream Man), John J. Fox (Warden), Kim Richards (Kathy), Marc Ross, Alan Koss, Henry Brandon, Peter Frankland, Gilbert de la Pena, Frank Doubleday, Al Nakauchi, James Johnson, Gilman Rankin, Cliff Battuello, Horace Johnson, Valentine Villareal, Kenny Miyamoto, Jerry Viramontes, Len Whitaker, Kris Young, Randy Moore, Warren Bradley III, Joe Woo, Jr. William Taylor, Breant Keast, Maynard Smith

THE ADVENTURES OF FRONTIER FREMONT (Sun Classic) Executive Producer, Raylan Jensen; Producer, Charles Sellier, Jr.; Director, Richard Friedenberg; Photography, George Stapleford; Assistant Director, Alan Burks; Screenplay, David O'Malley; In Techniscope and color; Rated G; October release. CAST: Dan Haggerty, Denver Pyle

FIGHTING MAD (20th Century-Fox) Producer, Roger Corman; Co-Producer, Evelyn Purcell; Written and Directed by Jonathan Demme; Photography, Michael Watkins; Editor, Anthony Magro; Music, Bruce Langhorne; Assistant Director, David Osterhout; In DeLuxe Color; Rated R; 90 minutes; October release. CAST: Peter Fonda (Tom), Lynn Lowry (Lorene), John Doucette (Jeff), Philip Carey (Pierce), Scott Glen (Charlie), Kathleen Miller (Carolee), Harry Northrup (Sheriff), Ted Markland (Hal) Gino Franco (Dylan), Nobel Willingham (Senator)

JOE PANTHER (Artist Creation) Producer, Stewart H. Beveridge; Executive Producer, Leroy C. Taylor; Director, Paul Krasny; Screenplay, Dale Eunson, from novel by Zachary Ball; Photography, Robert L. Morrison; Editors, Mike Vejar, Millie Moore; Music, Fred Karlin; In CFI Color; Rated R; 110 minutes; October release. CAST: Brian Keith (Capt. Harper), Ricardo Montalban (Turtle), Alan Feinstein (Rocky), Cliff Osmond (Rance), A. Martinez (Billy), Ray Tracey (Joe Panther), Robert W. Hoffman (George), Gem Thorpe Osceola (Tommy), Lois Red Elk (Mother), Monika Ramirez (Jenny)

THE KILLER INSIDE ME (Warner Bros.) Producer, Michael W. Leighton; Executive Producer, Irving Cohen; Director, Burt Kennedy; Screenplay, Edward Mann, Robert Chamblee, from novel by Jim Thompson; Photography, William A. Fraker; Music, Tim McIntire, John Rubinstein; Editors, Danford B. Greene, Aaron Stell; Assistant Director, Ray Marsh; In Metrocolor; Rated R; 99 minutes; October release. CAST: Stacy Keach (Lou), Susan Tyrrell (Joyce), Tisha Sterling (Amy), Keenan Wynn (Chester), Charles McGraw (Howard), John Dehner (Bob), Pepe Serna (Johnny), Royal Dano (Father), Julie Adams (Mother), John Carradine (Dr. Smith), Don Stroud (Elmer)

BLAST (New World) Produced, Directed and Written by Frank Arthur Wilson; Music, Wade Marcus; Played by Grant Green; In Metrocolor; Rated R; November release. CAST: Billy Dee Williams, D'Urville Martin, Sam Laws, Celia Kaye, Raymond St. Jacques, Pamela Jones, Madie Norman

THE SPIRIT OF SEVENTY-SEX (Artemis) Produced, Directed and Written by Ricki Krelmn; In Eastmancolor; 72 minutes; November release. CAST: Annette Haven, Tyler Reynolds, John C. Holmes, Desiree, Ken Scutter, Brit Britain, Randy Barns, Abigail Clayton, John Toland, Radio Ray

NIGHT OF THE SPANISH FLY No credits available; In color; Rated X; November release. CAST: Angel Barrett, Beerbohm Tree, Jeff Eagle, Jennifer Jordan

GOD TOLD ME TO (New World) Produced, Directed and Written by Larry Cohen; Photography, Paul Glickman; Music, Frank Cordell; A Larco Production; In color; Rated R; 90 minutes; November release. CAST: Tony LoBianco, Deborah Raffin, Sandy Dennis, Sylvia Sidney, Sam Levene, Robert Drivas, Mike Kellin, Richard Lynch, Sammy Williams, Jo Flores Chase, William Roerick, Lester Rawlins, Harry Bellaver, George Patterson, Walter Steele, John Heffernan

Abigail Clayton, Mark McIntire
in "Naked Afternoon"

JIVE TURKEY (Goldstone) Director, Bill Brame; A Ransom Production; In color; Rated R; November release. CAST: Paul Harris, Frank De Kova, Serene

TAPESTRY OF PASSION (Essex) Producer-Director, Alan B. Colberg; Screenplay, Alan B. Coldberg, Billy Thornberg; Story, Alan B. Colberg; Music, Flambe; Photography, Franklin DeCeco; In Eastmancolor; Rated X; November release. CAST: John C. Holmes, Sharon Thorpe, Leslie Bovee, Annette Haven, Patricia Lee, Mike Jones, John Leslie Dupre

THE TROUBLE WITH YOUNG STUFF Written and Directed by Odus Hamlin; Music, Jack Justis; In color; Rated X; November release. CAST: Christine Williams, Marlene Willoughby, Sara Barnes, Sonny Landham, Gloria Leonard, Nancy Dare, Roger Caine, Richard Bolla

THE AMAZING WORLD OF PSYCHIC PHENOMENA (Sun Classic) Producer, Charles E. Sellier, Jr.; Directed and Written by Robert Guenette; Narrator, Raymond Burr; In Technicolor; Rated G; November release.

THE AFFAIRS OF JANICE (Leisure Time) Direction and Screenplay, Zebedy Colt; Music, The Zodiacs; Photography, William Moody; Executive Producer, Leon DeLeon; A Taurus Production; In Eastmancolor; Rated X; 72 minutes; November release. CAST: C. J. Laing, Zebedy Colt, Crystal Harris, Ras Kean, Bobby Astyr, Annie Sprinkle, Renee Sanz

THE STARLETS (Quadravision International) Produced and Written by M. C. Von Hellen: Directors, David Summers, Joseph Tebber; In 4-D and color; Rated X; November release. CAST: Dorothy Newkirk, Monique Cardin, Patricia Lee, Spring Finely, Susan Devlin, Kitty Moore, David Scharf, Kenny Cotton, Virginia Baker, Lee Forest, Roger Seeman

GUMS (Masada) Directed and Written by Robert J. Kaplan; Producer, Paul Cohen; In color; November release. CAST: Terri Hall (Mermaid), Brother Theodore (Captain)

THE INCREDIBLE TORTURE SHOW (American Film) Producer, Alan C. Margolin; Direction and Screenplay, Joel M. Reed; Music, Michael Sahl; In color; Rated X; November release. CAST: Seamus O'Brien (Sardu), Louie DeJesus (Ralphus), Viji Krem, Lynette Sheldon, Karen Fraser, Michelle Craig

THE COCKTAIL HOSTESSES (S.C.A.) Producer-Director, A. C. Stephen; In Eastmancolor; Rated R; November release. CAST: Rene Bond, Terri Johnson, Lynn Harris, Kathy Hilton, Forman Shane

LES NYMPHO TEENS (Troma) Producer, Louis Su; Director, David Stitt; In color; Rated X; November release. CAST: Gloria Leonard, Sherril Karp, Cindy Greenstreet

LOVE IN STRANGE PLACES (Pendulus) Produced, Directed and Written by Robert D. Walters; Music, Harold Hindgrind; In Eastmancolor; Rated X; November release. CAST: John C. Holmes, Crystal Sync, Jeffrey Hurst, Eric Edwards, Marlene Willoughby, Slim Pickins Band

SOUPERMAN (Unique) Directed by Fred Lincoln; In Color; Rated X; November release. CAST: Marc Stevens, Brenda Bassie, Susan McBain

THE MUTHERS (Dimension) Producer-Director, Cirio H. Santiago; Screenplay, Cyril St. James; Story, Leonard Hermes; Music, Edd Villanueva; In color; Rated R; 83 minutes; November release. CAST: Jeanne Bell (Kelly), Rosanne Katon (Angie), J. Antonio Carrion (Montiero), Trina Parks (Marcie), Jayne Kennedy (Serena), John Montgomery, Sam Sharruff

PONY EXPRESS RIDER (Doty-Dayton) Producers, Dan Greer, Hal Harrison, Jr; Executive Producer, Robert Totten; Screenplay, Lyman Dayton, Dan Greer, Hal Harrison, Jr., Robert Totten; Director, Hal Harrison, Jr.; Music, Robert O. Ragland; Photography, Bernie Abramson; Editor, Marsh Hendry; Art Director, Elayne Cedar; Assistant Directors, Hall Galli, Gene Sulton; Costumes, Campbel; In DeLuxe Color; Rated G; November release. CAST: Stewart Petersen (Jimmy), Henry Wilcoxon (Trevor), Buck Taylor (Bovey), Maureen McCormick (Rose), Ken Curtis (Jed), Joan Caulfield (Charlotte), Slim Pickens (Bob), Dub Taylor (Boomer), Ace Reid (Bullfrog), Jack Elam (Crazy), Larry D. Mann (Blackmore), James Almanzar (Puddin), Bea Morris (Marquette), Tom Waters (Button), Cliff Brand (Capt.), Bleu McKenzie (Bill), Pamela D'On Thompson (Rebecca), Burtrust T. Wilson (Geech)

Shari Eubank
in "Chesty Anderson, U.S. Navy"

PANAMA RED (American Films) Executive Producer, Roland Miller; Producer, Linda Adrain; Direction and Screenplay, Robert C. Chinn; Photography, Dan Goodman; Editor, Lawrence Avery; Associate Producer, Donna Lee Wingert; Music and Lyrics, Jim Wingert; A Pantheon Production; In AGFA-Gevaert Color; Rated PG; 87 minutes; November release. CAST: Jim Wingert (Randy), Barbara Mills (Barbara), Alain Patrick (Marchaud), Henry Sanders (John), Rene Bond (Shari), Roland Miller (Rogers), Richard Weissman (Repossessor), Dan Soref (Chief), Glade Lee (McCord), Ed Crane (Ludwig), Andy Hernandez (Percy) Howard Tobar Mayo, Michael Conte, Rama Stagner, John Holmes, Ghuy Valdes, Walt Davis, Sandy Dempsey, Rick Cassidy, Jack Morgan, Cynthia Laurent

HARD CANDY (Debonair) Executive Producer, Tom Kenyon; Produced and Directed by Norm De Plume; Screenplay, Mark Thunderbuns, Ann Onymous; Music, The Luscious Lickers; Photography, D. W. Griffin; Costumes, Silky Sommers; Editor, Noel Pickett; In Eastmancolor; Rated X; 75 minutes; November release. CAST: Synthia Starr, John Holmes, Brenda Ram, Hal Walker, Heather Grant, Tyler Horn, William Margold, Barbara Brown, Candy Collins, Laura Raymond, Vicki Cunningham

HOLLYWOOD ON TRIAL (Lumiere) Producers, James Gutman, David Helpern, Jr.; Director, David Helpern; Associate Producers, Frank Galvin, Juergen Hellwig; Photography, Barry Abrams; Screenplay, Arnie Reisman; Editor, Frank Galvin; In black and white and color; Rated PG; 105 minutes; November release. A documentary.

CHESTY ANDERSON, U. S. NAVY (Atlas) Producer, Paul Pompian; Executive Producer, Philip J. Hacker; Screenplay, Paul Pompian, H. F. Green; Director, Ed Forsyth; In Eastmancolor; Rated R; 88 minutes; November release. CAST: Chari Eubank (Chesty), Dorri Thomson (Tina), Rosanne Katon (Cocoa), Marcie Barkin (Pucker), Timothy Agoglia Carey (Vincent), Frank Campanella (Baron), Scatman Crothers (Ben), Fred Willard (FBI Agent)

Lee Montgomery
in "Baker's Hawk"

Rosalind Cash, Yaphet Kotto
in "The Monkey Hustle"

KENNY & CO. (20th Century-Fox) Written, Produced, Directed, Photographed and Edited by Don Coscarelli; Music, Fred Myrow; Art Director, S. T. Coscarelli; Costumes, Cyndie Coscarelli; Assistant Director, Paul Pepperman; In color; Rated PG; 90 minutes; November release. CAST: Dan McCann (Kenny), Mike Baldwin (Doug), Jeff Roth (Sherman), Ralph Richmond (Big Doug), Reggie Bannister (Donovan), Clay Foster (Brink), Ken Jones (Soupy), Willy Masterson (Johnny), David Newton (Pudwell), James E. dePriest (Dad), S. T. Coscarelli (Mom), Terri Kalbus (Marcie)

FREEWHEELIN' (Turtle) Producer-Director, Scott Dittrich; Executive Producer, Daniel Rosenthal; Screenplay, Editing, George Van Noy; Photography, Pat Darrin; Music, Stephen Freud; In color; Rated G; 80 minutes; November release. CAST: Stacy Peralta, Camille Darrin, Russ Howell, Ken Means, Tom Sims, Mike Weed, Paul Coustantineau, Bobby Pierce, Stevie Monahan, Desiree Von Essen, Guy Grundy, Waldo Autrey

GETTING TOGETHER (Total Impact) Producers, Joey Asaro, David Sector; Written and Directed by David Secter; Photography, Marty Knopf; Editor, Jane Brodsky Altschuler; Design, Theodore S. Hammer; Art Director, Gerald Holbrook; Music, Tony Camillo; Costumes, Neil Cooper; In color; 110 minutes; November release. CAST: Malcolm Groome (David), Kathleen Seward (Shiela), Rhonda Hansome (Reb), Tony Collado (Carlos), Charles Douglass (Randy), Helga Kopperl (Vivian)

JAMES DEAN, THE FIRST AMERICAN TEENAGER (Ziv Tel) Producers, David Puttnam, Sandy Lieberson; Written and Directed by Ray Connolly; Narrated by Stacy Keach; Editor, Peter Hollywood; Music, Elton John, David Bowie; Rated PG; In Eastmancolor; 80 minutes; November Release. Documentary.

A CHILD IS A WILD YOUNG THING (Skinner) Produced, Written, Directed by Peter Skinner; Editors, Peter Skinner, Vincent Suprynowicz; Music, Derek Wadsworth; Lyrics, Peter Skinner; In color; 88 minutes; November release. CAST: Marie Antoinette Skinner (Miette), George S. Irving (Professor's Voice), Paulette Rubinstein (Miette's Voice)

**Heather Rattray, Mark Edward Hall
in "Across the Great Divide"**

HOLLYWOOD HIGH (Peter Perry) Director, Patrick Wright; Producer, Peter Perry; Music, Scott Gale; Photography, Jonathan Silveira; In color; Rated R; December release. CAST: Marcy Albrecht, Sherry Hardin, Rae Sperling, Susanne, Kevin Mead, John Young, Joseph Butcher, Richard Hynes

FUNK (Independent) Director, Julian Marsh; In 3-D and color; Rated X; December release, CAST: Annie Sprinkle, Alan Marlow, Claire Sable, Nikki Hilton, Ralph Waters, Mike Jefferson, Sue Rowan, Rita Davis, Don Allen, Alex Mann

GUARDIAN OF THE WILDERNESS (Sun Classic) Producer, Charles E. Sellier, Jr.; Director, David O'Malley; In Technicolor; Rated G; December release. CAST: Denver Pyle, Ken Berry, John Dehner, Cheryl Miller, Cliff Osmond, Ford Rainey, Jack Kruschen, Norman Fell

CANDY LIPS (Honeypot) Director, Cecil B. Damill; Rated X; December release. CAST: Suzy Humphree, Gloria Leonard, Ras Kean, Marlene Willoughby, Dominatia, Jake Teague, April May, Jeanette Sinclair

CHERRY TRUCKERS (Art Mart) Director, Rik Taziner; In color; Rated X; December release. CAST: Azure Te, Dean Gary

BAKER'S HAWK (Doty-Dayton) Producer-Director, Lyman D. Dayton; Screenplay, Dan Greer, Hal Harrison, Jr.; Associate Producers, Rick Thiriot, Dan Greer; Photography, Bernie Abramson; Music, Lex De Azevedo; Editor, Parkie Singh; Design, Bill Kenney; Assistant Directors, Bill Lukather, Edward Markley; In DeLuxe Color; Rated G; 98 minutes; December release. CAST: Clint Walker (Dan Baker), Burl Ives (McGraw), Diane Baker (Jenny), Lee H. Montgomery (Billy), Alan Young (Carson), Taylor Lacher (Sweeney), Bruce M. Fischer (Blacksmith), Cam Clarke (Morrie), Phil Hoover (Sled), Danny Bonaduce (Robertson), Brian Williams (Jeremy), Burt Mustin (General), Martin Eric (Wattle)

THE MONKEY HUSTLE (American International) Producer-Director, Arthur Marks; Screenplay, Charles Johnson; Story, Odie Hawkins; Photography, Jack L. Richards; Associate Producer, Robert E. Schultz; Editor, Art Seid; Music, Jack Conrad; In Movielab Color; Rated PG; 90 minutes; December release. CAST: Yaphet Kotto (Daddy Fox), Rudy Ray Moore (Goldie), Rosalind Cash (Mama), Randy Brooks (Win), Debbi Morgan (Vi), Thomas Carter (Player), Donn Harper (Tiny), Lyn Caridine (Jan), Patricia McCaskill (Shirl), Lynn Harris (Sweet Potato), Fuddle Bagley (Molet), Frank Rice (Black Knight), Carl Crudup (Joe), Duchyll Smith (Beatrice), Kirk Calloway (Baty D)

ALL THIS AND WORLD WAR II (20th Century-Fox) Producers, Sandy Lieberson, Martin J. Machat; Executive Producer, Russ Regan; Director, Susan Winslow; Music, Lou Reizner; Words and Music, John Lennon, Paul McCartney; A Martin J. Machat/Eric Kronfeld Presentation; In color and black and white; Rated PG; 88 minutes; December release. A documentary coverage of the "last of the great world conflagrations.

THE JOY OF LETTING GO (Summer Brown) Executive Producer, Edwin Scott Brown; Director, John Gregory; Screenplay, Cynthia Holm; Photography, Kurt Stem, Patrick Riley; Editor, David Peoples; Music, Bob Maser; In Eastmancolor; Rated X. 86 minutes; December release. CAST: Dominique St. Pierre (Michele), Leslie Hughes (David), James Kral (Dancer), Pamela Strasser (Annette), Susie Sung Lee (Topaz)

ACROSS THE GREAT DIVIDE (Pacific International) Producer, Arthur R. Dubs; Written and Directed by Stewart Raffill; Music, Gene Kauer, Douglas Lackey; In color; Rated G; December release. CAST: Robert Logan (Zachariah), Heather Rattray (Holly), Mark Hall (Jason), George Flower (Indian Chief)

JOSHUA (Lone Star) Producer-Director, Larry Spangler; Story and Screenplay, Fred Williamson; In color; Rated PG; 80 minutes; December release. CAST: Fred Williamson, Isela Vega, Calvin Bartlett, Brenda Venus

GARAGE SALE (Independent) Producers, Bruce Yonemoto, Norman Yonemoto; Directed, Written and Edited by Norman Yonemoto; Photography, Nick Ursin; Music, Sunset Boulevard, The Dreaded Mr. Twister; Title Song, Gordon Skene; Assistant Director, Steven McGrew; In Eastmancolor; Rated X; December release. CAST: Goldie Glitters (Herself-Michael Heesy), Ruth Hagopian, Paul Mathews, Anastasia, Steven McGrew, Bruce Lovern, Bob Opel, L. E. Coulter, Loren Rhodes, Don Soker, Nick Ursin

GOIN' HOME (Prentiss) Written, Produced, Directed, Edited by Chris Prentiss; Photography, Chris Prentiss, Christopher Sloan Nibley III; Music, Lee Holdridge; In DeLuxe Color; Rated G; 97 minutes; December release. CAST: Todd Christiansen (Todd), Bernard Triche (Bernard), Kevin Oliver (Kevin), Melvin Ruffin (Ruffin), Robert Dale Poole (Dusty), Marion Forbes (Evil), Delia Bradford (Delia)

PROMISING NEW ACTORS OF 1976

ROBBY BENSON

MEREDITH BAXTER BIRNEY

IRENE CARA

SAM ELLIOTT

FARRAH FAWCETT-MAJORS

SYLVESTER STALLONE

BO SVENSON

JODIE FOSTER

ANDREA MARCOVICCI

JOHN TRAVOLTA

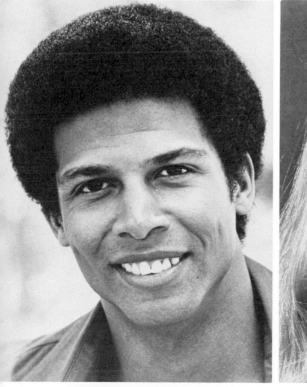

MICHAEL WARREN

SISSY SPACEK

ONE FLEW OVER THE CUCKOO'S NEST

(UNITED ARTISTS) Producers, Saul Zaentz, Michael Douglas; Director, Milos Forman; Screenplay, Lawrence Hauben, Bo Goldman; Based on novel of same title by Ken Kesey; Photography, Haskell Wexler, William Fraker, Bill Butler; Music, Jack Nitzsche; Editors, Richard Chew, Lynzee Klingman, Sheldon Kahn; Associate Producer, Martin Fink; Designer; Paul Sylbert; Art Director, Edwin O'Donovan; Assistant Directors, Irby Smith, William St. John; In color; Rated R; 129 minutes; November 1975 release

CAST

R. P. McMurphy	Jack Nicholson
Nurse Ratched	Louise Fletcher
Harding	William Redfield
Ellis	Michael Berryman
Billy Bibbit	Brad Dourif
Col. Matterson	Peter Brocco
Dr. Spivey	Dean R. Brooks
Miller	Alonzo Brown
Turkle	Sherman "Scatman" Crothers
Warren	Mwako Cumbuka
Martini	Danny De Vito
Sefelt	William Duell
Bancini	Josip Elic
Nurse Itsu	Lan Fendors
Washington	Nathan George
Beans Garfield	Ken Kenny
Harbor Master	Mel Lambert
Cheswick	Sydney Lassick
Night Supervisor	Kay Lee
Taber	Christopher Lloyd
Ellsworth	Dwight Marfield
Hap Arlich	Ted Markland
Rose	Louisa Moritz
Woolsey	Phil Roth
Chief Bromden	Will Sampson
Nurse Pilbow	Mimi Sarkisian
Fredrickson	Vincent Schiavelli
Candy	Marya Small
Scanlon	Delos V. Smith, Jr
Ruckley	Tin Welch

Left: Jack Nicholson, also top with Bob Milam

Louise Fletcher, Jack Nicholson, Ted Markland

Danny DeVito, Brad Dourif, Jack Nicholson, Christopher Lloyd

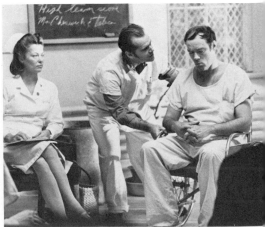

1975 Academy Awards for Best Picture, Best Actor (Jack Nicholson), Best Actress (Louise Fletcher), Best Director, Best Screenp

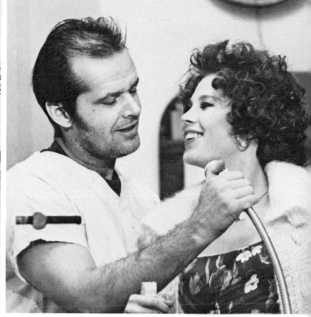

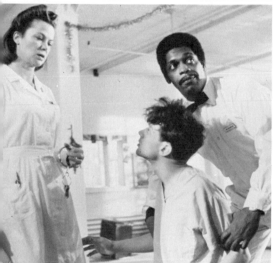

William Duell, Vincent Schiavelli, Delos V. Smith, Jr., Jack Nicholson, Brad Dourif, William Redfield Above: Louise Fletcher, Dourif, Nathan George

Mimi Sarkisian, Louise Fletcher, Jack Nicholson Above: Nicholson, Will Sampson Top: Nicholson, Marya Small

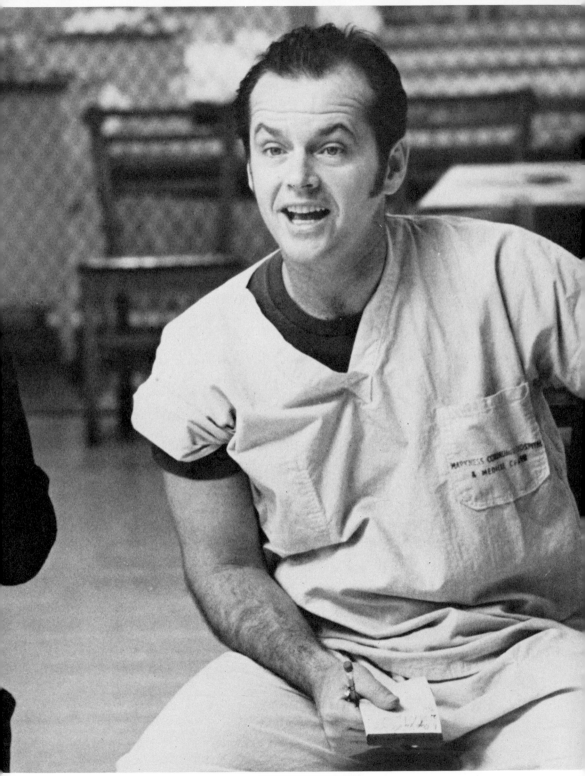

JACK NICHOLSON
in "One Flew over the Cuckoo's Nest"
1975 ACADEMY AWARD FOR BEST PERFORMANCE BY AN ACTOR

LOUISE FLETCHER
in "One Flew over the Cuckoo's Nest"
1975 ACADEMY AWARD FOR BEST PERFORMANCE BY AN ACTRESS

Academy Award for Best Foreign Language Film went to "Dersu Uzala" (no material available)

GEORGE BURNS
in "The Sunshine Boys"
1975 ACADEMY AWARD FOR BEST SUPPORTING PERFORMANCE BY AN ACTOR

LEE GRANT
in "Shampoo"
1975 ACADEMY AWARD FOR BEST SUPPORTING PERFORMANCE BY AN ACTRESS　　159

| Bing Crosby | Patty Duke | Jack Lemmon | Katharine Hepburn | Walter Matthau | Glenda Jackson |

PREVIOUS ACADEMY AWARD WINNERS

(1) Best Picture, (2) Actor, (3) Actress, (4) Supporting Actor, (5) Supporting Actress, (6) Director, (7) Special Award, (8) Best Foreign Language Film

1927–28: (1) "Wings" (2) Emil Jannings in "The Way of All Flesh", (3) Janet Gaynor in "Seventh Heaven", (6) Frank Borzage for "Seventh Heaven", (7) Charles Chaplin.

1928–29: (1) "Broadway Melody", (2) Warner Baxter in "Old Arizona", (3) Mary Pickford in "Coquette", (6) Frank Lloyd for "The Divine Lady".

1929–30: (1) "All Quiet on the Western Front", (2) George Arliss in "Disraeli", (3) Norma Shearer in "The Divorcee", (6) Lewis Milestone for "All Quiet on the Western Front".

1930–31: (1) "Cimarron", (2) Lionel Barrymore in "A Free Soul", (3) Marie Dressler in "Min and Bill", (6) Norman Taurog for "Skippy".

1931–32: (1) "Grand Hotel", (2) Fredric March in "Dr. Jekyll and Mr. Hyde" tied with Wallace Beery in "The Champ", (3) Helen Hayes in "The Sin of Madelon Claudet", (6) Frank Borzage for "Bad Girl".

1932–33: (1) "Cavalcade", (2) Charles Laughton in "The Private Life of Henry VIII", (3) Katharine Hepburn in "Morning Glory", (6) Frank Lloyd for "Cavalcade".

1934: (1) "It Happened One Night", (2) Clark Gable in "It Happened One Night", (3) Claudette Colbert in "It Happened One Night", (6) Frank Capra for "It Happened One Night", (7) Shirley Temple.

1935: (1) "Mutiny on the Bounty", (2) Victor McLaglen in "The Informer" (3) Bette Davis in "Dangerous", (6) John Ford for "The Informer", (7) D. W. Griffith.

1936: (1) "The Great Ziegfeld", (2) Paul Muni in "The Story of Louis Pasteur", (3) Luise Rainer in "The Great Ziegfeld", (4) Walter Brennan in "Come and Get It", (5) Gale Sondergaard in "Anthony Adverse", (6) Frank Capra for "Mr. Deeds Goes to Town".

1937: (1) "The Life of Emile Zola", (2) Spencer Tracy in "Captains Courageous", (3) Luise Rainer in "The Good Earth", (4) Joseph Schildkraut in "The Life of Emile Zola", (5) Alice Brady in "In Old Chicago", (6) Leo McCarey for "The Awful Truth", (7) Mack Sennett, Edgar Bergen.

1938: (1) "You Can't Take It with You", (2) Spencer Tracy in "Boys' Town", (3) Bette Davis in "Jezebel", (4) Walter Brennan in "Kentucky", (5) Fay Bainter in "Jezebel", (6) Frank Capra for "You Can't Take It with You", (7) Deanna Durbin, Mickey Rooney, Harry M. Warner, Walt Disney.

1939: (1) "Gone with the Wind", (2) Robert Donat in "Goodbye, Mr. Chips", (3) Vivien Leigh in "Gone with the Wind", (4) Thomas Mitchell in "Stagecoach", (5) Hattie McDaniel in "Gone with the Wind", (6) Victor Fleming for "Gone with the Wind", (7) Douglas Fairbanks, Judy Garland.

1940: (1) "Rebecca", (2) James Stewart in "The Philadelphia Story", (3) Ginger Rogers in "Kitty Foyle", (4) Walter Brennan in "The Westerner", (5) Jane Darwell in "The Grapes of Wrath", (6) John Ford for "The Grapes of Wrath", (7) Bob Hope.

1941: (1) "How Green Was My Valley", (2) Gary Cooper in "Sergeant York", (3) Joan Fontaine in "Suspicion", (4) Donald Crisp in "How Green Was My Valley", (5) Mary Astor in "The Great Lie", (6) John Ford for "How Green Was My Valley", (7) Leopold Stokowski, Walt Disney.

1942: (1) "Mrs. Miniver", (2) James Cagney in "Yankee Doodle Dandy", (3) Greer Garson in "Mrs. Miniver", (4) Van Heflin in "Johnny Eager", (5) Teresa Wright in "Mrs. Miniver", (6) William Wyler for "Mrs. Miniver", (7) Charles Boyer, Noel Coward.

1943: (1) "Casablanca", (2) Paul Lukas in "Watch on the Rhine", (3) Jennifer Jones in "The Song of Bernadette", (4) Charles Coburn in "The More the Merrier", (5) Katina Paxinou in "For Whom the Bell Tolls", (6) Michael Curtiz for "Casablanca".

1944: (1) "Going My Way", (2) Bing Crosby in "Going My Way", (3) Ingrid Bergman in "Gaslight", (4) Barry Fitzgerald in "Going My Way", (5) Ethel Barrymore in "None but the Lonely Heart", (6) Leo McCarey for "Going My Way", (7) Margaret O'Brien, Bob Hope.

1945: (1) "The Lost Weekend", (2) Ray Milland in "The Lost Weekend", (3) Joan Crawford in "Mildred Pierce", (4) James Dunn in "A Tree Grows in Brooklyn", (5) Anne Revere in "National Velvet", (6) Billy Wilder for "The Lost Weekend", (7) Walter Wanger, Peggy Ann Garner.

1946: (1) "The Best Years of Our Lives", (2) Fredric March in "The Best Years of Our Lives", (3) Olivia de Havilland in "To Each His Own", (4) Harold Russell in "The Best Years of Our Lives", (5) Anne Baxter in "The Razor's Edge", (7) Laurence Olivier, Harold Russell, Ernst Lubitsch, Claude Jarman, Jr.

1947: (1) "Gentleman's Agreement", (2) Ronald Colman in "A Double Life", (3) Loretta Young in "The Farmer's Daughter", (4) Edmund Gwenn in "Miracle On 34th Street", (5) Celeste Holm in "Gentleman's Agreement", (6) Elia Kazan for "Gentleman's Agreement", (7) James Baskette, (8) "Shoe Shine."

1948: (1) "Hamlet", (2) Laurence Olivier in "Hamlet", (3) Jane Wyman in "Johnny Belinda", (4) Walter Huston in "The Treasure of the Sierra Madre", (5) Claire Trevor in "Key Largo", (6) John Huston for "The Treasure of the Sierra Madre", (7) Ivan Jandl, Sid Grauman, Adolph Zukor, Walter Wanger, (8) "Monsieur Vincent".

1949: (1) "All the King's Men", (2) Broderick Crawford in "All the King's Men", (3) Olivia de Havilland in "The Heiress", (4) Dean Jagger in "Twelve O'Clock High", (5) Mercedes McCambridge in "All the King's Men", (6) Joseph L. Mankiewicz for "A Letter to Three Wives", (7) Bobby Driscoll, Fred Astaire, Cecil B. DeMille, Jean Hersholt, (8) "The Bicycle Thief."

1950: (1) "All about Eve", (2) Jose Ferrer in "Cyrano de Bergerac", (3) Judy Holliday in "Born Yesterday", (4) George Sanders in "All about Eve", (5) Josephine Hull in "Harvey", (6) Joseph L. Mankiewicz for "All about Eve", (7) George Murphy, Louis B. Mayer, (8) "The Walls of Malapaga."

1951: (1) "An American in Paris", (2) Humphrey Bogart in "The African Queen", (3) Vivien Leigh in "A Streetcar Named Desire", (4) Karl Malden in "A Streetcar Named Desire", (5) Kim Hunter in "A Streetcar Named Desire", (6) George Stevens for "A Place in the Sun", (7) Gene Kelly, (8) "Rashomon."

1952: (1) "The Greatest Show on Earth", (2) Gary Cooper in "High Noon", (3) Shirley Booth in "Come Back, Little Sheba", (4) Anthony Quinn in "Viva Zapata", (5) Gloria Grahame in "The Bad and the Beautiful", (6) John Ford for "The Quiet Man", (7) Joseph M. Schenck, Merian C. Cooper, Harold Lloyd, Bob Hope, George Alfred Mitchell, (8) "Forbidden Games."

| Sidney Poitier | Ginger Rogers | John Wayne | Elizabeth Taylor | Orson Welles | Shirley Temple |

1953: (1) "From Here to Eternity", (2) William Holden in "Stalag 17", (3) Audrey Hepburn in "Roman Holiday", (4) Frank Sinatra in "From Here to Eternity", (5) Donna Reed in "From Here to Eternity", (6) Fred Zinnemann for "From Here to Eternity", (7) Pete Smith, Joseph Breen.

1954: (1) "On the Waterfront", (2) Marlon Brando in "On the Waterfront", (3) Grace Kelly in "The Country Girl", (4) Edmond O'Brien in "The Barefoot Contessa", (5) Eva Marie Saint in "On the Waterfront", (6) Elia Kazan for "On the Waterfront", (7) Greta Garbo, Danny Kaye, Jon Whitely, Vincent Winter, (8) "Gate of Hell."

1955: (1) "Marty", (2) Ernest Borgnine in "Marty", (3) Anna Magnani in "The Rose Tattoo", (4) Jack Lemmon in "Mister Roberts", (5) Jo Van Fleet in "East of Eden", (6) Delbert Mann for "Marty", (8) "Samurai."

1956: (1) "Around the World in 80 Days", (2) Yul Brynner in "The King and I", (3) Ingrid Bergman in "Anastasia", (4) Anthony Quinn in "Lust for Life", (5) Dorothy Malone in "Written on the Wind", (6) George Stevens for "Giant", (7) Eddie Cantor (8) "La Strada."

1957: (1) "The Bridge on the River Kwai", (2) Alec Guinness in "The Bridge on the River Kwai", (3) Joanne Woodward in "The Three Faces of Eve", (4) Red Buttons in "Sayonara", (5) Miyoshi Umeki in "Sayonara", (6) David Lean for "The Bridge on the River Kwai", (7) Charles Brackett, B. B. Kahane, Gilbert M. (Bronco Billy) Anderson, (8) "The Nights of Cabiria."

1958: (1) "Gigi", (2) David Niven in "Separate Tables", (3) Susan Hayward in "I Want to Live", (4) Burl Ives in "The Big Country", (5) Wendy Hiller in "Separate Tables", (6) Vincente Minnelli for "Gigi", (7) Maurice Chevalier, (8) "My Uncle."

1959: (1) "Ben-Hur", (2) Charlton Heston in "Ben-Hur", (3) Simone Signoret in "Room at the Top", (4) Hugh Griffith in "Ben-Hur", (5) Shelley Winters in "The Diary of Anne Frank", (6) William Wyler for "Ben-Hur", (7) Lee de Forest, Buster Keaton, (8) "Black Orpheus."

1960: (1) "The Apartment", (2) Burt Lancaster in "Elmer Gantry", (3) Elizabeth Taylor in "Butterfield 8", (4) Peter Ustinov in "Spartacus", (5) Shirley Jones in "Elmer Gantry", (6) Billy Wilder for "The Apartment", (7) Gary Cooper, Stan Laurel, Hayley Mills, (8) "The Virgin Spring."

1961: (1) "West Side Story", (2) Maximilian Schell in "Judgment at Nuremberg", (3) Sophia Loren in "Two Women", (4) George Chakiris in "West Side Story", (5) Rita Moreno in "West Side Story", (6) Robert Wise for "West Side Story", (7) Jerome Robbins, Fred L. Metzler, (8) "Through a Glass Darkly."

1962: (1) "Lawrence of Arabia", (2) Gregory Peck in "To Kill a Mockingbird", (3) Anne Bancroft in "The Miracle Worker", (4) Ed Begley in "Sweet Bird of Youth", (5) Patty Duke in "The Miracle Worker", (6) David Lean for "Lawrence of Arabia", (8) "Sundays and Cybele."

1963: (1) "Tom Jones", (2) Sidney Poitier in "Lilies of the Field", (3) Patricia Neal in "Hud", (4) Melvyn Douglas in "Hud", (5) Margaret Rutherford in "The V.I.P's", (6) Tony Richardson for "Tom Jones", (8) "8½".

1964: (1) "My Fair Lady", (2) Rex Harrison in "My Fair Lady", (3) Julie Andrews in "Mary Poppins", (4) Peter Ustinov in "Topkapi", (5) Lila Kedrova in "Zorba the Greek", (6) George Cukor for "My Fair Lady", (7) William Tuttle, (8) "Yesterday, Today and Tomorrow."

1965: (1) "The Sound of Music", (2) Lee Marvin in "Cat Ballou", (3) Julie Christie in "Darling", (4) Martin Balsam in "A Thousand Clowns", (5) Shelley Winters in "A Patch of Blue", (6) Robert Wise for "The Sound of Music", (7) Bob Hope, (8) "The Shop on Main Street".

1966: (1) "A Man for All Seasons", (2) Paul Scofield in "A Man for All Seasons", (3) Elizabeth Taylor in "Who's Afraid of Virginia Woolf?", (4) Walter Matthau in "The Fortune Cookie", (5) Sandy Dennis in "Who's Afraid of Virginia Woolf?", (6) Fred Zinnemann for "A Man for All Seasons", (8) "A Man and A Woman."

1967: (1) "In the Heat of the Night", (2) Rod Steiger in "In the Heat of the Night", (3) Katharine Hepburn in "Guess Who's Coming to Dinner", (4) George Kennedy in "Cool Hand Luke", (5) Estelle Parsons in "Bonnie and Clyde", (6) Mike Nichols for "The Graduate", (8) "Closely Watched Trains."

1968: (1) "Oliver!", (2) Cliff Robertson in "Charly", (3) Katharine Hepburn in "The Lion in Winter" tied with Barbra Streisand in "Funny Girl", (4) Jack Albertson in "The Subject Was Roses", (5) Ruth Gordon in "Rosemary's Baby", (6) Carol Reed for "Oliver!", (7) Onna White for "Oliver!" choreography, John Chambers for "Planet of the Apes" make-up, (8) "War and Peace."

1969: (1) "Midnight Cowboy", (2) John Wayne in "True Grit", (3) Maggie Smith in "The Prime of Miss Jean Brodie", (4) Gig Young in "They Shoot Horses, Don't They?", (5) Goldie Hawn in "Cactus Flower", (6) John Schlesinger for "Midnight Cowboy", (7) Cary Grant, (8) "Z."

1970: (1) "Patton", (2) George C. Scott in "Patton", (3) Glenda Jackson in "Women in Love", (4) John Mills in "Ryan's Daughter," (5) Helen Hayes in "Airport", (6) Franklin J. Schaffner for "Patton," (7) Lillian Gish, Orson Welles, (8) "Investigation of a Citizen above Suspicion."

1971: (1) "The French Connection," (2) Gene Hackman in "The French Connection," (3) Jane Fonda in "Klute," (4) Ben Johnson in "The Last Picture Show," (5) Cloris Leachman in "The Last Picture Show," (6) William Friedkin for "The French Connection," (7) Charles Chaplin, (8) "The Garden of the Finzi-Continis."

1972: (1) "The Godfather," (2) Marlon Brando in "The Godfather," (3) Liza Minnelli in "Cabaret," (4) Joel Grey in "Cabaret," (5) Eileen Heckart in "Butterflies Are Free," (6) Bob Fosse for "Cabaret," (7) Edward G. Robinson, (8) "The Discreet Charm of the Bourgeoisie."

1973: (1) "The Sting," (2) Jack Lemmon in "Save the Tiger," (3) Glenda Jackson in "A Touch of Class," (4) John Houseman in "The Paper Chase," (5) Tatum O'Neal in "Paper Moon," (6) George Roy Hill for "The Sting," (8) "Day for Night"

1974: (1) "The Godfather Part II," (2) Art Carney in "Harry and Tonto," (3) Ellen Burstyn in "Alice Doesn't Live Here Anymore," (4) Robert DeNiro in "The Godfather Part II," (5) Ingrid Bergman in "Murder on the Orient Express," (6) Francis Ford Coppola for "The Godfather Part II," (7) Howard Hawks, Jean Renoir, (8). "Amarcord"

1975: (1) "One Flew over the Cuckoo's Nest," (2) Jack Nicholson in "One Flew over the Cuckoo's Nest," (3) Louise Fletcher in "One Flew over the Cuckoo's Nest," (4) George Burns in "The Sunshine Boys," (5) Lee Grant in "Shampoo," (6) Milos Forman for "One Flew over the Cuckoo's Nest," (7) Mary Pickford, (8) "Dersu Uzala."

1976: (1) "Rocky," (2) Peter Finch in "Network," (3) Faye Dunaway in "Network," (4) Jason Robards in "All the President's Men," (5) Beatrice Straight in "Network," (6) John G. Avildsen for "Rocky," (7) "Black and White in Color"

FOREIGN FILMS

SEVEN BEAUTIES

(CINEMA 5) Directed and Written by Lina Wertmuller; Photography, Tonino Delli Colli; Art Director, Enrico Job; Music, Enzo Iannacci; In Technicolor; Rated R; 115 minutes; January release.

CAST

Pasqualino Frafuso	Giancarlo Giannini
Pedro	Fernando Rey
Commandant	Shirley Stoler
Concettina	Elena Fiore
Don Raffaele	Enzo Vitale
Totonno	Mario Conti
Francesco	Piero DiOrio
Mother	Ermelinda DeFelice
Carolina	Francesca Marciano
Lawyer	Lucio Amelio
Socialist	Roberto Herlitzka
Doctor	Doriglia Palmi

Left: Giancarlo Giannini

Giancarlo Giannini

ALL SCREWED UP

(NEW LINE CINEMA) Formerly "All in Place, Nothing in Order"; Producer, Romano Cardarelli; Direction and Screenplay, Lina Wertmuller; Photography, Giuseppe Rotunno; Sets and Costumes, Enrico Job; Music, Piero Piccioni; Assistant Director, Giovanni Arduini; Editor, Franco Fraticelli; Sound, Mario Bramonti; Euro International Film in Italian with English subtitle; In Technicolor; Rated PG; 105 minutes; January release.

CAST

Gigi	Luigi Diberti
Mariuccia	Lina Polito
Carletto	Nino Bignamini
Adelina	Sara Rapisarda
Biki	Guiliana Calandra
Isotta	Isa Danieli
Bagonghi	Eros Pagni

FRENCH PROVINCIAL

(NEW YORKER) Director, Andre Techine; Screenplay, Andre Techine, Marilyn Goldin; Photography, Bruno Muytten; Editor, Anne-Marie Deshayes; Music, Philippe Sarde; Design, Philippe Galland; Costumes, Christian Gasc; In color; 95 minutes; February release.

CAST

Berthe	Jeanne Moreau
Hector	Michel Auclair
Regina	Marie-France Pisier
Prosper	Claude Mann
Augustine	Orane Demazis
Pedret	Aram Stephan
Lucie	Helene Surgere
Victor	Julien Guiomar
Pierrette	Michele Moretti
Pierre	Pierre Baillot
Young Pedret	Marc Chapiteau
Young Augustine	Francoise Lebrun
Valnoble	Jean Rougeul

Right: Jeanne Moreau, Michel Auclair

Michel Auclair, Jeanne Moreau
Above: Marie-France Pisier

Jeanne Moreau

CHER VICTOR

(PEPPERCORN-WORMSER) Director, Robin Davis; Producer, Denise Petitdidier Les Productions Du Daunou; Color by Movielab; French with English subtitles; Rated PG; 95 minutes; February release.

CAST

Victor	Jacques Dufilho
Anselme	Bernard Blier
Singer	Alida Valli

Right: Jacques Dufilho, Bernard Blier, Alida Valli

Alida Valli, Jacques Dufilho
Above: Bernard Blier, Alida Valli

Jacques Dufilho, Bernard Blier

DEVIL WITHIN HER

(AMERICAN INTERNATIONAL) Director, Peter Sasdy; Executive Producer, Nato De Angeles; Screenplay, Stanley Price; Story, Nato De Angeles; Music, Ron Grainer; Photography, Kenneth Talbot; Art Director, Roy Stannard; Editor, Keith Palmer; Choreographer, Mia Nadasi; Assistant Director, David Bracknell; In Movielab Color; Rated R; 90 minutes; February release

CAST

Lucy	Joan Collins
Sister Albana	Eileen Atkins
Dr. Finch	Donald Pleasence
Gino	Ralph Bates
Mandy	Caroline Munro
Mrs. Hyde	Hilary Mason
Tommy	John Steiner
Jill	Janet Key
Hercules	George Claydon
Sheila	Judy Buxton
Police Inspector	Derek Benfield
Police Sergeant	Stanley Lebor
Priest	John Moore
Nun	Phyllis McMahon
Delivery Boy	Andrew Secombe
Old Lady	Susan Richards

Top: George Claydon, Joan Collins
Below: Hilary Mason, Joan Collins

Joan Collins, Ralph Bates Above: Joan
Collins, Eileen Atkins

SALUT L'ARTISTE

(EXXEL) Director, Yves Robert; Executive Producers, Alain Poire, Yves Robert; Screenplay, Jean-Loup Dabadie, Yves Robert; Photography, Jean Penzer; Music, Vladimir Cosma; English subtitles; In color; 96 minutes; February release.

CAST

Nicholas .... Marcello Mastroianni
Peggy .... Francoise Fabian
Clement .... Jean Rochefort
Elisabeth .... Carla Gravina
Zeller .... Xavier Gelin

ROBIN AND MARIAN

(COLUMBIA) Producer, Denis O'Dell; Director, Richard Lester; Executive Producer, Richard Shepherd; Screenplay, James Goldman; Music, John Barry; Photography, David Watkin; Designer, Michael Stringer; Costumes, Yvonne Blake; Editor, John Victor Smith; Art Director, Gil Perondo; Assistant Director, Jose Lopez Rodero; In color; Rated PG; 107 minutes; March release

CAST

Robin Hood	Sean Connery
Maid Marian	Audrey Hepburn
Sheriff of Nottingham	Robert Shaw
King Richard	Richard Harris
Little John	Nicol Williamson
Will Scarlett	Denholm Elliott
Sir Ranulf	Kenneth Haigh
Friar Tuck	Ronnie Barker
King John	Ian Holm
Mercadier	Bill Maynard
Old Defender	Esmond Knight
Sister Mary	Veronica Quilligan
Surgeon	Peter Butterworth
Jack	John Barrett
Jack's Apprentice	Kenneth Cranhan
Queen Isabella	Victoria Merida Roja
First Sister	Montserrat Julio
Second Sister	Victoria Hernandez Sanguino
Third Sister	Margarita Minguillon

Richard Harris
Top: Sean Connery, Audrey Hepburn

Top: Sean Connery

Richard Harris, Sean Connery Above: Audrey
Hepburn, Connery, Nicol Williamson Top:
Robert Shaw, Kenneth Haigh

Audrey Hepburn, and top
with Sean Connery

MOSES

(AVCO EMBASSY) Producer, Vincenzo Labellq; Director, Gianfranco de Bosio; Screenplay, Anthony Burgess, Vitorio Bonicelli, Gianfranco de Bosio; Photography, Marcello Gatti; Editors, Gerry Hambling, Peter Bolta, John Guthridge, Alberto Gallitti, Freddie Wilson; Music, Ennio Morricone; Design, Pierluigi Basile; Costumes, Enrico Sabbatini; Assistant Director, Francesco Cinieri; In Technicolor; Rated PG; 140 minutes; March release

CAST

Moses	Burt Lancaster
Aaron	Anthony Quayle
Miriam	Ingrid Thulin
Zipporah	Irene Papas
Princess Bithia	Mariangela Melato
Young Moses	William Lancaster
Mernefta	Laurent Terzieff
Joshua	Aharon Ipale
Eliseba	Marina Berti
Pharaoh Ramses II	Mario Ferrari
Dathan	Yousef Shiloah
Jethro	Shmuel Rodnesky

Left: Burt Lancaster

Irene Papas, Burt Lancaster
Above: Anthony Quayle, Ingrid Thulin

Burt Lancaster, Anthony Quayle
Above: Laurent Terzieff

**Marina Berti (L) Above: Burt Lancaster,
Anthony Quayle Top: Burt Lancaster**

**Anthony Quayle Top: Burt
Lancaster, Irene Papas**

CRIME AND PASSION

(AMERICAN INTERNATIONAL) Executive Producer, Barney Bernhard; Producer, Robert L. Abrams; Director, Ivan Passer; Screenplay, Jesse Laskey, Jr., Pat Silver; Photography, Denis C. Lewiston; Editors, John Jympson, Bernard Gribble; Costumes, Yvonne Blake; Associate Producer, Pia I. Arnold; Art Director, Herta Pischinger; Music, Vangelis Papathanassiou; A Samuel Z. Arkoff and Gloria Films presentation in Movielab Color; Rated R; 92 minutes; April release

CAST

Andre	Omar Sharif
Susan	Karen Black
Larry	Joseph Bottoms
Herman Rolf	Bernhard Wicki
Henkel	Heinz Ehrenfreund
Masseuse	Elma Karlowa
Innkeeper	Volker Prechtel
Car Salesman	Erich Padalewski
Mr. Blatt	Robert Abrams
Priest	Franz Muxeneder
Sylvia	Margarete Soper

Top: Karen Black, Omar Sharif
Below: Omar Sharif

Karen Black, Omar Sharif Above: Karen
Black, Joseph Bottoms

BOESMAN AND LENA

(NEW YORKER) Producer, Johan Wright; Director, Ross Devenish; Screenplay from his play, Athol Fugard; Photography, David Muir; Editors, John Scott, Roger Harris; In color; 102 minutes; April release.

CAST

Lena	Yvonne Bryceland
Boesman	Athol Fugard
Outa	Sandy Tube
Bait-Shop Owner	Val Donald
Fisherman	Percy Sieff
Official	Frank Zietsman
Bulldozer Driver	Robert Pennacchini
Bottle-Store Owner	Bert Coppin

Right: Yvonne Bryceland, Athol Fugard

**Athol Fugard, and above
with Yvonne Bryceland**

Yvonne Bryceland

THE SAILOR WHO FELL FROM GRACE WITH THE SEA

(AVCO EMBASSY) Producer, Martin Poll; Written and Directed by Lewis John Carlino; Based on novel by Yukio Mishima; Associate Producer, David White; Photography, Douglas Slocombe; Designer, Ted Haworth; Costumes, Lee Poll; Editor, Anthony Gibbs; Music, John Mandel; Art Director, Brian Ackland-Snow; Assistant Directors, Gerry Gavigan, Pamela Davies; Costumes, Lee Poll; In CFI Color; Rated R; 105 minutes; April release.

CAST

Anne Osborne	Sarah Miles
Jim Cameron	Kris Kristofferson
Jonathan Osborne	Jonathan Kahn
Mrs. Palmer	Margo Cunningham
Chief	Earl Rhodes
Number 2	Paul Tropea
Number 4	Gary Lock
Number 5	Stephen Black
Richard Pettit	Peter Clapham
Mary Ingram	Jennifer Tolman

Left: Kris Kristofferson, Sarah Miles

Kris Kristofferson, Jonathan Kahn, Sarah Miles

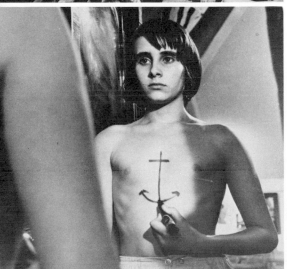

Jonathan Kahn Above: Earl Rhodes, Paul Tropea, Gary Locke, Stephen Black, Kahn Top: Sarah Miles, Kris Kristofferson

Kris Kristofferson, Sarah Miles, and above with Jonathan Kahn Top: Sarah Miles

Liv Ullmann

FACE TO FACE

(PARAMOUNT) Written, Directed and Produced by Ingmar Bergman; Photography, Sven Nykvist; Editor, Siv Lundgren; Music, Mozart; Design, Anne Hagegard; In Eastmancolor; Rated R; 136 minutes; April release

CAST

Dr. Jenny Isaksson .... Liv Ullmann
Dr. Thomas Jacobi .... Erland Josephson
Grandpa .... Gunnar Bjornstrand
Grandma .... Aino Taube-Henrikson
Maria .... Karl Sylwan
Mrs. Elizabeth Wankel .... Siv Ruud
Dr. Erik Isaksson .... Sven Lindberg
The Lady .... Tore Segelcke
Dr. Helmuth Wankel .... Ulf Johansson
Veronica .... Kristina Adolphson
Mickael Stromberg .... Gosta Ekman
Concert Pianist .... Kabi Laretei

Top: Erland Josephson, Liv Ullmann

Liv Ullman, and top with Ulf Johansson

THE MAN WHO FELL TO EARTH

(BRITISH LION) Producers, Michael Deeley, Barry Spikings; Director, Nicolas Roeg; Screenplay, Paul Mayersberg; From the novel by Walter Tevis; Executive Producer, Si Litvinoff; Musical Director, John Phillips; In color; Rated R; 140 minutes; May release

CAST

Thomas Jerome Newton	David Bowie
Nathan Bryce	Rip Torn
Mary-Lou	Candy Clark
Oliver Farnsworth	Buck Henry
Peters	Bernie Casey
Prof. Canutti	Jackson D. Kane
Trevor	Rick Riccardo
Arthur	Tony Mascia
Elaine	Linda Hutton
Jill	Hilary Holland
Helen	Adrienne Larussa
Jewelry Store Owner	Lilybelle Crawford
Receptionist	Richard Breeding
Waiter	Albert Nelson
Peters' Associate	Peter Prouse
Capt. James Lovell	Himself

Left: David Bowie, Lilybelle Crawford

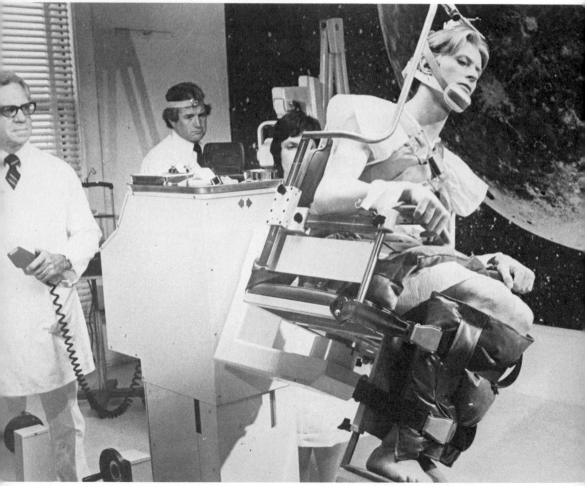

David Bowie

David Bowie, Candy Clark
Top: Rip Torn, David Bowie

END OF THE GAME

(20th CENTURY-FOX) Producers, Maximilian Schell, Arlene Sellers; Executive Producer, Alex Winitsky; Director, Maximilian Schell; Screenplay, Maximilian Schell, Bo Goldmann, Friedrich Duerrenmatt; Based on Duerrenmatt's "The Judge and His Hangman"; Photography, Ennio Guarnieri, Robert Gerardi, Klaus Koenig; Editor, Dagmar Hirtz; Art Director, Mario Garbuglia; In color; Rated PG; 106 minutes; May release

CAST

Walter Tschantz	Jon Voight
Anna Crawley	Jacqueline Bisset
Hans Barlach	Martin Ritt
Richard Gastmann	Robert Shaw
von Schwendi	Helmut Qualtinger
Dr. Lutz	Gabriele Ferzetti
Nadine	Rita Calderoni
Friedrich	Friedrich Duerrenmatt
Clenin	Willy Huegli
Dr. Hungertobel	Norbert Schiller
Coroner	Guido Cerniglia
Mrs. Schoenler	Margarethe Schell von Noe
Blatter	Otto Ryser
Guards	Rudolf Hunsperger, Edy Hubacher
Violinist	Pinchas Zukerman
Mrs. Gastman	Lil Dagover
Old Lady	Toni Roth
Taxi Driver	Wieland Liebske
Dr. Schallert	Anton Netzer
Cleaning Girl	Kathrin Brunner

**Right: Jacqueline Bisset, Robert Shaw
Top: Jacqueline Bisset, Jon Voight**

**Jacqueline Bisset, Jon Voight
Above: Robert Shaw, Martin Ritt**

**Pinchas Zukerman, Maximilian Schell
Above: Martin Ritt, Jon Voight**

SHOOT

(AVCO EMBASSY) Producer, Harve Sharman; Executive Producer, Dick Berg; Director, Harvey Hart; Screenplay, Dick Berg from the novel by Douglas Fairbairn; Photography, Zale Magder; Editors, Ron Wisman, Peter Shatalow; Music, Doug Riley; Art Director, Earl Preston; Assistant Director, Tim Rowse; In technicolor; Rated R; 92 minutes; June release

CAST

Maj. Rex Jeanette	Cliff Robertson
Lou Jonkheer	Ernest Borgnine
Zeke Springer	Henry Silva
Pete	James Blendick
Bob	Larry Reynolds
Jim	Les Carlson
Paula	Helen Shaver
Ellen	Gloria Carlin Chetwynd
Mrs. Graham	Kate Reid
Billy Platt	Alan McRae
Sgt. Bellows	Ed MacNamara
Marshall Flinn	Peter Langley
Helen Newhouse	Helena Hart

Above: Gloria Carlin Chetwynd Top: Ernest Borgnine Below: Helen Shaver Top Right: Cliff Robertson, Henry Silva Below: Robertson, James Blendick

Cliff Robertson, and above with Kate Reid

183

COUSIN, COUSINE

(LIBRA) Producer, Bertrand Javal; Direction, Screenplay, Dialogue, Jean-Charles Tacchella; Photography, Georges Lendi; Editor, Anges Guillemot; Music, Gerard Anfosso; Presented by Albert Schwartz and Imre J. Rosenthal; In color; French with English subtitles; Rated R; 95 minutes; July release

CAST

Marthe	Marie-Christine Barrault
Ludovic	Victor Lanoux
Karine	Marie-France Pisier
Pascal	Guy Marchand
Biju	Ginette Garcin
Diane	Sybil Maas
Sacy	Jean Herbert
Gobert	Pierre Plessis
Nelsa	Cathernine Verlor
Thomas	Hubert Gignoux

Victor Lanoux, Marie-Christine Barrault

Top: Marie-Christine Barrault, Victor Lanoux, Marie-France Pisier, Guy Marchand

Victor Lanoux, Marie-Christine Barrault,
also at top

Marie-France Pisier

BREAKING POINT

(20th CENTURY-FOX) Producers, Claude Heroux, Bob Clark; Executive Producers, Harold Greenberg, Alfred Pariser; Director, Bob Clark; Screenplay, Roger E. Swaybill, Stanley Mann, from story by Roger Swaybill; Photography, Marc Champion; Editor, Stan Cole; Music, David McLey; Art Director, Wolf Kroeger; Design, Dave Deyell; Assistant Director, Bud Cordos; In DeLuxe Color; Rated R; 92 minutes; June release.

CAST

Michael McBain	Bo Svenson
Frank Sirrianni	Robert Culp
Vincent Karbone	John Colicos
Diana McBain	Belinda J. Montgomery
Peter Stratis	Stephen Young
Helen McBain	Linda Sorenson
Andy Stratis	Jeffrey Lynas
Vigorito	Gerry Salsberg
Hirsch	Richard M. Davidson
Redpath	Jonathan White
Ted Buchanan	Alan McRae
Petrucci	Dwayne McLean
Gilligan	Doug Lennox
Domani	Jim Hunter
Fleming	Bud Cardos
Sarah	Joanna Noyes
Assistant D. A.	Ken Camroux
Hagerty	Ken James
Commissioner McGuire	Bill Kemp
Policeman	David Mann

Left: Bo Svenson

Robert Culp

**Bo Svenson, also above
with Gerry Salsberg**

ALPHA BETA

(CINE III) Producer, Timothy Burrill; Director, Anthony Page; Screenplay, E. A. Whitehead; Based on his play; Editor, Tom Priestley; Photography, Charles Stewart; In Technicolor; Rated PG; 70 minutes; August release

CAST

Frank Elliot .... Albert Finney
Nora Elliot .... Rachel Roberts

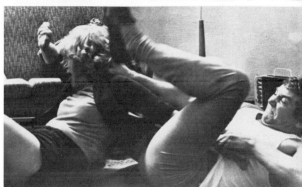

Above: Rachel Roberts, Albert Finney, and also at top

Rachel Roberts, Albert Finney, and also above

LET'S TALK ABOUT MEN

(ALLIED ARTISTS) Producer, Pietro Notorianni; Direction and Screenplay, Lina Wertmuller; Photography, Ennio Guarnieri; Music, Louis Enriquez Bacalov; Rated PG; 93 minutes; August release

CAST

The Man .... Nino Manfredi
The Wife:
    1st Episode .... Luciana Paluzzi
    2nd Episode .... Milena Vukotic
    3rd Episode .... Margaret Lee
    4th Episode .... Patrizia DeClara

**Nino Manfredi, Luciana Paluzzi Above: Nino
Manfredi Top: Manfredi, Margaret Lee**

**Top: Patrizia DeClara, Nino Manfredi
Below: Milena Vukotic, Nino Manfredi**

THE SUNDAY WOMAN

(20th CENTURY-FOX) Director, Luigi Comencini; Written by
Age and Scarpelli; Photography, Luciano Tovoli; Editor, Antonio
Siciliano; In color; Rated R; 110 minutes; September release

CAST

Santamaria	Marcello Mastroianni
Ana Maria	Jacqueline Bisset
Massimo	Jean-Louis Trintignant
Lello Rivera	Aldo Reggiani
De Palma	Pino Caruso
Virginia Tabusso	Maria Theresa Albani
Benito	Omero Antonutti
Vollero	Gigi Ballista
Nicosia	Renato Cecilia
Garrone	Claudio Gora

Right: Marcello Mastroianni, Jacqueline Bisset

Jean-Louis Trintignant, Marcello Mastroianni, Jacqueline Bisset

SHADOW OF THE HAWK

(COLUMBIA) Executive Producer, Henry Gellis; Producer, John Kemeny; Director, George McCowan; Screenplay, Norman Thaddeus Vane, Herbert J. Wright; Story, Peter Jensen, Lynette Cahill, Norman Thaddeus Vane; Music, Robert McMullin; Photography, John Holbrook, Reginald Morris; Associate Producer, Ronald L. Schwary; Editor, O. Nicholas Brown; Art Director, Keith Pepper; Assistant Directors, Roland L.Schwary, Jim Scott; Costumes, Ilse Richter, Bobby Watts; In Panavision and color; Rated PG; 92 minutes; October release

CAST

Mike	Jan-Michael Vincent
Maureen	Marilyn Hassett
Old Man Hawk	Chief Dan George
Faye	Pia Shandel
Dsonoqua	Marianne Jones
Andak	Jacques Hubert
Secretary	Cindi Griffith
Desk Nurse	Anna Hagan
Intern	Murray Lowry

Right: Jan-Michael Vincent

Marilyn Hassett, Chief Dan George, Jan-Michael Vincent Above: Vincent, Hassett

Jan-Michael Vincent, Marilyn Hassett Above: Marianne Jones

190

THE MARQUISE OF O . . .

(NEW LINE CINEMA) Director, Eric Rohmer; Story, Heinrich Von Kleist; Screenplay, Eric Rohmer; Photography, Nestor Almendros; Costumes, Moidele Bickel; Art Directors, Rolf Kaden, Helo Gutschwager; Editor, Cecile Decugis; A French-German Co-Production with English subtitles; In color; Rated PG; 102 minutes; October release

CAST

The Marquise	Edith Clever
The Count	Bruno Ganz
The Father	Peter Luhr
The Mother	Edda Seippel
The Brother	Otto Sander
The Midwife	Ruth Drexel
The Doctor	Eduard Linkers
The Servant	Hezzo Huber
The Russian General	Erich Schachinger
The Russian Officer	Richard Rogner
The Messenger	Thomas Straus
The Priest	Volker Prachtel
The Chambermaids	Marion Muller, Heidi Moller
The Townsmen	Franz Pikola, Theo DeMaal
The Children	Petra Meier, Manuela Mayer

Edith Clever

SMALL CHANGE

(NEW WORLD) Director, Francois Truffaut; Screenplay, Mr. Truffaut, Suzanne Schiffman; French with English titles; Photography, Pierre-William Glenn; Music, Maurice Jaubert; Editors, Yann Dedet, Martine Barraque, Jean Gargonne, Stephanie Granel, Muriel Zeleny; In color; Rated PG; 104 minutes; October release

CAST

Patrick	Geory Desmouceaux
Julien	Philippe Goldman
Mathieu Deluca	Claudio Deluca
Frank Deluca	Frank Deluca
Richard Golfier	Richard Golfier
Laurent Riffle	Laurent Devlaeminck
Bruno Rouillard	Bruno Staab
Oscar	Sebastien Marc
Sylvie	Sylvie Grezel
Martine	Pascale Bruchon
Corinne	Corinne Boucart
Patricia	Eva Truffaut
Jean-Francois Richet	Jean-Francois Stevinin
Chantal Petit	Chantal Mercier
Mr. Riffle	Francis Devlaeminck
Nadine Riffle	Tania Torrens
Lydie Richet	Virginie Thevenet
Madeleine Doinel	Laura Truffaut

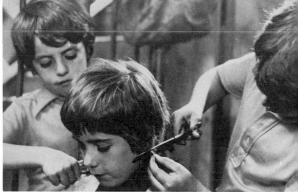

THE SLIPPER AND THE ROSE

(UNIVERSAL) Producer, Stuart Lyons; Director, Bryan Forbes; Screenplay, Bryan Forbes, Robert B. Sherman, Richard M. Sherman; Music and Lyrics, Richard M. Sherman, Robert B. Sherman; Executive Producer, David Frost; Choreographer, Marc Breaux; Photography, Tony Imi; Design, Raymond Simm; Costumes, Julie Harris; Editor, Timothy Gee; Assistant Director, Jack Causey; In Panavision and Technicolor; Rated G; 146 minutes; November release

CAST

Prince	Richard Chamberlain
Cinderella	Gemma Craven
Fairy Godmother	Annette Crosbie
Dowager Queen	Edith Evans
John	Christopher Gable
King	Michael Hordern
Stepmother	Margaret Lockwood
Chamberlain	Kenneth More
Montague	Julian Orchard
Queen	Lally Bowers
Palatine	Sherrie Hewson
Isabella	Rosalind Ayres
Major Domo	John Turner
Willoughby	Keith Skinner
Lady Caroline	Polly Williams
Dress Shop Proprietor	Norman Bird
General	Peter Graves
First Lord of the Navy	Gerald Sim
Lady in Waiting	Elizabeth Mansfield

and Roy Barraclough, Geoffrey Bayldon, Valentine Dyall, Tim Barrett, Vivienne McKee, Andre Morell, Myrtle Reed, Ludmilla Nova, Peter Leeming, Marianne Broome, Tessa Dahl, Lea Dreghorn, Eva Reuber-Staier, Ann Rutherford, Suzette St. Claire, Jenny Lee Wright, Patrick Jordan, Rocky Taylor, Paul Schmitzburger

Left: Gemma Craven, Sherrie Hewson, Rosalind Ayres, Margaret Lockwood Top: Annette Crosbie, Gemma Craven

Lally Bowers, Michael Hordern, Kenneth More

Richard Chamberlain

Richard Chamberlain, Gemma Craven

Gemma Craven, Annette Crosbie

LOVING COUSINS

(INDEPENDENT INTERNATIONAL) Producer, Carlo Ponti; Director, Sergio Martino; Screenplay, Sergio Martino, Savro Scavocini, Fernando Poli; Editor, Eugenio Alabiso; Music, Claudio Mattone; In Eastmancolor; Rated R; 87 minutes; November release

CAST

Sonia	Susan Player
Baron Roccadura	Hugh Griffith
Professor	Riccardo Cucciola
Nico	Alfredo Pea

Susan Player, Hugh Griffith

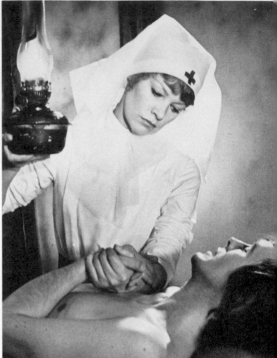

THE INCREDIBLE SARAH

(READERS DIGEST) Producer, Helen M. Strauss; Director, Richard Fleischer; Screenplay, Ruth Wolff; Photography, Christopher Challis; Editor, John Jympson; Music, Elmer Bernstein; Design, Elliot Scott; Art Director, Terry Marcel; In Technicolor and Panavision; Rated PG; 105 minutes; November release

CAST

Sarah Bernhardt	Glenda Jackson
Sardou	Daniel Massey
Mam'selle	Yvonne Mitchell
Montigny	Douglas Wilmer
Duc de Morny	David Langton
Henri de Ligne	Simon Williams
Damala	John Castle
Jarrett	Edward Judd
Mrs. Bernhardt	Rosemarie Dunham
Thierry	Peter Sallis
Marie	Bridget Armstrong
Madame Nathalie	Margaret Courtenay

John Castle, Glenda Jackson Above: Glenda Jackson, David Langton Top: Glenda Jackson

Top: Glenda Jackson, and below with Daniel Massey (L), Douglas Wilmer (R)

SHOUT AT THE DEVIL

(AMERICAN INTERNATIONAL) Producer, Michael Klinger; Director, Peter Hunt; Screenplay, Wilbur Smith, Alistair Reid, Stanley Price; From the novel by Wilbur Smith; Associate Producers, Stanley Sopel, Robert Sterne; Music, Maurice Jarre; Design, Sid Cain, Assistant Director, Frank Ernst; Editor, Michael Duthie; In color; Rated PG; 128 minutes; November release

CAST

Flynn	Lee Marvin
Sebastian	Roger Moore
Rosa	Barbara Parkins
Fleischer	Rene Kolldehoff
Mohammed	Ian Holm
Von Kleine	Karl Michael Vogler
Kyller	Horst Janson
Braun	Gernot Endemann
Mr. Smythe	Maurice Denham
Mrs. Smythe	Jean Kent
Cynthia	Heather Wright
Capt. Joyce	Bernard Horsfall
Capt. Henry	Robert Lang
Admiral Howe	Peter Copley
Lt. Phipps	Murray Melvin
Mackintosh	Geoff Davidson
French Pilot	Gerard Paquis
El Keb	George Coulouris
Mr. Raji	Renu Setna

Right: Roger Moore

Lee Marvin, Roger Moore Above: Moore
Barbara Parkins, Marvin

Barbara Parkins, Roger Moore,
Lee Marvin

197

LUMIERE

(NEW WORLD) Written and Directed by Jeanne Moreau; Photography, Richard Aronovitch; Editor, Albert Jurgenson; Music, Astor Piazzola; In Eastmancolor; Rated R; 95 minutes; November release

CAST

Sarah	Jeanne Moreau
Julienne	Francine Racette
Laura	Lucia Bose
Caroline	Caroline Cartier
Flora	Marie Henriau
Claire	Monique Tarbes
David	Keith Carradine
Henrich Grun	Bruno Ganz
Gregoire	Francois Simon
Thomas	Francis Huster
Nano	Niels Arestrup
Saint-Loup	Jacques Spiesser

Left: Francine Racette, Jeanne Moreau

Keith Carradine, Francine Racette
Above: Bruno Ganz, Jeanne Moreau

Francois Simon, Jeanne Moreau Above: Francine Racette, Lucia Bose, Jeanne Moreau

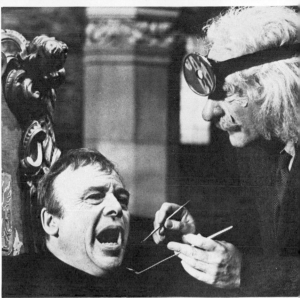

THE PINK PANTHER STRIKES AGAIN

(UNITED ARTISTS) Producer-Director, Blake Edwards; Screenplay, Frank Waldman, Blake Edwards; Music, Henry Mancini; Photography, Harry Waxman; Editor, Alan Jones; "Come to Me" sung by Tom Jones; In Panavision and DeLuxe Color; Rated PG; 103 minutes; December release

CAST

Inspector Clouseau	Peter Sellers
Dreyfus	Herbert Lom
Alec Drummond	Colin Blakely
Quinlin	Leonard Rossiter
Olga	Lesley-Anne Down
Kato	Burt Kwouk
Francois	Andre Maranne
Deputy Commissioner	Marne Maitland
Dr. Fassbender	Richard Vernon
Jarvis	Michael Robbins
Margo Fassbender	Briony McRoberts
President	Dick Crockett
Secretary of State	Byron Kane

Top: Peter Sellers, Lesley-Anne Down
Below: Herbert Lom, Peter Sellers,
and also top right

Peter Sellers
Above: Herbert Lom

199

ESCAPE FROM ANGOLA

(DOTY-DAYTON) Executive Producers, Ivan Tors, J. Van Zyl Alberts; Associate Producers, Thys Heyns, Alan L. Girney; Producer, George Gale; Director, Leslie Martinson; Photography, Hanro Mohr; Screenplay, Barry Clark; Story, George Gale, In color; Rated G; December release.

CAST

James Mallory	Stan Brock
Karen Mallory	Anne Collings
Lars Olaffson	Ivan Tors
Steve	Steven Tors
Peter	Peter Tors
Dave	David Tors
Tshoma	Mackson Ngobeni
Ogamo Woman	Shirley Pelle
Kruse	Jannie Wienand
Patrol Leader	Joe Mafela
Kende	Adijae Sasthu
Tom	Tom Mabinda

Right: Stan Brock, also at top

David Tors, Peter Tors, Steven Tors, Stan Brock, Ivan Tors

THE SLAP (Silver Screen Enterprises) Producer, Alain Poire; Director, Claude Pinoteau; Screenplay, Jean-Loup Dabadie, Claude Pinoteau; Photography, Jean Collomb; Music, Georges Delerue; A Franco-Italian Co-Production with English subtitles; In color; Rated PG; 104 minutes; January release. CAST: Lino Ventura (Jean), Annie Girardot (Helene), Isabelle Adjani (Isabelle), Francis Perrin (Marc), Jacques Spiesser (Remy), Nicole Courcel (Madeleine), Georges Wilson (Pierre)

EXIT THE DRAGON ENTER THE TIGER (Dimension Pictures) Producers, Jimmy Shaw, R. P. Shah; Director Lee Tse Nam; Screenplay, Chang Shun Yee; Adaptation, Hugo Grimaldi; Music, Chow Fook Leung; A Mickey Zide Presentation; Rated R; 84 minutes; January release. CAST: Bruce Li (David), Lung Fei, Ma Chi Chiang, San Moo, An Ping, Chang Sing Yee, Tsao Shao Jung

INSIDE OUT (Warner Bros.) Producer, Judd Bernard; Director, Peter Duffell; Screenplay, Judd Bernard, Stephen Schneck; Photography, John Coquillon; Editor, Thom Nobel; Music, Konrad Elfers; Art Directors, Peter Lamont, Jan Schlubach; Assistant Director, Wolfgang Glattes; A Kettledrum Production in Technicolor; 97 minutes; January release. CAST: Telly Savalas (Harry), Robert Culp (Sly), James Mason (Ernest), Aldo Ray (Sgt. Prior), Guenter Meisner (Schmidt). Adrian Hoven (Dr. Maar), Wolfgang Lukschy (Reinhold), Charles Korvin (Dohlberg), Constantin De Goguel (Colonel), Richard Warner (Wilhelm), Don Fellows (U.S. Colonel), Lorna Dallas (Meredith), Sigrid Hanack (Siggi), Peter Schlesinger (Udo)

THE LOVE MATES (New Line Cinema) Producer, Alain Delon; Director, Roger Kahane; Music, Francis Lai; In color; January release; no other credits available. CAST: Alain Delon, Mireille Darc, Jane Davenport

DOOMWATCH (Avco Embassy) Producer, S. Tony Tenser; Director, Peter Sasdy; Screenplay, Clive Exton; Story, Dr. Kit Pedler, Gerry Davis; A Tigon British Film Production in Technicolor; 92 minutes; January release. CAST: Ian Bannen, Judy Geeson, John Paul, Simon Oates, George Sanders, Jean Trend, Joby Blanshard, Percy Herbert, Geoffrey Keen, Joseph O'Connor, Shelagh Frazer

DEMONS OF THE MIND (Cinemation) Producer, Frank Godwin; Director, Peter Sykes; Screenplay, Christopher Wicking; Story, Frank Godwin, Christopher Wicking; Music, Harry Robinson; Photography, Arthur Grant; In color; Rated R; 89 minutes; January release. CAST: Paul Jones (Carl), Patrick Magee (Falkenberg), Yvonne Mitchell (Hilda), Robert Hardy (Friedrich), Gillian Hills (Elizabeth), Michael Hordern (Priest), Kenneth J. Warren (Klaus), Shane Briant (Emil), Virginia Wetherall (Inge)

GOODYE BRUCE LEE: HIS LAST GAME OF DEATH (Aquarius) A Robert Chow/Atlas International Production; Presented by Terry Levene; Rating R; In color; January release. CAST: Bruce Lee, Kareem Abdul Jabbar, Lee Roy, Ronald Brown, Johnny "Big" Floyd

THE FOUR DEUCES (Avco Embassy) Producer, Yuram Globus; Director, William H. Bushnell, Jr.; Executive Producer, Menachem Golan; Screenplay, C. Lester Franklin; Story, Don Martin; In DeLuxe Color; Rated R; 87 Minutes; January release. CAST: Jack Palance (Vic), Carol Lynley (Wendy), Warren Berlinger (Chico), Adam Roarke (Russ), E. J. Peaker (Lory), Gianni Russo, H. B. Haggerty, John Haymer, Cherie Latimer, Martin Kove

WHAT CHANGED CHARLEY FARTHING? (Stirling Gold) Producers, Sidney Hayers, Tristam Cones; Director, Sidney Hayers; Screenplay, David Pursall, Jack Seddon; In color; Rated PG; January release. CAST: Hayley Mills, Doug McClure, Lionel Jeffries

THE CHINESE MACK (Ellman Enterprises) Producer, David Chen, Jr.; Director, Herman Hsu; In color and Superscope; A Clark Film; Rated R; January release. CAST: Wu Chin, Chan Wei-Min, Travador Ramos, Lee Fung Lang

SHANGHAI JOE (United International) Producers, Renato Angiolini, Roberto Bessi; Director, Mario Caiano; Music, Bruno Nicolai; In Techniscope and Technicolor; Rated R; 98 minutes; January release. CAST: Chen Lee, Gordon Mitchell, Pancho Del Rio, Klaus Kinski, Carla Romanelli, Piero Lulli, Katsutoschi Mikuriya

Isabelle Adjani, Lino Ventura
in "The Slap"

GIRLS IN TROUBLE (Group One) Directed by E. Schroder; Rated R; In color; January release. CAST: Sandra Carney, Erica Arnoud, Lee Bishop

THE INTIMATE PLAYMATES (Hemisphere) An MPD Associates Film; In Eastmancolor; No other credits; January release. CAST: Carole Parker, Lynn Ross

WHOSE CHILD AM I? (Brian Distributing Corp.) Producer, Jesse Vogel; Director, Lawrence Britten; Screenplay, James Stevens; A Mara Co. Film in Eastmancolor and Panavision; Rated R; January release. CAST: Kate O'Mara, Paul Freeman, Edward Judd, Felicity Devonshire

LIZA (Horizon) Director, Marco Ferreri; Screenplay, Marco Ferreri, Jean-Claude Carriere from book by Ennio Flaiano; Photography, Mario Vulpiano; Music, Philippe Sarde; Art Director, Theo Meurisse; In Eastmancolor; 100 minutes; January release. CAST: Catherine Deneuve (Liza), Marcello Mastroianni (Giorgio), Corrine Marchand (Wife), Michel Piccoli (Friend), Pascal Laperrousaz (Son)

HER FAMILY JEWELS (M. Shuffey) Director, Martin Campbell; Music, Mike Vickers, Chris Spierer, Michael Kaufman; In color; Rated X; 86 minutes; January release. CAST: Nigel Evans, Elizabeth Aubrey, Edmond Searle, Colin Taylor, Megan Ross

WAITING FOR FIDEL (Open Circle) Producers, Geoffrey Stirling, Joseph Smallwood, Michael Rubbo; Directed and Edited by Michael Rubbo; In color; 57 minutes; January release. A documentary about three Canadians' trip to Cuba.

SCENT OF A WOMAN (United Artists) Director, Dino Risi; Screenplay, Ruggero Macari, Dino Risi; Based on novel by Giovanni Arpino; Photography, Claudio Cirillo; Editor, Alberto Gallitti; Music, Armando Trovaioli; In color; Rated R; 104 minutes; January release. CAST: Vittorio Gassman (Blind Captain), Allessandro Momo (Ciccio), Agostina Belli (Sara)

Robert Hardy, Patrick Magee
in "Demons of the Mind"

**Franco Nero
in "The Anonymous Avenger"**

**Sylvia Kristel, Umberto Orsini
in "Emmanuelle—The Joys of a Woman"**

LINDA (Lanir) Director, Rick Deconinck; In color; Rated X; February release. CAST: Lina Romay, Jacqueline Laurent, Pamela Stanford, Howard Vernon, Alice Arno, Catherine Leferiere, Pierre Taylou

THE HUNTED (Atlas) No credits available; In color; Rated PG; February release. CAST: Lee Remick, Michael Hinz, Ivan Desny, Jose Caffarel, Ingrid Garbo

THE KILLING MACHINE (Cinema Shares International) Director, Noribumi Suzuki; Screenplay, Isao Matsumoto; Photography, Yoshio Nakajima; In color; Rated R; 89 minutes; February release. CAST: Sonny Chiba, Makato Sato, Yutaka Nakajima, Nyoya Sei

THE ANONYMOUS AVENGER (Hallmark) Producer, Mario Cecchi Gori; Director, Enzo G. Castellari; Screenplay, Dino Maiuri, Massimo DeRita; A Capital Film Production; In color; Rated R; 88 minutes; February release. CAST: Franco Nero, Barbara Bach, Renzo Palmer, Giancarlo Prete, Romano Puppo, Marne Maitland

RETURN OF THE PANTHER (In-Frames Films) Director, Wu Ma; A First Films Production; In color; Rated R; February release. CAST: Kam Kang, Yen Nan Shee, Lung Fei, Lei Chen, Sung Lai

GIRLS AND THE LOVE GAMES (Atlas) Directed by F. G. Gottlieb; In Eastmancolor; Rated X; February release. CAST: Karin Gotz, Christine Schuberth

THE BLACK DRAGON VS. THE YELLOW TIGER (Aquarius) Presented by Terry Levene; In Technicolor; Rated R; February release. No other details available.

STATELINE MOTEL (International Cinefilm) formerly "Last Chance for a Born Loser"; Director, Maurizio Lucidi; A Fral Production and Nicholas Demetroules Presentation; In Eastmancolor; Rated R; 86 minutes; February release. CAST: Ursula Andress, Eli Wallach, Fabio Testi, Massimo Girotti, Barbara Bach, Howard Ross, Carlo De Mejo

EMMANUELLE—THE JOYS OF A WOMAN (Paramount) Director, Francis Giacobetti; Screenplay, Francis Giacobetti, Bob Elia from book by Emmanuelle Arsan; Photography, Robert Fraisse; Editor, Marie Sophie Dubus; Music, Francis Lai; In Eastmancolor; Rated X; 90 minutes; February release. CAST: Sylvia Kristel (Emmanuelle), Umberto Orsini (Jean), Catherine Rivet (Anna-Maria), Frederic Lagache (Christopher), Caroline Laurence

CARAVAN TO VACCARES (Bryanston) Producers, Geoffrey Reeve, Richard Morris-Adams; Director, Geoffrey Reeve; Screenplay, Paul Wheeler; Based on novel by Alistair MacLean; Photography, John Cabrera, David Bevan, Ted Deason; Design, Frank White; Art Director, George Petitot; Music, Stanley Myers; Assistant Director, Bert Batt; Executive Producer, John McNab; Associate Producer, George Davis; In Panavision and Eastmancolor; Rated PG; 98 minutes; February release. CAST: Charlotte Rampling (Lila), David Birney (Neil), Michel Lonsdale (Duc de Croytor), Marcel Bozuffi (Henri), Michael Bryant (Stefan), Manitas de Plata (Ricardo), Serge Marquand (Ferenc), Marianne Eggericks (Cecile), Francoise Brion (Stella), Vania Vilers (Guardian), Graham Hill (Pilot)

SOMETHING TO HIDE (Atlantic) Producer, Michael Klinger; Written and Directed by Alistair Reid; Based on novel by Nicholas Monsarrat; Associate Producer, Peter Shaw; Photography, Wolfgang Suschitzky; Music, Roy Budd; Art Director, Anthony Pratt; Editor, Reggie Beck; In Eastmancolor; 100 minutes; February release. CAST: Peter Finch (Harry), Shelley Winters (Gabriella), Colin Blakely (Blagdon), John Stride (Tom), Linda Hayden (Lorelei), Harold Goldblatt (Didbick), Rosemarie Dunham (Elsie), Helen Fraser, Graham Crowden, Jack Shepherd

SNUFF (Monarch Releasing Corp.) No credits, and no other details available. February release.

**Sylvia Kristel, Venantino Venantini, Catherine
Rivet in "Emmanuelle—The Joys of a Woman"**

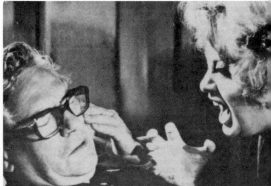

**Peter Finch, Shelley Winters
in "Something to Hide"**

Jean-Claude Brialy, Jane Birkin
in "Catherine & Co."

"Fox and His Friends"

CATHERINE & CO. (Warner Bros.) Producer, Leo L. Fuchs; Director, Michel Boisrond; Screenplay, Leo L Fuchs, Catherine Breillat; Based on novel by Edouard DeSegonzac; Assistant Directors, Chantal Larouette-Debelmas, Francis Herrgott; Photography, Richard Suzuki; Editor, Jacques Witta; Music, Vladimir Cosma; Art Director, Francois de Lamothe; Costumes, Simone Baron; In Technicolor; Rated R; 99 minutes; February release. CAST: Jane Birkin (Catherin), Patrick Dewaere (Francois), Jean-Claude Brialy (Guillaume), Vittorio Caprioli (Moretti), Jean-Pierre Aumont (Marquis), Mehdi (Thomas), Henri Garcin (Grandin), Nathalie Courval (Mauve), Jacques Marin, Jacques Rosny, Jean Barney, Marion Thebaud, Andre Thorent, Fabienne Arel, Lydia Dalbert, Alexandra Gorski, Madeleine Ganne, Bernard Musson, Dora Doll, Jose Lucioni, Jean Valmence, Carlo Nell, Jean-Pierre Moreux, Gerard Denizot, Catherine Ohotnikoff, Pipo Merisi, Angelina Alias, Pierre Hentz, Gerard Lemaire, Jean-Gabriel Molle.

FOX AND HIS FRIENDS (New Yorker) formerly "Fist-Right of Freedom"; Director, Rainer Werner Fassbinder, Executive Producer, Christian Hohoff; Screenplay, Rainer Werner Fassbinder, Christian Hohoff; Photography, Michael Ballhaus; Editor, Thea Eymesz; Music, Peer Raben; Costumes, Helga Kempke; In color; 123 minutes; February release. CAST: Rainer Werner Fassbinder (Fox), Peter Chatel (Eugen), Karl-Heinz Bohm (Max), Harry Baer (Philip), Adrian Hoven (Father), Ulla Jacobsen (Mother), Christiane Maybach (Hedwig)

JULIA: INNOCENCE ONCE REMOVED (Cine-Media) Executive Producer, Erich Tomak; Director, Sigi Rothemund; Screenplay, Wolfgang Bauer; Photography, Heinz Holscher; Editor, Eva Zeyn; Music, Gerhard Heinz; Art Director, Robert Fablankovich; Assistant Director, Ulrich Strobel; In Technicolor; Rated R; 83 minutes; February release. CAST: Sylvia Kristel (Julia), Jean-Claude Bouillon (Ralph), Terry Torday (Yvonne), Ekkehardt Belle (Patrick), Gisela Hahn (Miriam), Peter Berling, Rose-Renee Roth, Christine Glasner, Alois Mittermayer, Dominique del Pierre, Manfred Spies

CHINO (Intercontinental) Producer-Director, John Sturges; Screenplay, Clair Huffaker; Based on novel "The Valdez Horses" by Lee Hoffman; Presented by Sandy Cobe and David Baughn; In Eastmancolor; Rated PG; 98 minutes; February release. CAST: Charles Bronson, Jill Ireland, Marcel Bozzuffi, Vincent Van Patten, Fausto Tozzi, Melissa Chimenti

KARATE: ONE BY ONE (In-Frame Films) Director, Kin Lung; A First Films Production; In color; Rated R; February release. CAST: Kam Kung, Yasuai Kurata

MS. DON JUAN (Scotia American) Director, Roger Vadim; Screenplay, Jean Cau and Roger Vadim; In Eastmancolor; Rated R; 87 minutes; February release. CAST: Brigitte Bardot (Jeanne), Maurice Ronet (Pierre), Matthieu Carriere (Paul), Robert Hossein (Prevost), Jane Birkin (Clara), Michelle Sand (Leporella)

DR. TARR'S TORTURE DUNGEON (Group 1) Producers, Robert Viskin, J. G. Elster; Director, Juan L. Moctezuma; Screenplay, Charles Illescas; Based on Edgar Allen Poe's "The System of Dr. Tarr and Prof. Feather"; In color; Rated R; 88 minutes; March release. CAST: Claude Brook, Ellen Sherman, Martin LaSalle, Robert Dumont, Arthur Hansel

THE MAKING OF A LADY (Sunset International) Producer, Wolf C. Hartwig; Director, Christian Jacque; Jameson Brewer, Christian Jacque; Based on novel by Alexandre Dumas; In Panavision and Technicolor; Rated R; 93 minutes; March release. CAST: Michele Mercier, Richard Johnson, John Mills

CONFRONTATION (New Yorker) Director, Rolf Lyssy; Screenplay, Rolf Lyssy, George Janett; Photography, Fritz Maeder; Editor, George Janett; Music, Arthur Paul Huber; In black and white; 115 minutes; March release. CAST: Peter Bollag (David), Gert Haucke (Wilhelm), Marianne Kehlau (Frau Gustloff), Hilde Ziegler (Doris), Wolfram Berger (Zvonko), Michael Rittermann, Alfred Schlageter (Rabbis), Max Knapp (Court President), Peter Arens (Attorney), Klaus Knuth (Dr. Ursprung), Siegfried Meissner (Psychiatrist), Wolfgang Hiller (Dr. Furrier), Gunter Strack (Grimm)

Jean-Claude Bouillon, Sylvia Kristel
in "Julia: Innocence Once Removed"

Rainer Werner Fassbinder (L)
in "Fox and His Friends"

Edmund Purdom
in "Night Child"

Yves Montand, Michel Piccoli
in "Vincent, Francois, Paul and the Others"

TERROR FROM UNDER THE HOUSE (Hemisphere) Formerly "Revenge"; Director, Sidney Hayers; Screenplay, John Kruse; In color; Rated PG; 89 minutes; March release. CAST: Joan Collins (Carol), James Booth (Jim), Ray Barrett (Harry), Kenneth Griffith (Seely), Tom Marshall (Lee), Sinead Cusack (Rose), Zuleika Robson (Jill)

NIGHT CHILD (Film Ventures International) Directed and Written by Max Dallamano; Presented by Edward L. Montoro; In Deluxe Color; Rated R; 91 minutes; March release. CAST: Richard Johnson, Joanna Cassidy, Edmund Purdom, Evelyne Stewart, Nicole Elmi, Lila Kedrova

LOVE ME STRANGELY (Sunset International) Director, Sergio Gobbi; Based on novel by Dominique Fabre; In Eastmancolor; Rated R; 96 minutes; March release. CAST: Virna Lisi, Helmut Berger, Charles Aznavour

BEYOND THE DARKNESS (Mid-Broadway) Director, Michael Walter; Screenplay, August Reiger; A Constantin Film; An ABCO Enterprises presentation in color; Rated R; March release. CAST: Dagmar Hedrich, Werner Bruhns, Rudolf Schundler, Peter Martin Urtel, Michael Hinz, Elizabeth Volkmann, Eva Kinsky

FOURTEEN AND UNDER (Atlas) Producer, Wolf C. Hartwig; Director, Ernst Hofbauer; Executive Producer, Ludwig Spitaler; In color; Rated X; March release. CAST: Delphie Nouwen, Guinella Stern, Cynthia Horton, Mimita Lonero

THE SWINGING SWAPPERS (Hemisphere) Music, Rolf Bauer; In color; Rated R; March release. CAST: Carl Heinz, Gunther Kiezlich

BIRDS ORPHANS AND FOOLS (Golden) Producer, Samy Halfon; Direction and Story, Juri Jakubisko; Presented by Joseph R. Juliano and Terence Young; In Eastmancolor; Rated R; March release. CAST: Jiri Sykora (Yorick), Philippe Avron (Andre), Magda Vacaryova (Martha)

VINCENT, FRANCOIS, PAUL AND THE OTHERS (Joseph Green) Producer, Raymond Danon; Director, Claude Sautet; Screenplay, Jean-Loup Dabadie, Claude Neron, Claude Sautet; From novel "La Grande Marrade" by Claude Neron; Photography, Jean Boffety; Music, Philippe Sarde; Assistant Producer, Ralph Baum; In Eastmancolor; 118 minutes; March release. CAST: Yves Montand (Vincent), Michel Piccoli (Francois), Serge Reggiani (Paul), Gerard Depardieu (Jean), Stephane Audran (Catherine), Ludmilla Mikael (Marie), Marie Dubois (Lucie), Antonella Lauldi (Julia), Catherine Allegret (Colette), Umberto Orsini (Jacques)

IMMORAL TALES (New Line Cinema) Direction and Screenplay, Walerian Borowczyk; Assistant Director, Dominique Duverge; Producer, Anatole Dauman; Costumes, Piet Bolscher; Settings, Walerian Borowczyk; Music, Maurice LeRoux; In Eastmancolor; Rated X; 90 minutes; March release. CAST: Lise Danvers (Julie), Fabrice Luchini (Andre), Charlotte (Therese), Paloma Picasso (Erzsebet), Pascale Christophe (Istvan), Florence Ballamy (Lucrezia), Jacopo Berinizi (Pope), Lorenzo Berinizi (Cesar)

THE LOVES AND TIMES OF SCARAMOUCHE (Avco Embassy) Producer, Federico Aicardi; Director, Enzo G. Castellari; Screenplay, Tito Carpi, Enzo Castellari; Photography, Giovanni Bergamini; Editor, Gian-franco Amicucci; Music, Dammico Bixio; Art Director, Enzo Bulgarelli; Assistant Director, Roberto Pariante; In Telecolor; Rated PG; 91 minutes; March release. CAST: Michael Sarrazin (Scaramouche), Ursula Andress (Josephine), Aldo Macclone (Napoleon), Giancarlo Prete, Michael Forest, Nico Il Grande, Romano Puppo, Massimo Vanni, Alex Togni, Damir Mejovsek, Lucia De Oliveira

FROM BEYOND THE GRAVE (Howard Mahler) Producers, Max J. Rosenberg, Milton Subotsky; Director, Kevin Connor; Screenplay, Robin Clarke, Raymond Christodoulou, based on stories by R. Chetwynd-Hayes; Photography, Alan Hume; In color; Rated PG; 100 minutes; March release. CAST: Margaret Leighton, Donald Pleasence, David Warner, Ian Carmichael, Peter Cushing, Diana Dors, Ian Bannen

"Birds, Orphans and Fools"

Ursula Andress, Michael Sarrazin
in "The Loves and Times of Scaramouche"

**Jacque Rigby, Heather Deely
in "Diversions"**

**Lee Van Cleef, Lo Lieh
in "The Stranger and the Gunfighter"**

DIVERSIONS (Artemis) Producer, Valerie Ford; Directed and Written by Derek Ford; Photography, Geoffrey Glover; Editor, Pat Foster; Music, DeWolfe; In color; Rated X; 87 minutes; March release. CAST: Heather Deeley (Imogene), Jeffrey Morgan (Student), Tim Blackstong, James Lister, Tim Burr, Terry Walsh, Christopher Gilbert, Tony Kenyon, Gilly Sykes, Jacky Rigby, Derek Martin

MY MICHAEL (Alfred Plaine) Executive Producers, Shlomi Cohen, David Lipkind; Producer, Alfred Plaine; Direction and Screenplay, Dan Wolman; Photography, Adam Greenberg; Music, Alex Cogan; In color; 88 minutes; March release. CAST: Oded Kotler (Michael), Efrat Lavi (Wife)

GODZILLA VS. MEGALON (Cinema Shares International) Direction and Screenplay, Jun Fukuda; Produced by Toho-Eizo Ltd.; In color; Rated G; 85 minutes; April release. CAST: Katsuhiko Sasaki, Kiroyuki Kawase, Mori Mikita, Yutaka Hayashi

VIRGIN AND THE LOVER (Kemal International) Produced, Directed and Edited by Kemal Horulu; Screenplay, Kenneth Schwartz; Based on novelette "La Vierge et L'Amureaux"; In color; Rated X; April release. CAST: Olinka Podany, Eric Edwards, Leah Marlon, Jonothan John, Jennifer Welles, Darby Lloyd Rains, Marc Stevens

FRENCH HEAT (Cine Paris) Presented by Henri-Pierre Duval; Rated X; in color; April release. CAST: Antoinette Zoe Lucien, Debra D. Amnette, Emile Devos, Angela Fourastie

THE RETURN OF THE TALL BLOND MAN WITH ONE BLACK SHOE (Lanir) Producers, Yves Robert, Alain Poire; Director, Yves Robert; Screenplay, Yves Robert, Francis Verber; Music, Vladimir Cosma; Editor, Guislaine Desjonqueres; A Gaumont International-LaGueville Production; In color; Rated R; 84 minutes; April release. CAST Pierre Richard (Francois), Mireille Darc (Christine), Jean Rochefort (Toulouse), Jean Carmet (Maurice), Michel Duchaussoy (Cambrai), Paul Le Person (Perrache), Colette Castel (Paulette), Jean Bouise (Minister)

LOVE GAMES (Manuel S. Conde) Directed by Ed DePriest; In Eastmancolor; April release. CAST: Claudine Benet

THE STRANGER AND THE GUNFIGHTER (Columbia) Producers, Run Run Shaw, Gustave Berne; Director, Anthony Dawson; Story and Screenplay, Barth Jules Sussman; Music, Carlo Savina; In Panavision and Technicolor; Rated PG; 107 minutes; April release. CAST: Lee Van Cleef (Dakota), Lo Lieh (Wang), Karen Yeh (Lia), Julian Ugarte (Yancy), Goyo Peralto (Indio), Al Tung (Wang), Patty Sheppard (Russian), Erika Blanc (American), Femi Benussi (Italian), George Rigaud (Barclay), Richard Palacios (Calico), Alfred Boreman (Laundryman), Bart Barry (Sheriff), Paul Costello (Lawyer)

THE NOVICES (Monarch) Producer-Director, Guy Casaril; In color; Rated R; April release. CAST: Brigitte Bardot, Annie Girardot

SIXTEEN (United International) Director, Tiziano Longo; In color; Rated R; April release. CAST: Eli Galleani, Eva Czemerys, Anthony Steffen

MERRY GO ROUND (New Line) Director, Otto Schenk; Based on play "Reigan" by Arthur Schnitzler; Music, Francis Lai; Photography, Wolfgang Treu; In color; Rated R; 90 minutes; April release. CAST: Maria Schneider (Girl), Helmut Berger (Employer), Sydne Rome (Maid), Senta Berger (Mistress), Hans Brenner (Soldier), Peter Weck (Husband), Erika Pluhar (Actress), Gertraud Jesserer (Prostitute), Michael Heltau (Poet), Helmut Lohner (Count)

SUPER DRAGON (In-Frame) Directed by Kin Lung; A First Films Production; In color; Rated PG; April release. CAST: Jimmy Wang Yu

DON'T OPEN THE WINDOW (Newport) formerly "The Living Dead at Manchester Morgue"; Director, Jorge Grau; Screenplay, Sandro Continenza, Marcello Coscia, Jorge Grau; Special Effects, Gianetto DeRossi; In color; Rated R; 88 minutes; April release. CAST: Ray Lovelock (George), Christina Galbo (Edna), Arthur Kennedy (Inspector), Fernando Hilbeck

HORROR RISES FROM THE TOMB (Avco Embassy) Director, Carlos Aured; In color; Rated R; 95 minutes; April release. CAST: Paul Naschy, Emma Cohen, Helga Line

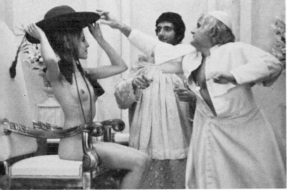

"Immoral Tales"

**Helmut Berger
in "Merry Go Round"**

**Marc Porel, Turi Ferro, Agostina Belli
in "Virility"**

VIRILITY (Athena/Coliseum) Director, Paolo Cavara; Screenplay, Gian Paolo Callegari; Photography, Claudio Cirillo; Music, Daniele Patucchi; Presented by Vincent Bejtman and Artwood Associates; Rated R; 87 minutes; April release. CAST: Turi Ferro (Vito), Agostina Belli (Cettina), Marc Porel (Roberto), Anna Bonaiuto (Lucia), Mario Carrara (L'Arciprete), Geraldine Hooper (Pat), Giuseppe Lo Presti (Bartolo), Tuccio Musumeci (Fisichella), Maria Tolu (Illuminata)

BAMBINA (Buckley Bros.) Producer, Silvio Clementelli; Director, Alberto Lattuada; Photography, Lamberto Caimi; Music, Fred Bongusto; Screenplay, Ottavio Jemma, Alberto Lattuada, Bruno Di Geronimo; In Technicolor; Rated R; 97 minutes; April release. CAST: Luigi Proietti (Severio), Irene Papas (Donna Raimonda), Teresa Ann Saboy (Clotilde), Bruno Cirino (Peppe), Mario Scaccia (Amilcare), Lina Polito (Concetta), Isa Miranda (Elisa), Clelia Mantania (Lore)

OH! ALFIE (Cinema National) formerly "Alfie Darling"; Producer, Dugald Rankin; Written and Directed by Ken Hughes; Based on novel "Alfie Darling" by Bill Naughton; Photography, Ousama Rawi; Music and Songs, Alan Price; Editor, John Trumper; Design, Harry Pottle; Assistant Director, Peter Cotton; In Technicolor; A Signal Films production; Rated R; 102 minutes; April release. CAST: Alan Price (Alfie), Jill Townsend (Abby), Paul Copley (Bakey), Joan Collins (Fay), Sheila White (Norma), Annie Ross (Claire), Hannah Gordon (Dora), Roger Lumont (Pierre), Rula Lenska, Minah Bird, Derek Smith, Vicki Michelle, Brian Wilde, Robin Parkinson, Rosalind Elliott, Jenny Hanley, Timothy Peters, Ben Aris, Hugh Walters, Sally Bulloch, Brian Anthony, Sean Roantree, Constantin de Goguel, Graham Ashley, Patsy Kensitt, Mark Scoones, Terence Taplin, Ian Woodward, Marianne Broom

RUM RUNNER (Libert Films International) Director, Robert Enrico; Screenplay, Pierre Pelegri, Robert Enrico from book by J. Porcheral; Photography, Jean Boffety; Editor, Michel Lewin; Art Director, Max Douy; In Eastmancolor; 125 minutes; Rated R; April release. CAST: Brigitte Bardot (Linda), Lino Ventura (Corny), Bill Travers (Gerry), Clive Revill (Hammond), Guy Marchand (Actor), Jess Hahn (Big Dutch)

**Irene Papas, Teresa Ann Savoy
in "Bambina"**

LES SUSPECTS (S. J. International) Director, Michel Wyn; Screenplay, Michel Wyn, Paul Adreota, Michel Sales, from book by Paul Andreota; Photography, Didier Tarot; Editor, Maryse Siclier; In Eastmancolor; Rated PG; 90 minutes; April release. CAST: Mimsy Farmer (Candice), Paul Meurisse (Kerchner), Michel Bouquet (Procurer), Renaud Verley (Bernard), Bruno Cremer (Inspector), Michel Lonsdale (Judge), Jean-Claude Dauphin (Christian)

LA CHIENNE (Ajay) Producer, Graunberger-Richebe; Director, Jean Renoir; Screenplay, Jean Renoir, Andre Girard, from novel by Georges de la Fouchardiere; Photography, Theodore Sparkuhl, Roger Hubert; Editor, Marguerite Renoir; 100 minutes; April release. CAST: Michel Simon (Maurice), Janie Mareze (Lulu), Georges Flamant (Dede), Madeleine Berubet (Adele), Gaillard (Alexis), Jean Gehret (Dagodet)

GET MEAN (Cee Note) Producer, Tony Anthony; Director, Ferdinando Baldi; Screenplay, Lloyd Batista, Wolfe Lowenthal; Executive Producer, C. B. Selnik; Associate Producer, Terrance McGovern; In Techniscope and Technicolor; Rated PG; May release. CAST: Tony Anthony, Lloyd Battista

THE GODFATHER SQUAD (Cannon) Executive Producer, Paul Ming; Director, M. Cardinal; In color; Rated R; May release. CAST: Bruce Liang, Shirley Corrigan, Gordon Mitchell, Maria Coronato

ANNIE (Map) Producers, Fulvio Lucisano, Harry Alan Towers; Director, Massimo Dallamano; Based on story by Annie Belle; In Movielab Color; Rated X; May release. CAST: Annie Belle (Annie), Charles Fawcett (Michael), Felicity Devonshire (Linda), Al Cliver (Philip), Ciro Ippolito (Angelo), Maria Rohm (Susan), Linda Ho (Genevieve), Chan Yiu Lan (Chen), Ted Thomas, Ines Pellegrini, Tim Street, Linda Slade

MASSAGE PARLOR WIFE (Boxoffice International) Produced, Directed and· Written by Barry Spinello; In color; 90 minutes; May release. CAST: Jenn Gillian, Brandi Saunders, Steve Rogers, Yvonne DeLacroux, Horst Vincent, Susan Snow, Martha Del Rio, Solly Stoner

PHARAOH (Hallmark) Director, Jerzy Kawalerowicz; Screenplay, Tadeusz Konwicki, Jerzy Kawalerowicz; Based on novel by Boleslaw Prus; In Eastmancolor; Rated R; 134 minutes; May release. CAST: George Zelnik (Ramses), Barbara Bryl (Kama), Krystyna Mikolajewska (Sara), Piotr Pawloski (Herhor), Leszek Herdegen, Jerzy Buczachi

CANDY'S CANDY (Variety) Direction and Screenplay, Renau Pieri; Music, Laurent Voulzy; In Eastmancolor; Rated X; 90 minutes; May release. CAST: Sylvia Bourdon, Beatrice Harnois, Richard Lemieuvre, Martine Grimaud

WATCH OUT, WE'RE MAD (Columbia) Producer, Mario Cecchi Gori; Director, Marcello Fondato; Screenplay, Marcello Fondato, Francesco Scarmaglia; Based on story by Marcello Fondato; In color; Rated G; May release. CAST: Terence Hill, Bud Spencer, Donald Pleasence

CHECK MY OIL, BABY (French) Produced and Directed by Norbert Terry; In color; Rated X; May release. CAST: Evelyne Scott, Laure Moutoussamy, Francois Gabriel

THE SUPER WEAPON (Howard Mahler) Producer, Serafim Karalexis; Screenplay, Norbert Albertson; A Madison World Film; In color; Rated PG; May release. CAST: Ron Van Clief, Charles Bonet, Jason Pai Pow

THE ROGUE (Group 1) Director, Gregory Simpson; Producer, Franco Bandinni; Executive Producer, Charles Driscall; Photography, Sesto Andriatti; In color; Rated R; 84 minutes; May release. CAST: Milan Galvonic, Barbara Bouchet, Margaret Lee

A PIECE OF PLEASURE (Joseph Green) Producer, Andre Genoves; Director, Claude Chabrol; Screenplay, Paul Gegauff; Photography, Jean Rabier; In color; English subtitles; Rated R; 100 minutes; May release. CAST: Paul Gegauff (Philippe), Danielle Gegauff (Esther), Paula Moore (Sylvia), Michel Valette (Katkof), Pierre Santini (Michel), Giancarlo Sisti (Habib)

GUERNICA (New Line Cinema) Producers, Harry Blum, Federico Mueller; Written and Directed by Fernando Arrabal; Photography, Ramon Suarez; Editor, Renzo Lucidi; 110 minutes; May release. CAST: Mariangela Melato (Vandale), Ron Faber (Goya), Bento Urago (Count), Cosimo Cinieri (Raphael), Franco Rossel (Onesimo), Mario Novelli (Ramiro), Cyril Spiga (Angel), Rocco Fontana (Antonio)

**Elizabeth Taylor, Ava Gardner
in "The Blue Bird"**

**Mariangela Melato
in "Guernica"**

THE BLUE BIRD (20th Century-Fox) Producer, Paul Maslansky; Director, George Cukor; Executive Producer, Edward Lewis; Screenplay, Hugh Whitemore, Alfred Hayes; Based on play "The Blue Bird" by Maurice Maeterlinck; Photography, Freddie Young, Ionas Gritzus; Music, Irwin Kostal; Songs and Ballet Numbers, Andrei Petrov; Lyrics, Tony Harrison; Editor, Ernest Walter; In DeLuxe Color; Rated G; 100 minutes; May release. CAST: Elizabeth Taylor (Mother, Maternal Love, Witch, Light), Jane Fonda (Night), Ava Gardner (Luxury), Cicely Tyson (Cat), Robert Morley (Father Time), Harry Andrews (Oak), Todd Lookinland (Tvityl), Patsy Kensit (Myltyl), Will Geer (Grandfather), Mona Washbourne (Grandmother), George Cole (Dog), Richard Pearson (Bread), Nadia Pavlova (Blue Bird), George Vitzin (Sugar), Margareta Terechova (Milk), Oleg Popov (Fat Laughter), Leonid Nevedomsky (Father), Valentina Ganilae Ganibalova (Water), Yevgeny Scherbakov (Fire), and the Leningrad Kirov Ballet

THE JEWISH GAUCHOS (Julio Tanjcloff) Producer-Director, Juan Jose Jusid; Screenplay, Juan Jose Jusid, Oscar Viale, Alejandro Saderman; Based on Alberto Gerehunoff's novel; Photography, Juan Carlos Desanzo; Music, Gustaveo Beytelman; In Eastmancolor; Rated PG; 92 minutes; May release. CAST: Pepe Soriano (Dr. Naum), Luis Politti (Remigio), Luisina Brando, Gustavo Luppi, Raul Lavie, Maria Rosa Gallo, Ginamaria Hidalgo, China Zorrilla, Dora Baret, Oscar Viale, Osvaldo Terranova, Eduardo Ruderman, Victor Laplace, Adrian Ghio, Maria Jose Demare, Jorge Barreiro, Zelmar Guenol, Martha Gam, Zulema Katz, Carlota Bonefoux, Maurice Jouvet, Golde Flami, Max Berliner, Claudio Lucero, Ignacio Finder

THE DAYDREAMER (Joseph Green) Director, Pierre Richard; Screenplay, Pierre Richard, Andre Ruellan; Photography, Daniel Vogel; Editor, Marie-Josephe Voyette; Art Director, Michel De Broin; Music, Vladimir Cosma; Associate Producers, Alain Poire, Yves Robert; In color; Rated PG; 90 minutes; May release. CAST: Pierre Richard (Pierre), Bernard Blier (Alexander), Marie-Christine Barrault (Lisa), Maria Pacome (Glycia), Paul Presboist (Klerdene), Catherine Samie (Clarisse), Robert Dalban (Mazelin)

RECOMMENDATION FOR MERCY (Cinema Shares International) Producers, James P. Lewis, Murray Markowitz; Director, Murray Markowitz; Executive Producer, Alfred M. Berman; Associate Producer, Edward Wachta; Screenplay, Fabian Jennings, Joel Weisenfeld, Murray Markowitz; Photography, Richard Leiterman; Editor, George Appleby; Music, Don Gillis; Art Director, Tony Hall; In color; Rated R; 94 minutes; May release. CAST: Andrew Skidd, Robb Judd, Mike Upmalis, Karen Martin, Michele Fansett, Michael Lewis, Jim Millington, Carl Gall, Ruth Peckham, Rod Rekofski, Howard Wilson, Lawrence Elion, Terry Doyle, Bill Koski, Jack Zimmerman, Arnold Wild, David Wideman, David Murray, Tom Brennan, George Cunnihgmfee, Henry Cohen, Barry Belchamber, Michael Lambert, Billey Anderson, Tom Story

ADAM AND NICOLE (United Pictures) Producer, Ken Coles; Director, Trevor Wrenn; In Eastmancolor; Rated X; June release. CAST: Jenny Westbrook, Chris Chittell, Michael Watkins, Jeannie Collings, Karl Lanchbury

SYMPTOMS (Bryanston) Producer, Jean L. Dupuis; Director, Joseph Larraz; Screenplay, Joseph Larraz, Stanley Miller; Music, John Scott; In color; Rated R; 81 minutes; June release. CAST: Angela Pleasence, Lorna Heilbron, Peter Vaughan

MEAN FRANK AND CRAZY TONY (Aquarius) Director, Michele Lupo; Music, Riz Ortolani; In Technicolor; Rated R; June release. CAST: Lee Van Cleef, Tony LoBianco, Edwige Fenech, Jess Hahn, Jean Rochefort, Joe Scedi

LIFE SIZE (Dimension) title changed to "Love Doll"; Director, Luis Berlanga; Screenplay, Rafael Azcona, Luis Berlanga; Music, Maurice Jarre; Photography, Alain Derobe; In color; Rated X; June release. CAST: Michel Piccoli (Michel), Valentine Tessier (Mother), Rada Rassimov (Isabelle), Claudi Bianchi (Girl), Queta Clavar (Maria), Manola Alexandre (Jose), Lucienne Hamon (Juliette) Jenny Astruc (Janine)

WEEKEND GIRLS Director, Ted Roter; In Eastmancolor; June release. CAST: Lena Lane, Lindan Dander, Alberta Ross

**Pierre Richard
in "The Daydreamer"**

**Michel Piccoli
in "Life Size"**

Romy Schneider, Philippe Noiret
in "The Old Gun"

"Spasmo"

TOM THUMB (Paramount) Director, Michel Boisrond; Screenplay, Marcel Julian; Music, Francis Lai; In color; Rated G; June release. CAST: Marie La Foret, Jean-Pierre Marielle, Michel Robin, Marie Henriau, Jean-Marie Proslier, Jean-Luc Bideau

MALE OF THE CENTURY (Joseph Green) Directed and Written by Claude Berri; From an idea by Milos Forman; In color; English subtitles; 95 minutes; June release. CAST: Claude Berri, Juliet Berto

THE OLD GUN (Surrogate) Director, Robert Enrico; Screenplay, Pascal Jardin, Robert Enrico, Claude Veillot; French with English subtitles; Story, Robert Enrico; Photography, Etienne Beckar; Music, Francois de Roubaix; A Carmen F. Zollo presentation; In color; 104 minutes; June release. CAST: Philippe Noiret (Julien), Romy Schneider (Clara), Jean Bouise (Francois), Madeline Ozeray (Mother)

SPASMO (Libra) Producer, Ugo Tucci; Director, Umberto Lenzi; Music, Ennio Morricone; In Eastmancolor; In English; 88 minutes; June release. CAST: Suzy Kendall (Barbara), Robert Hoffman (Christian), Monica Monet (Clorinda), Ivan Rassimov, Guido Alberti

DEMON WITCH CHILD (Coliseum) Director, Amando Ossorio; A Keystone Enterprises presentation; In Technicolor; Rated R; June release. CAST: Julian Mateos, Fernando Sancho, Marian Salgado, Lone Fleming, Angel Del Pozo

THE BITTER TEARS OF PETRA VON KANT (New Yorker) Executive Producer-Director-Screenplay, Rainer Werner Fassbinder; Photography, Michael Ballhaus; Music, Giuseppe Verdi, The Platters, Walker Brothers; Art Director, Kurt Raab; Editor, Thea Eymes; In color; 124 minutes; June release. CAST: Margit Carstensen (Petra), Irm Hermann (Marlene), Hanna Schygulla (Karin), Eva Mattes (Gabriele), Katrin Schaake (Sidonie), Gisela Fachelday (Valerie)

THE CLOCKMAKER (Joseph Green) Written and Directed by Bertrand Tavernier; From the novel by Georges Simenon; In color; English subtitles; 105 minutes; June release. CAST: Philippe Noiret, Jean Rochefort, Julien Bertheau

VERONIQUE OR THE SUMMER OF MY 13th YEAR (Levitt-Pickman) Written and Directed by Claudine Guillemin; Photography, Jean-Jacques Rochut; Editor, Nicole Saulnier; In Eastmancolor; 90 minutes; June release. CAST: Anne Teyssedre (Veronique), Anouk Ferjac (Anne), Michel Peyleron (Jean), Anne Kerylene (Mother), Edith Loria (Friend), Jean-Pierre Moulin (Sylvain)

PACO (Cinema National) Produced and Written by Andre Marquis; Director, Robert Vincent O'Neil; Photography, Andrew Davis; Music, Mariano and Mauro Bruno; Editor, Gene Ruggiero; In DeLuxe Color; 100 minutes; June release. CAST: Jose Ferrer, Allen Garfield, Pernell Roberts, Andre Marquis, Panchito Gomes

DEEP RED (Mahler) Executive Producer, Claudio Argento; Producer, Salvatore Argento; Director, Dario Argento; Screenplay, Giuseppe Bassan from story by Dario Argento, Bernardo Zapponi; Photography, Luigi Kuveiller; Costumes, Elena Mannini; Music, Giorgio Gaslini; In color; Rated R; 98 minutes; June release. CAST: David Hemmings (Marcus), Daria Nicolodi (Gianna), Gabriele Lavia (Carlo), Clara Calamai (Marta), Macha Meril (Helga), Glauco Mauri (Giordani), Eros Pagni (Calcabrini), Giuliana Calandra (Amanda)

THE LAST WOMAN (Columbia) Producer, Jacques Roitfeld; Director, Marco Ferreri; Screenplay, Rafael Azacona, Dante Matelli, Marco Ferreri; Photography, Luciano Tovoli; Editor, Enzo Meniconi; Music, Philippe Sarde; In color; Rated X; 112 minutes; June release. CAST: Gerard Depardieu (Gerard) Ornella Muti (Valerie), Michel Piccoli (Michel), Zouzou (Wife), Renato Salvatori (Friend), Giuliana Calandra (Friend's Wife)

DEATH-OF A STRANGER (I.P.C.) A Burbank International presentation; Rated PG; 90 minutes; June release; No other credits available. CAST: Jason Robards, Hardy Kruger, Gila Almagor

Philippe Noiret
in "The Clockmaker"

Margit Carstensen, Hanna Schygulla
in "The Bitter Tears of Petra von Kant"

"Rape of Innocence

Peter Cushing, Caroline Munro, Doug McClure
in "At the Earth's Core"

DUEL IN THE TIGER DEN (Tower) Producer, Kem Chair; Director, Yu Ming Ho; In Technicolor; Rated R; June release. CAST: Hui Tin, Yee Jan, Lo Lun

DICK DEADEYE (Intercontinental) Producer, Steven Melendez; Director, Bill Melendez; Screenplay, Leo Rost, Robin Miller; Executive Producer, Leo Rost; Based on drawings by Ronald Searle; Music, Gilbert and Sullivan; New Lyrics, Robin Miller; Music Arranged and Conducted by Jimmy Horowitz; In Technicolor; Rated G; 90 Minutes; July release. An animated rock opera featuring the voices of Victor Spinetti, Linda Lewis, Miriam Karlin

BRUCE LEE—SUPER DRAGON (Allied Artists) No credits available; In color; Rated R; July release. CAST: Lee Hsiao Lung, Jimmy Wang Yu

HOUSE OF EXORCISM (Peppercorn-Wormser) Director, Mickey Lion (Mario Bava); Producer, Alfred Leone; Screenplay, Alberto Cittini, Alfred Leone; Music, Carlo Savina; Movielab Color; Rated R; 90 minutes; July release. CAST: Telly Savalas, Elke Sommer, Robert Alda, Sylva Koscina, Alida Valli, Alessio Orano, Gabriele Tinti, Kathy Leone, Eduardo Fajardo, Carmen Silva, Franz Von Treuberg, Espartaco Santoni

THE GIRL FROM THE RED CABARET (Independent International) Producer, Jose Frade; Director, Eugenio Martin; Music, Tony Hatch, Jackie Trent; Art Director, Gil Parrondo; In Eastmancolor; Rated PG; July release. CAST: Marisol, Mel Ferrer, Renaud Verley

THE KINGFISH CAPER (Cinema Shares International) Producer, Ben Vlok; Director, Dirk DeVilliers; Adapted by Roy Boulting; Based on novel by Wilbur Smith; A Cavalier Film; In color; Rated PG; July release. CAST: David McCallum (Benedict), Hayley Mills (Tracy), Jon Cypher (Johnny)

THE RAPE KILLER (Joseph Brenner) Director, Dacosta Carayan; Screenplay, Telly Livadas; Music, Yani Spanos; In color; Rated R; 80 minutes; July release. CAST: Dorothy Moore, Larry Daniels, Leslie Bowman, Angela Clianto, Anthony Carr

AT THE EARTH'S CORE (American International) Producer, John Dark; Executive Producer, Harry N. Blum; Director, Kevin Connor; Screenplay, Milton Subotsky; Based on novel by Edgar Rice Burroughs; Photography, Alan Hume; Designer, Maurice Carter; Art Director, Bert Davey; Editors, John Ireland, Barry Peters; Music, Mike Vickers; Presented by Samuel Z. Arkoff; In Movielab Color; Rated PG; 89 minutes; July release. CAST: Doug McClure (David), Peter Cushing (Dr. Perry), Caroline Munro (Dia), Cy Grant (Ra), Godfrey James (Ghak), Sean Lynch (Hooja)

RAPE OF INNOCENCE (New Line Cinema) Director, Yves Boisset; Screenplay, Jean-Pierre Bastid, Michel Martens; Adaptation, Yves Boisset, Jean Curtelin; Photography, Jacques Loiseleux; Music, Vladimir Coema; Executive Producers, Catherine Winter, Gisele Rebillon; In color; 95 minutes; July release. CAST: Jean Carmet (George), Pierre Tornade (Colin), Jean Bouise (Boular), Michel Peyrelon (Schumacher), Ginette Garcia (Ginnette), Pascale Roberts (Mme. Colin), Jean-Pierre Marielle (Leo), Robert Castel (Loulou), Pina Caruso (Vigerelli), Isabelle Huppert (Brigitte), Jacques Chailleux, Henri Garcin, Odile Poisson, Victor Lanoux, Mohamed Zimet, Jacques Villeret

EMILIENNE & NICOLE (Joseph Green) Director, Guy Casaril; From novel by Claude des Olbes; Music, Nino Ferrer; In Eastmancolor; Rated X; 95 minutes; July release. CAST: Betty Mars, Pierre Oudry, Nathalie Guerin

SEX WITH A SMILE (Surrogate) Producer, Lucio Martino; Director, Sergio Martino; A Medusa Film; Rated R; CFI Color; 95 minutes; July release. CAST: Marty Feldman, Barbara Bouchet, Dayle Haddon, Sydne Rome

THE MARTYR (Joseph Green) Producer, Artur Brauner; Director, Aleksander Ford; Music, Moshe Wilensky; Photography, Jerzy Lipman; Editor, C. O. Bartning; Screenplay, Josef Gross; Based on Scenario by Alexander Ramati; The first Israeli-German Co-Production; In color; 90 minutes; July release. CAST: Leo Genn (Dr. Korczak), Orna Porat (Stefa), Efrat Lavi (Ruth), Ohad Kaplan (Yakov), Benjamin Volz (Michael), Carlos Werner (Adam)

"Emilienne & Nicole"

Leo Genn
in "The Martyr"

**Adolfo Celi, Ugo Tognazzi
in "My Friends"**

MY FRIENDS (Allied Artists) Producer, Carlo Nebiolo; Director, Mario Monicelli; Screenplay, Pietro Germi, Piero de Barnardi, Leo Benvenuti, Tullio Pinelli; Presented by Emanuel Wolf; In color; 113 minutes; July release. CAST: Ugo Tognazzi (Mascetti), Gastone Moschin (Melandri), Philippe Noiret (Perozzi), Duilio Del Prete (Necchi), Adolfo Celi (Sassaroli), Bernard Blier (Righi)

MANNEQUIN (Joseph Brenner) Producer, Alain Vallier; Directors, Alain Van Damme, Alex Nubarr, Gerard Kikoine; Screenplay, Alain Van Damme; In Eastmancolor; Rated X; 90 minutes; July release. CAST: Nadine Perles, Alain Schwartz, Elton Frame, Karin Mayer

THE WILD GOOSE CHASE (EDP) Written and Directed by Claude Zidi; Photography, Henri Decae; Editor, Robert Isnardon; Music, Vladimir Cosma; In Eastmancolor; 100 minutes; July release. CAST: Pierre Richard (Pierre), Jane Birkin (Janet), Michel Aumont (Inspector), Claude Dauphin (Rovere), Amedeus August (Gay One), Jean Martin (Director)

THE COUSIN (Cambist) Producer, Undis T. Gay; Director, Aldo Lado; In Technicolor; Rated R; July release. CAST: Massino Ranieri, Dayle Haddon

LE MAGNIFIQUE (Cine III) Directed and Written by Philippe De Brora; Producers, Alexandre Mnouchkine, Georges Dancigers; Photography, Maurice Chapiron; Music, Tomas Sosa; French with English subtitles; In color; 86 minutes; July release. CAST: Jean-Paul Belmondo, Jacqueline Bisset, Vittorio Capriolo

TIFFANY JONES (Cineworld) Producer-Director, Pete Walker; Screenplay, Alfred Shaughnessy; Music, Cyril Ornadel; In color; Rated R; 90 minutes; August release. CAST: Anouska Hempel, Ray Brooks, Eric Pohlmann, Martin Benson, Susan Sneers

THE AWAKENING OF ANNIE (Atlas) Produced, Directed and Written by Zygmunt Sulistrowski; Music, Hareton Salvanini, Beto Ruschel; Co-Producer, Joel Lifschutz; In Eastmancolor; Rated X; August release. CAST: Anne Friedmann, Hugo Jorge, Simon Kennedy, Sylvia Maria, Edy Maury

"The Awakening of Annie"

HELENA (Euram) Producer, Jean-Pierre Sammut; Director, Alain Maury; In color; Rated X; August release. CAST: Valerie Boisgel, Yan Brian

BAMBOO HOUSE OF DOLLS (Peppercorn-Wormser) Producer, Run Run Shaw; Movielab Color; Rated R; August release. CAST: Lo Lieh, Birte Tove

NINE LIVES OF A WET PUSSYCAT (Navaron) Producer, Richard Taylor; Director, Jimmy Laine; Screenplay, Nicholas George; Photography, Francis X. Wolfe; In color; Rated X; August release. CAST: Pauline La Monde, Dominique Santos, Joy Silver, David Pirell, Everett East, Ack Ming, Shaker Lewis, Nicholas George

THE FLOWER WITH THE DEADLY STING (P. A. B.) Director, Gianfranco Piccioli; Producers, Riccardo Cerro, Mauro Berardi; In color; Rated R; August release. CAST: Carroll Baker, Gianni Garko

LOVERS AND OTHER RELATIVES (Crystal) Producer, Silvio Clementelli; Director, Salvatore Samperi; Screenplay, Allessandro Parenzo, Ottavio Jemma; Presented by Sidney Tager; In Technicolor; Rated R; 98 minutes; August release. CAST: Laura Antonelli, Alessandro Momo, Orazio Orlando, Tino Carraro, Lilla Brignone, Monica Guerritore, Lino Toffolo

THEY'RE COMING TO GET YOU (Independent International) Director, Sergio Martino; In color; Rated R; August release. CAST: George Hilton, Susan Scott

SEVEN-MAN ARMY (Shaw Brothers) Produced by Shaw Brothers; Director, Chang Cheh; Screenplay, I. Kuang, Chang Cheh; Photography, Kung Mu To; Editor, Kuo Ting-hung; Music, Chen Yung-Yu; In color; 100 minutes; August release. CAST: David Chiang, Ti Lung, Chen Kuan-tai, Alexander Fu Sheng

TWO AGAINST THE LAW (Joseph Green) Written and Directed by Jose Giovanni; Photography, Jean-Jacques Tarbes; Editor, Francoise Javet; In Eastmancolor; 100 minutes; August release. CAST: Alain Delon (Gino), Jean Gabin (Germaine), Mimsy Farmer (Lucie), Michel Bouquet (Goitreau), Ilaria Occhini (Sophie), Victor Lanoux (Marcel), Christine Fabrega (Genevieve), Bernard Giraudeau (Frederic), Malka Ribovska (Lawyer), Jacques Monod (Prosecutor)

THE BAWDY ADVENTURES OF TOM JONES (Universal) Producer, Robert Sadoff; Director, Cliff Owen; Screenplay, Jeremy Lloyd; Based on musical "Tom Jones"; Photography, Douglas Slocombe; Art Director, Jack Shampan; Editor, Bill Blunden; Costumes, Beatrice Dawson; Score, Ron Grainer; Assistant Director, Anthony Wayne; In Technicolor; Rated R; 94 minutes; August release. CAST: Nicky Henson (Tom), Trevor Howard (Squire Western), Terry-Thomas (Square), Arthur Lowe (Thwackum), Georgia Brown (Jenny), Joan Collins (Bess), William Mervyn, Murray Melvin, Madeline Smith, Geraldine McEwan, Jeremy Lloyd, Janie Greenspun, Michael Bates, Hilda Fenemore, Patricia MacPherson, Isabel Dean, James Hayter, Frank Thornton, Gladys Henson, Joan Cooper, Maxine Casson, Judy Buxton, Arthur Howard, John Forrest, Arnold Diamond, Claire Davenport, Griffith Davies, Christine Ozanne

SURVIVE! (Paramount) Written, Produced and Directed by Rene Cardona, Jr.; Based on book by Clay Blair, Jr.; A Robert Stigwood/Allan Carr presentation; In color; Music, Gerald Fried; English version edited by Marshall M. Borden; Rated R; 85 minutes; August release. CAST: Pablo Ferrel (Raul), Hugo Stiglitz (Francisco), Luz Maria Aguilar (Mrs. Madero), Fernando Larranga (Madero), Norma Lazareno (Sylvia), Lorenzo de Rodas, Gloria Chavez, Jose Elias Moreno, Carlos Camara, Fernando Palaviccini, Sara Guash

HIGH VELOCITY (Turtle) Producer, Takashi Ohashi; Director, Remi Kramer; Executive Producer, Joseph Wolfe; Screenplay, Remi Kramer, Michael J. Parson; Music, Jerry Goldsmith; In Metrocolor; Rated PG; September release. CAST: Ben Gazzara, Brit Ekland, Paul Winfield, Keenan Wynn, Alejandro Rey, Victoria Racimo

FINDHORN (Moving Pictures) Producers, Randi Johnson, Victoria Mudd; Director, Peter Werner; Photography, Rhoden Streeter, Rowena Pattee; Music, Hans Poulson; Editor, Lisa Fruchtman; In color; Rated G; 62 minutes; September release. A documentary.

HOUSE OF PSYCHOTIC WOMEN (Independent International) Director, Carlos Aured; In color; Rated R; September release. CAST: Paul Naschy, Maria Perschy, Diana Lorys

Sonny Chiba
in "The Bodyguard"

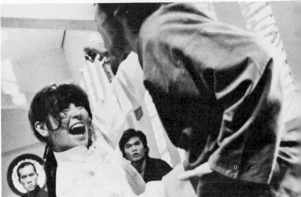

"Sister Street Fighter"

SPANISH FLY (Emerson) Director, Bob Kellett; A Nat Cohen presentation of an EMI film; In Technicolor; Rated R; September release. CAST: Terry-Thomas, Leslie Phillips, Sue Lloyd, Nadiuska, Sally Farmiloe, Nina Francis, Jelah Haddah

THE BODYGUARD (Aquarius) Director, Simon Nuchtern; Executive Producer, Terry Levene; Music, Maurice Sarli; In Technicolor; Rated R; 86 minutes; September release. CAST: Sonny Chiba, Aaron Banks, Bill Louie, Judy Lee

THE OTHER SIDE OF THE UNDERNEATH (Jack Bond) Producer, Jack Bond; Direction and Screenplay, Jane Arden; Music, Sally Minford; Photography, Aubrey Dewar, Jack Bond; Editor, David Mingay; Associate Producer, Prue Faull; In color; Rated R; 100 minutes; September release. CAST: Sheila Allen, Liz Danciger, Elaine Donovan, Susanka Fraey, Ann Lyn, Jenny Moss, Penny Slinger

AFFAIR (Intercontinental) Director, Andree Marchand; Screenplay, Elisabeth Reclair; In Eastmancolor; Rated X; 81 minutes; September release. CAST: Paulo Senatore, Lucretia Love, Mauro Parenti

XALA (New Yorker) Written and Directed by Ousmane Sembene; Based on Mr. Sembene's novel of same title; Photography, Georges Caristan; Editor, Florence Eymon; In color; 116 minutes; September release. CAST: Thierno Leye (El Hadji Abdoukader Beye), Seun Samb (First Wife), Younouss Seye (Second Wife), Miriam Niamg (Rama), Douta Seck, Fatim Diagne, Moustapha Toure, Ilimane Sagnan, Makhouredia Gueye, Adboulaye Seck, Doudou Gueye, Farba Sarr

YOUR HEAVEN, MY HELL (Athena) formerly "Between Heaven and Hell"; Director, Rafaello R. Marchent; Rated PG; 90 minutes; September release. CAST: John Philip Law, Ana Liagade

THE CONSPIRACY OF TORTURE (Athena) Produced by Film Ena; Director, L. Fulci; Rated R; 95 minutes; September release. CAST: Thomas Milian, Adrienne LaRossa, George Wilson

GENERAL IDI AMIN DADA (Tinc) Producers, Jean-Pierre Rassam, Charles-Henri Favrod; Director, Barbet Schroeder; Photography, Nestor Almendros; In color; 90 minutes; September release. A documentary on the military dictator of Africa's Uganda.

SISTER STREET FIGHTER (New Line) Producer, Toei Co.; Screenplay, Norifumi Suzuki, Masahiro Kakefuda; Director, Kazuhiko Yamaguchi; Photography, Yoshio Nakajima; Rated R; 86 minutes; September release. CAST: Shinichi Chiba, Etsuko Shiomi, Mie Hayakawa, Sanae Obori, Hsieh Hsiu Yung, Hiroshi Kondo, Tatsuya Nanjo

EDVARD MUNCH (New Yorker) Written and Directed by Peter Watkins; Photography, Odd Geir Saether; Art Director, Grethe Hajer; Costumes, Ada Skolmen; In color; 167 minutes; September release. CAST: Geir Westby (Edvard Munch), Gro Fraas (Mrs. Heiberg), Erik Allum (Edvard 1868), Amund Berge (Edvard 1875), Kerstii Allum (Sophie 1969), Inger-Berit Oland (Sophie 1875), Susan Troldmyr (Laura 1868), Camilla Falk (Laura 1875), Gro Jarto (Laura 1884), Ragnvald Caspari (Peter 1868), Erik Kristiansen (Peter 1875), Gunnar Skjetre (Peter 1884), Katja Pedersen (Inger 1868), Anne-Marie Daehli (Inger 1875), Berit Rytter Hasle (Inger 1884)

KASEKI (New Yorker) Producer, Masayki Sato; Director, Masaki Kobayashi; Screenplay, Shun Inagaki; Photography, Kouzo Okazaki; Music, Touru Takemitsu; In color; 213 minutes. September release. CAST: Shin Saburi, Keiko Kishi, Hasashi Igawa, Kei Yamamoto, Orie Sato, Komaki Jurihara, Mayimi Ogawa, Shigeru Kouyama, Haruko Sugimura, Ichiro Nakatani, Jukichi Uno, Goh Kato

THE BELSTONE FOX (Cine III) Producer, Sally Shuter; Written and Directed by James Hill; Based on "The Ballad of the Belstone Fox" by David Rook; Photography, John Wilcox; Art Director, Hazel Peizer; Music, Laurie Johnson; Editor, Peter Tanner; Assistant Director, Dickie Bamber; In color; Rated G; 103 minutes; September release. CAST: Eric Porter (Asher), Rachel Roberts (Cathie), Jeremy Kemp (Kendrick), Bill Travers (Tod), Dennis Waterman (Stephen), Heather Wright (Jenny)

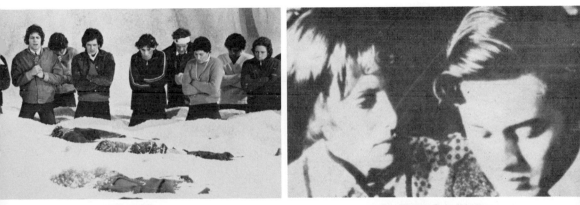

"Survive"

Gro Fraas, Geir Westby
in "Edvard Munch"

Romy Schneider
in "Dirty Hands"

"The Holes"

DIRTY HANDS (New Line) Written and Directed by Claude Chabrol; Photography, Jean Rabier; Editor, Jacques Gaillard; Music, Pierre Jansen; Based on book by Richard Neely; In color; Rated R; 102 minutes; September release. CAST: Rod Steiger (Louis), Romy Schneider (Julie), Paolo Giusti (Jeff), Jean Rochefort (Legal), Francois Maistre (Lamy), Pierre Santini (Villon), Francois Perrot (Thorent), Hans Christian Blech (Judge)

CONVERSATION PIECE (New Line) Producer, Rusconi Films and Gaumont International; Director, Luchino Visconti; Screenplay, Suso Checchi D'Amico, Enrico Medioli, Luchino Visconti; Executive Producer, Giovanni Bertolucci; Photography, Pasqualino de Santis; Editor, Ruggero Mastroianni; Music, Franco Manno; In color; Rated R; 122 minutes; September release. CAST: Burt Lancaster (Professer), Silvana Mangano (Bianca), Helmut Berger (Konrad), Claudia Marsani (Lietta), Stefano Patrizi (Stefano), Elvira Cortese (Erminia), Dominique Sanda (Mother), Claudia Cardinale (Wife)

IT SEEMED LIKE A GOOD IDEA AT THE TIME (Selective Cinema) Producer, David Pellutter; Director, John Trent; Screenplay, David Main, John Trent, from story by Claude Harz; Photography, Harry Makin; Art Director, Claude Bonniere; Editor, Tony Lower; Music, William McCauley; In color; Rated PG; 106 minutes; September release. CAST: Anthony Newley (Sweeney), Stefanie Powers (Georgina), Isaac Hayes (Moriarty), Lloyd Bochner (Burton), Yvonne DeCarlo (Julia), Henry Ramer (Prince), Lawrence Dane (Broom), John Candy (Kopek), Moya Fenwick (Mrs. Chorley)

MAD DOG (Cinema Shares International) Producer, Jeremy Thomas; Directed and Written by Philippe Mora; Based on "Morgan and Bold Bushranger" by Margaret Carnegie; Photography, Mike Molloy; Editor, John Scott; Music, Patrick Flynn; Art Director, Bob Hilditch; Assistant Director, Michael Lake; In Panavision and color; Rated R; 102 minutes; September release. CAST: Dennis Hopper (Morgan), Jack Thompson (Manwaring), David Gulpilil (Billy), Frank Thring (Cobham), Michael Pate (Winch), Wallas Eaton (Macpherson), Bill Hunter (Smith), John Hargreaves (Baylis), Martin Harris (Wendlan), Robin Ramsay (Roget)

THE SPIRIT OF THE BEE-HIVE (Janus) Producer, Elias Querejeta; Director, Victor Erice; Screenplay, Victor Erice, Angel Fernandez Santos; Music, Luis de Pablo; Editor, Tablo G. del Amo; Photography, Luis Cuadrado; In Eastmancolor; 95 minutes; September release. CAST: Fernando Fernan Gomez (Fernando), Teresa Gimpera (Teresa), Ana Torreni (Ana), Isabel Telleria (Isabel), Laly Soldevilla (Lucia), Miguel Picazo (Doctor), Jose Villasante (Frankenstein), Juan Margallo (Outlaw)

KEETJE TIPPEL (Cinema National) Producer, Bob Houwer; Director, Paul Verhoeven; Screenplay, Gerard Goetman; In Dutch with English subtitles; Based on writings of Neel Doff; Photography, Jan de Bont; Music, Roger van Oterloo; Editor, Jane Speer; In color; 104 minutes; September release. CAST: Monique van de Ven (Keetje), Andrea Domburg (Mother), Jan Blaaser (Father), Hannah de Leeuwe (Minna), Eddie Brugman (Andre), Rutger Hauer (Hugo), Peter Faber (George)

THE HOLES (Burbank International) Original title "Les Gaspards" changed to "The Down-in-the-Hole Gang"; A Pierre Tchernia film in color; Rated PG; 90 minutes; September release; No other credits available. CAST: Philippe Noiret, Charles Denner, Michel Serrault, Gerard Depardieu

CRIME BOSS (Cinema Shares International) Producer, Gino Mordini; Director, Alberto De Martino; A Moorehead Properties Film presentation; In color; Rated PG; October release. CAST: Telly Savalas, Lee Van Cleef, Antonio Sabato, Paola Tedesco

DRAGONS NEVER DIE (JMG) Producer, Jimmy L. Pascual; Director, Charlie Chen; In color; Rated R; October release. CAST: Alex Lung, Hong Ying Kit, Hon Kwok Choi

FEMALES FOR HIRE (Independent International) Director, Rolf Olsen; In Metrocolor; Rated R: 90 minutes; October release. CAST: Curt Kurgens, Christine Rucker, Marrianne Hoffman, Fritz Wepper, Monica Zinnenberg, Suzanne Roquet, Heintz Reincke

Burt Lancaster (L), Helmut Berger (R)
in "Conversation Piece"

Curt Jurgens
in "Females for Hire"

JOURNEY INTO FEAR (Stirling Gold) Producer, Trevor Wallace; Director, Daniel Mann; Screenplay, Trevor Wallace; Based on novel by Eric Ambler; Music, Alex North; Lyrics, Hal David; Associate Producer, John Creery; Photography, Harry Waxman; In Technicolor; Rated R; 97 minutes; October release. CAST: Sam Waterston (Graham), Zero Mostel (Kopelkin), Yvette Mimieux (Josette), Scott Marlowe (Jose), Ian McShane (Banat), Joseph Wiseman (Col. Haki), Shelley Winters (Mrs. Mathews), Stanley Holloway (Mathews), Donald Pleasence (Kuvetlin), Vincent Price (Dervos), Alicia Amman (Old Lady)

SUPERBUG, SUPER AGENT (Central Park) Direction and Screenplay, Rudolf Zehetgruber; A Barbara Films Production; In color; Rated G; October release. CAST: Robert Mark, Heidi Hansen, George Goodman, Kathrin Ogen

BEHIND THE SHUTTERS (Cine III) Producer, Xavier Armet; Director, Juan Antonio Bardem; Screenplay, Santiago Moncada; In Eastmancolor; Rated R; 87 minutes; October release. CAST: Jean Seberg, Barry Stokes, Marisol, Perla Cristal, Gerard Tichy

DEVIL WOMAN (JMG) Producer, Jimmy L. Pascual; Executive Producer, Tommy L. Pascual; Directors, Albert Yu, Felix Villars; In color; Rated R; October release. CAST: Rosemarie Gil, Alex Tang Lec, Romy Diax, Robert Chen

EXECUTION SQUAD (Fanfare) Producer, Roberto Infascelli; Director, Stefano Vanzina; Screenplay, Lucio DeCaro, Steno; Photography, Riccardo Pallottini; Music, Stelvio Cipriani; In Techniscope and Metrocolor; Rated R; 100 minutes; October release. CAST: Enrico Maria Salerno (Bertone), Mariangela Melato (Reporter), Franco Fabrizi (Criminal), Mario Adorf (D. A.), Cyril Cusack (Stolfi)

HOW FUNNY CAN SEX BE? (In-Frame) Director, Dino Risi; Screenplay, Dino Risi, Ruggero Maccari; Photography, Alfio Contini; Music, Armando Trovaioli; In Technicolor; Rated R; 97 minutes; October release. CAST: Giancarlo Giannini, Laura Antonelli, Alberto Lionelli, Duilio Del Prete, Paola Barbone, Carla Mancini

THE GIRL FROM STARSHIP VENUS (Intercontinental) Producer, Morton Lewis; Direction and Screenplay, Derek Ford; In Eastmancolor; 90 minutes; Rated R; October release. CAST: Monika Ringwald, Andrew Grant, Mark Jones, Tanya Ferova

HARD WOMAN (Independent International) Director, Alfred Vohrer; In Eastmancolor; Rated R; 81 minutes; October release. CAST: Horst Tappert, Werner Peters, Erika Pluhar, Judy Winter

BLACK EMANUELLE (Stirling Gold) Producer, Mario Mariani; Director, Albert Thomas; Screenplay, Bitto Albertini; Music, Nico Fidenco; Photography, Carlo Carlini; In Eastmancolor; Rated X; 95 minutes; October release. CAST: Emanuelle (Emanuelle), Karin Schubert (Ann), Angelo Infanti (Gianni), Isabelle Marchall (Gloria), Don Powell (Kamau), Venantino Venantini (Richard), Gabriele Tinti

THE SONG REMAINS THE SAME (Warner Bros.) Producer, Swan Song Inc.; Directors, Peter Clifton, Joe Massot; Executive Producer, Peter Grant; In color; Rated PG; 136 minutes; October release. CAST: Led Zepplin: Jimmy Page, Robert Plant, John Paul Jones, John Bonham

JUSTINE DE SADE (Cinema International) Director, Claude Pierson; Screenplay, Huguette Boisvert from book by Marquis de Sade; Photography, Jean-Jacques Tarbes; Music, Francoise and Roger Cotte; In Eastmancolor; Rated X; 110 minutes; October release. CAST: Alice Arno (Justine), Yves Arcanel (Count), Diana Leperier (Wife), Dominique Santarelli (Sister), Mauro Parenti (Man)

SOLARIS (Magna) Written and Directed by Andrei Tarkovsky; From book by Stanislas Lemm; Photography, Vadim Youssov; In color; 165 minutes; October release. CAST: Nathalie Bondarchouk (Harey), Youri Yarvet (Snaut), Donatas Banionys (Kris), Anatoli Sonlinitsin (Sartorius), Vladislav Dvorjetzki (Burton), Nikolai Grinko (Father), Sos Sarkissian (Gibarian)

PEOPLE OF THE WIND (Carolyn) Producers, Anthony Howarth, David Koff; Director, Anthony Howarth; Screenplay, David Koff; Executive Producer, Elizabeth E. Rogers; Photography, Mike Dodds; Music, G. T. Moore and Susha; Editor, Carolyn Hicks; In color; 127 minutes; October release. A documentary on the spring migration of the Babadi Tribe of Persia.

KUNG FU MASTER: BRUCE LEE STYLE (Goldstone) Producer, Philip Kang; Director, Chang Hung; In color; Rated R; November release. CAST: David Chen, Robert Chang, Yu Tang, Chen S. Ming, Peter Fang

Robert Plant, Jimmy Page
in "The Song Remains the Same"

ELIZA'S HOROSCOPE (O-Zali) Produced, Directed, Edited and Written by Gordon Sheppard; Photography, Jean Boffety, Paul Van Der Linden, Michel Brault; In color; 120 minutes; November release. CAST: Elizabeth Moorman (Eliza), Tom Lee Jones (Tommy), Lila Kedrova (Lila), Rose Quong (Astrologer), Richard Manuel (Composer)

BIM (Sharc) Producers, Hugh A. Robertson, Suzanne C. Robertson; Director, Hugh A. Robertson; Screenplay, Raoul Pantin; Photography, Bruce G. Sparks; Editor, Paul L. Evans; Music, Andre Tanker; Theme Song, Andrew Beddoe; Assistant Director, Wilbert Holder; In color; 100 minutes; November release. CAST: Ralph Maharaj, Hamilton Parris, Wilbert Holder, Joseph Gilbert, Lawrence Goldstraw, Anna Seerattan

MAITRESSE (Tinc) Director, Barbet Schroeder, Screenplay, Barbet Schroeder, Paul Voujargol; Photography, Nestor Almendros; Editor, Denise De Casablanca; Music, Carlos D'Carlos D'Alessio; In Eastmancolor; Rated X; 112 minutes; November release. CAST: Gerard Depardieu (Olivier), Bulle Ogier (Arian), Andre Rouyer (Mario), Nathalie Keryan (Lucienne), Tony Taffin (Emilie), Holger Lowenadler (Gautier)

STORY OF A SIN (Tinc) Written and Directed by Walerian Borowczyk; Photography, Zygmunt Samosiuk; Editor, Lidia Pacewiez; In Eastmancolor; Rated R; 130 minutes; November release. CAST: Graznya Dlugolecka (Ewa), Jerzy Zelnik (Lukasz), Olgierd Lukaszewicz (Count), Marek Walczewski (Heavy), Roman Wilhelmi

IT IS RAINING ON SANTIAGO (Films Marquise) Written and Directed by Helvio Soto; Photography, Georges Barsky; Editor, Cecile Ducugis; In Eastmancolor; 110 minutes; November release. CAST: Bibi Andersson (Monique), John Abbey (CIA Man), Ricardo Cucciola (Olivares), Andre Dussolier (Hugo), Annie Girardot (Maria), Henri Poirier (Pinochet), Laurent Terzieff (Calve), Jean-Louis Trintignant (Senator)

"Solaris"

**Jack Palance, Joan Collins
in "The Great Adventure"**

THE GREAT ADVENTURE (Pacific International) Producers, Elliot Geisinger, Joseph Allegro; Director, Paul Elliotts; Title song sung by Joseph Allegro; Color by CFI; Rated G; November release. CAST: Jack Palance, Joan Collins, Fred Romer

THE HAPPY HOUSEWIVES (Cannon) Producer, Kenneth F. Rowles; Director, John Sealy; Screenplay, Derrick Slater; In color; November release. CAST: Barry Stokes, Gay Soper, Sue Lloyd, Bob Todd

COME WITH ME MY LOVE Director, Luigi Manicottale; Story, Bran Toulose; In color; Rated X; November release. CAST: Ursula Austin, Jeffrey Hurst, Michael Gaunt, Vanessa Del Rio, Mike Jeffries, Annie Sprinkle, Ed Marshall, John Livermore

FELICIA (Mature Pictures) Produced, Directed and Written by Max Pecas; Music, Derry Hall; Photography, Roger Fellous; In Eastmancolor; Rated X; November release. CAST: Mary Mendem, Beatrice Harnois, Jean Roche, Ray Prevet, Roland Charbaux

MIDNIGHT PLEASURES (Film Ventures) Presented by Edward L. Montoro; Written and Directed by Marc Fondato; Music, Maurice Angels; In Movielab Color; Rated PG; 90 minutes; November release. CAST: Claudia Cardinale, Vittorio Gassman, Monica Vitti

JONAH WHO WILL BE 25 IN THE YEAR 2000 (New Yorker) Producers, Yves Gasser, Yves Peyrot; Director, Alain Tanner; Screenplay, John Berger, Alain Tanner; Photography, Renato Berta; Editor, Brigitte Sousselier; Music, Jean-Marie Senia; In color; French with English subtitles; 110 minutes; November release. CAST: Jean-Luc Bideau (Max), Myriam Meziere (Madeleine), Miou-Miou (Marie), Jacques Denis (Marco), Rufus (Mathieu), Dominique Labourier (Marguerite), Roger Jendly (Marcel), Myriam Boyer (Mathilde), Raymond Bussieres (Old Charles), and Jonah

THE PROPHET (Joseph Green) Director, Dino Risi; In Technicolor; Rated PG; 90 minutes; November release. CAST: Ann-Margret, Vittorio Gassman

DREAM CITY (Peppercorn-Wormser) Producer, Heinz Angermeyer; Direction and Screenplay, Johannes Schaaf; Based on novel "The Other Side" by Alfred Kubin; Music, Eberhard Schoener; Photography, Gerard Vandernberg; Executive Producer, Raymond P. Homer; A Durham Production in color; Rated R; 96 minutes; December release. CAST: Per Oscarsson (Florian), Rosemarie Fendel (Anna), Olimpia (Madchen), Eva Marie Meineke (Frau Lampenbogen), Alexander May (Lampenbogen)

KINKY LADIES OF BOURBON STREET (Mature) Director, Frederic Lansac; Presented by Robert Sumner; In color; Rated X; December release. CAST: Dawn Cummings, Helga Trixi, Penelope Lamour, Veronique Monod

THE PINK TELEPHONE (S. J. International) Producer, Alain Poire; Director, Edouard Molinaro; Screenplay, Francis Veber; Music, Vladimir Cosma; Rated R; In color; 95 minutes; December release. CAST: Pierre Mondy, Francoise Prevost, Mireille Darc, Michel Lonsdale, Daniel Ceccaldi

THE SENSUOUS HOUSEWIFE (Cineworld) Producer, Fred Zenker; Director, E. Schroeder; In color; December release. CAST: Angelica Johnson, Eva Garden. Peter Capell

LOVE COMES QUIETLY (Libert Films International) Producers, Henk Bos, Andre Thomas; Direction and Screenplay, Nikolai van der Heyde; Music, Georges Delerue; Photography, Jorgen Persson; Editor, Gust Verschueren; In Eastmancolor; Rated R; 103 minutes; December release. CAST: Sandy van der Linden (Harm), Barbara Hershey (Angela), Ralph Meeker (Ben), Ward de Ravet (Menno), Kitty Janssen (Louise), Onno Molenkamp (deVries), Fanny Winkeler (Geesje), Hanne Reynders (Reenske), Romain Deconinck (Waard)

THAT GIRL IS A TRAMP (Cineworld) Producer, S. A. Redinter; Director, Jack Guy; In color; A Vocalis presentation; December release. CAST: Bette Nielson, Laura Viala, Isabelle Coppens

BOTTOMS UP (Burbank International) Music, Don Great; In color; Rated X; December release. CAST: Alena Penz, Rinaldo Talamonti, Alexander Grill, Eva Garden

SERAIL (Caribou) Director, Eduardo DeGregorio; Screenplay, Michael Graham, Eduardo De Gregorio; Photography, Ricardo Aronovitch; Editor, Alberto Yaccelini; Music, Michel Portal; In Panavision and Eastmancolor; Rated R; 90 minutes; December release. CAST: Leslie Caron (Celeste), Bulle Ogier (Ariane), Marie-France Pisier (Agathe), Corin Redgrave (Eric)

TO THE DEVIL A DAUGHTER (EMI) Producer, Roy Skeggs; Director, Peter Sykes; Screenplay, Chris Wicking, based on novel by Dennis Wheatley; Photography, David Watkin; Art Director, Don Picton; Editor, John Trumper; Assistant Director, Barry Langley; In Technicolor; Rated R; 92 minutes; December release. CAST: Richard Widmark (John), Christopher Lee (Father Michael), Honor Blackman (Anna), Denholm Elliott (Henry), Michael Goodliffe (George), Nastassja Kinski (Catherine), Eva-Maria Meineke (Eveline), Anthony Valentine (David), Derek Francis (Bishop), Isabella Telezynska (Margaret), Constantin de Goguel (Kolide), Anna Bentinck (Isabel)

**Ann-Margret, Vittorio Gassman
in "The Prophet"**

**Leslie Caron
in "Serail"**

Anouk Aimee

Edward Albert

Bibi Andersson

Dana Andrews

Diane Baker

BIOGRAPHICAL DATA

(Name, real name, place and date of birth, school attended)

ABBOTT, JOHN: London, June 5, 1905.

ABEL, WALTER: St. Paul, Minn., June 6, 1898, AADA.

ADAMS, EDIE: (Elizabeth Edith Enke) Kingston, Pa., Apr. 16, 1929. Juilliard, Columbia.

ADAMS, JULIE: (Betty May) Waterloo, Iowa, Oct. 17, 1928. Little Rock Jr. College.

ADAMS, MAUD: (Maud Wikstrom) Lulea, Sweden.

ADDAMS, DAWN: Felixstowe, Suffolk, Eng., Sept. 21, 1930. RADA.

ADJANI, ISABELLE: Paris, 1955.

ADLER, LUTHER: NYC, May 4, 1903.

ADRIAN, IRIS: (Iris Adrian Hostetter) Los Angeles, May 29, 1913.

AGAR, JOHN: Chicago, Jan. 31, 1921.

AGUTTER, JENNY: London, 1953.

AHERNE, BRIAN: Worcestershire, Eng., May 2, 1902. Malvern College, U. of London.

AHN, PHILIP: Los Angeles, Mar. 29, 1911. U. of Calif.

AIMEE, ANOUK: Paris, Apr. 27, 1934. Bauer-Therond.

AKINS, CLAUDE: Nelson, Ga., May 25, 1936. Northwestern U.

ALBERGHETTI, ANNA MARIA: Pesaro, Italy, May 15, 1936.

ALBERT, EDDIE: (Eddie Albert Heimberger) Rock Island, Ill, Apr. 22, 1908. U. of Minn.

ALBERT, EDWARD: Los Angeles, Feb. 20, 1951. UCLA.

ALBERTSON, JACK: Malden, Ma. 1910.

ALBRIGHT, LOLA: Akron, Ohio, July 20, 1925.

ALDA, ALAN: NYC, Jan. 28, 1936, Fordham.

ALDA, ROBERT: (Alphonso D'Abruzzo) NYC, Feb. 26, 1914. NYU.

ALEJANDRO, MIGUEL: NYC, 1958.

ALEXANDER, JANE: Boston, Mass., Oct. 28, 1939, Sarah Lawrence.

ALLBRITTON, LOUISE: Oklahoma City, July 3, 1920. U. of Okla.

ALLEN, REX: Wilcox, Ar., Dec. 31, 1922.

ALLEN, STEVE: New York City, Dec. 26, 1921.

ALLEN, WOODY: Brooklyn, Dec. 1, 1935.

ALLENTUCK, KATHERINE: NYC, Oct. 16, 1954: Calhoun.

ALLYSON, JUNE: (Ella Geisman) Westchester, N.Y., Oct. 7, 1923.

AMECHE, DON: (Dominic Amichi) Kenosha, Wisc., May 31, 1908.

AMES, ED: Boston, July 9, 1929.

AMES, LEON: (Leon Wycoff) Portland, Ind., Jan. 20, 1903.

AMOS, JOHN: Newark, NJ., Dec. 27, Bronx Com. Col.

ANDERSON, JUDITH: Adelaide, Australia, Feb. 10, 1898.

ANDERSON, MICHAEL, JR.: London, Eng., 1943.

ANDERSSON, BIBI: Stockholm, Nov. 11, 1935, Royal Dramatic Sch.

ANDES, KEITH: Ocean City, N.J., July 12, 1920. Temple U., Oxford.

ANDRESS, URSULA: Switz., Mar. 19, 1936.

ANDREWS, DANA: Collins, Miss., Jan. 1, 1912. Sam Houston Col.

ANDREWS, EDWARD: Griffin, Ga., Oct. 9, 1914. U. VA.

ANDREWS, HARRY: Tonbridge, Kent, Eng., Nov. 10, 1911.

ANDREWS, JULIE: (Julia Elizabeth Wells) Surrey, Eng. Oct. 1, 1935.

ANGEL, HEATHER: Oxford, Eng., Feb. 9, 1909. Wycombe Abbey.

ANN-MARGRET: (Olsson) Valsjobyn, Sweden, Apr. 28, 1941. Northwestern U.

ANSARA, MICHAEL: Lowell, Mass., Apr. 15, 1922. Pasadena Playhouse.

ANTHONY, TONY: Clarksburg, W. Va., Oct 16, 1937. Carnegie Tech.

ARCHER, JOHN: (Ralph Bowman) Osceola, Neb., May 8, 1915. U. of S. Calif.

ARDEN, EVE: (Eunice Quedens) Mill Valley, Calif., Apr. 30, 1912.

ARKIN, ALAN: NYC, Mar. 26, 1934. LACC.

ARNAZ, DESI: Santiago, Cuba, Mar. 2, 1917, Colegio de Dolores.

ARNAZ, DESI, JR.: Los Angeles, Jan. 19, 1953.

ARNESS, JAMES: (Aurness) Minneapolis, Minn., May 26, 1923. Beloit College.

ARTHUR, BEATRICE: NYC, May 13, 1926, New School.

ARTHUR, JEAN: NYC, Oct. 17, 1908.

ARTHUR, ROBERT: (Robert Arthaud) Aberdeen, Wash., June 18. U. of Wash.

ASHLEY, ELIZABETH: Ocala, Fla., Aug. 30, 1939.

ASTAIRE, FRED: (Fred Austerlitz) Omaha, Neb., May 10, 1899.

ASTIN, JOHN: Baltimore, Md., Mar. 30, 1930, UMinn.

ASTOR, MARY: (Lucile V. Langhanke) Quincy, Ill., May 3, 1906. Kenwood-Loring School.

ATHERTON, WILLIAM: New Haven, Conn., July 30, 1947, Carnegie Tech.

ATTENBOROUGH, RICHARD: Cambridge, Eng., Aug. 29, 1923. RADA.

AUBERJONOIS, RENE: NYC, June 1, 1940, Carnegie Tech.

AUGER, CLAUDINE: Paris, Apr. 26, Dramatic Cons.

AULIN, EWA: Stockholm, Sweden, Feb. 14, 1950.

AUMONT, JEAN PIERRE: Paris, Jan. 5, 1913. French Nat'l School of Drama.

AUTRY, GENE: Tioga, Texas, Sept. 29, 1907.

AVALON, FRANKIE: (Francis Thomas Avallone) Philadelphia, Sept. 18, 1940.

AYLMER, FELIX: Corsham, Eng., Feb. 21, 1889. Oxford.

AYRES, LEW: Minneapolis, Minn., Dec. 28, 1908.

AZNAVOUR, CHARLES: (Varenagh Aznourian) Paris, May 22, 1924.

BACALL, LAUREN: (Betty Perske) NYC, Sept. 16, 1924. AADA.

BACKUS, JIM: Cleveland, Ohio, Feb. 25, 1913. AADA.

BADDELEY, HERMIONE: Shropshire, Eng., Nov. 13, 1908. Margaret Morris School.

BAILEY, PEARL: Newport News, Va., March 29, 1918.

BAIN, BARBARA: Chicago, Sept. 13, 1934. U. Ill.

BAKER, CARROLL: Johnstown, Pa., May 28, 1931. St. Petersburg Jr. College.

BAKER, DIANE: Hollywood, Calif., Feb. 25, USC

215

Marie-Christine Barrault   Keith Baxter   Jeannie Berlin   Stephen Boyd   Florinda Bolkan

BALABAN, ROBERT: Chicago, Aug. 16, 1945, Colgate.

BALIN, INA: Brooklyn, Nov. 12, 1937. NYU.

BALL, LUCILLE: Celaron, N.Y., Aug. 6, 1911. Chataqua Musical Inst.

BALSAM, MARTIN: NYC Nov. 4, 1919. Actors Studio.

BANCROFT, ANNE: (Anna Maria Italiano) Bronx, N.Y., Sept. 17, 1931. AADA.

BANNEN, IAN: Airdrie, Scot., June 29, 1928.

BARDOT, BRIGITTE: Paris, Sept. 28, 1934.

BARRAULT, MARIE-CHRISTINE: Paris, 1946.

BARRIE, WENDY: London, Apr. 18, 1913.

BARRON, KEITH: Mexborough, Eng., Aug. 8, 1936. Sheffield Playhouse.

BARRY, DONALD: (Donald Barry de Acosta) Houston, Tex. Texas School of Mines.

BARRY, GENE: (Eugene Klass) NYC, June 14, 1921.

BARRYMORE, JOHN BLYTH: Beverly Hills, Calif., June 4, 1932. St. John's Military Academy.

BARTHOLOMEW, FREDDIE: London, Mar. 28, 1924.

BASEHART, RICHARD: Zanesville, Ohio, Aug. 31, 1914.

BATES, ALAN: Allestree, Derbyshire, Eng., Feb. 17, 1934. RADA.

BAXTER, ANNE: Michigan City, Ind., May 7, 1923, Ervine School of Drama.

BAXTER, KEITH: South Wales, Apr. 29, 1933, RADA.

BEAL, JOHN: (J. Alexander Bliedung) Joplin, Mo., Aug. 13, 1909. Pa. U.

BEATTY, ROBERT: Hamilton, Ont., Can., Oct. 19, 1909. U. of Toronto.

BEATTY, WARREN: Richmond, Virginia, March 30, 1937.

BEERY, NOAH, JR.: NYC, Aug. 10, 1916. Harvard Military Academy.

BELAFONTE, HARRY: NYC, Mar. 1, 1927.

BELASCO, LEON: Odessa, Russia, Oct. 11, 1902.

BEL GEDDES, BARBARA: NYC, Oct. 31, 1922.

BELL, TOM: Liverpool, Eng., 1932.

BELLAMY, RALPH: Chicago, June 17, 1904.

BELMONDO, JEAN PAUL: Paris, Apr. 9, 1933.

BENEDICT, DIRK: Montana, 1945, Whitman Col.

BENJAMIN, RICHARD: NYC, May 22, 1938, Northwestern U.

BENNETT, BRUCE: (Herman Brix) Tacoma, Wash., U. of Wash.

BENNETT, JILL: Penang, Malay, Dec. 24, 1931.

BENNETT, JOAN: Palisades, N.J., Feb. 27, 1910. St. Margaret's School.

BENSON, ROBBY: Dallas, Tex., Jan. 21, 1956.

BERENSON, MARISSA: NYC, Feb. 15, 1948.

BERGEN, CANDICE: Los Angeles, May, 9, 1946. U. Pa.

BERGEN, EDGAR: Chicago, Feb. 16, 1903. Northwestern U.

BERGEN, POLLY: Knoxville, Tenn., July 14, 1930. Compton Jr. College.

BERGER, HELMUT: Salzburg, Aus., 1945.

BERGER, WILLIAM: Austria, Jan. 20, 1928, Columbia.

BERGERAC, JACQUES: Biarritz, France, May 26, 1927. Paris U.

BERGMAN, INGRID: Stockholm, Sweden, Aug. 29, 1915. Royal Dramatic Theatre School.

BERLE, MILTON: (Milton Berlinger) NYC, July 12, 1908. Professional Children's School.

BERLIN, JEANNIE: Los Angeles, Nov. 1, 1949.

BERLINGER, WARREN: Brooklyn, Aug. 31, 1937. Columbia.

BEST, JAMES: Corydon, Ind., July 26, 1926.

BETTGER, LYLE: Philadelphia, Feb. 13, 1915. AADA.

BETZ, CARL: Pittsburgh, Mar. 9. Duquesne, Carnegie Tech.

BEYMER, RICHARD: Avoca, Iowa, Feb. 21, 1939.

BIKEL, THEODORE: Vienna, May 2, 1924. RADA.

BISHOP, JOEY: (Joseph Abraham Gottlieb) Bronx, N.Y., Feb. 3, 1918.

BISHOP, JULIE: (formerly Jacqueline Wells) Denver, Colo., Aug. 30, 1917. Westlake School.

BISSET, JACQUELINE: Waybridge, Eng., Sept. 13, 1944.

BIXBY, BILL: San Francisco, Jan. 22, 1934. U. Cal.

BLACK, KAREN: (Ziegler) Park Ridge, Ill., July 1, 1942. Northwestern.

BLAINE, VIVIAN: (Vivian Stapleton) Newark, N.J., Nov. 21, 1923.

BLAIR, BETSY: (Betsy Boger) NYC, Dec. 11.

BLAIR, JANET: (Martha Jane Lafferty) Blair, Pa., Apr. 23, 1921.

BLAIR, LINDA: Westport, Ct., 1959.

BLAKE, AMANDA: (Beverly Louise Neill) Buffalo, N.Y., Feb. 20.

BLAKE, ROBERT: (Michael Gubitosi) Nutley, N.J., Sept. 18, 1933.

BLAKELY, SUSAN: Frankfurt, Germany 1950. U. Tex.

BLAKLEY, RONEE: Stanley, Id., 1946. Stanford U.

BLONDELL, JOAN: NYC, Aug. 30, 1909.

BLOOM, CLAIRE: London, Feb. 15, 1931. Badminton School.

BLYTHE, ANN: Mt. Kisco, N.Y., Aug. 16, 1928. New Wayburn Dramatic School.

BOGARDE, DIRK: London, Mar. 28, 1921. Glasgow & Univ. College.

BOLGER, RAY: Dorchester, Mass., Jan. 10, 1906.

BOLKAN, FLORINDA: (Florinda Soares Bulcao) Ceara, Brazil, Feb. 15, 1941.

BOND, DEREK: Glasgow, Scot., Jan. 26, 1920. Askes School.

BONDI, BEULAH: Chicago, May 3, 1892.

BOONE, PAT: Jacksonville, Fla., June 1, 1934. Columbia U.

BOONE, RICHARD: Los Angeles. June 18, 1916, Stanford U.

BOOTH, SHIRLEY: (Thelma Ford) NYC, Aug. 30, 1907.

BORGNINE, ERNEST: (Borgnino) Hamden, Conn., Jan. 24, 1918. Randall School.

BOTTOMS, TIMOTHY: Santa Barbara, Ca., Aug. 30, 1951.

BOULTING, INGRID: Transvaal, SF, 1947.

BOWKER, JUDI: Shawford, Eng., Apr. 6, 1954.

BOWMAN, LEE: Cincinnati, Dec. 28, 1914. AADA.

BOYD, STEPHEN: (William Miller) Belfast, Ire., July 4, 1928.

BOYER, CHARLES: Figeac, France, Aug. 28, 1899. Sorbonne.

BOYLE, PETER: Philadelphia, Pa., 1937, LaSalle Col.

BRACKEN, EDDIE: NYC, Feb. 7, 1920. Professional Children's School.

BRADY, SCOTT: (Jerry Tierney) Brooklyn, Sept. 13, 1924. Bliss-Hayden Dramatic School.

BRAND, NEVILLE: Kewanee, Ill., Aug. 13, 1921.

| Beau Bridges | Coral Browne | Carleton Carpenter | Catherine Burns | Jean-Pierre Cassel |

BRANDO, JOCELYN: San Francisco, Nov. 18, 1919. Lake Forest College. AADA.

BRANDO, MARLON: Omaha, Neb., Apr. 3, 1924. New School.

BRASSELLE, KEEFE: Elyria, Ohio, Feb. 7, 1923.

BRAZZI, ROSSANO: Bologna, Italy, 1916. U. of Florence.

BRENT, GEORGE: Dublin, Ire., Mar. 15, 1904. Dublin U.

BRIAN, DAVID: NYC, Aug. 5, 1914. CCNY.

BRIDGES, BEAU: Los Angeles, Dec. 9, 1941. UCLA.

BRIDGES, JEFF: Los Angeles, Dec. 4, 1949.

BRIDGES, LLOYD: San Leandro, Calif., Jan. 15, 1913.

BRITT, MAY: (Maybritt Wilkins) Sweden, March 22, 1936.

BRODIE, STEVE: (Johnny Stevens) Eldorado, Kan., Nov. 25, 1919.

BROLIN, JAMES: Los Angeles, July 18, 1940. UCLA.

BROMFIELD, JOHN: (Farron Bromfield) South Bend, Ind., June 11, 1922. St. Mary's College.

BRONSON, CHARLES: (Buchinsky) Ehrenfield, Pa., Nov. 3, 1920.

BROOKS, GERALDINE: (Geraldine Stroock) NYC, Oct. 29, 1925. AADA.

BROWN, BARRY: San Jose, Cal., Apr. 19, 1951, LACC.

BROWN, JAMES: Desdemona, Tex., Mar. 22, 1920. Baylor U.

BROWN, JIM: St. Simons Island, N.Y., Feb. 17, 1935 Syracuse U.

BROWN, TOM: NYC, Jan. 6, 1913. Professional Children's School.

BROWNE, CORAL: Melbourne, Aust., July 23, 1913.

BRUCE, DAVID: (McBroom) Kankakee, IL., Jan. 6, 1914.

BRUCE, VIRGINIA: Minneapolis, Sept. 29, 1910.

BRYNNER, YUL: Sakhalin Island, Japan, July 11, 1915.

BUCHHOLZ, HORST: Berlin, Ger., Dec. 4, 1933. Ludwig Dramatic School.

BUETEL, JACK: Dallas, Tex., Sept. 5, 1917.

BUJOLD, GENEVIEVE: Montreal, Can., July 1, 1942.

BUONO, VICTOR: San Diego, Ca., 1939. Villanova.

BURKE, PAUL: New Orleans, July 21, 1926. Pasadena Playhouse.

BURNETT, CAROL: San Antonio, Tex., Apr. 26, 1933. UCLA.

BURNS, CATHERINE: NYC, Sept. 25, 1945, AADA.

BURNS, GEORGE: (Nathan Birnbaum) NYC, Jan. 20, 1896.

BURR, RAYMOND: New Westminster, B.C., Can., May 21, 1917. Stanford, U. of Cal., Columbia.

BURSTYN, ELLEN: (Edna Rae Gillooly) Detroit, Mich., Dec. 7, 1932.

BURTON, RICHARD (Richard Jenkins) Pontrhydyfen, S. Wales, Nov. 10, 1925. Oxford.

BUTTONS, RED: (Aaron Chwatt) NYC, Feb. 5, 1919.

BUZZI, RUTH: Wequetequock, R.I., July 24, 1936. Pasadena Playhouse.

BYGRAVES, MAX: London, Oct. 16, 1922. St. Joseph's School.

BYRNES, EDD: NYC, July 30, 1933. Haaren High.

CAAN, JAMES: Bronx, NY, Mar. 26, 1939.

CABOT, SUSAN: Boston, July 6, 1927.

CAESAR, SID: Yonkers, N.Y., Sept. 8, 1922.

CAGNEY, JAMES: NYC, July 1, 1904. Columbia.

CAGNEY, JEANNE: NYC, Mar. 25, 1919. Hunter.

CAINE, MICHAEL: (Maurice Michelwhite) London, Mar. 14, 1933.

CAINE, SHAKIRA: (Baksh) Guyana, Feb. 23, 1947. Indian Trust Col.

CALHOUN, RORY: (Francis Timothy Durgin) Los Angeles, Aug. 8, 1923.

CALLAN, MICHAEL: (Martin Calinieff) Philadelphia, Nov. 22, 1935.

CALVERT, PHYLLIS: London, Feb. 18, 1917. Margaret Morris School.

CALVET, CORRINE: (Corrine Dibos) Paris, Apr. 30. UParis.

CAMERON, ROD: (Rod Cox) Calgary, Alberta, Can., Dec. 7, 1912.

CAMP, COLLEEN: San Francisco, 1953.

CAMPBELL, GLEN: Delight, Ark. Apr. 22, 1935.

CANALE, GIANNA MARIA: Reggio Calabria, Italy, Sept. 12.

CANNON, DYAN: (Samille Diane Friesen) Jan. 4, 1929, Tacoma, Wash.

CANOVA, JUDY: Jacksonville, Fla., Nov. 20, 1916.

CAPERS, VIRGINIA: Sumter, SC, 1925, Juilliard.

CAPUCINE: (Germaine Lefebvre) Toulon, France, Jan. 6, 1935.

CARDINALE, CLAUDIA: Tunis, N. Africa, Apr. 15, 1939; College Paul Cambon.

CAREY, HARRY, JR.: Saugus, Calif., May 16, Black Fox Military Academy.

CAREY, MACDONALD: Sioux City, Iowa, Mar. 15, 1913. U. of Wisc., U. of Iowa.

CAREY, PHILIP: Hackensack, N.J., July 15, 1925. U. of Miami.

CARMICHAEL, HOAGY: Bloomington, Ind., Nov. 22, 1899. Ind. U.

CARMICHAEL, IAN: Hull, Eng., June 18, 1920. Scarborough Col.

CARNE, JUDY: (Joyce Botterill) Northampton, Eng., 1939. Bush-Davis Theatre School.

CARNEY, ART: Mt. Vernon, N.Y., Nov. 4, 1918.

CARON, LESLIE: Paris, July 1, 1931. Nat'l Conservatory, Paris.

CARPENTER, CARLETON: Bennington, Vt., July 10, 1926. Northwestern.

CARR, VIKKI: (Florence Cardona) July 19, 1942. San Fermardo Col.

CARRADINE, DAVID: Hollywood, Dec. 8, 1936. San Francisco State.

CARRADINE, JOHN: NYC, Feb. 5, 1906.

CARRADINE, KEITH: Los Angeles, Aug. 8, 1951.

CARREL, DANY: Tourane, Indochina, Sept. 20, 1936. Marseilles Cons.

CARROLL, DIAHANN: (Johnson) NYC, July 17, 1935. NYU.

CARROLL, MADELEINE: West Bromwich, Eng., Feb. 26, 1906. Birmingham U.

CARROLL, PAT: Shreveport, La., May 5, 1927. Catholic U.

CARSON, JOHN DAVID: 1951, Calif. Valley Col.

CARSON, JOHNNY: Corning, Iowa, Oct. 23, 1925. U. of Neb.

CARSTEN, PETER: (Ransenthaler) Weissenberg, Bavaria, Apr. 30, 1929; Munich Akademie.

CASH, ROSALIND: Atlantic City, NJ, Dec. 31, 1938, CCNY.

CASON, BARBARA: Memphis, Tenn., Nov. 15, 1933, UIowa.

CASS, PEGGY: (Mary Margaret) Boston, May 21, 1925.

CASSAVETES, JOHN: NYC, Dec. 9, 1929. Colgate College, AADA.

CASSEL, JEAN-PIERRE: Paris, Oct. 27, 1932.

Joanna Cassidy

George Chakiris

Jill Clayburgh   Keene Curtis   Joan Collins

CASSIDY, DAVID: NYC, Apr. 12, 1950.

CASSIDY, JOANNA: Camden, NJ, 1944, Syracuse U.

CASTELLANO, RICHARD: Bronx, NY, Sept. 3, 1934.

CAULFIELD, JOAN: Orange, N.J., June 1. Columbia U.

CAVANI, LILIANA: Bologna, Italy, Jan. 12, 1937; UBologna.

CELI, ADOLFO: Sicily, July 27, 1922, Rome Academy.

CHAKIRIS, GEORGE: Norwood, O., Sept. 16, 1933.

CHAMBERLAIN, RICHARD: Beverly Hills, Cal., March 31, 1935. Pomona.

CHAMPION, GOWER: Geneva, Ill., June 22, 1921.

CHAMPION, MARGE: Los Angeles, Sept. 2, 1926.

CHANNING, CAROL: Seattle, Jan. 31, 1921. Bennington.

CHANNING, STOCKARD: (Susan Stockard) NYC, 1944. Radcliffe

CHAPLIN, CHARLES: London, Apr. 16, 1889.

CHAPLIN, GERALDINE: Santa Monica, Cal. July 31, 1944. Royal Ballet.

CHAPLIN, SYDNEY: Los Angeles, Mar. 31, 1926. Lawrenceville.

CHARISSE, CYD: (Tula Ellice Finklea) Amarillo, Tex., Mar. 3, 1923. Hollywood Professional School.

CHASE, ILKA: NYC, Apr. 8, 1905.

CHER: (Cheryl La Piere) May 20, 1946.

CHIARI, WALTER: Verona, Italy, 1930.

CHRISTIAN, LINDA: (Blanca Rosa Welter) Tampico, Mex., Nov. 13, 1923.

CHRISTIAN, ROBERT: Los Angeles, Dec. 27, 1939. UCLA.

CHRISTIE, JULIE: Chukua, Assam, India, Apr. 14, 1941.

CHRISTOPHER, JORDAN: Youngstown, O., Oct. 23, 1940. Kent State.

CHURCHILL, SARAH: London, Oct. 7, 1916.

CILENTO, DIANE: Queensland, Australia, Oct. 5, 1933. AADA.

CLAPTON, ERIC: London, Mar. 30, 1945.

CLARK, DANE: NYC, Feb. 18, 1915. Cornell, Johns Hopkins U.

CLARK, DICK: Mt. Vernon, N.Y., Nov. 30, 1929. Syracuse U.

CLARK, MAE: Philadelphia, Aug. 16, 1910.

CLARK, PETULA: Epsom England, Nov. 15, 1932.

CLARK, SUSAN: Sarnid, Ont., Can., Mar. 8. RADA

CLAYBURGH, JILL: NYC, Apr. 30, 1944; Sarah Lawrence.

CLEMENTS, STANLEY: Long Island, N.Y., July 16, 1926.

CLERY, CORINNE: Italy, 1950.

CLOONEY, ROSEMARY: Maysville Ky., May 23, 1928.

COBURN, JAMES: Laurel, Neb., Aug. 31, 1928. LACC.

COCA, IMOGENE: Philadelphiá, Nov. 18, 1908.

COCO, JAMES: NYC, Mar. 21, 1929.

CODY, KATHLEEN: Bronx, NY, Oct. 30, 1953.

COLBERT, CLAUDETTE: (Lily Chauchoin) Paris, Sept. 13, 1907. Art Students League.

COLE, GEORGE: London, Apr. 22, 1925.

COLLINS, JOAN: London, May 23, 1933. Francis Holland School.

COMER, ANJANETTE: Dawson, Tex., Aug. 7, 1942. Baylor, Tex. U.

CONANT, OLIVER: NYC, Nov. 15, 1955; Dalton.

CONNERY, SEAN: Edinburgh, Scot. Aug. 25, 1930.

CONNORS, CHUCK: (Kevin Joseph Connors) Brooklyn, Apr. 10, 1924. Seton Hall College.

CONNORS, MIKE: (Krekor Ohanian) Fresno, Ca., Aug. 15, UCLA.

CONRAD, WILLIAM: Louisville, Ky., Sept. 27, 1920.

CONVERSE, FRANK: St. Louis, Mo., May 22, 1938. Carnegie Tech.

CONWAY, TIM: (Thomas Daniel) Willoughby, Oh., Dec. 15, 1933. Bowling Green State.

COOGAN, JACKIE: Los Angeles, Oct. 25, 1914. Villanova College.

COOK, ELISHA, JR.: San Francisco, Dec. 26, 1907. St. Albans.

COOPER, BEN: Hartford, Conn., Sept. 30. Columbia U.

COOPER, JACKIE: Los Angeles, Sept. 15, 1921.

COOTE, ROBERT: London, Feb. 4, 1909. Hurstpierpont College.

CORBY, ELLEN: (Hansen) Racine, Wisc., June 13, 1914.

CORCORAN, DONNA: Quincy, Mass., Sept. 29.

CORD, ALEX: (Viespi) Floral Park, N.Y., Aug. 3, 1931. NYU, Actors Studio.

CORDAY, MARA: (Marilyn Watts) Santa Monica, Calif., Jan. 3, 1932.

COREY, JEFF: NYC, Aug. 10, 1914. Fagin School.

CORRI, ADRIENNE: Glasgow, Scot., Nov. 13, 1933. RADA.

CORTESA, VALENTINA: Milan, Italy, Jan. 1, 1925.

COSBY, BILL: Philadelphia, July 12, 1937. Temple U.

COTTEN, JOSEPH: Petersburg, Va., May 13, 1905.

COURTENAY, TOM: Hull, Eng., Feb. 25, 1937. RADA.

CORLAN, ANTHONY: Cork City, Ire., May 9, 1947; Birmingham School of Dramatic Arts.

COURTLAND, JEROME: Knoxville, Tenn., Dec. 27, 1926.

CRABBE, BUSTER (LARRY): (Clarence Linden) Oakland, Calif., U. of S. Cal.

CRAIG, JAMES: (James H. Meador) Nashville, Tenn., Feb. 4, 1912. Rice Inst.

CRAIG, MICHAEL: India in 1929.

CRAIN, JEANNE: Barstow, Cal., May 25, 1925.

CRANE, BOB: Waterbury, Conn., July 13.

CRAWFORD, BRODERICK: Philadelphia, Dec. 9, 1911.

CRAWFORD, JOAN: (Billie Cassin) San Antonio, Tex., Mar. 23, 1908.

CRENNA, RICHARD: Los Angeles, Nov. 30, 1927. USC.

CRISTAL, LINDA: (Victoria Moya) Buenos Aires, 1935.

CROSBY, BING: (Harry Lillith Crosby) Tacoma, Wash., May 2, 1904. Gonzaga College.

CROWLEY, PAT: Olyphant, Pa., Sept. 17, 1933.

CULLUM, JOHN: Knoxville, Tenn., Mar. 2, 1930. UTenn.

CULP, ROBERT: Oakland, Calif., Aug. 16, 1930. U. Wash.

CULVER, CALVIN: Canandaigua, NY, 1943.

CUMMINGS, CONSTANCE: Seattle, Wash., May 15, 1910.

CUMMINGS, ROBERT: Joplin, Mo., June 9, 1910. Carnegie Tech.

CUMMINS, PEGGY: Prestatyn, N. Wales, Dec. 18, 1926. Alexandra School.

CURTIS, KEENE: Salt Lake City, U., Feb. 15, 1925, U. Utah.

CURTIS, TONY: (Bernard Schwartz) NYC, June 3, 1925.

CUSACK, CYRIL: Durban, S.F., Nov. 26, 1910. Univ. Col.

CUSHING, PETER: Kenley, Surrey, Eng., May 26, 1913.

DAHL, ARLENE: Minneapolis, Aug. 11, 1925. U. Minn.

Joe Dallesandro

Catherine Deneuve

Michael Douglas

Angie Dickinson

Robert Drivas

DALLESANDRO, JOE: Pensacola, Fla., Dec. 31, 1948.

DALTON, TIMOTHY: Wales, 1945; RADA.

DALTREY, ROGER: London, Mar. 1, 1945.

DALY, JAMES: Wisconsin Rapids, Wis., Oct. 23, 1918. U Wis.

DAMONE, VIC: (Vito Farinola) Brooklyn, June 12, 1928.

DANIELS, WILLIAM: Bklyn, Mar. 31, 1927. Northwestern.

DANNER, BLYTHE: Philadelphia, Pa., Bard Col.

DANO, ROYAL: NYC, Nov. 16, 1922, NYU.

DANTE, MICHAEL: (Ralph Vitti) Stamford, Conn., 1935. U Miami.

DANTINE, HELMUT: Vienna, Oct. 7, 1918. U. Calif.

DANTON, RAY: NYC, Sept. 19, 1931. Carnegie Tech.

DARBY, KIM: (Deborah Zerby) North Hollywood, Cal., July 8, 1948.

DARCEL, DENISE: (Denise Billecard) Paris, Sept. 8, 1925. U. Dijon.

DARREN, JAMES: Philadelphia, June 8, 1936. Stella Adler School.

DARRIEUX, DANIELLE: Bordeaux, France, May 1, 1917. Lycee LaTour.

DA SILVA, HOWARD: Cleveland, Ohio, May 4, 1909. Carnegie Tech.

DAUPHIN, CLAUDE: Crobeil, France, Aug. 19, 1903. Beaux Arts.

DAVIDSON, JOHN: Pittsburgh, Dec. 13, 1941. Denison U.

DAVIES, RUPERT: Liverpool, Eng., 1916.

DAVIS, BETTE: Lowell, Mass., Apr. 5, 1908. John Murray Anderson Dramatic School.

DAVIS, OSSIE: Cogdell, Ga., Dec. 18, 1917. Howard U.

DAVIS, SAMMY, JR.: NYC, Dec. 8, 1925.

DAY, DENNIS: (Eugene Dennis McNulty) NYC, May 21, 1917. Manhattan College.

DAY, DORIS: (Doris Kappelhoff) Cincinnati, Apr. 3, 1924.

DAY, LARAINE: (Johnson) Roosevelt, Utah, Oct. 13, 1920.

DAYAN, ASSEF: Israel, 1945: U. Jerusalem.

DEAN, JIMMY: Plainview, Tex., Aug. 10, 1928.

DE CARLO, YVONNE: (Peggy Yvonne Middleton) Vancouver, B.C., Can., Sept. 1, 1924. Vancouver School of Drama.

DEE, FRANCES: Los Angeles, Nov. 26, 1907. Chicago U.

DEE, JOEY: (Joseph Di Nicola) Passaic, N.J., June 11, 1940. Patterson State College.

DEE, RUBY: Cleveland, O., Oct. 27, Hunter Col.

DEE, SANDRA: (Alexandra Zuck) Bayonne, N.J., Apr. 23, 1942.

DE FORE, DON: Cedar Rapids, Iowa, Aug. 25, 1917. U. Iowa.

DE HAVEN, GLORIA: Los Angeles, July 23, 1925.

DE HAVILLAND, OLIVIA: Tokyo, Japan, July 1, 1916. Notre Dame Convent School.

DELL, GABRIEL: Barbados, BWI, Oct. 7, 1930.

DELON, ALAIN: Sceaux, Fr., Nov. 8, 1935.

DE LUISE, DOM: Brooklyn, Aug. 1, 1933. Tufts Col.

DEL RIO, DOLORES: (Dolores Ansunsolo) Durango, Mex., Aug. 3, 1905. St. Joseph's Convent.

DEMAREST, WILLIAM: St. Paul, Mi., Feb. 27, 1892.

DE NIRO, ROBERT: NYC, Aug. 17, 1943, Stella Adler.

DENISON, MICHAEL: Doncaster, York, Eng., Nov. 1, 1915. Oxford.

DENEUVE, CATHERINE: Paris, Oct. 22, 1943.

DENNER, CHARLES: Tarnow, Poland, May 29, 1926.

DENNIS, SANDY: Hastings, Neb., Apr. 27, 1937. Actors Studio.

DEREK, JOHN: Hollywood, Aug. 12, 1926.

DERN, BRUCE: Chicago, June 4, 1936, UPa.

DEVINE, ANDY: Flagstaff, Ariz., Oct. 7, 1905. Ariz. State College.

DEWHURST, COLLEEN: Montreal, June 3, 1926, Lawrence U.

DEXTER, ANTHONY: (Walter Reinhold Alfred Fleischmann) Talmadge, Neb., Jan. 19, 1919. U. Iowa.

DHIEGH, KHIGH: New Jersey 1910.

DICKINSON, ANGIE: Kulm, N. Dak., Sept. 30, 1932. Glendale College.

DIETRICH, MARLENE: (Maria Magdalene von Losch) Berlin, Ger., Dec. 27, 1904. Berlin Music Academy.

DILLER, PHYLLIS: Lima, O., July 17, 1917. Bluffton College.

DILLMAN, BRADFORD: San Francisco, Apr. 14, 1930. Yale.

DOBSON, TAMARA: Baltimore, Md., 1947, Md. Inst. of Art.

DOMERGUE, FAITH: New Orleans, June 16, 1925.

DONAHUE, TROY: (Merle Johnson) NYC, Jan. 27, 1937. Columbia U.

DONNELL, JEFF: (Jean Donnell) South Windham, Me., July 10, 1921. Yale Drama School.

DONNELLY, RUTH: Trenton, N.J., May 17, 1896.

DORS, DIANA: (Fluck) Swindon, Wilshire, Eng., Oct. 23, 1931. London Academy of Music.

D'ORSAY, FIFI: Montreal, Can., Apr. 16, 1904.

DOUGLAS, KIRK: (Issur Danielovitch) Amsterdam, N.Y., Dec. 9, 1916. St. Lawrence U.

DOUGLAS, MELVYN: (Melvyn Hesselberg) Macon, Ga., Apr. 5, 1901.

DOUGLAS, MICHAEL: Hollywood, Sept. 25, 1944, U. Cal.

DOURIF, BRAD: Huntington, W.Va., Mar. 18, 1950. Marshall U.

DOWN, LESLEY ANN: London, Mar. 17, 1954.

DRAKE, BETSY: Paris, Sept. 11, 1923.

DRAKE, CHARLES: (Charles Rupert) NYC, Oct. 2, 1914. Nichols College.

DREW, ELLEN: (formerly Terry Ray) Kansas City, Mo., Nov. 23, 1915.

DREYFUSS, RICHARD: Brooklyn, NY, 1948.

DRIVAS, ROBERT: Chicago, Oct. 7, 1938. U. Chi.

DRU, JOANNE: (Joanne LaCock) Logan, W. Va., Jan. 31, 1923. John Robert Powers School.

DUBBINS, DON: Brooklyn, N.Y., June 28.

DUFF, HOWARD: Bremerton, Wash., Nov. 24, 1917.

DUKE, PATTY: NYC, Dec. 14, 1946.

DULLEA, KEIR: Cleveland, N.J., May 30, 1936. Neighborhood Playhouse, SF State Col.

DUNAWAY, FAYE: Bascom, Fla., Jan, 14, 1941. Fla. U.

DUNCAN, SANDY: Henderson, Tex., Feb. 20, 1946; Len Morris Col.

DUNNE, IRENE: Louisville, Ky., Dec. 20, 1904. Chicago College of Music.

DUNNOCK, MILDRED: Baltimore, Jan. 25, 1906. Johns Hopkins and Columbia U.

DURANTE, JIMMY: NYC, Feb. 10, 1893.

DURBIN, DEANNA: (Edna) Winnipeg, Can., Dec. 4, 1922.

Barbara Eden

Hector Elizondo

Sally Field

Al Freeman, Jr.

Rhonda Fleming

DURNING, CHARLES: Highland Falls, NY, Feb. 28, 1933, NYU.

DUSSOLLIER, ANDRE: Annecy, France, Feb. 17, 1946.

DUVALL, ROBERT: San Diego, Cal., 1930, Principia Col.

DVORAK, ANN: (Ann McKim) NYC, Aug. 2, 1912.

EASTON, ROBERT: Milwaukee, Nov. 23, 1930. U. of Texas.

EASTWOOD, CLINT: San Francisco, May 31, 1930 LACC.

EATON, SHIRLEY: London, 1937. Aida Foster School.

EBSEN, BUDDY: (Christian, Jr.) Belleville, Ill. Apr. 2, 1910. UFla.

ECKEMYR, AGNETA: Karlsborg, Swed., July 2. Actors Studio.

EDEN, BARBARA: (Moorhead) Tucson, Ariz., 1934.

EDWARDS, VINCE: NYC, July 9, 1928. AADA.

EGAN, RICHARD: San Francisco, July 29, 1923. Stanford U.

EGGAR, SAMANTHA: London, Mar. 5, 1939.

EKBERG, ANITA: Malmo, Sweden, Sept. 29, 1931.

EKLAND, BRITT: Stockholm, Swed., 1942.

ELIZONDO, HECTOR: NYC, Dec. 22, 1936.

ELLIOTT, DENHOLM: London, May 31, 1922. Malvern College.

ELSOM, ISOBEL: Cambridge, Eng., Mar. 15, 1894.

ELY, RON: (Ronald Pierce) Hereford, Tex. June 21, 1938.

EMERSON, FAYE: Elizabeth, La., July 8, 1917. San Diego State Col.

ENSERRO, MICHAEL: Soldier, Pa., Oct. 5, 1918. Allegheny Col.

ERDMAN, RICHARD: Enid, Okla., June 1, 1925.

ERICKSON, LEIF: Alameda, Calif., Oct. 27, 1911. U. of Calif.

ERICSON, JOHN: Dusseldorf, Ger., Sept. 25, 1926. AADA.

ESMOND, CARL: Vienna, June 14, 1906. U. of Vienna.

EVANS, DALE: (Francis Smith) Uvalde, Texas, Oct. 31, 1912.

EVANS, GENE: Holbrook, Ariz., July 11, 1922.

EVANS, MAURICE: Dorchester, Eng., June 3, 1901.

EVERETT, CHAD: (Ray Cramton) South Bend, Ind., June 11, 1936.

EWELL, TOM: (Yewell Tompkins) Owensboro, Ky., Apr. 29, 1909. U. of Wisc.

FABARES SHELLEY: Los Angeles, Jan. 19, 1944.

FABIAN: (Fabian Forte) Philadelphia, Feb. 6, 1940.

FABRAY, NANETTE: (Ruby Nanette Fabares) San Diego, Oct. 27, 1920.

FAIRBANKS, DOUGLAS JR.: NYC, Dec. 9, 1909, Collegiate School.

FALK, PETER: NYC, Sept. 16, 1927, New School.

FARENTINO, JAMES: Brooklyn, Feb. 24, 1938. AADA.

FARR, DEREK: London, Feb. 7, 1912.

FARR, FELICIA: Westchester, N.Y., Oct. 4, 1932. Penn State Col.

FARRELL, CHARLES: Onset Bay, Mass., Aug. 9, 1901. Boston U.

FARROW, MIA: Los Angeles, Feb. 9, 1945.

FAULKNER, GRAHAM: London, Sept. 26, 1947, Webber-Douglas.

FAYE, ALICE: (Ann Leppert) NYC, May 5, 1915.

FELDON, BARBARA: (Hall) Pittsburgh, Mar. 12, 1941. Carnegie Tech.

FELLOWS, EDITH: Boston, May 20, 1923.

FERRER, JOSE: Santurce, P.R., Jan. 8, 1909. Princeton U.

FERRER, MEL: Elberon, N.J., Aug. 25, 1917. Princeton U.

FERRIS, BARBARA: London 1943.

FERZETTI, GABRIELE: Italy 1927; Rome Acad. of Drama.

FIELD, SALLY: Pasadena, Cal., Nov. 6, 1946.

FIGUEROA, RUBEN: NYC 1958.

FINNEY, ALBERT: Salford, Lancashire, Eng., May 9, 1936. RADA.

FISHER, EDDIE: Philadelphia, Aug. 10, 1928.

FITZGERALD, GERALDINE: Dublin, Ire., Nov. 24, 1914. Dublin Art School.

FLANNERY, SUSAN: Jersey City, N.J. July 31, 1943.

FLEMING, RHONDA: (Marilyn Louis) Los Angeles, Aug. 10, 1922.

FLEMYNG, ROBERT: Liverpool, Eng., Jan. 3, 1912. Haileybury Col.

FLETCHER, LOUISE: Birmingham, Al., July 1934.

FOCH, NINA: Leyden, Holland, Apr. 20, 1924.

FONDA, HENRY: Grand Island, Neb., May 16, 1905. Minn. U.

FONDA, JANE: NYC, Dec. 21, 1937. Vassar.

FONDA, PETER: NYC, Feb. 23, 1939. U. of Omaha.

FONTAINE, JOAN: Tokyo, Japan, Oct. 22, 1917.

FORAN, DICK: Flemington, N.J., June 18, 1910. Princeton.

FORD, GLENN: (Gwyllyn Samuel Newton Ford) Quebec, Can., May 1, 1916.

FOREST, MARK: (Lou Degni) Brooklyn, Jan. 1933.

FORREST, STEVE: Huntsville, Tex., Sept. 29. UCLA.

FORSTER, ROBERT: (Foster, Jr.) Rochester, N.Y., July 13, 1941. Rochester U.

FORSYTHE, JOHN: Penn's Grove, N.J., Jan. 29, 1918.

FOSTER, JODIE: Bronx, NY, 1963.

FOX, EDWARD: London, 1937, RADA.

FOX, JAMES: London, 1939.

FOXX, REDD: St. Louis, Mo., Dec. 9, 1922.

FRANCIOSA, ANTHONY: NYC, Oct. 25, 1928.

FRANCIS, ANNE: Ossining, N.Y., Sept. 16.

FRANCIS, ARLENE: (Arlene Kazanjian) Boston, Oct. 20, 1908. Finch School.

FRANCIS, CONNIE: (Constance Franconero) Newark, N.J., Dec. 12, 1938.

FRANCISCUS, JAMES: Clayton, Mo., Jan. 31, 1934, Yale.

FRANCKS, DON: Vancouver, Can., Feb. 28, 1932.

FRANKLIN, PAMELA: Tokyo, Feb. 4, 1950.

FRANZ, ARTHUR: Perth Amboy, N.J., Feb. 29, 1920. Blue Ridge College.

FRANZ, EDUARD: Milwaukee, Wisc., Oct. 31, 1902.

FRAZIER, SHEILA: NYC, 1949.

FREEMAN, AL, JR.: San Antonio, Texas, 1934. CCLA.

FREEMAN, MONA: Baltimore, Md., June 9, 1926.

FREY, LEONARD: Brooklyn, Sept. 4, 1938, Neighborhood Playhouse.

FURNEAUX, YVONNE: Lille, France, 1928. Oxford U.

GABEL, MARTIN: Philadelphia, June 19, 1912. AADA.

GABOR, EVA: Budapest, Hungary, Feb. 11, 1925.

GABOR, ZSA ZSA: (Sari Gabor) Budapest, Hungary, Feb. 6, 1923.

GAM, RITA: Pittsburgh, Pa., Apr. 2, 1928.

| Ben Gazzara | Ava Gardner | Chief Dan George | Tammy Grimes | George Grizzard |

GARBER, VICTOR: Montreal, Can., Mar. 16, 1949.

GARBO, GRETA: (Greta Gustafson) Stockholm, Sweden, Sept. 18, 1905.

GARDENIA, VINCENT: Naples, Italy, Jan. 7, 1922.

GARDINER, REGINALD: Wimbledon, Eng., Feb. 27, 1903. RADA.

GARDNER, AVA: Smithfield, N.C., Dec. 24, 1922. Atlantic Christian College.

GARFIELD, ALLEN: Newark, N.J., Nov. 22, 1939. Actors Studio.

GARLAND, BEVERLY: Santa Cruz, Ca., Oct. 17, 1930. Glendale Col.

GARNER, JAMES: (James Baumgarner) Norman, Okla., Apr. 7, 1928. Okla. U.

GARNER, PEGGY ANN: Canton, Ohio, Feb. 3, 1932.

GARR, TERI: Lakewood, Ohio, 1952.

GARRETT, BETTY: St. Joseph, Mo., May 23, 1919. Annie Wright Seminary.

GARRISON, SEAN: NYC, Oct. 19, 1937.

GARSON, GREER: Ireland, Sept. 29, 1908.

GASSMAN, VITTORIO: Genoa, Italy, Sept. 1, 1922. Rome Academy of Dramatic Art.

GAVIN, JOHN: Los Angeles, Apr. 8, 1935. Stanford U.

GAYNOR, JANET: Philadelphia, Oct. 6, 1906.

GAYNOR, MITZI: (Francesca Marlene Von Gerber) Chicago, Sept. 4, 1930.

GAZZARA, BEN: NYC, Aug. 28, 1930. Actors Studio.

GEER, WILL: Frankfort, Ind., Mar. 9, 1902. Columbia.

GEESON, JUDY: Arundel, Eng., Sept. 10, 1948, Corona.

GENN, LEO: London, Aug. 9, 1905. Cambridge.

GEORGE, CHIEF DAN: (Geswanouth Slaholt) North Vancouver, Can., June 24, 1899.

GHOLSON, JULIE: Birmingham, Ala., June 4, 1958.

GIANNINI, GIANCARLO: Spezia, Italy, Aug. 1, 1942; Rome Acad. of Drama.

GIELGUD, JOHN: London, Apr. 14, 1904. RADA.

GILLIS, ANNE: (Alma O'Connor) Little Rock, Ar., Feb. 12, 1927.

GILLMORE, MARGALO: London, May 31, 1897. AADA.

GILMORE, VIRGINIA: (Sherman Poole) Del Monte, Calif., July 26, 1919. U. of Calif.

GINGOLD, HERMIONE: London, Dec. 9, 1897.

GISH, LILLIAN: Springfield, Ohio, Oct. 14, 1896.

GLEASON, JACKIE: Brooklyn, Feb. 26, 1916.

GODDARD, PAULETTE: (Levy) Great Neck, N.Y., June 3, 1911.

GONZALES-GONZALEZ, PEDRO: Aguilares, Tex., Dec. 21, 1926.

GORDON, GALE: (Aldrich) NYC, Feb. 2, 1906.

GORDON, RUTH: (Jones) Wollaston, Mass., Oct. 30, 1896. AADA.

GORING, MARIUS: Newport, Isle of Wright; 1912; Cambridge; Old Vic.

GORMAN, CLIFF: Jamaica, NY, Oct. 13, 1936, NYU.

GORTNER, MARJOE: Long Beach, Ca., 1944.

GOSSETT, LOUIS: Brooklyn, May 27, 1936; NYU.

GOULD, ELLIOTT: (Goldstein); Bklyn, Aug. 29, 1938. Columbia U.

GOULET, ROBERT: Lawrence, Mass., Nov. 26, 1933. Edmonton.

GRAHAME, GLORIA: (Gloria Grahame Hallward) Los Angeles, Nov. 28, 1925.

GRANGER, FARLEY: San Jose, Calif., July 1, 1925.

GRANGER, STEWART: (James Stewart) London, May 6, 1913. Webber-Douglas School of Acting.

GRANT, CARY: (Archibald Alexander Leach) Bristol, Eng., Jan. 18, 1904.

GRANT, KATHRYN: (Olive Grandstaff) Houston, Tex., Nov. 25, 1933. UCLA.

GRANT, LEE: NYC, Oct. 31, 1929, Juilliard.

GRANVILLE, BONITA: NYC, Feb. 2, 1923.

GRAVES, PETER: (Aurness) Minneapolis, Mar. 18, 1926. U. of Minn.

GRAY, COLEEN: (Doris Jensen) Staplehurst, Neb., Oct. 23, 1922. Hamline U.

GRAYSON, KATHRYN: (Zelma Hedrick) Winston-Salem, N.C., Feb. 9, 1923.

GREENE, LORNE: Ottawa, Can., Feb. 12, 1915. Queens U.

GREENE, RICHARD: Plymouth, Eng., Aug. 25, 1918. Cardinal Vaughn School.

GREENWOOD, JOAN: London, 1919. RADA.

GREER, JANE: Washington, D.C., Sept. 9, 1924.

GREER, MICHAEL: Galesburg, Ill., Apr. 20, 1943.

GREY, JOEL: (Katz) Cleveland, O., Apr. 11, 1932.

GREY, VIRGINIA: Los Angeles, Mar. 22, 1923.

GRIEM, HELMUT: Hamburg, Ger. UHamburg.

GRIFFITH, ANDY: Mt. Airy, N.C., June 1, 1926. U.N.C.

GRIFFITH, HUGH: Marian Glas, Anglesey, N. Wales, May 30, 1912.

GRIFFITH, MELANIE: NYC, Aug. 9, 1957. Pierce Col.

GRIMES, GARY: San Francisco, June 2, 1955.

GRIMES, TAMMY: Lynn, Mass., Jan. 30, 1934, Stephens Col.

GRIZZARD, GEORGE: Roanoke Rapids, N.C., Apr. 1, 1928. U.N.C.

GRODIN, CHARLES: Pittsburgh, Pa., Apr. 21, 1935.

GROH, DAVID: NYC, May 21, 1939. Brown U., LAMDA.

GUARDINO, HARRY: Brooklyn, Dec. 23, 1925, Haaren High.

GUINNESS, ALEC: London, Apr. 2, 1914. Pembroke Lodge School.

GUNN, MOSES: St. Louis, Mo., Oct. 2, 1929. TN. State U.

GWILLIM, DAVID: Plymouth, Eng., Dec. 15, 1948, RADA.

HACKETT, BUDDY: (Leonard Hacker) Brooklyn, Aug. 31, 1924.

HACKETT, JOAN: NYC, May 1, 1942. Actors Studio.

HACKMAN, GENE: San Bernardino, Jan. 30, 1931.

HADDON, DALE: Montreal, Can., May 26, 1949, Neighborhood Playhouse.

HAGMAN, LARRY: (Hageman) Texas, 1939. Bard Col.

HALE, BARBARA: DeKalb, Ill., Apr. 18, 1922. Chicago Academy of Fine Arts.

HAMILTON, GEORGE: Memphis, Tenn., Aug. 12, 1939. Hackley.

HAMILTON, MARGARET: Cleveland, Ohio, Dec. 9, 1902. Hathaway-Brown School.

HAMILTON, NEIL: Lynn, Mass., Sept. 9, 1899.

HAMPSHIRE, SUSAN: London, May 12, 1941.

HARDIN, TY: (Orison Whipple Hungerford II) NYC, 1930.

Rosemary Harris **David Hartman** **Wendy Hiller** **Robert Hooks** **Gayle Hunnicutt**

HARDING, ANN: (Dorothy Walton Gatley) Fort Sam Houston, Texas, Aug. 17, 1904.

HAREWOOD, DORIAN: Dayton, OH, Aug. 6.

HARPER, VALERIE: Suffern, NY, Aug. 22.

HARRINGTON, PAT: NYC, Aug. 13, 1929, Fordham U.

HARRIS, BARBARA: (Sandra Markowitz) Evanston, Ill., 1937.

HARRIS, JULIE: Grosse Pointe, Mich., Dec. 2, 1925. Yale Drama School.

HARRIS, RICHARD: Limerick, Ire., Oct. 1, 1930. London Acad.

HARRIS, ROSEMARY: Ashby, Eng., Sept. 19, 1930. RADA

HARRISON, NOEL: London, Jan. 29, 1936.

HARRISON, REX: Huyton, Cheshire, Eng., Mar. 5, 1908.

HARTMAN, DAVID: Pawtucket, RI., May 19. .Duke U.

HARTMAN, ELIZABETH: Youngstown, O., Dec. 23, 1941. Carnegie Tech.

HAVER, JUNE: Rock Island, Ill., June 10, 1926.

HAVOC, JUNE: (June Hovick) Seattle, Wash., Nov. 8, 1916.

HAWN, GOLDIE: Washington, DC, Nov. 21, 1945.

HAYDEN, LINDA: Stanmore, Eng., Aida Foster School.

HAYDEN, STERLING: (John Hamilton) Montclair, N.J., March 26, 1916.

HAYES, HELEN: (Helen Brown) Washington, D.C., Oct. 10, 1900. Sacred Heart Convent.

HAYES, MARGARET: (Maggie) Baltimore, Dec. 5, 1925.

HAYWORTH, RITA: (Margarita Cansino) NYC, Oct. 17, 1918.

HEATHERTON, JOEY: NYC, Sept. 14, 1944.

HECKART, EILEEN: Columbus, Ohio, Mar. 29, 1919. Ohio State U.

HEDISON, DAVID: Providence, R.I., May 20, 1929. Brown U.

HEMMINGS, DAVID: Guilford, Eng.; Nov. 18, 1938.

HENDERSON, MARCIA: Andover, Mass., July 22, 1932. AADA.

HENDRIX, WANDA: Jacksonville, Fla., Nov. 3, 1928.

HENDRY, GLORIA: Jacksonville, Fla., 1949.

HENREID, PAUL: Trieste, Jan. 10, 1908.

HENRY, BUCK: (Zuckerman) NYC, 1931; Dartmouth.

HEPBURN, AUDREY: Brussels, Belgium, May 4, 1929.

HEPBURN, KATHARINE: Hartford, Conn., Nov. 8, 1909. Bryn Mawr.

HESTON, CHARLTON: Evanston, Ill., Oct. 4, 1924. Northwestern U.

HEYWOOD, ANNE: (Violet Pretty) Birmingham, Eng., Dec. 11, 1933.

HICKMAN, DARRYL: Hollywood, Cal., July 28, 1931. Loyola U.

HICKMAN, DWAYNE: Los Angeles, May 18, 1934. Loyola.

HILL, ARTHUR: Saskatchewan, Can., Aug. 1, 1922. U. Brit. Col.

HILL, STEVEN: Seattle, Wash., Feb. 24, 1922. U. Wash.

HILL, TERENCE: (Mario Giotti) Venice, Italy, 1941, URome.

HILLER, WENDY: Bramhall, Cheshire, Eng., Aug. 15, 1912. Winceby House School.

HINGLE, PAT: Denver, Co., July 19, 1923. Tex. U.

HOFFMAN, DUSTIN: Los Angeles, Aug. 8, 1937. Pasadena Playhouse.

HOLBROOK, HAL: (Harold) Cleveland, O., Feb. 17, 1925. Denison.

HOLDEN, WILLIAM: O'Fallon, Ill., Apr. 17, 1918. Pasadena Jr. Coll.

HOLLIMAN, EARL: Tennessee Swamp, Delhi, La., Sept. 11, UCLA.

HOLLOWAY, STANLEY: London, Oct. 1, 1890.

HOLM, CELESTE: NYC, Apr. 29, 1919.

HOMEIER, SKIP: (George Vincent Homeier) Chicago, Oct. 5, 1930. UCLA.

HOMOLKA, OSCAR: Vienna, Aug. 12, 1898. Vienna Dramatic Academy.

HOOKS, ROBERT: Washington, D.C., Apr. 18, 1937. Temple.

HOPE, BOB: London, May 26, 1903.

HOPPER, DENNIS: Dodge City, Kan., May 17, 1936.

HORNE, LENA: Brooklyn, June 30, 1917.

HORTON, ROBERT: Los Angeles, July 29, 1924. UCLA.

HOUGHTON, KATHARINE: Hartford, Conn., Mar. 10, 1945. Sarah Lawrence.

HOUSER, JERRY: Los Angeles, July 14, 1952; Valley Jr. Col.

HOUSEMAN, JOHN: Bucharest, Sept. 22, 1902.

HOUSTON, DONALD: Tonypandy, Wales, 1924.

HOVEY, TIM: Los Angeles, June 19, 1945.

HOWARD, KEN: El Centro, Cal., Mar. 28, 1944, Yale.

HOWARD, RON: Duncan, Okla., Mar. 1, 1954. USC.

HOWARD, RONALD: Norwood, Eng., Apr. 7, 1918. Jesus College.

HOWARD, TREVOR: Kent, Eng., Sept. 29, 1916. RADA

HOWELLS, URSULA: London, Sept. 17, 1922.

HOWES, SALLY ANN: London, July 20, 1934.

HUDSON, ROCK: (Roy Scherer Fitzgerald) Winnetka, Ill., Nov. 17, 1925.

HUGHES, BARNARD: Bedford Hills, NY, July 16, 1915, Manhattan Col.

HUGHES, KATHLEEN: (Betty von Gerkan) Hollywood, Ca., Nov. 14, 1928. UCLA

HUNNICUTT, ARTHUR: Gravelly, Ark., Feb. 17, 1911. Ark. State.

HUNNICUTT, GAYLE: Ft. Worth, Tex., Feb. 6, 1943, UCLA.

HUNT, MARSHA: Chicago, Oct. 17, 1917.

HUNTER, IAN: Cape Town, S.A., June 13, 1900. St. Andrew's Col.

HUNTER, KIM: (Janet Cole) Detroit, Nov. 12, 1922.

HUNTER, TAB: (Arthur Galien) NYC, July 11, 1931.

HUSSEY, RUTH: Providence , R.I., Oct. 30, 1917. U. of Mich.

HUSTON, JOHN: Nevada, Mo., Aug. 5, 1906.

HUTTON, BETTY: (Betty Thornberg) Battle Creek, Mich., Feb. 26, 1921.

HUTTON, LAUREN: (Mary) Charleston, S.C., Nov. 17, 1943. Newcomb Col.

HUTTON, ROBERT: (Winne) Kingston, N.Y., June 11, 1920. Blair Academy.

HYDE-WHITE, WILFRID: Gloucestershire, Eng., May 13, 1903. RADA.

HYER, MARTHA: Fort Worth, Tex., Aug. 10, 1930. Northwestern U.

INGELS, MARTY: Brooklyn, NY, Mar. 9, 1936.

IRELAND, JOHN: Vancouver, B.C., Can., Jan. 30, 1915.

IVES, BURL: Hunt Township, Ill., June 14, 1909. Charleston Ill. Teachers College.

Page Johnson   **Carolyn Jones**   **David Janssen**   **Diane Ladd**   **Aron Kincaid**

JACKSON, ANNE: Alleghany, Pa., Sept. 3, 1926. Neighborhood Playhouse.

JACKSON, GLENDA: Hoylake, Cheshire, Eng., May 9, 1936. RADA.

JACOBI, LOU: Toronto, Can., Dec. 28, 1913.

JACOBY, SCOTT: Chicago, Nov. 19, 1956.

JAECKEL, RICHARD: Long Beach, N.Y., Oct. 10, 1926.

JAFFE, SAM: NYC, Mar. 8, 1896.

JAGGER, DEAN: Lima, Ohio, Nov. 7, 1903. Wabash College.

JAMES, CLIFTON: NYC, May 29, 1921. Ore. U.

JANSSEN, DAVID: (David Meyer) Naponee, Neb., Mar. 27, 1930.

JARMAN, CLAUDE, JR.: Nashville, Tenn., Sept. 27, 1934.

JASON, RICK: NYC, May 21, 1926. AADA.

JEAN, GLORIA: (Gloria Jean Schoonover) Buffalo, N.Y. Apr. 14, 1928.

JEFFREYS, ANNE: (Carmichael) Goldsboro, N.C., Jan. 26, 1923. Anderson College.

JEFFRIES, LIONEL: London, 1927, RADA.

JERGENS, ADELE: Brooklyn, Nov. 26, 1922.

JESSEL, GEORGE: NYC, Apr. 3, 1898.

JOHNS, GLYNIS: Durban, S. Africa, Oct. 5, 1923.

JOHNSON, CELIA: Richmond, Surrey, Eng., Dec. 18, 1908. RADA.

JOHNSON, PAGE: Welch, W. Va., Aug. 25, 1930. Ithaca.

JOHNSON, RAFER: Hillsboro, Tex., Aug. 18, 1935. UCLA.

JOHNSON, RICHARD: Essex, Eng., 1927. RADA.

JOHNSON, VAN: Newport, R.I., Aug. 28, 1916.

JONES, CAROLYN: Amarillo, Tex., Apr. 28, 1933.

JONES, CHRISTOPHER: Jackson, Tenn., Aug. 18, 1941, Actors Studio.

JONES, DEAN: Morgan County, Ala., Jan. 25, 1936. Ashburn College.

JONES, JACK: Bel-Air, Calif., Jan. 14, 1938.

JONES, JAMES EARL: Arkabutla, Miss., Jan 17, 1931. U. Mich.

JONES, JENNIFER: (Phyllis Isley) Tulsa, Okla., Mar. 2, 1919. AADA.

JONES, SHIRLEY: Smithton, Pa., March 31, 1934.

JONES, TOM: (Thomas Jones Woodward) Pontypridd, Wales, June 7, 1940.

JORDAN, RICHARD: NYC, July 19, 1938, Harvard.

JORY, VICTOR: Dawson City, Can., Nov. 28, 1902, CalU.

JOURDAN, LOUIS: Marseilles, France, June 18, 1921.

JURADO, KATY: (Maria Christina Jurado Garcia) Guadalajara, Mex., 1927.

KAHN, MADELINE: Boston, Mass., Sept. 29, 1942, Hofstra U.

KANE, CAROL: Cleveland, O., 1952.

KASZNAR, KURT: Vienna, Aug. 12, 1913. Gymnasium, Vienna.

KAUFMANN, CHRISTINE: Lansdorf, Graz, Austria, Jan. 11, 1945.

KAYE, DANNY: (David Daniel Kominski) Brooklyn, Jan. 18, 1913.

KAYE, STUBBY: NYC, Nov. 11, 1918.

KEACH, STACY: Savannah, Ga., June 2, 1941; UCal., Yale.

KEATON, DIANE: (Hall) Los Angeles, Ca., Jan. 5, 1946. Neighborhood Playhouse.

KEDROVA, LILA: Greece, 1918.

KEEL, HOWARD: (Harold Keel) Gillespie, Ill., Apr. 13, 1919.

KEELER, RUBY: (Ethel) Halifax, N.S. Aug. 25, 1909.

KEITH, BRIAN: Bayonne, N.J., Nov. 14, 1921.

KELLERMAN, SALLY: Long Beach, Cal., June 2, 1938; Actors Studio West.

KELLY, GENE: Pittsburgh, Aug. 23, 1912. U. of Pittsburgh.

KELLY, GRACE: Philadelphia, Nov. 12, 1929. AADA.

KELLY, JACK: Astoria, N.Y., Sept. 16, 1927. UCLA.

KELLY, NANCY: Lowell, Mass., Mar. 25, 1921. Bentley School.

KELLY, PATSY: Brooklyn, Jan. 12, 1910.

KEMP, JEREMY: Chesterfield, Eng., 1935, Central Sch.

KENNEDY, ARTHUR: Worcester, Mass., Feb. 17, 1914. Carnegie Tech.

KENNEDY, GEORGE: NYC, Feb. 18, 1925.

KERR, DEBORAH: Helensburg, Scot., Sept. 30, 1921. Smale Ballet School.

KERR, JOHN: NYC, Nov. 15, 1931. Harvard, Columbia.

KHAMBATTA, PERSIS: Bombay, 1950.

KIDDER, MARGOT: Yellow Knife, Can., Oct. 17, 1948; UBC.

KIER, UDO: Germany, Oct. 14, 1944.

KILEY, RICHARD: Chicago, Mar. 31, 1922. Loyola.

KILIAN, VICTOR: Jersey City, N.J., Mar. 6, 1898.

KINCAID, ARON: (Norman Neale Williams III) Los Angeles, June 15, 1943. UCLA.

KING, ALAN: (Irwin Kniberg) Brooklyn, Dec. 26, 1927.

KITT, EARTHA: North, S.C., Jan. 26, 1928.

KLEMPERER, WERNER: Cologne, Mar. 22, 1920.

KLUGMAN, JACK: Philadelphia, Pa., Apr. 27, 1925. Carnegie Tech.

KNIGHT, ESMOND: East Sheen, Eng., May 4, 1906.

KNIGHT, SHIRLEY: Goessel, Kan., July 5, 1937. Wichita U.

KNOWLES, PATRIC: (Reginald Lawrence Knowles) Horsforth, Eng., Nov. 11, 1911.

KNOX, ALEXANDER: Strathroy, Ont., Can., Jan. 16, 1907.

KNOX, ELYSE: Hartford, Conn., Dec. 14, 1917. Traphagen School.

KOHNER, SUSAN: Los Angeles, Nov. 11, 1936. U. of Calif.

KORMAN, HARVEY: Chicago, IL., Feb. 15, 1927. Goodman.

KORVIN, CHARLES: (Geza Korvin Karpathi) Czechoslovakia, Nov. 21. Sorbonne.

KOSLECK, MARTIN: Barkotzen, Ger., Mar. 24, 1907. Max Reinhardt School.

KOTTO, YAPHET: NYC, Nov. 15, 1937.

KREUGER, KURT: St. Moritz, Switz., July 23, 1917. U. of London.

KRISTOFFERSON, KRIS: 1936, Brownsville, Tx., Pomona Col.

KRUGER, HARDY: Berlin, Ger., April. 12, 1928.

KUNTSMANN, DORIS: Hamburg, 1944.

KWAN, NANCY: Hong Kong, May 19, 1939. Royal Ballet.

LACY, JERRY: Sioux City, I., Mar. 27, 1936, LACC.

LADD, DIANE: (Ladnier) France, Nov. 29, 1932.

LAMARR, HEDY: (Hedwig Kiesler) Vienna, Sept. 11, 1915.

LAMAS, FERNANDO: Buenos Aires, Jan. 9, 1920.

LAMB, GIL: Minneapolis, June 14, 1906. U. of Minn.

Piper Laurie Herbert Lom Michelle Lee Cleavon Little Shirley MacLaine

LAMOUR, DOROTHY: Dec. 10, 1914. Spence School.

LANCASTER, BURT: NYC, Nov. 2, 1913. NYU.

LANCHESTER, ELSA: (Elsa Sullivan) London, Oct. 28, 1902.

LANDAU, MARTIN: Brooklyn, NY, 1931. Actors Studio.

LANDON, MICHAEL: (Eugene Orowitz) Collingswood, N.J., Oct. 31, 1936. USC.

LANE, ABBE: Brooklyn, Dec. 14, 1935.

LANGAN, GLENN: Denver, Colo., July 8, 1917.

LANGE, HOPE: Redding Ridge, Conn., Nov. 28, 1933. Reed Col.

LANGE, JESSICA: Minnesota, 1950. UMinn.

LANGTON, PAUL: Salt Lake City, Apr. 17, 1913. Travers School of Theatre.

LANSBURY, ANGELA: London, Oct. 16, 1925. London Academy of Music.

LANSING, ROBERT: (Brown) San Diego, Cal., June 5.

LAURIE, PIPER: (Rosetta Jacobs) Detroit, Jan. 22, 1932.

LAW, JOHN PHILLIP: Hollywood, Sept. 7, 1937. Neighborhood Playhouse., UHawaii.

LAWFORD, PETER: London, Sept. 7, 1923.

LAWRENCE, BARBARA: Carnegie, Okla., Feb. 24, 1930. UCLA.

LAWRENCE, CAROL: (Laraia) Melrose Park, Ill., Sept. 5, 1935.

LAWSON, LEIGH: Atherston, Eng., July 21, 1945, RADA.

LEACHMAN, CLORIS: Des Moines, Iowa, Apr. 30, 1930. Northwestern U.

LEDERER, FRANCIS: Karlin, Prague, Czech., Nov. 6, 1906.

LEE, CHRISTOPHER: London, May 27, 1922. Wellington College.

LEE, MICHELE: (Dusiak) Los Angeles, June 24, 1942. LACC.

LEIBMAN, RON: NYC, Oct. 11, 1937, Ohio Wesleyan.

LEIGH, JANET: (Jeanette Helen Morrison) Merced, Calif., July 6, 1927. College of Pacific.

LEMBECK, HARVEY: Brooklyn, Apr. 15, 1923. U. of Ala.

LEMMON, JACK: Boston, Feb. 8, 1925. Harvard.

LENZ, RICK: Springfield, Ill., Nov. 21, 1939. U. Mich.

LEONARD, SHELDON: (Bershad) NYC, Feb. 22, 1907, Syracuse U.

LEROY, PHILIPPE: Paris, Oct. 15, 1930; UParis.

LESLIE, BETHEL: NYC, Aug. 3, 1929. Breaney School.

LESLIE, JOAN: (Joan Brodell) Detroit, Jan. 26, 1925. St. Benedict's.

LESTER, MARK: Oxford, Eng., July 11, 1958.

LEVENE, SAM: NYC, Aug. 28, 1905.

LEWIS, JERRY: Newark, N.J., Mar. 16, 1926.

LIGON, TOM: New Orleans, La., Sept. 10, 1945.

LILLIE, BEATRICE: Toronto, Can., May 29, 1898.

LINCOLN, ABBEY: (Anna Marie Woolridge) Chicago, Aug. 6, 1930.

LINDFORS, VIVECA: Uppsala, Sweden, Dec. 29, 1920. Stockholm Royal Dramatic School.

LISI, VIRNA: Rome, 1938.

LITTLE, CLEAVON: Chickasha, Okla., June 1, 1939, San Diego State.

LOCKE, SONDRA: Shelbyville, Tenn., 1947.

LOCKHART, JUNE: NYC, June 25, 1925. Westlake School.

LOCKWOOD, GARY: Van Nuys, Cal., 1937.

LOCKWOOD, MARGARET: Karachi, Pakistan, Sept. 15, 1916. RADA.

LOLLOBRIGIDA, GINA: Subiaco, Italy, 1928. Rome Academy of Fine Arts.

LOM, HERBERT: Prague, Czechoslovakia, 1917. Prague U.

LONDON, JULIE: (Julie Peck) Santa Rosa, Calif., Sept. 26, 1926.

LOPEZ, PERRY: NYC, July 22, 1931. NYU.

LORD, JACK: (John Joseph Ryan) NYC, Dec. 30, 1928. NYU.

LOREN, SOPHIA: (Sofia Scicolone) Rome, Italy, Sept. 20, 1934.

LOUISE, TINA: (Blacker) NYC, Feb. 11, 1934. Miami U.

LOVELACE, LINDA: Bryan, Tex., 1952.

LOY, MYRNA: (Myrna Williams) Helena, Mont., Aug. 2, 1905. Westlake School.

LUND, JOHN: Rochester, N.Y., Feb. 6, 1913.

LUPINO, IDA: London, Feb. 4, 1918. RADA.

LYDON, JAMES: Harrington Park, N.J., May 30, 1923.

LYNDE, PAUL: Mt. Vernon, Ohio, June 13, 1926. Northwestern U.

LYNLEY, CAROL: (Jones) NYC, Feb. 13, 1942.

LYNN, JEFFREY: Auburn, Mass., 1909. Bates College.

LYON, SUE: Davenport, Iowa, July 10, 1946.

LYONS, ROBERT F.: Albany, N.Y.; AADA.

MacARTHUR, JAMES: Los Angeles, Dec. 8, 1937. Harvard.

MacGINNIS, NIALL: Dublin, Ire., Mar. 29, 1913. Dublin U.

MacGRAW, ALI: NYC, Apr. 1, 1938, Wellesley.

MacLAINE, SHIRLEY: (Beatty) Richmond, Va., Apr. 24, 1934.

MacMAHON, ALINE: McKeesport, Pa., May 3, 1899. Barnard College.

MacMURRAY, FRED: Kankakee, Ill., Aug. 30, 1908. Carroll Col.

MACNEE, PATRICK: London, Feb. 1922.

MacRAE, GORDON: East Orange, N.J., Mar. 12, 1921.

MADISON, GUY: (Robert Moseley) Bakersfield, Calif., Jan. 19, 1922. Bakersfield Jr. College.

MAHARIS, GEORGE: Astoria, N.Y., Sept. 1, 1928. Actors Studio.

MAHONEY, JOCK: (Jacques O'-Mahoney) Chicago, Feb. 7, 1919. U. of Iowa.

MALDEN, KARL: (Mladen Sekulovich) Gary, Ind., Mar. 22, 1914.

MALONE, DOROTHY: Chicago, Jan. 30, 1925. S. Methodist U.

MANN, KURT: Roslyn, NY, July 18, 1947.

MARAIS, JEAN: Cherbourg, France, Dec. 11, 1913. St. Germain.

MARGO: (Maria Marguerita Guadalupe Boldoay Castilla) Mexico City, May 10, 1918.

MARGOLIN, JANET: NYC, July 25, 1943. Walden School.

MARIN, JACQUES: Paris, Sept. 9, 1919. Conservatoire National.

MARLOWE, HUGH: (Hugh Hipple) Philadelphia, Jan. 30, 1914.

MARSHALL, BRENDA: (Ardis Anderson Gaines) Isle of Negros, P.I., Sept. 29, 1915. Texas State College.

MARSHALL, E. G.: Owatonna, Minn., June 18, 1910. U. of Minn.

MARSHALL, WILLIAM: Gary, Ind., Aug. 19, 1924, NYU.

MARTIN, DEAN: (Dino Crocetti) Steubenville, Ohio, June 17, 1917.

MARTIN, MARY: Weatherford, Tex., Dec. 1, 1914. Ward-Belmont School.

MARTIN, STROTHER: Kokomo, Ind., 1919, UMich.

MARTIN, TONY: (Alfred Norris) Oakland, Cal., Dec. 25, 1913. St. Mary's College.

James Mason	Yvette Mimieux	Malcolm McDowell	Kay Medford	James Mitchum

MARVIN, LEE: NYC, Feb. 19, 1924.

MARX, GROUCHO: (Julius Marx) NYC, Oct. 2, 1895.

MASON, JAMES: Huddersfield, Yorkshire, Eng., May 15, 1909. Cambridge.

MASON, MARSHA: St. Louis, Mo., Apr. 3, 1942, Webster Col.

MASON, PAMELA: (Pamela Kellino) Westgate, Eng., Mar. 10, 1918.

MASSEN, OSA: Copenhagen, Den., Jan. 13, 1916.

MASSEY, DANIEL: London, Oct. 10, 1933. Eaton and King's Col.

MASSEY, RAYMOND: Toronto, Can., Aug. 30, 1896. Oxford.

MASTERSON, PETER: Angleton, Tex., June 1, 1934; Rice U.

MASTROIANNI, MARCELLO: Fontana Liri, Italy, Sept. 28, 1924.

MATTHAU, WALTER: (Matuschanskayasky) NYC, Oct. 1, 1920.

MATURE, VICTOR: Louisville, Ky., Jan. 29, 1916.

MAY, ELAINE: (Berlin) Philadelphia, Apr. 21, 1932.

MAYEHOFF, EDDIE: Baltimore, July 7, Yale.

McCALLUM, DAVID: Scotland, Sept. 19, 1933. Chapman Coll.

McCAMBRIDGE, MERCEDES: Jolliet, Ill., March 17, 1918, Mundelein College.

McCARTHY, KEVIN: Seattle, Wash., Feb. 15, 1914. Minn. U.

McCLORY, SEAN: Dublin, Ire., March 8, 1924. U. of Galway.

McCLURE, DOUG: Glendale, Calif., May 11, 1938. UCLA.

McCOWEN, ALEC: Tunbridge Wells, Eng., May 26, 1925. RADA.

McCREA, JOEL: Los Angeles, Nov. 5, 1905. Pomona College.

McDERMOTT, HUGH: Edinburgh, Scot., Mar. 20, 1908.

McDOWALL, RODDY: London, Sept. 17, 1928. St. Joseph's.

McDOWELL, MALCOLM: (Taylor) Leeds, Eng., June 15, 1943. LAMDA.

McENERY, PETER: Walsall, Eng., Feb. 21, 1940.

McGAVIN, DARREN: Spokane, Wash., May 7, 1922. College of Pacific.

McGUIRE, BIFF: New Haven, Conn., Oct. 25, 1926, Mass. State Col.

McGUIRE, DOROTHY: Omaha, Neb., June 14, 1919.

McKAY, GARDNER: NYC, June 10, 1932. Cornell.

McKENNA, VIRGINIA: London, June 7, 1931.

McKUEN, ROD: Oakland, Cal., Apr. 29, 1933.

McLERIE, ALLYN ANN: Grand Mere, Can., Dec. 1, 1926.

McNAIR, BARBARA: Chicago, March 4, 1939. UCLA.

McNALLY, STEPHEN: (Horace McNally) NYC, July 29, Fordham U.

McNAMARA, MAGGIE: NYC, June 18. St. Catherine.

McQUEEN, BUTTERFLY: Tampa, Fla., Jan. 8, 1911. UCLA.

McQUEEN, STEVE: Slater, Mo., Mar. 24, 1932.

MEADOWS, AUDREY: Wuchang, China, 1924. St. Margaret's.

MEADOWS, JAYNE: (formerly, Jayne Cotter) Wuchang, China, Sept. 27, 1923. St. Margaret's.

MEDFORD, KAY: (Maggie O'Regin) NYC, Sept. 14, 1920.

MEDWIN, MICHAEL: London, 1925. Instut Fischer.

MEEKER, RALPH: (Ralph Rathgeber) Minneapolis, Nov. 21, 1920. Northwestern U.

MELL, MARISA: Vienna, Austria, 1942.

MERCOURI, MELINA: Athens, Greece, Oct. 18, 1915.

MEREDITH, BURGESS: Cleveland, Ohio, Nov. 16, 1909. Amherst.

MEREDITH, LEE: (Judi Lee Sauls) Oct. 1947. AADA.

MERKEL, UNA: Covington, Ky., Dec. 10, 1903.

MERMAN, ETHEL: (Ethel Zimmerman) Astoria, N.Y., Jan. 16, 1909.

MERRILL, DINA: (Nedinia Hutton) NYC, Dec. 9, 1925. AADA.

MERRILL, GARY: Hartford, Conn., Aug. 2, 1915. Bowdoin, Trinity.

MICHELL, KEITH: Adelaide, Aus., Dec. 1, 1926.

MIFUNE, TOSHIRO: Tsingtao, China, Apr. 1, 1920.

MILES, SARAH: Ingatestone, Eng., Dec. 31, 1941. RADA.

MILES, SYLVIA: NYC, Sept. 9, 1932.

MILES, VERA: (Ralston) Boise City, Okla., Aug. 23, 1929, UCLA.

MILLAND, RAY: (Reginald Truscott-Jones) Neath, Wales, Jan. 3, 1908. King's College.

MILLER, ANN: (Lucille Ann Collier) Chireno, Tex., Apr. 12, 1919. Lawler Professional School.

MILLER, JASON: Long Island City, NY, Apr. 22, 1939, Catholic U.

MILLER, MARVIN: St. Louis, July 18, 1913. Washington U.

MILLS, HAYLEY: London, Apr. 18, 1946. Elmhurst School.

MILLS, JOHN: Suffolk, Eng., Feb. 22, 1908.

MILNER, MARTIN: Detroit, Mich., Dec. 28, 1933.

MIMIEUX, YVETTE: Los Angeles, Jan. 8, 1941. Hollywood High.

MINNELLI, LIZA: Los Angeles, Mar. 12, 1946.

MIRANDA, ISA: (Isabella Sampietro) Milan, Italy, July 5, 1917.

MITCHELL, CAMERON: Dallastown, Pa., Nov. 4, 1918. N.Y. Theatre School.

MITCHELL, JAMES: Sacramento, Calif., Feb. 29, 1920. LACC.

MITCHUM, JAMES: Los Angeles, Cal., May 8, 1941.

MITCHUM, ROBERT: Bridgeport, Conn., Aug. 6, 1917.

MONTALBAN, RICARDO: Mexico City, Nov. 25, 1920.

MONTAND, YVES: (Yves Montand Livi) Mansummano, Tuscany, Oct. 13, 1921.

MONTGOMERY, BELINDA: Winnipeg, Can., July 23, 1950.

MONTGOMERY, ELIZABETH: Los Angeles, Apr. 15, 1933. AADA.

MONTGOMERY, GEORGE: (George Letz) Brady, Mont., Aug. 29, 1916. U. of Mont.

MONTGOMERY, ROBERT: (Henry, Jr.) Beacon, N.Y., May 21, 1904.

MOON, KEITH: London, Aug. 23, 1947.

MOOR, BILL: Toledo, O., July 13, 1931, Northwestern.

MOORE, CONSTANCE: Sioux City, Iowa, Jan. 18, 1922.

MOORE, DICK: Los Angeles, Sept. 12, 1925.

MOORE, KIERON: County Cork, Ire., 1925. St. Mary's College.

MOORE, MARY TYLER: Brooklyn, Dec. 29, 1936.

MOORE, ROGER: London, Oct. 14, 1927. RADA.

MOORE, TERRY: (Helen Koford) Los Angeles, Jan. 7, 1929.

MOORE, KENNETH: Gerrards Cross, Eng., Sept. 20, 1914. Victoria College.

Rita Moreno

Ken Norton

Patricia Neal

Don Nute

Tricia O'Neil

MORE, KENNETH: Gerrards Cross, Eng., Sept. 20, 1914.

MOREAU, JEANNE: Paris, Jan. 3, 1928.

MORENO, RITA: (Rosita Alverio) Humacao, P.R., Dec. 11, 1931.

MORGAN, DENNIS: (Stanley Morner) Prentice, Wisc., Dec. 10, 1920. Carroll College.

MORGAN, HARRY (HENRY): (Harry Bratsburg) Detroit, Apr. 10, 1915. U. of Chicago.

MORGAN, MICHELE: (Simone Roussel) Paris, Feb. 29, 1920. Paris Dramatic School.

MORIARTY, MICHAEL: Detroit, Mich., Apr. 5, 1941. Dartmouth.

MORISON, PATRICIA: NYC, 1919.

MORLEY, ROBERT: Wiltshire, Eng., May 26, 1908. RADA.

MORRIS, GREG: CLeveland, O., 1934. Ohio State.

MORRIS, HOWARD: NYC, Sept. 4, 1919, NYU.

MORROW, VIC: Bronx, N.Y., Feb. 14, 1932. Fla. Southern College.

MORSE, ROBERT: Newton, Mass., May 18, 1931.

MOSS, ARNOLD: NYC, Jan. 28, 1910. CCNY.

MOSTEL, ZERO: Brooklyn, Feb. 28, 1915. CCNY.

MULLIGAN, RICHARD: NYC, Nov. 13, 1932.

MURPHY, GEORGE: New Haven, Conn., July 4, 1902. Yale.

MURRAY, DON: Hollywood, July 31, 1929. AADA.

MURRAY, KEN: (Don Court) NYC, July 14, 1903.

MUSANTE, TONY: Bridgeport, Ct., June 30, 1936. Oberlin Col.

NADER, GEORGE: Pasadena, Calif., Oct. 19, 1921. Occidental College.

NAPIER, ALAN: Birmingham, Eng., Jan. 7, 1903. Birmingham University.

NATWICK, MILDRED: Baltimore, June 19, 1908. Bryn Mawr.

NAUGHTON, JAMES: Middletown, Conn., Dec. 6, 1945. Yale.

NEAL, PATRICIA: Packard, Ky., Jan. 20, 1926. Northwestern U.

NEFF, HILDEGARDE: (Hildegard Knef) Ulm, Ger., Dec. 28, 1925. Berlin Art Academy.

NELSON, BARRY: (Robert Nielsen) Oakland, Cal., 1920.

NELSON, DAVID: NYC, Oct. 24, 1936. USC.

NELSON, GENE: (Gene Berg) Seattle, Wash., Mar. 24, 1920.

NELSON, HARRIET HILLIARD: (Peggy Lou Snyder) Des Moines, Iowa, July 18.

NELSON, LORI: (Dixie Kay Nelson) Santa Fe, N.M., Aug. 15, 1933.

NELSON, RICK: (Eric Hilliard Nelson) Teaneck, N.J., May 8, 1940.

NESBITT, CATHLEEN: Cheshire, Eng., Nov. 24, 1889. Victoria College.

NEWHART, BOB: Chicago, IL., Sept. 5, 1929. Loyola U.

NEWLEY, ANTHONY: Hackney, London, Sept. 21, 1931.

NEWMAN, BARRY: Boston, Ma., Mar. 26, 1938. Brandeis U.

NEWMAN, PAUL: Cleveland, Ohio, Jan. 26, 1925. Yale.

NEWMAN, SCOTT: NYC 1954; Washington Col.

NEWMAR, JULIE: (Newmeyer) Los Angeles, Aug. 16, 1935.

NICHOLAS, PAUL: London, 1945.

NICHOLS, MIKE: (Michael Igor Peschkowsky) Berlin, Nov. 6, 1931. U. Chicago.

NICHOLSON, JACK: Neptune, N.J., Apr. 22, 1937.

NICOL, ALEX: Ossining, N.Y., Jan. 20, 1919. Actors Studio.

NIELSEN, LESLIE: Regina, Saskatchewan, Can., Feb. 11, 1926. Neighborhood Playhouse.

NIVEN, DAVID: Kirriemuir, Scot., Mar. 1, 1910. Sandhurst College.

NOLAN, LLOYD: San Francisco, Aug. 11, 1902. Stanford U.

NOLTE, NICK: 1941.

NORRIS, CHRISTOPHER: NYC, Oct. 7, 1943; Lincoln Square Acad.

NORTH, HEATHER: Pasadena, Cal., Dec. 13, 1950; Actors Workshop.

NORTH, SHEREE: (Dawn Bethel) Los Angeles, Jan. 17, 1933. Hollywood High.

NORTON, KEN: Aug. 9, 1945.

NOVAK, KIM: (Marilyn Novak) Chicago, Feb. 18, 1933. LACC.

NUGENT, ELLIOTT: Dover, Ohio, Sept. 20, 1900. Ohio State U.

NUTE, DON: Connellsville, Pa., Mar. 13, Denver U.

NUYEN, FRANCE: (Vannga) Marseilles, France, July 31, 1939. Beaux Arts School.

OATES, WARREN: Depoy, Ky., July 5, 1928.

OBERON, MERLE: (Estelle Merle O'Brien Thompson) Tasmania, Feb. 19, 1916.

O'BRIAN, HUGH: (Hugh J. Krampe) Rochester, N.Y., Apr. 19, 1928. Cincinnati U.

O'BRIEN, CLAY: Ray, Ariz., May 6, 1961.

O'BRIEN, EDMOND: NYC, Sept. 10, 1915. Fordham, Neighborhood Playhouse.

O'BRIEN, MARGARET: (Angela Maxine O'Brien) Los Angeles, Jan. 15, 1937.

O'BRIEN, PAT: Milwaukee, Nov. 11, 1899. Marquette U.

O'CONNELL, ARTHUR: NYC, Mar. 29, 1908. St. John's.

O'CONNOR, CARROLL: Bronx, N.Y., Aug. 2, 1925; Dublin National Univ.

O'CONNOR, DONALD: Chicago, Aug. 28, 1925.

O'CONNOR, GLYNNIS: NYC, Nov. 19, 1956, NYSU.

O'HANLON, GEORGE: Brooklyn, NY, Nov. 23, 1917.

O'HARA, MAUREEN: (Maureen FitzSimons) Dublin, Ire., Aug. 17, 1921. Abbey School.

O'HERLIHY, DAN: Wexford, Ire., May 1, 1919. National U.

OLIVIER, LAURENCE: Dorking, Eng., May 22, 1907. Oxford.

O'LOUGHLIN, GERALD S.: NYC, Dec. 23, 1921. U. Rochester.

OLSON, NANCY: Milwaukee, Wisc., July 14, UCLA.

O'NEAL, PATRICK: Ocala, Fla., Sept. 26, 1927. U. of Fla.

O'NEAL, RON: Utica, NY, Sept. 1, 1937, Ohio State.

O'NEAL, RYAN: Los Angeles, Apr. 20, 1941.

O'NEAL, TATUM: Los Angeles, Nov. 5, 1963.

O'NEIL, TRICIA: Shreveport, La., Mar. 11, 1945, Baylor U.

O'NEILL, JENNIFER: Rio de Janeiro, Feb. 20, 1949; Neighborhood Playhouse.

O'SULLIVAN, MAUREEN: Byle, Ire., May 17, 1911. Sacred Heart Convent.

O'TOOLE, PETER: Connemara, Ireland, Aug. 2, 1932. RADA.

OWEN, REGINALD: Wheathampstead, Eng., Aug. 5, 1887. Tree's Academy.

PACINO, AL: NYC, Apr. 25, 1940.

PAGE, GERALDINE: Kirksville, Mo., Nov. 22, 1924. Goodman School.

Jack Palance

Barbara Parkins

Anthony Quayle

Bernadette Peters

Thalmus Rasulala

PAGET, DEBRA: (Debralee Griffin) Denver, Aug. 19, 1933.

PAIGE, JANIS: (Donna Mae Jaden) Tacoma, Wash., Sept. 16, 1922.

PALANCE, JACK: (Walter Palanuik) Lattimer, Pa., Feb. 18, 1920. U. N.C.

PALMER, BETSY: East Chicago, Ind., Nov. 1, 1929. DePaul U.

PALMER, GREGG: (Palmer Lee) San Francisco, Jan. 25, 1927. U. Utah.

PALMER, LILLI: Posen, Austria, May 24, 1914. Ilka Gruning School.

PALMER, MARIA: Vienna, Sept. 5, 1924. College de Bouffement.

PAMPANINI, SILVANA: Rome, Sept. 25, 1925.

PAPAS, IRENE: Chiliomodion, Greece, 1929.

PARKER, ELEANOR: Cedarville, Ohio, June 26, 1922. Pasadena Playhouse.

PARKER, FESS: Fort Worth, Tex., Aug. 16, 1927. USC.

PARKER, JEAN: (Mae Green) Deer Lodge, Mont., Aug. 11, 1918.

PARKER, SUZY: (Cecelia Parker) San Antonio, Tex. Oct. 28, 1933.

PARKER, WILLARD: (Worster Van Eps) NYC, Feb. 5, 1912.

PARKINS, BARBARA: Vancouver, Can., May 22, 1945.

PARSONS, ESTELLE: Lynn, Mass. Nov. 20; 1927. Boston U.

PATRICK, DENNIS: Philadelphia, Mar. 14, 1918.

PATRICK, NIGEL: London, May 2, 1913.

PATTERSON, LEE: Vancouver, Can., 1929. Ontario College.

PAVAN, MARISA: (Marisa Pierangeli) Cagliari, Sardinia, June 19, 1932. Torquado Tasso College.

PEACH, MARY: Durban, S. Africa, 1934.

PEARSON, BEATRICE: Denison, Tex., July 27, 1920.

PECK, GREGORY: La Jolla, Calif., Apr. 5, 1916. U. of Calif.

PEPPARD, GEORGE: Detroit, Oct. 1, 1933. Carnegie Tech.

PERKINS, ANTHONY: NYC, Apr. 14, 1932. Rollins College.

PERREAU, GIGI: (Ghislaine) Los Angeles, Feb. 6, 1941.

PERRINE, VALERIE: Galveston, Tx., Sept. 3, 1944. UAriz.

PETERS, BERNADETTE: Jamaica, NY, Feb. 28, 1948.

PETERS, BROCK: NYC, July 2, 1927, CCNY.

PETERS, JEAN: (Elizabeth) Canton, Ohio, Oct. 15, 1926. Ohio State U.

PETTET, JOANNA: London, Nov. 16, 1944; Neighborhood Playhouse.

PHILLIPS, MacKENZIE: Hollywood, Ca. 1960.

PHILLIPS, MICHELLE: (Holly Gilliam) NJ, June 4, 1944.

PICERNI, PAUL: NYC, Dec. 1, 1922. Loyola U.

PICKENS, SLIM: (Louis Bert Lindley, Jr.) Kingsberg, Calif., June 29, 1919.

PICKFORD, MARY: (Gladys Mary Smith) Toronto, Can., Apr. 8, 1893.

PIDGEON, WALTER: East St. John, N.B., Can., Sept. 23, 1898.

PINE, PHILLIP: Hanford, Calif., July 16, 1925. Actors' Lab.

PLACE, MARY KAY: Port Arthur, Tx., Sept., 1947. UTulsa.

PLAYTEN, ALICE: NYC, Aug. 28, 1947, NYU.

PLEASENCE, DONALD: Workshop, Eng, Oct. 5, 1919. Sheffield School.

PLESHETTE, SUZANNE: NYC, Jan. 31, 1937. Syracuse U.

PLUMMER, CHRISTOPHER: Toronto, Can., Dec. 13, 1927.

PODESTA, ROSSANA: Tripoli, June 20, 1934.

POITIER, SIDNEY: Miami, Fla., Feb. 27, 1924.

POLITO, LINA: Naples, Italy, Aug. 11, 1954.

POLLARD, MICHAEL J.: Pacific, N.J., May 30, 1939.

PORTER, ERIC: London, Apr. 8, 1928, Wimbledon Col.

POWELL, ELEANOR: Springfield, Mass., Nov. 21, 1913.

POWELL, JANE: (Suzanne Burce) Portland, Ore., Apr. 1, 1929.

POWELL, ROBERT: London, June 1, 1944.

POWELL, WILLIAM: Pittsburgh, July 29, 1892. AADA.

POWERS, MALA: (Mary Ellen) San Francisco, Dec. 29, 1921. UCLA.

PRENTISS, PAULA: (Paula Ragusa) San Antonio, Tex., Mar. 4, 1939. Northwestern U.

PRESLE, MICHELINE: (Micheline Chassagne) Paris, Aug. 22, 1922. Rouleau Drama School.

PRESLEY, ELVIS: Tupelo, Miss., Jan. 8, 1935.

PRESNELL, HARVE: Modesto, Calif., Sept. 14, 1933. USC.

PRESTON, ROBERT: (Robert Preston Meservey) Newton Highlands, Mass., June 8, 1913. Pasadena Playhouse.

PRICE, VINCENT: St. Louis, May 27, 1911. Yale.

PRINCE, WILLIAM: Nicholas, N.Y., Jan. 26, 1913. Cornell U.

PRINCIPAL, VICTORIA: Tokyo, Jan. 3, 1945, Dade Jr. Col.

PROVINE, DOROTHY: Deadwood, S.D., Jan. 20, 1937. U. of Wash.

PROWSE, JULIET: Bombay, India, Sept. 25, 1936.

PRYOR, RICHARD: Peoria, Ill., Dec. 1, 1940.

PURCELL, LEE: Cherry Point, N.C., 1947; Stephens.

PURCELL, NOEL: Dublin, Ire., Dec. 23, 1900. Irish Christian Brothers.

PURDOM, EDMUND: Welwyn Garden City, Eng., Dec. 19, St. Ignatius College.

QUAYLE, ANTHONY: Lancashire, Eng., Sept. 7, 1913. Old Vic School.

QUINE, RICHARD: Detroit, Mi, Nov. 12, 1920.

QUINN, ANTHONY: Chihuahua, Mex., Apr. 21, 1915.

RAFFERTY, FRANCES: Sioux City, Iowa, June 16, 1922. UCLA.

RAFFIN, DEBORAH: Los Angeles, Mar. 13, 1953. Valley Col.

RAFT, GEORGE: NYC, 1903.

RAINES, ELLA: (Ella Wallace) Snoqualmie Falls, Wash., Aug. 6, 1921. U. of Wash.

RAMPLING, CHARLOTTE: Surmer, Eng., Feb. 5, 1946; UMadrid.

RAMSEY, LOGAN: Long Beach, Cal., Mar. 21, 1921; St. Joseph.

RANDALL, TONY: Tulsa, Okla., Feb. 26, 1920. Northwestern U.

RANDELL, RON: Sydney, Australia, Oct. 8, 1920. St. Mary's Col.

RASULALA, THALMUS: (Jack Crowder) Miami, Fla., Nov. 15, 1939. U. Redlands.

RAY, ALDO: (Aldo DeRe) Pen Argyl, Pa. Sept. 25, 1926. UCLA.

RAYE, MARTHA: (Margie Yvonne Reed) Butte, Mont., Aug. 27, 1916.

RAYMOND, GENE: (Raymond Guion) NYC, Aug. 13, 1908.

REAGAN, RONALD: Tampico, Ill., Feb. 6, 1911. Eureka College.

REASON, REX: Berlin, Ger., Nov. 30, 1928. Pasadena Playhouse.

REDDY, HELEN: Australia, Oct. 25, 1942.

Carl Reiner

Diana Rigg

Don Rickles

Maria Schell

Roy Scheider

REDFORD, ROBERT: Santa Monica, Calif., Aug. 18, 1937. AADA.

REDGRAVE, CORIN: London, July 16, 1939.

REDGRAVE, LYNN: London, Mar. 8, 1943.

REDGRAVE, MICHAEL: Bristol, Eng., Mar. 20, 1908. Cambridge.

REDGRAVE, VANESSA: London, Jan. 30, 1937.

REDMAN, JOYCE: County Mayo, Ire., 1919. RADA.

REED, DONNA: (Donna Mullenger) Denison, Iowa, Jan. 27, 1921. LACC.

REED, OLIVER: Wimbledon, Eng., Feb. 13, 1938.

REED, REX: Ft. Worth, Tex., Oct. 2, 1939, LSU.

REEMS, HARRY: (Herbert Streicher) Bronx, NY, 1947. UPittsburgh.

REEVES, STEVE: Glasgow, Mont., Jan. 21, 1926.

REID, ELLIOTT: NYC, Jan. 16, 1920.

REINER, CARL: NYC, Mar. 20, 1922. Georgetown.

REINER, ROBERT: NYC, 1945, UCLA.

REMICK, LEE: Quincy, Mass., Dec. 14, 1935. Barnard College.

RETTIG, TOMMY: Jackson Heights, N.Y., Dec. 10, 1941.

REVILL, CLIVE: Wellington, NZ, Apr. 18, 1930.

REYNOLDS, BURT: West Palm Beach, Fla. Feb. 11, 1936. Fla. State U.

REYNOLDS, DEBBIE: (Mary Frances Reynolds) El Paso, Tex., Apr. 1, 1932.

REYNOLDS, MARJORIE: Buhl, Idaho, Aug. 12, 1921.

RHOADES, BARBARA: Poughkeepsie, N.Y., 1947.

RICH, IRENE: Buffalo, N.Y., Oct. 13, 1897. St. Margaret's School.

RICHARDS, JEFF: (Richard Mansfield Taylor) Portland, Ore., Nov. 1. USC.

RICHARDSON, RALPH: Cheltenham, Eng., Dec. 19, 1902.

RICKLES, DON: NYC, May 8, 1926. AADA.

RIGG, DIANA: Doncaster, Eng., July 20, 1938. RADA.

ROBARDS, JASON: Chicago, July 26, 1922. AADA.

ROBBINS, GALE: Chicago, Il., May 7, 1932.

ROBERTS, TONY: NYC, Oct. 22, 1939. Northwestern U.

ROBERTS, RACHEL: Llanelly, Wales, Sept. 20, 1927. RADA.

ROBERTS, RALPH: Salisbury, NC, Aug. 17, 1922. UNC.

ROBERTSON, CLIFF: La Jolla, Calif., Sept. 9, 1925. Antioch Col.

ROBERTSON, DALE: Oklahoma City, July 14, 1923.

ROBINSON, CHRIS: 1938, West Palm Beach, Fla., LACC.

ROBINSON, ROGER: Seattle, Wash., May 2, 1941; USCal.

ROBSON, FLORA: South Shields, Eng., Mar. 28, 1902. RADA.

ROCHESTER: (Eddie Anderson) Oakland, Calif., Sept. 18, 1905.

ROGERS, CHARLES "BUDDY": Olathe, Kan., Aug. 13, 1904. U. of Kan.

ROGERS, GINGER: (Virginia Katherine McMath) Independence, Mo., July 16, 1911.

ROGERS, ROY: (Leonard Slye) Cincinnati, Nov. 5, 1912.

ROGERS, WAYNE: Birmingham, Ala., Apr. 7, 1933. Princeton.

ROLAND, GILBERT: (Luis Antonio Damaso De Alonso) Juarez, Mex., Dec. 11, 1905.

ROMAN, RUTH: Boston, Dec. 23. Bishop Lee Dramatic School.

ROMERO, CESAR: NYC, Feb. 15, 1907. Collegiate School.

ROONEY, MICKEY: (Joe Yule, Jr.) Brooklyn, Sept. 23, 1920.

ROSS, DIANA: Detroit, Mich., Mar. 26, 1945.

ROSS, KATHARINE: Hollywood, Jan. 29, 1943. Santa Rosa Col.

ROSSITER, LEONARD: Liverpool, Eng., Oct. 21, 1926.

ROTH, LILLIAN: Boston, Dec. 13, 1910.

ROUNDS, DAVID: Bronxville, NY, Oct. 9, 1938, Denison U.

ROUNDTREE, RICHARD: New Rochelle, N.Y., Sept. 7, 1942. Southern Ill.

ROWLANDS, GENA: Cambria, Wisc., June 19, 1936.

RULE, JANICE: Cincinnati, O., Aug. 15, 1931.

RUPERT, MICHAEL: Denver, Co. Oct. 23, 1951. Pasadena Playhouse.

RUSH, BARBARA: Denver, Colo., Jan. 4. U. of Calif.

RUSSELL, JANE: Bemidji, Minn., June 21, 1921. Max Reinhardt School.

RUSSELL, JOHN: Los Angeles, Jan. 3, 1921. U. of Calif.

RUSSELL, KURT: Springfield, Mass., March 17, 1951.

RUTHERFORD, ANN: Toronto, Can., 1924.

RUYMEN, AYN: Brooklyn, July 18, 1947, HB Studio.

SAINT, EVA MARIE: Newark, N.J., July 4, 1924. Bowling Green State U.

ST. JACQUES, RAYMOND: (James Arthur Johnson) Conn.

ST. JAMES, SUSAN: Los Angeles, Aug. 14. Conn. Col.

ST. JOHN, BETTA: Hawthorne, Calif., Nov. 26, 1929.

ST. JOHN, JILL: (Jill Oppenheim) Los Angeles, Aug. 19, 1940.

SALMI, ALBERT: Coney Island, NY. 1925. Actors Studio.

SALT, JENNIFER: Los Angeles, Sept. 4, 1944. Sarah Lawrence Col.

SANDS, TOMMY: Chicago, Aug. 27, 1937.

SAN JUAN, OLGA: NYC, Mar. 16, 1927.

SARANDON, CHRIS: Beckley, W.Va., July 24, 1942. UWVa. Catholic U.

SARANDON, SUSAN: (Tomaling) NYC, Oct. 4, 1946. Catholic U.

SARGENT, RICHARD: (Richard Cox) Carmel, Cal., 1933. Stanford.

SARRAZIN, MICHAEL: Quebec City, Can., May 22, 1940.

SAVALAS, TELLY: (Aristotle) Garden City, N.Y., Jan. 21, 1925. Columbia.

SAXON, JOHN: (Carmen Orrico) Brooklyn, Aug. 5, 1935.

SCHEIDER, ROY: Orange, N.J., Nov. 10, 1935, Franklin-Marshall.

SCHELL, MARIA: Vienna, Jan. 15, 1926.

SCHELL, MAXIMILIAN: Vienna, Dec. 8, 1930.

SCHNEIDER, MARIA: Paris, Mar. 27, 1952.

SCHNEIDER, ROMY: Vienna, Sept. 23, 1938.

SCOFIELD, PAUL: Hurstpierpoint, Eng., Jan. 21, 1922. London Mask Theatre School.

SCOTT, GEORGE C.: Wise, Va., Oct. 18, 1927. U. of Mo.

SCOTT, GORDON: (Gordon M. Werschkul) Portland, Ore., Aug. 3, 1927. Oregon U.

SCOTT, MARTHA: Jamesport, Mo., Sept. 22, 1914. U. of Mich.

SCOTT, RANDOLPH: Orange County, Va., Jan. 23, 1903. U. of N.C.

SEAGULL, BARBARA HERSHEY: (Herzstein) Hollywood, Feb. 5, 1948.

SEARS, HEATHER: London, 1935.

SEBERG, JEAN: Marshalltown, Iowa, Nov. 13, 1938. Iowa U.

SECOMBE, HARRY: Swansea, Wales, Sept. 8, 1921.

SEGAL, GEORGE: NYC, Feb. 13, 1934, Columbia.

Anne Seymour

Paul Sorvino

Alexis Smith

Peter Strauss

Gloria Swanson

SELLARS, ELIZABETH: Glasgow, Scot., May 6, 1923.

SELLERS, PETER: Southsea, Eng., Sept. 8, 1925. Aloysius College.

SELWART, TONIO: Watenberg, Ger., June 9, 1906. Munich U.

SERNAS, JACQUES: Lithuania, July 30, 1925.

SEYLER, ATHENE: (Athene Hannen) London, May 31, 1889.

SEYMOUR, ANNE: NYC, Sept. 11, 1909. American Laboratory Theatre.

SEYMOUR, JANE: Hillingdon, Eng., Feb. 15, 1951.

SHARIF, OMAR: (Michel Shalboub) Alexandria, Egypt, Apr. 10, 1933. Victoria Col.

SHATNER, WILLIAM: Montreal, Can., Mar. 22, 1931. McGill U.

SHAW, ROBERT: Orkney Isles, Scot., Aug. 9, 1925, RADA.

SHAW, SEBASTIAN: Holt, Eng., May 29, 1905. Gresham School.

SHAWLEE, JOAN: Forest Hills, N.Y., Mar. 5, 1929.

SHAWN, DICK: (Richard Shulefand) Buffalo, N.Y., Dec. 1. U. of Miami.

SHEARER, MOIRA: Dunfermline, Scot., Jan. 17, 1926. London Theatre School.

SHEARER, NORMA: Montreal, Can., Aug. 19, 1904.

SHEEN, MARTIN: (Ramon Estevez) Dayton, O., Aug. 3, 1940.

SHEFFIELD, JOHN: Pasadena, Calif., Apr. 11, 1931. UCLA.

SHEPHERD, CYBIL: Memphis, Tenn., Feb. 18, 1950. Hunter, NYU.

SHIRE, TALIA: Lake Success, NY. Yale.

SHORE, DINAH: (Frances Rose Shore) Winchester, Tenn., Mar. 1, 1917. Vanderbilt U.

SHOWALTER, MAX: (formerly Casey Adams) Caldwell, Kan., June 2, 1917. Pasadena Playhouse.

SIDNEY, SYLVIA: NYC, Aug. 8, 1910. Theatre Guild School.

SIGNORET, SIMONE: (Simone Kaminker) Wiesbaden, Ger., Mar. 25, 1921. Solange Sicard School.

SILVERS, PHIL: (Philip Silversmith) Brooklyn, May 11, 1912.

SIMMONS, JEAN: London, Jan. 31, 1929. Aida Foster School.

SIMON, SIMONE: Marseilles, France, Apr. 23, 1914.

SIMPSON, O. J.: (Orenthal James) San Francisco, CA., July 9, 1947. UCLA.

SINATRA, FRANK: Hoboken, N.J., Dec. 12, 1915.

SINDEN, DONALD: Plymouth, Eng., Oct. 9, 1923. Webber-Douglas.

SKELTON, RED: (Richard) Vincennes, Ind., July 18, 1913.

SLEZAK, WALTER: Vienna, Austria, May 3, 1902.

SMITH, ALEXIS: Penticton, Can., June 8, 1921. LACC.

SMITH, JOHN: (Robert E. Van Orden) Los Angeles, Mar. 6, 1931. UCLA.

SMITH, KATE: (Kathryn Elizabeth) Greenville, Va., May 1, 1909.

SMITH, KENT: NYC, Mar. 19, 1907. Harvard U.

SMITH, MAGGIE: Ilford, Eng., Dec. 28, 1934.

SMITH, ROGER: South Gate, Calif., Dec. 18, 1932. U. of Ariz.

SNODGRESS, CARRIE: Chicago, Oct. 27, 1946. UNI.

SNOWDEN, LEIGH: Memphis, Tn, June 28, 1932. Lambeth Col.

SOMMER, ELKE: Berlin, Nov. 5, 1941.

SONNY: (Salvatore Bono) 1935.

SORDI, ALBERTO: Rome, Italy, 1925.

SORVINO, PAUL: NYC, 1939, AMDA.

SOTHERN, ANN: (Harriet Lake) Valley City, N.D., Jan. 22, 1909. Washington U.

SPACEK, SISSY: Quitman, Tx, Dec. 25, 1949. Actors Studio.

SPENSER, JEREMY: Ceylon, 1937.

SPRINGER, GARY: NYC, July 29, 1954. Hunter Col.

STACK, ROBERT: Los Angeles, Jan. 13, 1919. USC.

STADLEN, LEWIS J.: Brooklyn, Mar. 7, 1947, Neighborhood Playhouse.

STALLONE, SYLVESTER: NYC, 1946. UMiami.

STAMP, TERENCE: London, 1940.

STANDER, LIONEL: NYC, Jan. 11, 1908. UNC.

STANG, ARNOLD: Chelsea, Mass., Sept. 28, 1925.

STANLEY, KIM: (Patricia Reid) Tularosa, N.M., Feb. 11, 1921. U. of Tex.

STANWYCK, BARBARA: (Ruby Stevens) Brooklyn, July 16, 1907.

STAPLETON, JEAN: NYC, Jan. 19, 1923.

STAPLETON, MAUREEN: Troy, N.Y., June 21, 1925.

STEEL, ANTHONY: London, May 21, 1920. Cambridge.

STEELE, TOMMY: London, Dec. 17, 1936.

STEIGER, ROD: Westhampton, N.Y., Apr. 14, 1925.

STERLING, JAN: (Jane Sterling Adriance) NYC, Apr. 3, 1923. Fay Compton School.

STERLING, ROBERT: (William Sterling Hart) Newcastle, Pa., Nov. 13, 1917. U. of Pittsburgh.

STEVENS, CONNIE: (Concetta Ann Ingolia) Brooklyn, Aug. 8, 1938. Hollywood Professional School.

STEVENS, KAYE: (Catherine) Pittsburgh, July 21, 1933.

STEVENS, MARK: (Richard) Cleveland, Ohio, Dec. 13, 1922.

STEVENS, STELLA: (Estelle Eggleston) Hot Coffee, Miss., Oct. 1, 1936.

STEWART, ALEXANDRA: Montreal, Can., June 10. Louvre.

STEWART, ELAINE: Montclair, N.J., May 31, 1929.

STEWART, JAMES: Indiana, Pa., May 20, 1908. Princeton.

STEWART, MARTHA: (Martha Haworth) Bardwell, Ky., Oct. 7, 1922.

STOCKWELL, DEAN: Hollywood, March 5, 1936.

STORM, GALE: (Josephine Cottle) Bloomington, Tex., Apr. 5, 1922.

STRAIGHT, BEATRICE: Old Westbury, NY, Aug. 2, 1916. Dartington Hall.

STRASBERG, SUSAN: NYC, May 22, 1938.

STRAUD, DON: Hawaii, 1943.

STRAUSS, PETER: NY, 1947.

STREISAND, BARBRA: Brooklyn, Apr. 24, 1942.

STRODE, WOODY: Los Angeles, 1914.

STRUDWICK, SHEPPERD: Hillsboro, N.C., Sept. 22, 1907. U. of N.C.

STRUTHERS, SALLY: Portland, Ore., July 28, 1948, Pasadena Playhouse.

SULLIVAN, BARRY: (Patrick Barry) NYC, Aug. 29, 1912. NYU.

SULLY, FRANK: (Frank Sullivan) St. Louis, 1910. St. Teresa's Col.

SUTHERLAND, DONALD: St. John, New Brunswick, Can., July 17, 1934. U. Toronto.

SVENSON, BO: Goteborg, Swed., Feb. 13, 1941. UCLA

SWANSON, GLORIA: (Josephine May Swenson) Chicago, Mar. 27, 1898. Chicago Art Inst.

SWINBURNE, NORA: Bath, Eng., July 24, 1902. RADA.

SWIT, LORETTA: Passaic, NJ, Nov. 4, AADA.

SYLVESTER, WILLIAM: Oakland, Calif., Jan. 31, 1922. RADA.

SYMS, SYLVIA: London, 1934. Convent School.

229

Russ Tamblyn

Marlo Thomas

Russ Thacker

Brenda Vaccaro

Ben Vereen

TABORI, KRISTOFFER: Los Angeles, Aug. 4, 1952.

TALBOT, LYLE: (Lysle Hollywood) Pittsburgh, Feb. 8, 1904.

TALBOT, NITA: NYC, Aug. 8, 1930. Irvine Studio School.

TAMBLYN, RUSS: Los Angeles, Dec. 30.

TANDY, JESSICA: London, June 7, 1909. Dame Owens' School.

TAYLOR, DON: Freeport, Pa., Dec. 13, 1920. Penn State U.

TAYLOR, ELIZABETH: London, Feb. 27, 1932. Byron House School.

TAYLOR, KENT: (Louis Weiss) Nashua, Iowa, May 11, 1907.

TAYLOR, ROD: (Robert) Sydney, Aust., Jan. 11, 1929.

TAYLOR-YOUNG, LEIGH: Wash., D.C., Jan. 25, 1945. Northwestern.

TEAGUE, ANTHONY SKOOTER: Jacksboro, Tex., Jan. 4, 1940.

TEMPLE, SHIRLEY: Santa Monica, Calif., Apr. 23, 1928.

TERRY-THOMAS: (Thomas Terry Hoar Stevens) Finchley, London, July 14, 1911. Ardingly College.

TERZIEFF, LAURENT: Paris, 1935.

THACKER, RUSS: Washington, DC, June 23, 1946, Montgomery Col.

THATCHER, TORIN: Bombay, India, Jan. 15, 1905. RADA.

THAXTER, PHYLLIS: Portland, Me., Nov. 20, 1921. St. Genevieve.

THOMAS, DANNY: (Amos Jacobs) Deerfield, Mich., Jan. 6, 1914.

THOMAS, MARLO: (Margaret) Detroit, Nov. 21, 1938. USC.

THOMAS, PHILIP: Columbus, O., May 26, 1949. Oakwood Col.

THOMAS, RICHARD: NYC, June 13, 1951. Columbia.

THOMPSON, JACK: (John Payne) Sydney, Aus., 1940. UBrisbane.

THOMPSON, MARSHALL: Peoria, Ill., Nov. 27, 1925. Occidental.

THOMPSON, REX: NYC, Dec. 14, 1942.

THOMPSON, SADA: Des Moines, Io., Sept. 27, 1929, Carnegie Tech.

THULIN, INGRID: Solleftea, Sweden, Jan. 27, 1929, Royal Drama Theatre.

TIERNEY, GENE: Brooklyn, Nov. 20, 1920. Miss Farmer's School.

TIERNEY, LAWRENCE: Brooklyn, Mar. 15, 1919. Manhattan College.

TIFFIN, PAMELA: (Wonso) Oklahoma City, Oct. 13, 1942.

TODD, RICHARD: Dublin, Ire., June 11, 1919. Shrewsbury School.

TOLO, MARILU': Rome, Italy, 1948.

TOMLIN, LILY: Detroit, Mi., Sept. 1939. Wayne State U.

TOPOL: (Chaim Topol) Tel-Aviv, Israel, Sept. 9, 1935.

TORN, RIP: Temple, Tex., Feb. 6, 1931. U. Tex.

TORRES, LIZ: NYC, 1947, NYU.

TOTTER, AUDREY: Joliet, Ill., Dec. 20.

TRAVERS, BILL: Newcastle-on-Tyne, Eng., Jan. 3, 1922.

TRAVIS, RICHARD: (William Justice) Carlsbad, N.M., Apr. 17, 1913.

TRAVOLTA, JOHN: Englewood, NJ., Feb. 18, 1954.

TREMAYNE, LES: London, Apr. 16, 1913. Northwestern, Columbia, UCLA.

TRINTIGNANT, JEAN-LOUIS: Pont-St. Esprit, France, Dec. 11, 1930. Dullin-Balachova Drama School.

TRYON, TOM: Hartford, Conn., Jan. 14, 1926. Yale.

TSOPEI, CORINNA: Athens, Greece, June 21, 1944.

TUCKER, FORREST: Plainfield, Ind., Feb. 12, 1919. George Washington U.

TURNER, LANA: (Julia Jean Mildred Frances Turner) Wallace, Idaho, Feb. 8, 1920.

TUSHINGHAM, RITA: Liverpool, Eng., 1942.

TUTIN, DOROTHY: London, Apr. 8, 1930.

TUTTLE, LURENE: Pleasant Lake, Ind., Aug. 20, 1906, USC.

TWIGGY: (Lesley Hornby) London, Sept. 19, 1949.

TYLER, BEVERLY: (Beverly Jean Saul) Scranton, Pa., July 5, 1928.

TYRRELL, SUSAN: San Francisco, 1946.

TYSON, CICELY: NYC, Dec. 19.

UGGAMS, LESLIE: NYC, May 25, 1943.

ULLMANN, LIV: Tokyo, Dec. 16, 1939, Webber-Douglas Acad.

USTINOV, PETER: London, Apr. 16, 1921. Westminster School.

VACCARO, BRENDA: Brooklyn, Nov. 18, 1939. Neighborhood Playhouse.

VALLEE, RUDY: (Hubert) Island Pond, Vt., July 28, 1901. Yale.

VALLI, ALIDA: Pola, Italy, May 31, 1921. Rome Academy of Drama.

VALLONE, RAF: Riogio, Italy, Feb. 17. Turin U.

VAN, BOBBY: (Stein) NYC, Dec. 6, 1930.

VAN CLEEF, LEE: Somerville, N.J., Jan. 9, 1925.

VAN DE VEN, MONIQUE: Holland, 1957.

VAN DEVERE, TRISH: (Patricia Dressel) Englewood Cliffs, NJ, Mar. 9, 1945, Ohio Wesleyan.

VAN DOREN, MAMIE: (Joan Lucile Olander) Rowena, S.D., Feb. 6, 1933.

VAN DYKE, DICK: West Plains, Mo., Dec. 13, 1925.

VAN FLEET, JO: Oakland, Cal., 1922.

VAN PATTEN, DICK: NYC, Dec. 9, 1928.

VAN PATTEN, JOYCE: NYC, Mar. 9, 1934.

VAUGHN, ROBERT: NYC, Nov. 22, 1932. USC.

VEGA, ISELA: Mexico, 1940.

VENTURA, LINO: Parma, Italy, July 14, 1919.

VENUTA, VENAY: San Francisco, Jan. 27, 1911.

VERA-ELLEN: (Rohe) Cincinnati, Feb. 16, 1926.

VERDON, GWEN: Culver City, Calif., Jan. 13, 1925.

VEREEN, BEN: Miami, Fl, Oct. 10, 1946.

VINCENT, JAN-MICHAEL: Denver, Col., July 15, 1944. Ventura Col.

VIOLET, ULTRA: (Isabelle Collin-Dufresne) Grenoble, France.

VITALE, MILLY: Rome, Italy, July 16, 1938. Lycee Chateaubriand.

VOHS, JOAN: St. Albans, NY, July 30, 1931.

VOIGHT, JON: Yonkers, N.Y., Dec. 29, 1938. Catholic U.

VOLONTE, GIAN MARIA: Milan, Italy, Apr. 9, 1933.

VON SYDOW, MAX: Lund, Swed., July 10, 1929, Royal Drama Theatre.

WAGNER, LINDSAY: Los Angeles, 1949.

WAGNER, ROBERT: Detroit, Feb. 10, 1930.

WAITE, GENEVIEVE: South Africa 1949.

WALKEN, CHRISTOPHER: Astoria, NY, Mar. 31, 1943, Hofstra.

WALKER, CLINT: Hartfold, Ill., May 30, 1927. USC.

WALKER, NANCY: (Ann Myrtle Swoyer) Philadelphia, May 10, 1921.

WALLACH, ELI: Brooklyn, Dec. 7, 1915. CCNY, U. of Tex.

WALLIS, SHANI: London, Apr. 5, 1941.

Jennifer Warren **Orson Welles** **Collin Wilcox-Horne** **Michael York** **Mary Woronov**

WALSTON, RAY: New Orleans, Nov. 22, 1918. Cleveland Playhouse.

WALTER, JESSICA: Brooklyn, NY, Jan. 31, 1940. Neighborhood Playhouse.

WANAMAKER, SAM: Chicago, June 14, 1919. Drake.

WARD, BURT: (Gervis) Los Angeles, July 6, 1945.

WARD, SIMON: London 1941.

WARDEN, JACK: Newark, N.J., Sept. 18, 1920.

WARREN, JENNIFER: NYC, Aug. 12, 1941. UWisc.

WARREN, LESLEY ANN: NYC, Aug. 16, 1946.

WARRICK, RUTH: St. Joseph, Mo., June 29, UMo.

WASHBOURNE, MONA: Birmingham, Eng., Nov. 27, 1903.

WATERS, ETHEL: Chester, Pa., Oct. 31, 1900.

WATERSTON, SAM: Cambridge, Mass., Nov. 15, 1940. Yale.

WATLING, JACK: London, Jan. 13, 1923. Italia Conti School.

WATSON, DOUGLASS: Jackson, Ga., Feb. 24, 1921. UNC.

WAYNE, DAVID: (Wayne McKeehan) Travers City, Mich., Jan. 30, 1914. Western Michigan State U.

WAYNE, JOHN: (Marion Michael Morrison) Winterset, Iowa, May 26, 1907. USC.

WAYNE, PATRICK: Los Angeles, July 15, 1939. Loyola.

WEAVER, DENNIS: Joplin, Mo., June 4, 1925. U. Okla.

WEAVER, MARJORIE: Crossville, Tenn., Mar. 2, 1913. Indiana U.

WEBB, ALAN: York, Eng., July 2, 1906. Dartmouth.

WEBB, JACK: Santa Monica, Calif. Apr. 2, 1920.

WEBBER, ROBERT: Santa Ana, Cal., Oct. 14, Compton Jr. Col.

WEISSMULLER, JOHNNY: Chicago, June 2, 1904. Chicago U.

WELCH, RAQUEL: (Tejada) Chicago, Sept. 5, 1940.

WELD, TUESDAY: (Susan) NYC, Aug. 27, 1943. Hollywood Professional School.

WELDON, JOAN: San Francisco, Aug. 5, 1933. San Francisco Conservatory.

WELLES, GWEN: NYC, Mar. 4.

WELLES, ORSON: Kenosha, Wisc., May 6, 1915. Todd School.

WERNER, OSKAR: Vienna, Nov. 13, 1922.

WEST, MAE: Brooklyn, Aug. 17, 1892.

WESTON, JACK: Cleveland, O., 1915.

WHITAKER, JOHNNY: Van Nuys, Cal., Dec. 13. 1959.

WHITE, CAROL: London, Apr. 1, 1944.

WHITE, CHARLES: Perth Amboy, NJ, Aug. 29, 1920, Rutgers U.

WHITE, JESSE: Buffalo, N.Y., Jan. 3, 1919.

WHITMAN, STUART: San Francisco, Feb. 1, 1929. CCLA.

WHITMORE, JAMES: White Plains, NY, Oct. 1, 1922, Yale.

WIDDOES, KATHLEEN: Wilmington, Del., Mar. 21, 1939.

WIDMARK, RICHARD: Sunrise, Minn., Dec. 26, 1914. Lake Forest.

WILCOX-HORNE, COLIN: Highlands N.C., Feb. 4, 1937. U. Tenn.

WILCOXON, HENRY: British West Indies, Sept. 8, 1905.

WILDE, CORNEL: NYC, Oct. 13, 1915. CCNY, Columbia.

WILDER, GENE: Milwaukee, Wis., June 11, 1935. U Iowa.

WILDING, MICHAEL: Westcliff, Eng., July 23, 1912. Christ's Hospital.

WILLIAMS, BILLY DEE: NYC, Apr. 6, 1937.

WILLIAMS, CINDY: Van Nuys, Ca., Aug. 22, 1948, LACC.

WILLIAMS, EMLYN: Mostyn, Wales, Nov. 26, 1905. Oxford.

WILLIAMS, ESTHER: Los Angeles, Aug. 8, 1923.

WILLIAMS, GRANT: NYC, Aug. 18, 1930. Queens College.

WILLIAMS, JOHN: Chalfont, Eng., Apr. 15, 1903. Lancing College.

WILLIAMSON, FRED: Gary, Ind., Mar. 5, 1938, Northwestern.

WILSON, DEMOND: NYC, Oct. 13, 1946, Hunter Col.

WILSON, FLIP: (Clerow Wilson) Jersey City, N.J., Dec. 8, 1933.

WILSON, NANCY: Chillicothe, O., Feb. 20, 1937.

WILSON, SCOTT: Atlanta, Ga., 1942.

WINDE, BEATRICE: Chicago, Jan. 6.

WINDOM, WILLIAM: NYC, Sept. 28, 1923, Williams Col.

WINDSOR, MARIE: (Emily Marie Bertelson) Marysvale, Utah, Dec. 11, 1924. Brigham Young U.

WINFIELD, PAUL: Los Angeles, 1940, UCLA.

WINKLER, HENRY: NYC, Oct. 30, 1945. Yale.

WINN, KITTY: Wash., D.C., 1944. Boston U.

WINTERS, JONATHAN: Dayton Ohio, Nov. 11, 1925. Kenyon Col.

WINTERS, ROLAND: Boston, Nov. 22, 1904.

WINTERS, SHELLEY: (Shirley Schrift) St. Louis, Aug. 18, 1922. Wayne U.

WINWOOD, ESTELLE: Kent, Eng., Jan. 24, 1883. Lyric Stage Academy.

WITHERS, GOOGIE: Karachi, India, Mar. 12, 1917. Italia Conti.

WITHERS, JANE: Atlanta, Ga., 1926.

WOOD, NATALIE: (Natasha Gurdin) San Francisco, July 20, 1938.

WOOD, PEGGY: Brooklyn, Feb. 9, 1894.

WOODLAWN, HOLLY: (Harold Ajzenberg) Juana Diaz, PR, 1947.

WOODS, JAMES: Vernal, U., Apr. 18, 1947, MIT.

WOODWARD, JOANNE: Thomasville, Ga., Feb. 27, 1931. Neighborhood Playhouse.

WOOLAND, NORMAN: Dusseldorf, Ger., Mar. 16, 1910. Edward VI School.

WORONOV, MARY: Brooklyn, Dec. 8, 1946. Cornell.

WRAY, FAY: Alberta, Can., Sept. 15, 1907.

WRIGHT, TERESA: NYC, Oct. 27, 1918.

WYATT, JANE: Campgaw, N.J., Aug. 10, 1912. Barnard College.

WYMAN, JANE: (Sarah Jane Fulks) St. Joseph, Mo., Jan. 4, 1914.

WYMORE, PATRICE: Miltonvale, Kan., Dec. 17, 1927.

WYNN, KEENAN: NYC, July 27, 1916. St. John's.

WYNN, MAY: (Donna Lee Hickey) NYC, Jan. 8, 1930.

WYNTER, DANA: London, June 8, Rhodes U.

YORK, DICK: Fort Wayne, Ind., Sept. 4, 1928. De Paul U.

YORK, MICHAEL: Fulmer, Eng., Mar. 27, 1942. Oxford.

YORK, SUSANNAH: London, Jan. 9, 1941. RADA.

YOUNG, ALAN: (Angus) North Shield, Eng., Nov. 19, 1919.

YOUNG, GIG: (Byron Barr) St. Cloud, Minn., Nov. 4, 1917. Pasadena Playhouse.

YOUNG, LORETTA: (Gretchen) Salt Lake City, Jan. 6, 1913. Immaculate Heart College.

YOUNG, ROBERT: Chicago, Feb. 22, 1907.

ZETTERLING, MAI: Sweden, May 27, 1925. Ordtuery Theatre School.

ZIMBALIST, EFREM, JR.: NYC, Nov. 30, 1918. Yale.

| Warner Anderson | Richard Arlen | Stanley Baker | Margaret Bannerman | Alan Baxter | Oscar Beregi |

OBITUARIES

ALYCE ALLYN, age unreported, died Feb. 11, 1976 in Santa Monica, CA. Her career covered many years in motion pictures and tv. Her films include "The Manchurian Candidate" and "The Wild Bunch." Among her many tv appearances were "Have Gun, Will Travel" and "Baretta." Her husband survives.

WARNER ANDERSON, 65, New York-born film, stage and tv actor, died Aug. 26, 1976 in Santa Monica, CA. Made first film appearance at 4, but performed on Broadway until 1943 when he went to Hollywood and appeared in over 50 films, including "Destination Tokyo," "Objective Burma," "Abbot and Costello in Hollywood," "Her Highness and the Bellboy," "Weekend at the Waldorf," "Tenth Avenue Angel," "Song of the Thin Man," "Command Decision," "Blue Veil," "Detective Story," "Only the Valiant," "The Star," "A Lion Is in the Streets," "Caine Mutiny," "Blackboard Jungle," and "Rio Conchos." He was probably best known for his appearances in the tv series "The Line-up." His wife and son survive.

RICHARD ARLEN, 75, (born Van Mattimore in Virginia) whose career spanned 52 years from silent to talking films, died March 28, 1976 in North Hollywood, CA, of emphysema. He appeared in over 280 films, including "Wings," "Old Ironsides," "She's a Sheik," "Manhattan Cocktail," "Four Feathers," "The Virginian," "All American," "Three-Cornered Moon," "Artists and Models," "Legion of Lost Flyers," "Come on Marines!," "Call of the Yukon," "Mutiny in the Arctic," "Power Dive," "Aerial Gunner," "Storm over Lisbon," "When My Baby Smiles at Me," "Torpedo Boat," "Alaska Highway," "Blood on the Sun," "Grand Canyon," "The Last Time I Saw Archie," "Young Fury," "Fort Utah," "Buckskin," and his last "Won Ton Ton, the Dog Who Saved Hollywood." Surviving are his third wife, a daughter, and a son.

ANGELA BADDELEY, 71, British actress, died in London Feb. 22, 1976. She was best known to U.S. audiences as the cook in the tv series "Upstairs, Downstairs." Her films include "The Speckled Band," "Quartet," "Ghost Train," and "Tom Jones." She was married twice and had a son and two daughters. She was the sister of actress Hermione Baddeley.

STANLEY BAKER, 49, British actor, died June 28, 1976 in Malaga, Spain, following an operation for lung cancer. His films include "The Cruel Sea," "Knights of the Round Table," "The Tell-Tale Heart," "Hell Below Zero," "Helen of Troy," "Richard III," "Alexander the Great," "Checkpoint," "Hell Divers," "Lili Marlene," "Paratrooper," "Guns of Navarone," "Concrete Jungle," "Zulu," "Dingaka," "Stiletto," "The Games," "Where's Jack?" "Moon Zero Two," "Butterfly Affair," "Innocent Bystanders." He had been knighted by Queen Elizabeth a month before his death. No reported survivors.

MARGARET BANNERMAN, 79, Canadian-born actress, died Apr. 25, 1976 in Englewood, NJ. After achieving stardom in London, she came to the U.S. in 1937 and appeared on Broadway. Her film credits include "The Loves of Madame duBarry," "Cluny Brown," and "The Homestretch." There were no survivors. She had been twice married and divorced.

ALAN BAXTER, 67, film and stage actor, died of cancer May 8, 1976 in Woodland Hills, CA. From 1935 he appeared in over 60 films including "Mary Burns, Fugitive," "Ramona," "Trail of the Lonesome Pine," "Parole," "Last Gangster," "Big Town Girl," "Gangs of New York," "Each Dawn I Die," "The Lone Wolf Strikes," "Abe Lincoln in Illinois," "Escape to Glory," "Pittsburgh Kid," "Shadow of the Thin Man," "Saboteur," "The Human Comedy," "Judgment at Nuremberg," "This Property Is Condemned," and "Paint Your Wagon." His widow, actress Christy Palmer, survives.

GEORGE DAVID BAXTER, 72, film, stage and tv actor, died Sept. 10, 1976 in New York City. Among his film credits are "Marianne," "The Right to Love," "Dinner at Eight," "Thirty Day Princess," "The Great Flirtation," "Sing Sing Nights," "Sofia," and "Lili." No immediate survivors.

OSCAR BEREGI, 58, Hungarian-born character actor, died of a heart attack Nov. 1, 1976 in Los Angeles, CA. His most prominent film roles were in "The Fiercest Heart," "The Incredible Mr. Limpet," "36 Hours," "Morituri," "Ship of Fools," "Panic in the City," "The Great White Hope," "The Christine Jorgenson Story," "Cactus in the Snow," "Everything You Always Wanted to Know about Sex," and "Young Frankenstein." No reported survivors.

BUSBY BERKELEY, 80, Los Angeles-born choreographer and director, died Mar. 14, 1976 at his home in Palm Springs, CA. He was noted for his extravagant musicals with hundreds of dancers, and his credits include "Babes in Arms," "Gold Diggers of 1935," "42nd Street," "Footlight Parade," "Stage Struck," "Hollywood Hotel," "Strike Up the Band," "Dames," "Wonder Bar," "Varsity Show," "Babes on Broadway," "For Me and My Gal," "The Gang's All Here," "Ziegfeld Girl," "Take Me Out to the Ball Game," "Girl Crazy," and his last in 1963 "Jumbo." He was survived by his sixth wife.

CONNEE BOSWELL, 68, popular singer and actress, died of cancer Oct. 10, 1976 in New York City. She was discovered in the late 1920's singing with her two sisters in their native New Orleans. In 1936 she became a single act after her sisters married, and her recordings sold over 75 million copies. Partially paralyzed by polio, she performed in a wheelchair throughout her career. Among the films in which she appeared are "Artists and Models," "Kiss the Boys Goodbye," "Syncopation," "Moulin Rouge," "Transatlantic Merry-Go-Round," "Senior Prom," "Swing Parade," and "The Big Broadcast." She leaves her sister Helvetia. Her husband died in 1975.

ROMNEY BRENT, 74, Mexican-born Romulo Larrade, film and stage actor, died Sept. 24, 1976 in Mexico City. His screen credits include "East Meets West," "Head over Heels in Love," "Dinner at the Ritz," "School for Husbands," "The Fugitive," "Adventures of Don Juan," "Don't Go Near the Water," "The Sign of Zorro." He is survived by a daughter.

DAVID BRUCE, 61, actor, died of a heart attack May 3, 1976 in Hollywood. Among the films in which he appeared are "The Man Who Talked Too Much," "Sea Hawk," "Sea Wolf," "Sgt. York," "Flying Tigers," "Gung Ho!," "Ladies Courageous," "Christmas Holiday," "Can't Help Singing," "Lady on a Train," "Prejudice," "Young Daniel Boone," "Masterson of Kansas," "Jungle Hell." Surviving is a daughter, actress Amanda McBroom.

GODFREY CAMBRIDGE, 43, New York-born film, stage and tv comedian, died of a heart attack Nov. 29, 1976 on a movie set in Burbank, CA. Adept at either serious or comic roles, his films include "The Last Angry Man," "Gone Are the Days!" "Troublemaker," "The Busy Body," "The President's Analyst," "The Biggest Bundle of Them All," "Bye Bye Braverman," "Watermelon Man," "Cotton Comes to Harlem," "Come Back Charleston Blue," "Whiffs," and "Friday Foster." His second wife and two daughters survive.

| Connee Boswell | Godfrey Cambridge | Jack Cassidy | Lee J. Cobb | Edith Evans | Walter Fitzgerald |

JACK CASSIDY, 49, whose career took him from Broadway musicals to films and tv, died Dec. 12, 1976 in a fire in his Los Angeles apartment. He had appeared in such movies as "Look in Any Window," "FBI Code 98," "Bunny O'Hare," "Eiger Sanction," and "W. C. Fields and Me." He was divorced from actresses Evelyn Ward and Shirley Jones. Surviving are two sons, singer David and actor Shaun Cassidy.

DAME AGATHA CHRISTIE, 85, prolific British writer, and creator of detectives Jane Marple and Hercule Poirot, died Jan. 12, 1976 at her home in Wallingford, Eng. Many of her more than 100 works were made into films, including "Witness for the Prosecution," "Alibi," "Ten Little Indians," "Murder on the Orient Express," "Love from a Stranger," "Murder at the Gallop," and "The Alphabet Murders." She is survived by her second husband, Sir Max Mallowan, and a grandson.

LEE J. COBB, 64, New York-born character actor of stage, screen and tv, died of a heart attack on Feb. 11, 1976 in his home in Woodland Hills, CA. Among his numerous film credits are "Golden Boy," "This Thing Called Love," "Men of Boys Town," "The Moon Is Down," "Song of Bernadette," "Winged Victory," "Anna and the King of Siam," "Captain from Castile," "Call Northside 777," "Miracle of the Bells," "On the Waterfront," "Man in the Gray Flannel Suit," "12 Angry Men," "Three Faces of Eve," "Brothers Karamazov," "Green Mansions," "Exodus," "How the West Was Won," "Come Blow Your Horn," "Our Man Flint," "Coogan's Bluff," "The Exorcist," and his last "The Man Who Loved Cat Dancing." His greatest fame came with the role of Judge Garth in the tv series "The Virginian." Surviving are his second wife, two sons, a daughter, and a step-son.

RAY CORRIGAN, 73, actor who had appeared in 105 films (mostly western), died of a heart attack Aug. 10, 1976 in his home in Brookings Harbor, Ore. Began career as stunt man and double for Tarzan series before being featured as Crash Corrigan in three series: "Darkest Africa," "The Undersea Kingdom," "Painted Stallion." Other films were "Night Life of the Gods," "The Three Mesquiteers" series, "Santa Fe Stampede," "Zamba," "Stagecoach," "Killer Ape," "The Range Busters" series, and "It! The Terror from Outer Space." He was host on a tv series "Danger Is My Business." He is survived by a son, a daughter, and his third wife.

KEVIN COUGHLIN, 30, New York-born film and tv actor for 23 years, died in Los Angeles Jan. 19, 1976 of multiple injuries from a hit-and-run auto accident. Before his Hollywood career, he appeared on Broadway, and the tv series "I Remember Mama." Picture credits include "Storm Center," "The Defiant Ones," "Happy Anniversary," "Duel at Diablo," "Mary Jane," "Wild in the Streets," "The Young Runaways," and "The Gay Deceivers." He is survived by his widow.

GEORGE CURZON, 77, British actor, died May 10, 1976 in London. His film appearances include "Woman in Chains," "After the Ball," "The Man Who Knew Too Much," "Java Head," "Scotland Yard Mystery," "White Angel," "Jamaica Inn," and "Inheritance." No reported survivors.

FRANKIE DARRO, 59, well known child actor who bridged the gap into adult roles, died of a heart attack Dec. 25, 1976 in Huntington Beach, CA. Among his film credits are "So Big," "Kiki," "Circus Kid," "Rainbow Man," "Mad Genius," "Three on a Match," "Wolf Dog," "Tugboat Annie," "Mayor of Hell," "Wild Boys of the Road," "Little Men," "No Greater Glory," "The Pay-Off," "Born to Fight," "Racing Blood," "Saratoga," "Thoroughbreds Don't Cry," "Juvenile Court," "Boy's Reformatory," "Up in the Air," "The Gang's All Here," "Junior Prom," "Angels' Alley," "Hold That Baby!," "Pride of Maryland," "Across the Wide Missouri," "Operation Petticoat," "Hook, Line and Sinker." He also appeared as the old lady on the Red Skelton tv shows. His widow survives.

PAUL DEHN, 63, Academy-Award-winning British screenwriter, died of cancer Sept. 30, 1976 in London. With his collaborator James Bernard he received an "Oscar" for "Seven Days to Noon" in 1952. His other credits include "Orders to Kill," "Goldfinger," "The Spy Who Came in from the Cold," "Night of the Generals," "Taming of the Shrew," "Fragment of Fear," "Orders to Kill," and "The Deadly Affair." No reported survivors.

DOROTHY DEVORE, 77, Texas-born Christie Comedies star in the 1920's died Sept. 10, 1976 in Woodland Hills, CA. She also appeared in such features as "The Narrow Street," "How Baxter Buttered In," "His Majesty Bunker Bean," "The Social Highwayman," and "Senor Daredevil." A sister survives.

CIRO JAMES DIGANGI, 65, film producer, died Aug. 26, 1976 in NYC. His credits include "Once Is Not Enough," "The Man in the Glass Booth," "Badge 373" and "Uptight." His widow and a son survive.

SONIA DRESDEL, 67, British actress, died Jan. 18, 1976 in Canterbury, Eng. Among her film credits are "This Was a Woman," "The Fallen Idol," "The Clouded Yellow," "Trials of Oscar Wilde," "The World Owes Me a Living," "Now and Forever," and "Lady Caroline Lamb." No reported survivors.

LIAM DUNN, 59, film and tv comedian, died of emphysema Apr. 11, 1976 in Granada Hills, CA. He had been working in "The Shaggy D. A." Other roles were in "What's Up, Doc?," "Blazing Saddles," "Young Frankenstein," "Gus," "The Love Bug Rides Again," "World's Greatest Athlete," "Bank Shot," "Peeper," and "Silent Movie." No immediate survivors.

LOUIS F. EDELMAN, 75, producer for more than 40 years, died of a heart ailment Jan. 6, 1976 in Los Angeles, CA. He produced among others, "White Heat," "The Jazz Singer," "You Were Never Lovelier," "Once upon a Time," "Hotel Berlin," "West Point Story," "Operation Pacific," "I'll See You in My Dreams," "Springfield Rifle," "Stop, You're Killing Me," and "Here Comes the Navy." For tv he produced "Make Room for Daddy," "The Big Valley," "Wyatt Earp," and "The Danny Thomas Show." Surviving are his widow and two daughters.

DAME EDITH EVANS, 88, one of the great British actresses of this century, died Oct. 14, 1976 at her home near London. After great acclaim on the stage, she began a film career at 60 and appeared in "Queen of Spades," "Dolwyn," "The Importance of Being Earnest," "The Nun's Story," "Look Back in Anger," "Tom Jones," "Chalk Garden," "Young Cassidy," "The Whisperers," "Fitzwilly," "Prudence and the Pill," "Crooks and Coronets," "Trog," and "The Abbess of Philadelphia." She was the widow of engineer George Booth.

ERNST FEGTE, 78, Academy-Award-winning art director, died of heart complications Dec. 15, 1976 in his Los Angeles home. He won an "Oscar" in 1945 for "Frenchman's Creek." Other credits include "Quebec," "Five Graves to Cairo," "Treasure Chest," "The Angel and the Badman," and "I Wonder Who's Killing Her Now." His widow and a daughter survive.

WALTER FIELD, 101, died June 5, 1976 in Hollywood, CA. He was the oldest American motion picture actor, and had appeared in more than 2000 films, including "Born to Fight," "Les Miserables," "Barbary Coast," "Too Hot to Handle." His last appearance was on tv's "Medical Center." No reported survivors.

WALTER FITZGERALD, 80, British film and stage character actor, died Dec. 20, 1976 in London. Among his credits are "Treasure Island," "In Which We Serve," "Blanche Fury," "This Was a Woman," "Mine Own Executioner," "Edward, My Son," "Fallen Idol," "Winslow Boy," "Pickwick Papers," "Lease of Life," "Third Man on the Mountain," and "Damn the Defiant." Twice married, his survivors include four sons and a daughter.

| James Flavin | Paul Ford | Norman Foster | Jean Gabin | James Wong Howe | Frieda Inescort |

JAMES FLAVIN, 69, character actor in more than 400 films, died of a ruptured aorta Apr. 23, 1976 in Los Angeles, CA. Born in Maine, and a successful Broadway actor, he began his film career in 1932 in "McKenna of the Mounted," followed by, among others, "Back Street," "King Kong," "Riot Squad," "Baby Take a Bow," "Affairs of Cellini," "After Office Hours," "G-Men," "West Point of the Air," "My Man Godfrey," "The Buccaneer," "Ride a Crooked Mile," "Duke of West Point," "Cisco Kid and the Lady," "The Great Profile," "Night of January 16," "Belle Starr," "Gentleman Jim," "Life Begins at 8:30," "Mission to Moscow," "So Proudly We Hail!," "Murder on the Water Front," "Abroad with Two Yanks," "Laura," "Hollywood Canteen," "Spellbound," "Tars and Spars," "Big Sleep," "Nora Prentiss," "Desert Fury," "Nightmare Alley," "One Touch of Venus," "Million Dollar Mermaid," "Here Come the Marines," "The Last Hurrah," "In Cold Blood," "Good Times," "Mister Roberts." His last role was as Pres. Eisenhower in tv's "The Gary Francis Story." He leaves his wife.

PAUL FORD, 74, film, stage and tv character actor, died Apr. 12, 1976 in Mineola, NY after a lengthy illness. He did not begin his acting career until almost 40, but became successful in all media. His greatest popularity was as Colonel Hall in "The Sgt. Bilko Show." His films include "House on 92nd Street," "Naked City," "All the King's Men," "Teahouse of the August Moon," "Matchmaker," "Missouri Traveler," "Advise and Consent," "The Music Man," "It's a Mad Mad Mad World," "Never Too Late," "The Russians Are Coming," "The Comedians," "Skidoo," and "Twinky." He is survived by his widow, two sons and two daughters.

FRANK FOREST, 80, popular singer on radio and in films, died Dec. 23, 1976 in Santa Monica, CA. His film credits include "The Big Broadcast of 1937," "Champagne Waltz," "I'll Take Romance," and "The Count of Luxembourg." His wife and a son survive.

NORMAN FOSTER, 72, popular actor who became a director and screenwriter, died of cancer July 7, 1976 in Santa Monica, CA. Born in Indiana, he went to NY and appeared in several Broadway productions before acting in his first film in 1928. His credits include "Gentlemen of the Press," "Young Man of Manhattan," "Up Pops the Devil," "Steady Company," "The Cohens and the Kellys in Hollywood," "Smilin' Through," "Week-End Marriage," "State Fair," "Pilgrimage," "Orient Express," "Strictly Dynamite," "Escape from Devil's Island," "Hoosier Schoolmaster," "The Bishop Misbehaves," "Behind Green Lights," "The Racket," "June Moon," "Merry Wives of Windsor," and "The Other Side of the Wind." He directed such pictures as "Think Fast, Mr. Moto," "Mr. Moto Takes a Chance," "Charlie Chan at Treasure Island," "Scotland Yard," "Journey into Fear," "Kiss the Blood off My Hands," "Father Is a Bachelor," "Woman on the Run," "Navajo," "Sombrero," and "The Sign of Zorro." Surviving are his wife, former actress Sally Blane, a son and a daughter.

ALBERTA FRANKLIN, 79, silent screen actress, died Mar. 14, 1976 in Mountain View, CA. She had appeared in "Birth of a Nation," "Sunset Strip," "Dance of the Seven Veils," "Devil's Trail," several films with Charlie Chaplin, Tom Mix, and Mary Pickford. She is survived by her husband Paul J. Levy, a son and a daughter.

JEAN GABIN, 72, internationally acclaimed French film star, died of a heart attack Nov. 15, 1976 at the American Hospital in Neuilly, France. His career began on stage at 18 and he was seldom idle thereafter. His greatest films were "They Were Five," "Grand Illusion," "Pepe le Moko," "Les Miserables," and "Port of Shadows." Others among his over 100 films include "Daybreak," "The Walls of Malapaga," "The Room Upstairs,"

"Crime and Punishment," "Inspector Maigret," "Love Is My Profession," "La Bete Humaine," "French Can-Can," and "Le Chat." He was cremated and his ashes scattered at sea. Surviving are two sons and two daughers, and his third wife.

RAY GILBERT, 63, composer and Academy-Award-winning song writer, died Mar. 3, 1976 after heart surgery in Los Angeles. He received the award for "Zip-a-Dee-Doo-Dah" in "Song of the South." He is survived by his wife actress Janis Paige, and a daughter, singer Joanne Gilbert.

MICHAEL GOODLIFFE, 61, British film, stage and tv actor, died of a heart attack Mar. 22, 1976 in London. Among his film credits are "Cry, the Beloved Country," "Sea Devils," "Rob Roy," "Front Page Story," "End of the Affair," "Quentin Durward," "Pursuit of the Graf Spee," "39 Steps," "Seventh Dawn," "Von Ryan's Express," "The Jokers," "A Night to Remember," "Jigsaw," "Cromwell," "Hitler: the Last 10 Days." His widow and three sons survive.

MICHAEL GWYNN, 59, British character actor, died of a heart attack Jan. 29, 1976 in London. His many film credits include "Dunkirk," "Camp on Blood Island," "A Doctor's Dilemma," "Question 7," "Barabbas," "Cleopatra," "The Revenge of Frankenstein," "The Village of the Damned," "No Place Like Homicide." No reported survivors.

BILLY HALOP, 56, leader of the Dead End Kids on Broadway and in films, died in his sleep Nov. 9, 1976. After the film "Dead End," he appeared in "Crime School," "Angels with Dirty Faces," "Little Tough Guy," "Hell's Kitchen," "Dust Be My Destiny," "Angels Wash Their Faces," "Tom Brown's School Days," "Give Us Wings," "Hit the Road," "Blues in the Night," "Tough as They Come," "Dangerous Years," "For Love or Money," "Mr. Buddwing," "Fitzwilly." Recently he had appeared as a barroom friend of Archie Bunker in tv's "All in the Family." Surviving are his mother, a brother, and a sister.

JOSEPH HENABERY, 88, director and actor in silent films, died Feb. 18, 1976 in Woodland Hills, CA. He appeared as Lincoln in "Birth of a Nation," and his directing credits include "Children of the Feud," "His Majesty, the American," "The Stranger," "A Sainted Devil," "Tongues of Flame," and "Moonlight and Honeysuckle." He is survived by his widow, a son, and a daughter.

ARTHUR HORNBLOW, JR., 83, producer, died July 17, 1976 in NYC. He gave up a legal career to become a Broadway producer, and then pictures for almost 40 years. His films include "Bulldog Drummond," "Limehouse Blues," "Ruggles of Red Gap," "Mississippi," "Waikiki Wedding," "High, Wide and Handsome," "Artists and Models Abroad," "Man about Town," "The Cat and the Canary," "Hold Back the Dawn," "Nothing but the Truth," "The Major and the Minor," "Gaslight," "Weekend at the Waldorf," "The Hucksters," "Cass Timberlane," "Asphalt Jungle," "Oklahoma!," "Witness for the Prosecution," and "The War Lovers." Surviving are his widow, and two sons.

FRANCES HOWARD, 73, former actress and widow of Samuel Goldwyn, died July 2, 1976 at her home in Beverly Hills, CA. After appearing in "The Swan," "Too Many Kisses," and "The Shock Punch," she cancelled her contract and married Mr. Goldwyn. She became his close collaborator in the production of many notable movies. She is survived by her son, Samuel Goldwyn, Jr.

JAMES WONG HOWE, 76, award-winning cinematographer who was born in China, died July 12, 1976 in his Hollywood home after a long illness. He was nominated 16 times for an Academy Award, and won for "The Rose Tattoo" and "Hud." Among his many other credits are "Trail of the Lonesome Pine," "Viva Villa," "Algiers," "King's Row," "Yankee Doodle Dandy," "North Star," "Body and Soul," "Come Back, Little Sheba," "Picnic," "Sweet Smell of Success," "The Old Man and the Sea," and his last "Funny Lady." His widow survives.

| Anissa
Jones | Margaret
Leighton | Ruth
McDevitt | Sal
Mineo | Mary
Nash | Barbara
Nichols |

HOWARD HUGHES, 70, former producer, who became a reclusive billionaire, died in a plane en route from Acapulco, Mex., to Houston, Tx. He produced such films as "The Front Page," "Cock of the Air," "Sky Devils," "The Outlaw," "Vendetta," and "Affair with a Stranger." An aunt survives.

FRIEDA INESCORT, 75, Scottish-born stage and screen actress, died of multiple sclerosis, Feb. 21, 1976 in Woodland Hills, CA. Her film career began in 1935 and among the many pictures in which she appeared were "Dark Angel," "Give Me Your Heart," "The King Steps Out," "Mary of Scotland," "Hollywood Boulevard," "Call It a Day," "The Great O'Malley," "Zero Hour," "Tarzan Takes a Son," "The Letter," "Pride and Prejudice," "Trial of Mary Dugan," "Sunny," "Remember the Day," "Courtship of Andy Hardy," "Sweater Girl," "Mission to Moscow," "Indian Summer," "The Judge Steps Out," "A Place in the Sun," "Never Wave at a Wac," "Casanova's Big Night," "Eddy Duchin Story," "Senior Prom," "Alligator People," "The Crowded Sky." A sister survives.

SIDNEY JAMES, 62, British tv and screen comedian, collapsed on stage in Sunderland, Eng, and died shortly thereafter on Apr. 26, 1976. His credits include "Give Us This Day," "The Lavendar Hill Mob," "The Assassin," "Miss Robin Hood," "A King in New York," "Iron Petticoat," "Too Many Crooks," "Upstairs and Downstairs," "The Pure Hell of St. Trinian's," "No Place like Homicide," "Carry on Cleo." No reported survivors.

ANISSA JONES, 18, who played Buffy in the tv series "Family Affair," was found dead Aug. 29, 1976 from an overdose of barbiturates. She had also appeared in the Elvis Presley film "The Trouble with Girls."

FUZZY KNIGHT, 74, Virginia-born comedian of western films, died in his sleep Feb. 23, 1976 in Hollywood. His credits include many western films with Johnny Mack Brown, Tex Ritter, Russ Hayden and Bob Baker, and "She Done Him Wrong," "Moulin Rouge," "Music in the Air," "Trail of the Lonesome Pine," "And Sudden Death," "County Fair," "Spawn of the North," "The Cowboy and the Lady," "Union Pacific," "My Little Chickadee," "Johnny Apollo," "Butch Minds the Baby," "Juke Girl," "Corvette K-225," "Frisco Sal," "The Egg and I," "Down to the Sea in Ships," "Honeychile," and "Waco." His wife survives.

FRITZ LANG, 85, Viennese-born film director, died Aug. 2, 1976 in Los Angeles after a long illness. He was probably best known for "M" which he made before fleeing Nazi Germany. Other films are "Siegfried," "Metropolis," "Dr. Mabuse," "Spies," "Liliom," "Fury," "You Only Live Once," "Western Union," "Man Hunt," "The Last Will of Dr. Mabuse," "Hangmen Also Die," "The Woman in the Window," "Ministry of Fear," "Scarlet Street," "Clash by Night," "The Blue Gardenia," "The Big Heat," "While the City Cries," "Rancho Notorious," "Beyond a Reasonable Doubt," and "Journey to the Lost City." He was divorced from writer Thea von Harbou.

CHARLES LEDERER, 65, screenwriter, died Mar. 5, 1976 in Los Angeles. His screenplays include "Front Page," "Topaze," "Broadway Serenade," "Slightly Dangerous," "Kiss of Death," "Can-Can," "Mutiny on the Bounty," "Follow that Dream," and "A Global Affair." Surviving are his widow, former actress Anne Shirley, a son, and a step-daughter.

MARGARET LEIGHTON, 53, British stage and screen actress, died of multiple sclerosis Jan. 13, 1976 in Chichester, Eng. Among the 22 films in which she appeared are "The Astonished Heart," "Under Capricorn," "Winslow Boy," "The Holly and the Ivy," "The Constant Husband," "The Sound and the Fury," "Waltz of the Toreadors," "The Best Man," "7 Women," and "Madwoman of Chaillot." Her last performance was in the tv film "Great Expectations." She is survived by her third husband, Michael Wilding.

ROGER LIVESEY, 69, Welch-born character actor for 50 years on stage, film and tv, died Feb. 5, 1976 in Watford, Eng. His films include "Drums," "The Life and Death of Colonel Blimp," "Stairway to Heaven," "I Know Where I'm Going," "The Entertainer," "Of Human Bondage," "Oedipus the King," and "Hamlet." His wife, actress Ursula Jeans, died in 1973.

ROBERT LORD, 75, writer and producer, died of a heart attack Apr. 5, 1976 in Los Angeles, CA. He received an Academy Award in 1932 for his screenplay "One Way Passage." For Humphrey Bogart he produced "Knock on Any Door," "Tokyo Joe," "In a Lonely Place" and "Sirocco." Surviving are two daughters.

JUDITH LOWRY, 86, stage, screen and tv character actress, died of a heart attack Nov. 29, 1976 while walking with her son in NYC. She was best known for her Mother Dexter on the tv series "Phyllis." Her film appearances include "The Trouble with Angels," "The Tiger Makes Out," "Valley of the Dolls," "Popi," "The Night They Raided Minsky's," "Sweet Charity," "Ladybug, Ladybug," "On a Clear Day You Can See Forever," "Cold Turkey," "Anderson Tapes," "Superdad." She is survived by nine children.

NINO MARTINI, 72, lyric tenor of opera, concert, radio and film, died of a heart attack Dec. 9, 1976 in his native Verona, Italy. His motion pictures were "Paramount on Parade," "Here's to Romance," "Gay Desperado," "Music for Madame," and "One Night with You." His widow survives.

RUTH McDEVITT, 80, Michigan-born stage, screen and tv character actress, died May 27, 1976 in her Hollywood home. After the death of her husband in 1936 she decided to become an actress and made her Broadway debut in 1940. Her films include "The Guy Who Came Back," "The Trap," "Boys' Night Out," "Love Is a Ball," "The Birds," "Dear Heart," "The Out-of-Towners," "The Shakiest Gun in the West," "An Angel in My Pocket," "Change of Habit." Her last appearance was on the tv series "Phyllis." No reported survivors.

JOHNNY MERCER, 66, Academy-Award winning songwriter, died June 25, 1976 in his home in Bel Air, CA. His four songs to receive "Oscars" were "On the Atchison, Topeka and the Santa Fe," "In the Cool, Cool, Cool of the Evening," "Moon River," and "Days of Wine and Roses." He collaborated with the most outstanding composers of the last 50 years, and produced a multitude of hit songs. He was married to former dancer Ginger McHan.

SAL MINEO, 37, New York-born actor of stage, screen and tv, was stabbed to death Feb. 12, 1976 as he was returning home from a play rehearsal. He was nominated for an Academy Award for his performances in "Rebel without a Cause," and "Exodus." Other film credits include "Six Bridges to Cross," "Crime in the Streets," "Somebody Up There Likes Me," "Giant," "The Longest Day," "Greatest Story Ever Told," "Gene Krupa Story," "Who Killed Teddy Bear?," "The Challengers." Surviving are his mother, a sister, and two brothers.

MARY NASH, 92, stage and film actress whose career spanned 40 years, died Dec. 3, 1976 in her Brentwood, CA. home. After stardom on Broadway, she began her film-making in 1936. Among her pictures were "The King and the Chorus Girl," "Easy Living," "Heidi," "Wells Fargo," "The Little Princess," "The Rains Came," "The Philadelphia Story," "The Human Comedy," "Monsieur Beaucaire," and "Till the Clouds Roll By." She was married briefly to actor Jose Ruben. No immediate survivors.

BARBARA NICHOLS, 47, movie and tv actress, died Oct. 5, 1976 in Hollywood after a long coma caused by liver complications. She had appeared in 28 films, including "Miracle in the Rain," "Sweet Smell of Success," "Pal Joey," "Pajama Game," "The Naked and the Dead," "The Disorderly Orderly," "The Swinger," "The Power." Her parents survive.

| Rex O'Malley | Lily Pons | Ronald Radd | Paul Robeson | Gene Roth | Shimen Ruskin |

REX O'MALLEY, 75, British-born stage and film actor, died May 1, 1976 in NYC. He came to the U.S. in 1927 and appeared on Broadway before making his film debut. His picture credits include "Camille," "Zaza," "Midnight," "The Thief," and "Taxi." No known survivors.

LILY PONS, 71, French-born coloratura star of the Metropolitan Opera for 25 years, died of cancer Feb. 13, 1976 in Dallas, TX. She appeared in four films: "I Dream Too Much," "That Girl from Paris," "Hitting a New High," and "Carnegie Hall." She was divorced from Andre Kostelanetz. A sister survives.

MAUDIE PRICKETT, 62, character actress who appeared in over 400 films, died of uremic poisoning Apr. 14, 1976 in Pasadena, CA. Among her many credits are "Two-Fisted Stranger," "Lone Hand Texan," "Song of Idaho," "Messenger of Peace," "Her First Romance," "Stars and Stripes Forever," "A Man Called Peter," "Phantom Stagecoach," "Legend of Tom Dooley," "North by Northwest," "The Gnome-mobile," "Rascal," and "Maltese Bippy." Surviving are a son and a daughter.

RONALD RADD, 47, British-born actor, died of a brain hemorrhage Apr. 23, 1976 in Toronto, CAN. where he was appearing. His film credits include "Camp on Blood Island," "Where the Spies Are," "The Sea Gull," "Kremlin Letter," "Spiral Staircase," "Galileo," and "Operation Daybreak." His wife and three children survive.

WILLIAM REDFIELD, 49, actor on stage, film and tv, who began his career at age of 9, died Aug. 17, 1976 in NYC of a respiratory ailment complicated by leukemia. His film credits include "Back Door to Heaven," "The Proud and the Profane," "I Married a Woman," "Hamlet," "Morituri," "Duel at Diablo," "Fantastic Voyage," and "One Flew over the Cuckoo's Nest." Surviving are a son and a daughter, and his second wife.

SIR CAROL REED, 69, British director, died of a heart attack Apr. 25, 1976 in his London home. He received an Academy Award for "Oliver" in 1968. Other notable films include "The Third Man," "Odd Man Out," "The Fallen Idol," "Our Man in Havana," "The Stars Look Down," "Night Train," "Young Mr. Pitt," "The Man Between," "Outcast of the Islands," "The Key," "Kipps," "The Agony and the Ecstasy." He was knighted in 1952. Surviving are his second wife, actress Penelope Ward, and a son.

JULIAN RIVERO, 85, stage and screen actor, and director, died Feb. 24, 1976 in Hollywood, CA. He appeared in many westerns, and in "Kid from Spain," "Dancing Pirate," "Heroes of the Alamo," "That Night with You," "Amazon Quest," "The Reward." He also acted in several tv series. A daughter survives.

PAUL ROBESON, 77, internationally recognized singer and actor, died Jan. 23, 1976 in Philadelphia following a stroke. After Broadway success, he appeared in the films "The Emperor Jones," "Sanders of the River," "Show Boat," "King Solomon's Mines," "The Song of Freedom," "Dark Sands," "Jericho," "The Proud Valley," "Native Land," and "Tales of Manhattan." He is survived by a son, and a sister.

MAXIE ROSENBLOOM, 71, actor and former boxer, died of Paget's disease Mar. 6, 1976 in South Pasadena, CA. In 1932 he became the light-heavyweight champion of the world, but lost the title in 1934. He then devoted his time to films, including "Mr. Broadway," "King for a Night," "Don't Pull Your Punches," "Nothing Sacred," "The Kid Comes Back," "Each Dawn I Die," "Louisiana Purchase," "Follow the Boys," "Hazard," "Skipalong Rosenbloom," "Mr. Universe," "Beat Generation." Three brothers and two sisters survive.

GENE ROTH, 73, South Dakota-born character actor, died July 19, 1976 in Los Angeles after being struck by a car while crossing the street. He was born Gene Stutenroth and used that name for several years before shortening it. He appeared in over 190 films, including "Baron of Arizona," "Red Planet Mars," "The Farmer Takes a Wife," "Strange Death of Adolph Hitler," "Secret Agent X9," "Nightmare Alley," "Alaska Patrol," "Montana Belle," "Three Stooges Meet Hercules," "Tormented," "The Spider," "Ada," "Twice Told Tales," "Young Dillinger," and "Rosie." Surviving are a son and a daughter.

SHIMEN RUSKIN, 69, stage, screen and tv character actor, died of cancer Apr. 23, 1976 in Los Angeles, CA. Among his many screen appearances were roles in "Fiddler on the Roof," "The Producers," "Love and Death," "Body and Soul," "Murder My Sweet," "Letter to an Unknown Woman," and "Dark Passage." Surviving are his widow, and a son.

ROSALIND RUSSELL, 65, versatile star of stage and screen, died of cancer Nov. 28, 1976 in her Beverly Hills, CA. home. After her Hollywood career began in 1933, she appeared in such films as "Evelyn Prentice," "Forsaking All Others," "Reckless," "China Seas," "Craig's Wife," "Night Must Fall," "The Citadel," "Fast and Loose," "The Women," "His Girl Friday," "No Time for Comedy," "Woman of Distinction," "Picnic," "Gypsy," "Where Angels Go." She was nominated for an Academy Award for performances in "My Sister Eileen," "Sister Kenny," "Mourning Becomes Electra", and "Auntie Mame." She is survived by her husband, producer Frederick Brisson, and a son.

JEAN SERVAIS, 65, Belgian-born French actor, died of heart failure after an operation Feb. 17, 1976 in Paris. He had appeared in many plays, and over 50 films that include "Les Miserables," "La Danse de Mort," "Riptide," "Rififi," "He Who Must Die," "Tamango," "The World in My Pocket," "Crime Does Not Pay," "That Man from Rio," "Lost Command," "Every Man Is My Enemy," "Better a Widow," "They Came to Rob Las Vegas." No reported survivors.

LEO SHUKEN, 69, composer, died July 24, 1976 in Santa Monica, CA. He received an Academy Award in 1939 for his score for "Stagecoach." Other scores were "Waikiki Wedding," "Artists and Models Abroad," and "The Greatest Story Ever Told." He leaves his widow and two sons.

ALASTAIR SIM, 75, versatile British stage and screen actor, died of cancer Aug. 19, 1976 in London. During his 45 years of acting, he performed in over 30 films, including "Lavendar Hill Mob," "An Inspector Calls," "The Green Man," "The Happiest Day of Your Life," "Belles of St. Trinian's," "A Christmas Carol," "Green for Danger," "Hue and Cry," "Laughter in Paradise," "Folly to Be Wise," "Innocents in Paris," "Wee Geordie," "Escapade," "Blue Murder at St. Trinian's," "A School for Scoundrels," "The Millionairess," "The Anatomist," "Escape from the Dark." His widow and a daughter survive.

WILLIAM V. SKALL, 78, cinematographer, died Mar. 22, 1976 in Los Angeles after a long illness. He received an Academy Award in 1948 for "Joan of Arc," and was nominated nine times for works including "Quo Vadis" and "The Silver Chalice." His widow survives.

VIKTOR STANITSYN, 79, for 40 years a leading actor, producer and art director of the Moscow Art Theatre, died Dec. 24, 1976 in Moscow. Among his many film credits are "Men and Jobs," "Paris Commune," "Jubilee," "The First Front," and "War and Peace." No reported survivors.

| **Rosalind Russell** | **Alistair Sim** | **Sybil Thorndike** | **Victor Varconi** | **Bruno VeSota** | **Linda Watkins** |

LEONORA SUMMERS, 78, former dancer and comedienne, died June 29, 1976 in Woodland Hills, CA. She left Broadway for Hollywood in 1925 and appeared in many Mack Sennett comedies, co-starring with Billy Bevan and Alice Day, and in "Sea Beast," "Ben-Hur," "Hoboken to Hollywood," and "Her Actor Friend." She is survived by her husband, one-time junior welterweight champion Mushy Callahan, and a son.

WILLIAM TANNEN, 65, character actor, died Dec. 2, 1976 in Woodland Hills, CA. His film career began in his native NY in 1934 in "The Band Plays On," followed by, among others, "Crash Donovan," "When Love Is Young," "New Moon," "Flight Command," "Whistling in the Dark," "Dr. Jekyll and Mr. Hyde," "Woman of the Year," "Stand By for Action," "Alaska Patrol," "New Mexico," "Chain Gang," "Blue Blood," "Jungle Jim," "Dangerous Crossing," "Sitting Bull," "The Tijuana Story," "Noose for a Gunman." His wife survives.

RAY TEAL, 74, character actor in over 200 pictures, died Apr. 2, 1976 in Santa Monica, CA. For 13 years he was Sheriff Coffee on tv's "Bonanza" series. His films include "Western Jamboree," "Adventures of Red Ryder," "Northwest Passage," "They Died with Their Boots On," "A Wing and a Prayer," "Captain Kidd," "Along Came Jones," "The Best Years of Our Lives," "Bandit of Sherwood Forest," "Blondie Knows Best," "Till the Clouds Roll By," "Road to Rio," "Brute Force," "Driftwood," "Countess of Monte Cristo," "Joan of Arc," "Once More, My Darling," "No Way Out," "The Men," "Winchester 73," "Distant Drums," "Carrie," "Wild North," "About Mrs. Leslie," "A Band of Angels," "Decision at Sundown," "Girl on the Run," "Inherit the Wind," "One-Eyed Jacks," "Judgment at Nuremberg," "Bullet for a Badman," and "Taggart." No reported survivors.

DAME SYBIL THORNDIKE, 93, versatile British actress for 70 years, died from a heart attack June 9, 1976 in her home in London. Although she disliked films, she appeard in many of them, including "Dawn," "Nine Days a Queen," "Major Barbara," "Nicholas Nickleby," "Stage Fright," "Melba," "The Prince and the Showgirl," "Hand in Hand," "The Big Gamble." Her husband of 61 years, actor-manager Lewis Casson, died in 1969. Two sons and two daughters survive.

DALTON TRUMBO, 70, Colorado-born screenwriter, died of a heart attack Sept. 10, 1976 in his Los Angeles home. He was the most famous member of the imprisoned and blacklisted "Hollywood Ten." He received an Academy Award 25 years after it was awarded to Robert Rich, his pseudonym, for "The Brave One." Other screenplays were "Flying Irishman," "Five Came Back," "Bill of Divorcement," "Kitty Foyle," "A Guy Named Joe," "30 Seconds over Tokyo," "Our Vines Have Tender Grapes," "Spartacus," "Exodus," "Lonely Are the Brave," "Hawaii," "Papillon," and "The Fixer." Surviving are his widow, a son and two daughters.

VICTOR VARCONI, 80, versatile Hungarian-born actor, died of a heart attack June 16, 1976 in Santa Barbara, CA. He was brought to Hollywood in 1924 by Cecil B. DeMille for "Triumph," and subsequently appeared in "King of Kings," "Divine Lady," "Feet of Clay," "Changing Husbands," "Volga Boatman," "Chicago," "Roberta," "Big City," "Suez," "Submarine Patrol," "Strange Cargo," "My Story of Vernon and Irene Castle," "My Favorite Blond," "For Whom the Bell Tolls," "The Hitler Gang," "Samson and Delilah," "Atomic Submarine." No reported survivors.

BRUNO VeSOTA, 54, Chicago-born screen, stage, tv actor-director, died of a heart attack Sept. 24, 1976 in Culver City, CA. He was probably best known for his role as the bartender in tv's "Bonanza" series, but appeared in over 50 films, usually as the fat villain, in such pictures as "Daddy-O," "The Choppers," "Attack of the Giant Leeches," "The Wild One," "The Undead," "Hot Car Girl," "Cat Burglar," "Wild Rovers," and "Million Dollar Duck." He directed "Female Jungle," "Brain Eaters," and "Invasion of the Star Creatures." Surviving are his widow and six children.

LUCHINO VISCONTI, 69, Italian film director, died Mar. 30, 1976 at his home in Rome from influenza complicated by a cardiac ailment. Among his credits, are "Bellissima," "White Nights," "Rocco and His Brothers," "Boccaccio '70," "The Leopard," "La Terra Trema," "The Damned," "Death In Venice," "Ludwig," and his last "The Innocent." A bachelor, there are no reported survivors.

MURVYN VYE, 63, stage and screen character actor, died Aug. 17, 1976 in Pompano Beach, FL., while on vacation. He appeared in 47 films including "Golden Earrings," "Whispering Smith," "A Connecticut Yankee," "Road to Bali," "River of No Return," "Escape to Burma," "The Best Things in Life Are Free," "Al Capone," "King of the Roaring '20's," "Andy." No reported survivors.

NED WASHINGTON, 75, composer and songwriter, died of a heart ailment Dec. 20, 1976 in Los Angeles, CA. He won Academy Awards for his score for "Pinocchio," and the songs "When You Wish upon a Star," and "High Noon." Some of the best known of his hundreds of songs are "The Nearness of You," "My Foolish Heart," "Stella by Starlight," "I Don't Stand a Ghost of a Chance," "Smoke Rings," "I'm Getting Sentimental over You," "La Cucaracha," "Cosi-Cosa." He also wrote lyrics for 140 songs. He is survived by his widow and a daughter.

LINDA WATKINS, 68, Boston-born stage and screen actress, died Oct. 31, 1976 in Santa Monica, CA. She made her Broadway debut at 16 and went to Hollywood in 1931. Her films include "Sob Sister," "Good Sport," "Gay Caballero," "Cheaters at Play," "Going Steady," "10 North Frederick," "As Young as We Are," "Cash McCall," "The Parent Trap," and "Good Neighbor Sam." She was the widow of lawyer Gabriel Hess.

NILES WELCH, 88, Broadway actor, and leading man of many silent and early talking pictures, died Nov. 21, 1976 at his home in Laguna Niguel, CA. His film credits include "A Little Child Shall Lead Them," "Stepping Out," "From Rags to Riches," "May Man," "Wine of Youth," "Night Club Lady," "Silver Dollar," "Let's Fall in Love," "Singing Vagabond," "Empty Saddles." His widow survives.

CECIL WESTON, 86, actress, died of pneumonia Aug. 7, 1976 in Hollywood. Among her many screen credits are "Dude Ranch," "Huckleberry Finn," "Behold My Wife," "Banjo on My Knee," "This Land Is Mine," "Mr. Belvedere Rings the Bell." She was the widow of cameraman-producer Fred Balshofer.

ADOLPH ZUKOR, 103, Hungarian-born pioneer producer, died in his sleep June 10, 1976 in his Los Angeles apartment. His success began with penny arcades offering moving peepshows that evolved into nickelodeon theatres offering longer, larger moving pictures. On July 12, 1912 he premiered the first feature length film, "Queen Elizabeth" that starred French actress Sarah Bernhardt and ran for 40 minutes. Subsequently he became president of the giant movie production and distribution empire, Paramount Pictures Corporation. In 1914 he produced the first American-made feature film "The Prisoner of Zenda," followed by such other successes as "Count of Monte Cristo," "Tess of the D'Urbervilles," "The Sheik," and "The Covered Wagon." He was also credited with personally bringing to the screen some of the industry's great stars. Surviving are a son and a daughter, five grandchildren and 10 great-grandchildren.

INDEX

A Letter to Three Wives, 160
A Tree Grows in Brooklyn, 160
Aarons, Leroy, 18
Abbey, John, 213
Abbott, Christine, 144
Abbott, John, 215
Abel, Alan, 139
Abel, Jeanne, 139
Abel, Walter, 215
Abelew, Alan, 131
Abey, Dennis, 140
Able, Albert, 118
Abraham, F. Murray, 18, 78
Abrams, Barry, 149
Abrams, Drew, 134
Abrams, Rita, 114
Abrams, Robert L., 174
Abramson, Bernie, 149, 150
Ackerman, Jack, 129
Ackerman, Leslie, 131
Ackerman, Ron, 139
Ackland-Snow, Brian, 176
Across the Great Divide, 150
Actors, Allen J., 142
Adam and Nicole, 207
Adam, Ken, 94
Adams, Carol, 148
Adams, Dave, 140
Adams, Dorothy, 126
Adams, Edie, 215
Adams, Eve, 130
Adams, Julie, 148, 215
Adams, Maud, 215
Adams, Richard, 127
Adams, Stanley, 136, 145
Adams, Suzi, 129
Adamson, Al, 135, 140
Addams, Dawn, 215
Addison, John, 68, 94, 140
Addy, Wesley, 102
Adeolu, Funso, 135
Ader, Michele, 110
Ades, Dan, 34
Adetoye, Olubji, 134
Adios Amigo, 126
Adjani, Isabelle, 42, 201, 215
Adler, Bill, 138
Adler, Joseph, 145
Adler, Luther, 124, 127, 215
Adler, Michele, 120
Adlum, Ed, 128, 130
Adolphson, Kristina, 178
Adorf, Mario, 213
Adrain, Linda, 149
Adreota, Paul, 206
Adrian, Iris, 118, 215
Adrisano, Gui, 12
Adu, Jab, 135
Adventures of Frontier Fremont, The, 148
Affair, 211
Affairs of Janice, The, 149
African Queen, The, 160
Agar, John, 116, 215
Age, 189
Agony and Ecstasy of Michael, Angelo and David, The, 130
Aguilar, Luz Maria, 210
Agutter, Jenny, 58, 59, 215
Aherne, Brian, 215
Ahn, Philip, 215
Aicardi, Federico, 204
Aiello, Danny, 82
Aimee, Anouk, 215
Airhart, Ted, 147
Airport, 161
Ajaye, Franklyn, 86
Akins, Claude, 215
Alabiso, Eugenio, 195
Albani, Maria Theresa, 189
Alberghetti, Anna Maria, 215
Alberoni, Sherry, 127
Albert, Eddie, 31, 143, 215
Albert, Edward, 56, 57, 215
Albert, Jerry, 114
Albertini, Bitto, 213
Alberts, J. Van Zyl, 200
Albertson, Jack, 161, 215
Albertson, Norbert, 206
Albin, Andy, 128
Albrecht, Marcy, 150
Albright, Lola, 215
Alda, Alan, 215
Alda, Robert, 89, 130, 209, 215
Alda, Rutanya, 12
Alderman, John, 142
Aldredge, Theoni V., 44, 102
Aldredge, Tom, 135

Aldridge, James, 140
Alejandro, Miguel, 215
Alesia, Frank, 143
Alex & the Gypsy, 96
Alexander, Dick, 127
Alexander, Jane, 18, 215
Alexander, Sooren, 145
Alexander, Victor, 131
Alexandre, Manola, 207
Alexsandre, Patrice, 42
Alfie Darling, 206
Ali, Anne, 145
Alias, Angelina, 203
Alice, Mary, 133
Alice Doesn't Live Here Anymore, 161
Alice in Wonderland, 138
All about Eve, 160
All in Place, Nothing in Order, 164
All Night Long, 132
All Quiet on the Western Front, 160
All Screwed Up, 164
All the King's Men, 160
All the President's Men, 18, 161
All This and World War II, 150
All-American Woman, The, 136
Allen, Sean, 134
Allbritton, Louise, 215
Allegret, Catherine, 204
Allegro, Joseph, 214
Allen, Argy, 137
Allen, Dede, 34
Allen, Don, 215
Allen, Gary, 132
Allen, Jonelle, 134
Allen, Kip, 133
Allen, Nancy, 98, 99
Allen, Rex, 132, 215
Allen, Sheila, 211
Allen, Stanford C., 48
Allen, Steve, 215
Allen, Woody, 6, 82, 83, 215
Allentuck, Katherine, 215
Allison, Arlene, 129
Allison, Bart, 78
Allum, Erik, 211
Allum, Kerstii, 211
Allyn, Alyce, 232
Allyson, June, 215
Almagor, Gila, 208
Almanzar, James, 149
Almendros, Nestor, 191, 211, 213
Alonzo, John A., 28, 130
Alpha Beta, 187
Alraune, Lorraine, 130, 140
Alroe, Leslie, 140
Alsberg, Arthur, 10, 64
Altman, Robert, 52
Alto, Bobby, 148
Altschuler, Jane Brodsky, 150
Alvarez, Abraham, 137
Alves, Joe, 40
Amarcord, 161
Amateau, Rod, 136
Amazing Dr. Jekyll, The, 145
Amazing World of Psychic Phenomena, The, 149
Ambler, Eric, 213
Ameche, Don, 215
Amelio, Lucio, 162
Amend, Nick, 84
Ament, Donald S., 142
America at the Movies, 146
American Film Institute, 146
Ames, Don, 44
Ames, Ed, 215
Ames, Leon, 215
Ames, Lionel, 142
Amicucci, Gian-Franco, 204
Amman, Alicia, 213
Amnette, Debra D., 205
Amon, Glenn C., 30
Amorous Adventures of Don Quixote and Sancho Panza, The, 132
Amos, John, 215
Amos, Pharaoh, 126
Amsler, Joe, 114
An American in Paris, 160
Anastasia, 150, 161
Ancore, Joseph, Jr., 137
Anden, Mathew, 114
Anders, Darlene, 140
Anders, Luana, 34
Anderson, Bill, 118, 141, 207
Anderson, Christina, 118
Anderson, Edwina, 143
Anderson, Ernie, 143

Anderson, Gilbert M., 161
Anderson, Haskell V., III, 145
Anderson, Jamie, 144
Anderson, Judith, 215
Anderson, Michael, Jr., 58, 74, 134, 215
Anderson, Shelby, 141
Anderson, Steve, 36
Anderson, Sylvia, 140
Anderson, Warner, 232
Anderson, William, 135
Andersson, Bibi, 213, 215
Andes, Keith, 215
Andor-Palfi, Lotta, 92
Andre, E. J., 114
Andreota, Paul, 206
Andress, Ursula, 202, 204, 215
Andrews, Dana, 104, 215
Andrews, edward, 215
Andrews, Harry, 131, 207, 215
Andrews, Julie, 161, 215
Andrews, Marie, 129
Andrews, Sally, 131
Andrews, Tige, 104
Andriatti, Sesto, 206
Andros, Spiros, 88
Anfosso, Gerard, 184
Angel, Heather, 215
Angel on Fire, 141
Angels, 134
Angels, Maurice, 214
Angermeyer, Heinz, 214
Angiolini, Renato, 201
Ankrum, David, 136
Annerl, Mark, 129
Annie, 206
Ann-Margret, 214, 215
Anonymous Avenger, The, 202
Ansara, Michael, 215
Anthony, Bree, 126, 127, 130, 142, 145
Anthony, Brian, 206
Anthony, Frank, 145
Anthony, Marc, 126, 127, 132
Anthony, Tony, 206, 215
Anthony Adverse, 160
Antoinesse, Collette, 138
Antonelli, Laura, 210, 213
Antonio, Jim, 80
Antonutti, Omero, 189
Anzel, Hy, 144
Apanowicz, Kathryn, 84
Apartment, The, 161
A*P*E*, 147
Aplon, Boris, 107
Appleby, George, 207
Appleseth, Mary Ann, 145
Appleton, Peter, 52
Aprile, Salvatore, 129
Aragones, Sergio, 77
Arata, Frank, 127
Arbus, Allan, 20
Arcanel, Yves, 213
Archer, Anne, 55, 134
Archer, John, 215
Archer, Kate, 107
Archerd, Army, 128
Archerd, Selma, 44
Ardell, Deirdre, 142
Ardell, Gretchen, 142
Arden, Eve, 215
Arden, Jane, 211
Ardinger, H. T., Jr., 30
Ardito, Gino, 96
Arduini, Giovanni, 164
Arel, Fabienne, 203
Arens, Peter, 203
Arestrup, Niels, 198
Argento, Claudio, 208
Argento, Dario, 208
Argento, Salvatore, 208
Argenziano, Carmen, 134
Argiaga, Michael, 98
Aris, Ben, 78, 124, 206
Arkin, Adam, 137
Arkin, Alan, 94, 95, 215
Arkin, David, 18, 142
Arkoff, Louis S., 143
Arkoff, Samuel Z., 54, 80, 88, 139, 209
Arkush, Allan, 142
Arlen, Richard, 232
Arliss, George, 160
Armdexter, Bradford, 138
Armelino, Raymond, 147
Armet, Xavier, 213
Armitage, George, 134
Armstrong, Bridget, 196
Armstrong, Peter, 139
Armstrong, R. G., 22, 127, 136, 145
Armstrong, R. L., 34
Armstrong, William H., 147

Armus, Sidney, 114
Arnaz, Desi, 133, 215
Arnaz, Desi, Jr., 215
Arness, James, 215
Arnett, James, 133
Arno, Alice, 202, 213
Arnold, Christopher, 144
Arnold, Denny, 58
Arnold, Pia I., 174
Arnoud, Erica, 201
Aronis, Dimitri, 133
Aronoff, Maria, 132
Aronovitch, Ricardo, 198, 214
Aronson, Brad, 139
Around the World in 80 Days, 161
Arpino, Giovanni, 201
Arrabal, Fernando, 206
Arrants, Rod, 147
Arrick, Rose, 120
Arrigo, Frank, 131
Arsan, Emmanuelle, 202
Arthur, Beatrice, 215
Arthur, Carol, 48
Arthur, George, 136
Arthur, Jean, 215
Arthur, Karen, 134
Arthur, Maureen, 44
Arthur, Robert, 215
Arvanitis, George, 133
Asaro, Joey, 150
Ash, Carl, 126
Ashby, Hal, 122
Ashe, Michael, 133
Ashford, Emmett, 36
Ashley, Elizabeth, 139, 215
Ashley, Graham, 206
Ashley, Jennifer, 138
Ashley, Seymour, 126, 127
Asner, Edward, 64, 65
Assault on Agathon, 133
Assault on Precinct 13, 148
Asseyev, Tamara, 136
Ast, Pat, 22
Astaire, Fred, 38, 160, 215
Astin, John, 215
Astor, Mary, 160, 215
Astruc, Jenny, 207
Astyr, Bobby, 126, 127, 145, 148, 149
At the Earth's Core, 209
Atherton, William, 215
Atkin, Harvey, 112
Atkins, Eileen, 167
Atkins, Tom, 63
Atomettes, The, 65
Attenborough, Richard, 215
Attmore, Billy, 141
Atwater, Edith, 24
Auberjonois, Rene, 62, 116, 215
Aubrey, Elizabeth, 201
Aubrey, James T., 80
Auclair, Michel, 165
Audran, Stephane, 204
Auger, Claudine, 215
August, Amedeus, 210
Aulbaugh, Lynn, 84
Aulin, Ewa, 215
Aumont, Jean-Pierre, 203, 215
Aumont, Michel, 210
Aumont, Tina, 88
Aured, Carlos, 205, 210
Austin, Bud, 120
Austin, Dero, 36
Austin, Gary, 142
Austin, Gordon, 144
Austin, Ursula, 214
Autobiography of a Flea, The, 145
Autrey, Waldo, 150
Autry, Gene, 215
Avakian, Aram, 97
Avalon, Frankie, 215
Avedis, Hikmet, 147
Avery, Lawrence, 149
Avery, Margaret, 142
Avery, Val, 44, 129
Avildsen, Christopher, 107
Avildsen, John G., 100, 161
Avron, Philippe, 204
Awakening of Annie, The, 210
Awful Truth, The, 160
Axelrod, David A., 142
Axtell, Kirk, 69
Ayaye, Franklyn, 43
Ayers, Billy, 137
Aylmer, Felix, 215
Ayres, Lew, 215
Ayres, Rosalind, 194
Azcona, Rafael, 207, 208
Aznavour, Charles, 131, 204, 215
Bandage, Ace, 137

Baby Blue Marine, 137
Bacall, Lauren, 72, 73, 144, 215
Bacalov, Enriquez Louis, 188
Bach, Barbara, 202
Backes, Alice, 128
Backlar, Marshall, 144
Backus, Jim, 215
Bacon, James, 143
Bad and the Beautiful, The, 160
Bad Bunch, The, 147
Bad Girl, 160
Bad News Bears, The, 28
Baddeley, Angela, 232
Baddeley, Hermione, 215
Badham, John, 36
Baer, Harry, 203
Baer, Max, 45
Baerma, Bub, 140
Bagetta, Vincent, 40, 107
Bagley, Don, 136
Bagley, Fuddle, 141, 150
Bail, Chuck, 143
Bailbondsman, The, 96
Bailey, Charles, 82
Bailey, John, 134
Bailey, Pearl, 77, 215
Baillot, Pierre, 165
Bain, Barbara, 215
Bain, Sherry, 106, 146
Bainter, Fay, 160
Baio, Scott, 84, 85
Baird, Stuart, 60
Bakalyan, Dick, 118
Baker, Buddy, 10, 118, 141
Baker, Carroll, 210, 215
Baker, Diane, 150, 215
Baker, Lenny, 12, 13
Baker, Lisa, 144
Baker, Lynn, 147
Baker, Mark, 68
Baker, Stanley, 232
Baker, Virginia, 149
Baker's Hawk, 149, 150
Balaban, Robert, 216
Balachoff, Peter, 138
Baladimas, Kostas, 133
Balaski, Belinda, 54, 133, 142
Balasko, Josiane, 42
Balbo, Ennio, 145
Baldi, Ferdinando, 206
Baldwin, Bill, 100
Baldwin, Karen, 140
Baldwin, Mike, 150
Balin, Ina, 216
Ball, Lucille, 216
Ball, Robert E., 114
Ball, Zachary, 148
Ballad of the Belstone Fox, The, 211
Ballamy, Florence, 204
Ballantine, Carl, 137
Ballard, Kaye, 78, 79
Ballard, Lucien, 32, 74, 76, 143
Ballen, Tony, 132
Ballew, Jerry Lee, 106
Ballhaus, Michael, 203, 208
Ballista, Gigi, 189
Balsam, Martin, 18, 19, 107, 161, 216
Bamber, Dickie, 211
Bambina, 206
Bamboo House of Dolls, 210
Bancroft, Anne, 26, 27, 161, 216
Band, Charles, 146
Bandinni, Franco, 206
Bane, Monte, 146
Banionys, Donatas, 213
Banks, Aaron, 127, 211
Bannen, Ian, 201, 204, 216
Bannerman, Margaret, 232
Bannister, Reggie, 129, 150
Baptiste, Thomas, 195
Baran, Jack, 17
Barber, Ellen, 129
Barber, Phil, 129
Barbera, Joseph R., 41
Barbi, Vince, 129
Barbone, Paola, 213
Bardem, Juan Antonio, 213
Bardo, Joseph, 138
Bardot, Brigitte, 203, 205, 206, 216
Bare, Bobby, 133
Barefoot Contessa, The, 161
Baret, Dora, 207
Barinholtz, Alan J., 139
Barker, Richard, 145
Barker, Ronnie, 170

Barkin, Marcie, 131, 133, 149
Barn of the Naked Dead, 127
Barnes, Chris, 28, 94
Barnes, Derek, 139
Barnes, Henry, 140
Barnes, Jake, 128, 137
Barnes, Sara, 149
Barney, Jean, 203
Barnhardt, Faith, 136
Barns, Randy, 148
Baron, Red, 140
Baron, Simone, 203
Barr, Rev. William, 31
Barraclough, Roy, 194
Barraque, Martine, 192
Barrault, Marie-Christine, 184, 185, 207, 216
Barreiro, Jorge, 207
Barrett, Alan, 94
Barrett, Angel, 130, 138, 142, 148
Barrett, John, 170
Barrett, Ray, 204
Barrett, Tim, 194
Barrie, George, 127, 130
Barrie, Wendy, 216
Barron, Keith, 124, 216
Barry, Bart, 205
Barry, Donald, 216
Barry, Gene, 216
Barry, John, 116, 170
Barrymore, Ethel, 160
Barrymore, John Blyth, 38, 137, 216
Barrymore, Lionel, 160
Barsky, Georges, 213
Bartel, Paul, 135, 142
Bartel, Wendy, 142
Bartholomew, Freddie, 216
Bartkowiak, Andrzej, 17
Bartlett, Bonnie, 104
Bartlett, Calvin, 150
Bartning, C. O., 209
Barton, Amanda, 134, 148
Barton, Barbara, 131
Barty, Billy, 20, 21
Barwood, Hal, 36
Basch, Harry, 68
Basehart, Richard, 146, 216
Basil, Toni, 41
Basile, Pierluigi, 172
Baskette, James, 160
Baskin, Richard, 52
Bass, Billy, 86
Bass, Mike, 145
Bassan, Giuseppe, 208
Bastid, Jean-Pierre, 209
Batalla, George, 124
Bates, Alan, 216
Bates, Ben, 106
Bates, Michael, 210
Bates, Ralph, 167
Batista, Lloyd, 206
Batt, Bert, 202
Battuello, Cliff, 148
Bauer, Rolf, 204
Bauer, Wolfgang, 203
Baum, Ralph, 204
Baum, Tom, 127
Bawdy Adventures of Tom Jones, The, 17
Baxter, Alan, 232
Baxter, Anne, 160, 216
Baxter, George David, 232
Baxter, Keith, 216
Baxter, Meredith, 18
Baxter, Warner, 160
Baydon, Geoffrey, 194
Bayless, Luster, 72
Bayly, Lorraine, 140
Beagle, E. Hampton, 114
Beal, John, 216
Beal, Kay, 132
Beatty, Ned, 18, 62, 102, 103, 112, 113, 120
Beatty, Robert, 216
Beatty, Warren, 216
Beaudant, Jaqueline, 137
Becher, John C., 12
Beck, Billy, 114
Beck, Joe, 130
Beck, John, 62, 131
Beck, Kimberly, 144
Beck, Reggie, 202
Becker, Etienne, 208
Beckel, Graham, 137
Becker, Antonie, 86
Beckerman, Barry, 74
Beckerman, Sidney, 92, 134
Beckley, James, 148
Beckman, Henry, 112
Beddoe, Andrew, 213
Bedford, Patrick, 99
Beery, Noah, Jr., 216
Beery, Wallace, 160
Beetson, Frank, 143
Begley, Ed, 161
Begley, Ed, Jr., 22
Begun, Jeff, 133
Behind the Shutters, 213

Behling, Robert, 109
Behrens, Bernard, 68
Behrens, Inge, 87
Bel Geddes, Barbara, 216
Belafonte, Harry, 216
Belasco, Leon, 216
Belasco, William, 23
Belchamber, Barry, 207
Bell, Alfred, 140
Bell, Edward, 129
Bell, Jeanne, 149
Bell, Mary Beth, 114
Bell, Nancy, 80
Bell, Tita, 137
Bell, Tom, 216
Bellamy, Ralph, 216
Bellan, Jana, 140
Bellaver, Harry, 148
Belle, Annie, 206
Belle, Ekkehardt, 203
Bellflower, Nellie, 143
Belli, Agostina, 201, 206
Belling, Davina, 130
Bellwood, Pamela, 107
Belmondo, Jean-Paul, 210, 216
Belstone Fox, The, 211
Benally, Steven, Jr., 132
Bender, Bob, 70
Beneath the Mermaids, 130
Benedek, Lasic, 133
Benedict, Dirk, 216
Benet, Claudine, 205
Benfante, Dennea, 148
Benfield, Derek, 167
Ben-Hur, 161
Benides, Ted, 97
Benjamin, Paul, 14
Benjamin, Richard, 216
Benn, Harry, 130
Bennett, Bruce, 216
Bennett, Donnlynn, 18
Bennett, Jill, 216
Bennett, Joan, 216
Bennett, Michael, 136, 145
Bennett, Steven, 136
Bennett, Wallace C., 141
Benny, Troy, 135
Benson, Hugh, 58
Benson, Lucille, 112
Benson, Martin, 60, 210
Benson, Robby, 45, 151, 216
Benson, Taylor, 131
Bentinck, Anna, 214
Bentley, John, 82
Benton, Susanne, 139
Benussi, Femi, 205
Benvenuti, Leo, 210
Beny, Tony, 126
Berardi, Mauro, 210
Beregi, Oscar, 232
Berenson, Marissa, 216
Berg, Richard, 63, 183
Bergamini, Giovanni, 204
Berge, Amund, 211
Bergen, Candice, 216
Bergen, Edgar, 160, 216
Bergen, Polly, 216
Berger, Helmut, 204, 205, 212, 216
Berger, John, 214
Berger, Keith, 134
Berger, Mel, 17
Berger, Peter E., 133, 134
Berger, Richard, 44, 114
Berger, Senta, 205
Berger, Stephen M., 34, 77
Berger, William, 216
Berger, Wolfram, 203
Bergerac, Jacques, 216
Bergman, Alan, 44
Bergman, Ingmar, 178
Bergman, Ingrid, 88, 160, 161, 216
Bergman, Marilyn, 44
Berinizi, Jacopo, 204
Berinizi, Lorenzo, 204
Berkeley, Busby, 232
Berlanga, Luis, 207
Berle, Milton, 216
Berlin, Jeannie, 216
Berline, Byron, 22
Berliner, Max, 207
Berling, Peter, 203
Berlinger, Warren, 44, 118, 130, 201, 216
Berman, Alfred M., 207
Bernard, Jason, 86
Bernard, Judd, 201
Bernardi, Herschel, 10, 11, 82, 83
Berne, Gustave, 142, 205
Bernhard, Harvey, 60, 174
Berns, Norman C., 129
Bernstein, Andrew, 82
Bernstein, Carl, 18
Bernstein, Charles, 69, 134, 143
Bernstein, Elmer, 72, 76, 196
Bernstein, Jacob, 82
Bernstein, Walter, 82

Berri, Claude, 208
Berry, Bill, 145
Berry, Ken, 150
Berryman, Michael, 154
Berta, Renato, 214
Bertheau, Julien, 208
Berthron, Dierdre, 98
Berti, Marina, 172, 173
Berto, Juliet, 208
Bertolucci, Giovanni, 212
Berubet, Madeleine, 206
Beruh, Joseph, 141
Bessi, Roberto, 201
Best, James, 45, 114, 216
Best Years of Our Lives, The, 160
Besterman, Paul, 84
Bethune, Ivey, 130
Bettger, Lyle, 216
Bettles, Robert, 140
Between Heaven and Hell, 211
Betz, Carl, 216
Bevan, David, 202
Beveridge, Stewart H., 148
Bexley, Don, 133
Beymer, Richard, 216
Beyond Fulfillment, 131
Beyond the Darkness, 204
Beytelman, Gustaveo, 207
Bianchi, Claudi, 207
Bickel, Moidele, 191
Bickley, William, 30
Bicycle Thief, The, 160
Bideau, Jean-Luc, 208, 214
Biery, Edward A., 68
Big Abner, 144
Big Bus, The, 62
Big Country, The, 161
Bignamini, Nino, 164
Bijou, Adrianna, 135
Bikel, Theodore, 216
Bill, Tony, 44, 127
Billings, Earl, 147
Bim Robertson, Hugh A., 213
Bindon, John, 146
Bingo Long Traveling All-Stars and Motor Kings, The, 36
Binney, Geoffrey, 132, 133
Birch Interval, 31
Bird, John, 94
Bird, Minah, 206
Bird, Norman, 194
Birds, Orphans and Fools, 204
Birkin, Jane, 203, 210
Birman, Len, 112
Birney, David, 146, 202
Birney, Meredith Baxter, 89, 151
Biroc, Joseph, 22
Bishop, Jenifer, 135, 141
Bishop, Joey, 216
Bishop, Julie, 216
Bishop, Larry, 142
Bishop, Lee, 201
Bishop, Phillan, 135
Bishop, Wes, 136
Bisoglio, Val, 74
Bisset, Jacqueline, 73, 74, 75, 182, 189, 210, 216
Bitter Tears of Petra Von Kant, The, 208
Bittersweet Love, 89
Bixby, Bill, 216
Bixio, Dammico, 204
Biziou, Peter, 84
Bjornstrand, Gunnar, 178
Blaaser, Jan, 212
Black, Diane, 130
Black, Karen, 24, 90, 91, 174, 216
Black, Stephen, 176, 177
Black and White in Color, 161
Black Dragon vs. the Yellow Tiger, The, 202
Black Emanuelle, 213
Black Heat, 140
Black Orpheus, 161
Black Shampoo, 132
Black Street Fighter, The, 129
Blackman, Honor, 214
Blackman, Wanda, 70, 71
Blackstong, Tim, 205
Blackwell, John, 114
Blaine, Vivian, 216
Blair, Betsy, 216
Blair, Clay, Jr., 210
Blair, Edward, 139
Blair, Janet, 216
Blair, Linda, 216
Blair, Nicky, 44
Blake, Amanda, 216
Blake, Ellen, 44
Blake, James P., 145
Blake, Robert, 216
Blake, Yvonne, 170, 174
Blakely, Colin, 199, 202

Blakely, Susan, 216
Blakley, Ronee, 216
Blanc, Erika, 205
Blanc, Michel, 42
Blanshard, Joby, 201
Blast, 148
Blech, Hans Christian, 212
Bleeck, Oliver, 74
Bleier, Nancy, 131, 144
Blendick, James, 183
Blewitt, David, 38
Blier, Bernard, 166, 207, 210
Blitz, Rusty, 114
Bloch, Sam, 146
Blondell, Joan, 216
Bloom, Claire, 216
Bloom, Jeffrey, 68
Bloom, John, 78
Blot, Florence, 42
Bluc, Arlana, 126, 127, 130
Blue, Tony, 145
Blue Bird, The, 207
Blum, Harry N., 70, 136, 206, 209
Blum, Joel, 131
Blum, Stanford, 107
Blumenthal, Herman A., 107
Blumofe, Robert F., 122
Blunden, Bill, 210
Blunt, Erin, 28, 86
Blythe, Ann, 216
Blythe, Astrid, 146
Boas, Alexander, 145
Bobbie Jo and the Outlaw, 133
Bobrick, Sam, 77
Bochner, Lloyd, 212
Bod Squad, The, 147
Bodine, Charles, 132
Bodyguard, The, 211
Boesman and Lena, 175
Boffety, Jean, 204, 206, 213
Bogarde, Dirk, 216
Bogart, Humphrey, 160
Bogart, Peter, 68
Bogdanovich, Peter, 114
Bogert, William, 82
Bogot, Jean Pierre, 42
Bohm, Karl-Heinz, 203
Boisgel, Valerie, 210
Boisrond, Michel, 203, 208
Boisset, Yves, 209
Boisvert, Hughette, 213
Boland, Jim, 138
Bolden, Ronald, 147
Bolger, Ray, 216
Bolkan, Florinda, 216
Bolla, Richard, 149
Bollag, Peter, 203
Bologna, Joseph, 62
Bolscher, Piet, 204
Bolta, Peter, 172
Bonaduce, Danny, 150
Bonaiuto, Anna, 206
Bonar, Ivan, 128
Bond, Derek, 216
Bond, Jack, 211
Bond, Julian, 146
Bond, Laura, 128
Bond, Rene, 145, 149
Bond, Steve, 140, 144
Bondarchouk, Nathalie, 213
Bondi, Beulah, 216
Bonefous, Carlota, 207
Bonet, Charles, 206
Bonet, Nai, 142
Bongusto, Fred, 206
Bonham, John, 213
Boniceli, Vitorio, 172
Bonnell, Vivian, 14
Bonner, Frank, 127
Bonner, William, 142
Bonnie and Clyde, 161
Bonniere, Claude, 212
Bonnot, Francoise, 42
Booby Hatch, The, 145
Book, David, 128
Booke, Sorrell, 63
Bookwalter, DeVeren, 108
Boone, Pat, 216
Boone, Richard, 72, 216
Boorstin, Jon, 18
Booth, James, 204
Booth, Margaret, 50
Booth, Shirley, 160, 216
Boozer, Emerson, 140
Borden, Marshall M., 210
Borden, Roger, 58
Boreman, Alfred, 205
Borgnine, Ernest, 161, 183, 216
Borman, Gene, 147
Born to Dance, 39
Born Yesterday, 160
Borowczyk, Walerian, 204, 213
Borzage, Frank, 160
Bos, Henk, 214
Bose, Lucia, 198
Bosley, Tom, 64, 65

Boss, May, 143
Bossie, Brenda, 149
Bosso, Giorgio, 124
Boston, Myra, 138
Boswell, Connee, 232, 233
Bottoms, Joseph, 174
Bottoms, Sam, 46
Bottoms, Timothy, 143, 216
Bottoms Up, 214
Boucart, Corrine, 192
Bouchet, Barbara, 206, 209
Bouillon, Jean-Claude, 203
Bouise, Jean, 205, 208, 209
Bouldin, Kathy, 137
Boulting, Ingrid, 104, 105, 216
Boulting, Roy, 209
Bound for Glory, 122
Bouquet, Michel, 206, 210
Bourbon, Laura, 144
Bourdon, Sylvia, 206
Bourke, Rory, 131
Bourne, St. Clair, 140
Bouteille, Romain, 42
Bovee, Leslie, 126, 132, 135, 137, 146, 149
Bow, Simmy, 100, 134
Bowen, Roger, 143
Bower, Tom, 127
Bowers, George, 138
Bowers, Lally, 194
Bowie, David, 150, 180, 181
Bowker, Judi, 216
Bowles, Phil, 86, 129
Bowman, Lee, 216
Bowman, Leslie, 209
Box, Euel, 30
Boy and His Dog, A, 139
Boyar, Sully, 86
Boyd, Stephen, 144, 216
Boyd, Tanya, 131, 132, 140
Boyer, Charles, 88, 160, 216
Boyer, Myriam, 214
Boyle, Peter, 8, 68, 216
Boyle, Robert, 14, 20, 72
Boys' Town, 160
Bozuffi, Marcel, 202, 203
Brach, Gerard, 42
Bracken, Eddie, 216
Brackett, Charles, 161
Bracknell, David, 167
Bradford, Delia, 150
Bradford, Richard, 34
Bradley, Warren, III, 148
Bradsell, Mike, 130
Bradshaw, Carl, 137
Brady, Alice, 160
Brady, Buff, 21
Brady, Scott, 216
Brame, Bill, 149
Bramley, William, 137
Bramonti, Mario, 164
Brand, Anthony, 45
Brand, Cliff, 149
Brand, Neville, 216
Brand, Tony, 134
Branda, Richard, 107
Brandes, Elliott, 127
Brando, Jocelyn, 217
Brando, Luisina, 207
Brando, Marlon, 7, 34, 35, 161, 217
Brandon, Henry, 148
Brandon-Jones, Una, 146
Brandt, Buzz, 32
Brandun, Elizabeth, 144
Brashler, William, 36
Brasselle, Keefe, 217
Brault, Michel, 213
Brauner, Artur, 209
Braunsberg, Andrew, 42
Braverman, Bart, 144
Bray, Gillian, 147
Brazzi, Rossano, 217
Breakheart Pass, 32
Breaking Point, 186
Breaux, Marc, 194
Breaux, Walter, 147
Breeding, Richard, 133, 180
Breeding, Ron, 144
Breen, Joseph, 161
Breeze, Michelle, 44
Bregman, Martin, 97
Breillat, Catherine, 203
Bremson, Robert S., 70, 136
Brennan, Eileen, 50, 51
Brennan, Tom, 207
Brennan, Walter, 160
Brenner, Albert, 34, 126
Brenner, Dori, 217
Brenner, Hans, 205
Brent, Bill, 126
Brent, George, 217
Brent, Romney, 232
Brestoff, Richard, 86
Bretherton, David, 44, 112

Brewer, Jameson, 203
Brewer, Roxanne, 144
Brialy, Jean-Claude, 203
Brian, David, 217
Brian, Yan, 210
Briant, Shane, 201
Bridge on the River Kwai,
The, 161
Bridges, Beau, 16, 68, 107,
217
Bridges, Jeff, 22, 116, 117,
217
Bridges, Juli, 107
Bridges, Lloyd, 217
Bright, Richard, 92
Brigitte, 129
Brignone, Lilla, 210
Bring, Bob, 118
Brion, Francoise, 202
Brisebois, Danielle, 129
Brison, Sam "Birmingham",
36
Bristol, Alfred, 97
Britain, Brit, 148
Britt, Kelly, 106
Britt, May, 217
Brittany, Morgan, 128
Britten, Lawrence, 201
Britton, Burt, 82
Britton, George B., 144
Britton, Greg, 144
Britton, Michael, 18
Broadway Melody, 160
Broadway Melody of 1936,
38
Brocco, Peter, 154
Brock, Alan, 128
Brock, Stanley, 114, 200
Brodhead, James E., 14
Brodie, Don, 135
Brodie, Steve, 133, 217
Brodsky, Jack, 44, 107
Brody, Ronnie, 78
Brody, William J., 131
Brolin, James, 128, 217
Bromfeld, John, 217
Bronco Billy, 161
Bronson, Charles, 6, 32, 33,
73, 74, 75, 76, 203,
217
Brook, Claudio, 66, 203
Brooke, Rebecca, 140, 144,
148
Brooke, Walter, 62
Brooks, Albert, 8
Brooks, Dave, 126
Brooks, Dean R., 154
Brooks, Denny, 131
Brooks, Foster, 122
Brooks, Geraldine, 217
Brooks, James, 128
Brooks, Joe, 28
Brooks, Linda, 128
Brooks, Mel, 6, 48, 49
Brooks, Randy, 150
Brooks, Ray, 210
Broome, Marianne, 194,
206
Brost, Frederic, 20
Brotherhood of Death, 145
Brothers, Dr. Joyce, 40
Brown, Alonzo, 154
Brown, Barbara, 149
Brown, Barry, 217
Brown, Becky, 45
Brown, Christopher J., 78
Brown, Darcy, 128
Brown, Edwin Scott, 150
Brown, Emmett, 44
Brown, Georgia, 94, 210
Brown, Henry, 131
Brown, James, 126, 127,
217
Brown, Jophrey, 36
Brown, Judith, 132, 133
Brown, Lynn, 135
Brown, O. Nicholas, 190
Brown, Peter S., 131, 133
Brown, Robert, 147
Brown, Ronald, 201
Brown, Sarah, 132
Brown, Steve, 128, 130
Brown, Timothy, 140
Brown, Tom, 217
Brown, Vanessa, 128
Brown, Wes, 128
Browne, Coral, 217
Browne, Roscoe Lee, 58, 59
Browne, Tyrone, 145
Browning, Phillip, 137
Brownrigg, S. F., 140
Broyles, Robert, 135
Bruce, David, 217, 232
Bruce, Melba, 137, 142
Bruce, Virginia, 217
Bruce Lee—Super Dragon,
209
Bruchon, Pascale, 192
Brugman, Eddie, 212
Bruhns, Werner, 204
Brummer, Richard S., 132,
137
Bruni, Peter, 148

Brunner, Howard, 76
Brunner, Kathrin, 182
Brunner, Robert F., 64
Bruno, Mariano and Mauro,
208
Bruns, Philip, 114
Bryant, David, 134
Bryant, Michael, 202
Bryant, William, 107, 128
Bryceland, Yvonne, 175
Bryl, Barbara, 206
Brynner, Yul, 80, 139, 161,
217
Buchanan, Frances, 140
Buchanan, Frank, 129
Buchanan, Larry, 130
Buchholz, Horst, 217
Buck, Jules, 139
Buckley, Betty, 98
Buckley, Keith, 146
Buckner, Susan, 131
Buczachi, Jerzy, 206
Budd, Roy, 202
Buetel, Jack, 217
Buffalo Bill and the Indians,
52
Bugsy Malone, 84
Bujold, Genevieve, 68, 70,
71, 96, 217
Bukzin, Al, 132
Bulgarelli, Enzo, 204
Bulleit, James, 97
Bulloch, Sally, 206
Bumstead, Henry, 24
Buono, Victor, 217
Burch, Dick, 146
Burgess, Anthony, 172
Burgess, Catharine, 145
Burghardt, Arthur, 102
Burke, Martin, 16
Burke, Paul, 217
Burks, Alan, 148
Burnett, Carol, 217
Burnette, Dorsey, 136
Burns, Bill, 26
Burns, Brendan, 104
Burns, Catherine, 217
Burns, George, 158, 161,
217
Burns, Philip, 145
Burns, Steve, 55
Burnt Offerings, 90
Burr, Raymond, 149, 217
Burr, Robert, 129
Burr, Tim, 205
Burrill, Timothy, 187
Burroughs, Edgar Rice, 209
Burrows, Bill, 102
Burstyn, Ellen, 161, 217
Burton, Norman, 143, 147
Burton, Phil, 129
Burton, Richard, 217
Burton, Tony, 36, 100,
134, 148
Burton, Warren, 137
Busey, Gary, 110, 143
Bushelman, Jeff, 140
Bushelman, John, 140
Bushnell, William H., Jr.,
201
Bussieres, Raymond, 214
Butcher, Joseph, 150
Butkus, Dick, 41, 64
Butler, Artie, 134
Butler, Bill, 26, 36, 89, 96,
154
Butler, David, 124
Butler, Ella, 148
Butler, Jay, 86
Butler, Michael, 34
Butterfly 8, 161
Butterflies Are Free, 161
Butterworth, Peter, 78, 170
Buttons, Red, 128, 161,
217
Buxton, Judy, 167, 210
Buzzi, Ruth, 217
Byars, Joe, 140
Byers, Richard, 129
Bygraves, Max, 217
Bynum, Don, 147
Byrd, David, 106
Byrd-Nethery, Miriam, 62
Byrnes, Edd, 217
Byron, Jeffrey, 114
Byrum, John, 44, 130
C. B. Mamas, 132
Caan, James, 44, 217
Cabaret, 161
Cabot, Susan, 217
Cabrera, John, 202
Cactus Flower, 161
Cady, Daniel B., 135
Caesar, Sid, 48, 49, 217
Caffarel, Jose, 202
Cagney, James, 38, 160,
217
Cagney, Jeanne, 217
Cahill, Lynette, 190
Cahn, Jeff, 133
Caiano, Mario, 201
Caillou, Alan, 133
Caimi, Lamberto, 206

Cain, Sid, 197
Caine, Michael, 44, 126,
217
Caine, Roger, 136, 148,
149
Caine, Shakira, 217
Calamai, Clara, 208
Calandra, Giuliana, 164,
208
Calderoni, Rita, 182
Caldwell, Dan, 132
Calfa, Don, 114, 126
Calhoun, Rory, 217
Callaghan, Duke, 23
Callahan, Gene, 97, 104
Callan, Michael, 217
Callas, Charlie, 48
Callegari, Gian Paolo, 206
Calloway, Kirk, 150
Callum, B., 146
Callwood, Marquita, 134
Calnan, Matilda, 112, 114
Calvert, Henry, 18
Calvert, Phyllis, 217
Calvet, Corrine, 217
Calvin, John, 137
Camara, Carlos, 210
Cambern, Donn, 96
Cambridge, Godfrey, 232,
233
Cameron, John, 139
Cameron, Rod, 135, 217
Camilleri, Terry, 139
Camillo, Tony, 150
Camp, Colleen, 140, 217
Camp, Hamilton, 114
Campanella, Frank, 149
Campbel, 149
Campbell, Glen, 217
Campbell, Martin, 201
Campbell, Mike, 140
Campbell, Patrick, 48
Campbell, Sid, 139
Campos, Rafael, 145
Camps, Jean Pierre, 128
Camras, Roger, 45
Camroux, Ken, 186
Canale, Gianna Maria, 217
Candy, John, 212
Candy Lips, 150
Candy's Candy, 206
Cann, James, 7
Canning, Victor, 24
Cannon, Dyan, 217
Cannon, Gene, 139
Cannon, Norman, 144
Cannon, Orin, 90
Cannon, Vince, 134
Canova, Diana, 131
Canova, Judy, 142, 217
Canter, Stanley, 74
Cantor, Eddie, 161
Cantrell, Tom, 129
Capell, Peter, 214
Capelle, Frannye, 45
Capelle, Jack, 45
Capers, Virginia, 217
Capetanos, Leon, 143
Capote, Truman, 50
Capra, Frank, 160
Capri, Anna, 36
Caprioli, Vittorio, 203, 210
Captains Courageous, 160
Capucine, 217
Caputo, Bernard F., 136
Car Wash, 86
Cara, Irene, 133, 151
Caravan to Vaccares, 202
Carayan, Dacosta, 209
Carbis, Chris, 124
Carbone, Antony, 134
Cardarelli, Romano, 164
Cardiff, Jack, 140
Cardin, Monique, 149
Cardinal, M., 206
Cardinale, Claudia, 212,
214, 217
Cardona, Rene, Jr., 210
Carey, Harry, Jr., 114, 217
Carey, MacDonald, 217
Carey, Philip, 148, 217
Carey, Ron, 48
Carey, Timothy Agoglia,
126, 129, 149
Carfagno, Edward C., 23,
128
Caridi, Carmine, 86
Caridine, Lyn, 150
Caristan, Georges, 211
Carlin, Ed, 136
Carlin, Fred, 80
Carlin, George, 86
Carlin, Ric, 213
Carlino, Lewis John, 176
Carlson, Erika, 139
Carlson, Les, 183
Carlton, Mark, 133
Carmet, Jean, 205, 209
Carmichael, Hoagy, 217

Carmichael, Ian, 204, 217
Carnal Haven, 126
Carne, Judy, 217
Carnegie, Margaret, 212
Carney, Art, 40, 161, 217
Carney, Sandra, 201
Carnival of Blood, 126
Caron, Leslie, 214, 217
Carpenter, Carleton, 217
Carpenter, John, 102, 148
Carpenter, Keri, 128
Carpi, Tito, 204
Carr, Anthony, 209
Carr, Arnold, 107
Carr, Camilla, 58, 140
Carr, Vikki, 217
Carradine, David, 122, 123,
142, 217
Carradine, John, 72, 104,
148, 217
Carradine, Keith, 198, 217
Carradine, Robert, 133,
138, 142, 144
Carrara, Mario, 206
Carraro, Tino, 210
Carrel, Dany, 217
Carrera, Barbara, 40
Carrie, 98
Carriere, Jean-Claude, 201
Carriere, Matthieu, 203
Carrigan, Ana, 87
Carrington, Virginia, 129
Carrion, J. Antonio, 149
Carrol, Helen, 140
Carrol, Regina, 135, 140
Carrolli, Diahann, 217
Carroll, Larry, 100
Carroll, Lewis, 138
Carroll, Madeleine, 217
Carroll, Pat, 217
Carroll, Tony, 97
Carrott, Ric, 41
Carruth, William, 114
Cars That Eat People, The,
139
Carsetti, Gastogne, 145
Carson, John David, 22,
131, 217
Carson, Johnny, 217
Carson, Robert, 110
Carsten, Peter, 217
Carstensen, Margit, 208
Carter, Don, 140
Carter, Forrest, 46
Carter, John, 120
Carter, Lynda, 133
Carter, Maurice, 150
Carter, Thomas, 150
Cartier, Caroline, 198
Cartwright, Veronica, 130
Caruso, Fred, 102
Caruso, Pino, 189, 209
Caruso, Tony, 127
Carver, Steve, 143
Casablanca, 160
Casaril, Guy, 205, 209
Casas, Justin, 136
Case, Robert, 124
Casey, Bernie, 127, 180
Casey, Elana, 144
Casey, Sandra, 135
Cash, Rosalind, 127, 150,
217
Cason, Barbara, 217
Caspari, Ragnvald, 211
Cass, David, 107
Cass, Peggy, 217
Cassavetes, John, 107,
120, 121, 129, 217
Cassel, Jean-Pierre, 217
Cassel, Seymour, 104, 129
Cassidy, Bill, 100
Cassidy, David, 218
Cassidy, Jack, 20, 21, 233
Cassidy, Jim, 144
Cassidy, Joanna, 22, 204,
218
Cassidy, Rick, 149
Cassidy, Ted, 44
Cassisi, John, 84
Casson, Maxine, 210
Castel, Colette, 205
Castel, Robert, 209
Castellano, Richard, 218
Castellanos, Ralph, 139
Castellari, Enzo G., 202,
204
Castle, John, 196
Cat Ballou, 161
Cat Murkil and the Silks,
140
Cates, Gilbert, 16
Cates, Jim, 140
Catharine, Susan, 126, 144,
147
Catherine & Co., 203
Catti, James, 129
Catusi, James, 144
Cau, James, 203
Caulfield, Joan, 149, 218
Causey, Jack, 194
Cavagnaro, Gary Lee, 28,
136

Cavalcade, 160
Cavalier, Joe, 72, 108
Cavani, Liliana, 218
Cavara, Paolo, 206
Ceccaldi, Daniel, 214
Cecilia, Renato, 189
Cedar, Elayne, 143, 149
Cedar, Jon, 68
Cedergren, Ingrid, 147
Celi, Adolfo, 97, 210, 218
Cerniglia, Guido, 182
Cerro, Riccardo, 210
Chabrol, Claude, 206, 212
Chadwick, Nancy, 131
Chaffey, Don, 140
Chailleux, Jacques, 209
Chain, Coke, 144
Chair, Kem, 209
Chakiris, George, 161, 218
Challis, Christopher, 196
Chamberlain, Richard, 194,
195, 218
Chamberlain, Wilt, 142
Chambers, Candice, 142,
147
Chambers, John, 161
Chambers, Marilyn, 130
Chamblee, Robert, 148
Chameleon, A., 141
Champ, The, 160
Champion, Gill, 128
Champion, Gower, 218
Champion, John, 131
Champion, Marc, 186
Champion, Marge, 218
Chance, John T., 148
Chandler, John David, 141,
147
Chandler, Mandy, 146
Chandler, Vern, 34
Chaney, Barbara, 147
Chang, Robert, 213
Channing, Carol, 218
Channing, Stockard, 43, 62,
218
Chapiron, Maurice, 210
Chapiteau, Marc, 165
Chaplin, Charles, 160, 161,
218
Chaplin, Geraldine, 52, 53,
218
Chaplin, Saul, 38
Chaplin, Sydney, 218
Chapman, Dianne Finn, 141
Chapman, Lonny, 128, 143
Chapman, Michael, 8, 82,
97
Chapman, Wayne, 144
Chappell, John, 114
Charbakshi, Henri, 145
Charbaux, Roland, 214
Charisse, Cyd, 218
Charity, C. C., 139
Charity Ball, The, 127
Charles, Beau, 150
Charly, 161
Charney, Jordan, 102
Chartoff, Robert, 100, 114,
126
Chase, Annazette, 129, 147
Chase, Chevy, 143
Chase, Ilka, 218
Chase, Jo Flores, 148
Chase, Libbie, 146
Chatel, Peter, 203
Chatman, Xavier, 137
Chauvet, Elizabeth, 132,
134
Chavez, Gloria, 210
Chayefsky, Paddy, 102
Chazel, Louba, 42
Chebier, Sam, 147
Check My Oil, Baby, 206
Cheese, 145
Cheesman, Ron, 140
Cheh, Chang, 210
Chen, Charlie, 212
Chen, David, 213
Chen, David, Jr., 201
Chen, Lei, 202
Chen, Robert, 213
Chen, Sherry, 133
Cher, 218
Cher Victor, 166
Chermayeff, Ivan, 146
Chernus, Sonia, 46
Cherry Truckers, 150
Chesney, Diana, 68
Chesty Anderson, U.S. Navy,
149
Chetwynd, Gloria Carlin,
183
Chetwynd-Hayes, R., 204
Chevalier, Maurice, 161
Chew, Richard, 154
Chew, Sam, 132
Chianese, Dominic, 28
Chiang, David, 210
Chiang, Ma Chi, 201
Chiari, Mario, 116
Chiari, Walter, 218
Chiba, Shinichi, 211
Chiba, Sonny, 202, 211

Chihara, Paul, 43
Child is a Wild Young Thing, A, 150
Childress, Alvin, 36
Childs, Betty, 145
Childs, Peter, 146
Chimenti, Melissa, 203
Chin, Wu, 201
Chinese Mack, The, 201
Chinich, Michael, 36
Chinn, Robert C., 142, 147, 149
Chino, 203
Chirelstein, Paul, 84
Chittell, Chris, 207
Chitty, Erik, 94
Choi, Hon Kwok, 212
Chong, Michael, 139
Christenberry, Chris, 62
Christian, Anne, 128
Christian, Damon, 142, 147
Christian, Dana, 145
Christian, Hans, 126, 140
Christian, Linda, 218
Christian, Robert, 218
Christiansen, Todd, 150
Christie, Dame Agatha, 233
Christie, Julie, 161, 218
Christmas, Eric, 104
Christodoulou, Raymond, 204
Christophe, Pascale, 204
Christopher, Faith, 138
Christopher, Jordan, 218
Christy, 128
Chulack, Fred, 23
Churchett, Stephen, 124
Churchill, Sarah, 218
Cilento, Diane, 218
Ciletti, Miles, 129
Cili, Adolfo, 210
Cimarron, 160
Cimber, Matt, 128
Cinieri, Cosimo, 206
Cinieri, Francesco, 172
Cioffi, Charles, 97
Cipriani, Stelvio, 213
Cirillo, Claudio, 201, 206
Cirino, Bruno, 206
Citges, Luis, 124
Cittini, Alberto, 209
Civera, Joe, 148
Civitello, Linda, 142
Claire, Adele, 130
Clancy, Tom, 68
Clapham, Peter, 176
Clapton, Eric, 218
Clark, Barry, 200
Clark, Bob, 186
Clark, Bryan E., 18
Clark, Candy, 130, 180, 181
Clark, Dane, 218
Clark, Dick, 218
Clark, Greydon, 132, 147
Clark, Jim, 92
Clark, John, 130
Clark, Mae, 218
Clark, Oliver, 110
Clark, Petula, 218
Clark, Ron, 48, 77
Clark, Susan, 218
Clarke, Cam, 150
Clarke, Caprice, 128
Clarke, David, 82
Clarke, Robin, 204
Clatworthy, Robert, 76, 86, 141
Clausen, Richard, 129
Clavar, Queta, 207
Clay, Stanley, 18, 142
Clayburgh, Jill, 112, 113, 128, 218
Claydon, George, 167
Clayton, Abigail, 128, 148
Clementelli, Silvio, 206, 210
Clements, Richard, 126
Clements, Stanley, 218
Clery, Corinne, 218
Clever, Edith, 191
Clianto, Angela, 209
Clift, Brooks, 36
Clifton, Peter, 213
Climax of Blue Power, The, 145
Cline, Sheryl, 144
Cliver, Al, 206
Clockmaker, The, 208
Clooney, Rosemary, 218
Close, Del, 145
Closely Watched Trains, 161
Clouse, Robert, 139
Cobb, Lee J., 233
Cobert, Robert, 90
Cobham, Billy, 133
Coblenz, Walter, 18
Coburn, Brian, 146
Coburn, Charles, 160
Coburn, James, 23, 56, 131, 218
Coca, Imogene, 218

Cocktail Hostesses, The, 149
Coco, James, 50, 51, 218
Cody, Kathleen, 218
Coe, Peter, 134
Coema, Vladimir, 209
Coffin, Fredrick, 16
Cogan, Alex, 205
Coggans, Tony, 142
Coggin, Carol, 18
Cohen, Alison, 131
Cohen, Emma, 205
Cohen, Henry, 207
Cohen, Irving, 148
Cohen, Jerry, 136
Cohen, Lawrence D., 62, 98
Cohen, Norman I., 144
Cohen, Paul, 149
Cohen, Rob, 36
Cohen, Shlomi, 205
Colasanti, Veniero, 88
Colasanto, Nicholas, 24
Colberg, Alan B., 132, 149
Colbert, Claudette, 160, 218
Cole, Betty, 76
Cole, Byron, 135
Cole, George, 207, 218
Cole, Jacquelin, 147
Cole, Joel, 140
Cole, Lori, 31
Cole, Stan, 186
Coleman, Madelyn, 31
Coles, Ken, 207
Colicos, John, 143, 186
Collado, Tony, 150
Colli, Tonino Delli, 162
Collicut, J. Craig, 130
Collier, Ian, 97
Collings, Anne, 200
Collings, Jeannie, 207
Collins, Candy, 149
Collins, Elaine, 146
Collins, Joan, 167, 204, 206, 210, 214, 218
Collins, Stephen, 18
Collis, Jack, 104
Collomb, Jean, 201
Colman, Ronald, 160
Colt, Zebedy, 126, 145, 148, 149
Columbia, Anthony, 44
Colvin, Jack, 40
Combo, El Gran, 133
Come and Get It, 160
Come Back, Little Sheba, 160
Come with Me my Love, 214
Comencini, Luigi, 189
Comer, Anjanette, 218
Commitment, The, 127
Compton, Spencer, 134
Compton, Todd, 146
Comway, Tim, 218
Conant, Oliver, 218
Conde, Manuel S., 135, 136
Cones, Tristam, 201
Confessions of a Teenage Peanut Butter Freak, 140
Confessions of a Young American Housewife, 140
Conforti, Gene, 30
Confrontation, 203
Congregation, Mike Curb, 136
Conley, Rene, 139
Connelly, Christopher, 30
Conners, Jim, 142
Connery, Sean, 97, 170, 171, 218
Connolly, Ray, 150
Connor, Kevin, 146, 204, 209
Connors, Chuck, 218
Connors, Mike, 218
Conrad, Jack, 150
Conrad, Michael, 44, 137
Conrad, Sid, 116
Conrad, William, 218
Conreid, Hans, 118
Conroy, Bert, 80, 137
Considine, John, 52
Conspiracy of Torture, The, 211
Constantine, Michael, 124, 126
Conte, Michael, 149
Conti, Bill, 12, 100
Conti, Mario, 162
Continenza, Sandro, 205
Contini, Alfio, 213
Conversation Piece, 212
Converse, Frank, 218
Conway, James L., 141, 142
Conway, Tim, 64, 65, 118, 119
Coogan, Jackie, 218
Cook, Ancil, 127
Cook, Elisha, Jr., 74, 218

Cook, Frederic, 133
Cooke, Melissa, 132
Cool Hand Luke, 161
Coop, Denys, 130
Cooper, Ben, 218
Cooper, Gary, 160, 161
Cooper, Jackie, 218
Cooper, Joan, 210
Cooper, Merian C., 160
Cooper, Neil, 150
Cooper, Tamar, 114
Cooper, Wilmuth, 129
Coote, Robert, 218
Copelan, Jodie, 143
Copeland, Lisa, 133
Copeland, Maurice, 97
Copley, Paul, 206
Copley, Peter, 197
Coppens, Isabelle, 214
Coppin, Bert, 175
Coppola, Carmine, 44
Coppola, Francis Ford, 161
Coquette, 160
Coquillon, John, 134, 201
Corbett, Glenn, 56, 131
Corbett, Pamela, 147
Corbett, Ray, 84
Corby, Ellen, 218
Corcoran, Donna, 218
Cord, Alex, 218
Corday, Mara, 218
Cordell, Frank, 146, 148
Cordos, Bud, 186
Corey, Jeff, 104, 129, 218
Corey, Phil, 135
Corey, Prof. Irwin, 86
Cori, Bob, 139
Corlan, Anthony, 218
Corman, Cary, 128
Corman, Gene, 134
Corman, Julie, 143
Corman, Roger, 133, 135, 142, 143, 148
Cormier, Al, 127
Cormier, Gerald, 127
Cornberg, Peter, 142
Cornelius, Don, 137
Cornell, Major, 144
Cornthwaite, Robert, 80
Cornwell, Tom, 129
Coronato, Maria, 206
Corran, Helen, 84
Correll, Charles, 143
Corri, Adrienne, 218
Corrigan, Ray, 233
Corrigan, Shirley, 206
Corso, Chris, 131
Corso, Robert, 106
Cortesa, Valentina, 218
Cortese, Elvira, 212
Cortese, Joseph, 148
Cosby, Bill, 41, 218
Coscarelli, Cyndie, 129, 150
Coscarelli, Don, 129, 150
Coscarelli, Shirley, 129, 150
Coscia, Marcello, 205
Cosell, Howard, 107
Cosma, Vladimir, 168, 203, 205, 207, 210, 214
Costello, Paul, 205
Coster, Nicholas, 18
Cotte, Francoise, 213
Cotte, Roger, 213
Cotten, Joseph, 218
Cotton, Kenny, 126, 137, 148, 149
Cotton, Peter, 206
Cotts, Gerald, 144
Coughlin, Kevin, 233
Coulouris, George, 78, 197
Coulter, L. E., 150
Countdown at Kusini, 135
Counterpoint, Media, 140
Country Girl, The, 161
Couples, 142
Courcel, Nicole, 201
Courtenay, Margaret, 196
Courtenay, Tom, 218
Courtland, Jerome, 140, 218
Courtney, Chuck, 54
Courval, Nathalie, 203
Cousin, Cousine, 184
Cousin, The, 210
Coustantineau, Paul, 150
Covan, DeForest, 100
Covington, Fred, 36
Covington, Laurence, 18
Covington, Suzanne, 44
Coward, Noel, 160
Cox, Ashley, 136
Cox, Doug, 98
Cox, Joel, 108
Cox, Ronny, 122, 123, 127
Cox, Roy, 139
Crabbe, Buster (Larry), 218
Crabe, James, 100
Crabtree, Glenda, 132
Craig, George, 137
Craig, James, 218
Craig, Michael, 140, 218

Craig, Michelle, 149
Crain, Jeanne, 218
Crain, William, 127
Crampton, Gerry, 124
Crandall, Brad, 141
Crane, Bob, 64, 218
Crane, Ed, 149
Crane, Kenneth, 142
Cranhan, Kenneth, 170
Craven, Gemma, 194, 195
Crawford, Broderick, 160, 218
Crawford, Joan, 39, 160, 218
Crawford, Joanna, 31
Crawford, John, 108, 144
Crawford, Lilybelle, 180
Creature from Black Lake, The, 131
Creery, John, 213
Cremer, Bruno, 206
Crenna, Richard, 32, 218
Cresciman, Vince, 89
Crews, The, 148
Crime and Passion, 174
Crime Boss, 212
Criscuola, Lou, 148
Crisp, Donald, 160
Cristal, Linda, 218
Cristal, Perla, 213
Critchlow, Keith, 145
Crockett, Dick, 199
Croghan, Terrance, 136
Cromwell, James, 50
Cronenberg, David, 141
Cronenweth, Jordan S., 218
Cronjager, William, 134
Cronkite, Kathy, 102
Crookham, Wade, 131
Crosbie, Annette, 194, 195
Crosby, Bing, 160, 218
Crosby, Cathy Lee, 134
Crosby, Joan, 118
Crosskill, Vaughn, 137
Crothers, Scatman, 22, 72, 112, 149
Crothers, Sherman *Scatman*, 154
Crouse, Lindsay Ann, 18
Crowden, Graham, 202
Crowley, Ed, 102
Crowley, Lawrence P., 140
Crowley, Pat, 218
Crudup, Carl, 141, 150
Cruiser, Roy, 138
Crusin, Dave, 82
Cruz, Brandon, 28
Cry for Cindy, 137
Cuadrado, Luis, 212
Cucciola, Ricardo, 195, 213
Cukor, George, 161, 207
Cullen, Ian, 124
Cullum, John, 218
Culman, E. G., 129
Culp, Robert, 131, 139, 186, 201, 218
Culver, Calvin, 218
Cumbuka, Ji-Tu, 122, 127
Cumbuka, Mwako, 154
Cummings, Constance, 218
Cummings, Dawn, 214
Cummings, Robert, 218
Cummins, Jack, 106
Cummins, Peggy, 218
Cunningham, George, 207
Cunningham, Margo, 176
Cunningham, Vicki, 149
Curcio, Amadeo, 130
Curcio, Frank, 130
Currie, Sondra, 135
Currin, Valerie, 48
Curry, Mark, 84
Curtelin, Jean, 209
Curtin, Valerie, 18, 41, 112
Curtis, Dan, 90
Curtis, Keene, 218
Curtis, Ken, 149
Curtis, Leslie, 104
Curtis, Tony, 104, 218
Curtiz, Michael, 160
Curzon, George, 233
Cusack, Cyril, 213, 218
Cusack, Sinead, 204
Cushing, Peter, 146, 204, 209, 218
Cutaia, Jon, 143
Cybbers, Charles, 134
Cypher, Jon, 54, 209
Cyphers, Charles, 148
Cyrano de Bergerac, 160
Czemerys, Eva, 205
Da Silva, Howard, 219
Daalder, Renee, 144
Daarstadt, Eric, 142
Dabadie, Jean-Loup, 168, 201, 204
Daehli, Anne-Marie, 211
Dagenhart, Carl, 141
Dagle, Reep, 145
Dagover, Lil, 182
Dahan, Armand, 97
Dahl, Arlene, 218
Dahl, Tessa, 194

Daigler, Gary D., 20
Daker, David, 124
Dalban, Robert, 207
Dalbert, Lydia, 203
D'Alessio, Carlos D'Carlos, 213
Daley, Robert, 46, 108
Dallamano, Massimo, 206
Dallamano, Max, 204
Dallas, Lorna, 201
Dallenbach, Walter, 127
Dallenback, Emilia, 127
Dallesandro, Joe, 219
Dalton, Diane, 148
Dalton, Jeanine, 144
Dalton, Phyllis, 124
Dalton, Timothy, 219
Daltrey, Roger, 219
Daly, Cindy, 98
Daly, James, 219
Daly, Jonathan, 118
Daly, Tyne, 108, 109
Damian, Michael, 124
D'Amico, Suso Checchi, 212
Damien, Pedro, 66, 67
Damill, Cecil B., 150
Damone, Vic, 219
Dan, Debbie, 145
Dana, Bunny, 132
Dana, Jonathan, 132
Dancer, William, 126
Danciger, Liz, 211
Dancigers, Georges, 210
Dander, Lindan, 207
D'Andrea, John, 127
Dandy, The All American Girl, 43
Dane, Lawrence, 212
Dangerous, 160
Daniel, Dave, 131
Daniel, Sean, 144
Danieli, Isa, 164
Daniels, Eugene, 107
Daniels, John, 132
Daniels, Larry, 209
Daniels, William, 140, 219
Danner, Blythe, 80, 81, 219
Dano, Royal, 143, 148, 219
Danon, Raymond, 204
Danova, Cesare, 147
Dante, Joe, 142
Dante, Michael, 219
Dantine, Helmut, 219
Danton, Ray, 219
Danvers, Lise, 204
Daprato, William, 139
D'Aquila, Marjorie, 147
Darby, Kim, 219
Darc, Mireille, 201, 205, 214
Darcel, Denise, 219
Darcy, Gene, 129
Darden, Philip, 147
Darden, Severn, 41, 133
Dare, Nancy, 148, 149
Dark, Danny, 143
Dark, John, 209
Darling, 161
Darren, James, 219
Darrieux, Danielle, 219
Darrin, Camille, 150
Darro, Frankie, 233
Darwell, Jane, 160
Darwin, Jeff, 128
Dauman, Anatole, 204
Dauphin, Claude, 42, 206, 210, 219
Davenport, Claire, 210
Davenport, Jane, 201
Daves, Michael, 137
Davey, Bert, 209
Davian, Joseph, 135, 140
David, Brad, 135
David, Hal, 213
David, Saul, 58
David, Thayer, 22, 100, 126
Davidson, Ben, 44
Davidson, David, 131
Davidson, Geoff, 197
Davidson, Jack, 82, 97
Davidson, John, 219
Davidson, Richard M., 186
Davies, Griffith, 129
Davies, Pamela, 176
Davies, Rupert, 219
Davies, Stephen, 130
Davis, Altovise, 106
Davis, Andrew, 146, 208
Davis, Bette, 90, 91, 160, 219
Davis, Cal, 131
Davis, Derna Wong, 129
Davis, George, 202
Davis, Gerry, 201
Davis, Jesse, 30
Davis, Keith, 148
Davis, Mary, 140
Davis, Mike, 87
Davis, Mimi, 127
Davis, Ossie, 135, 219
Davis, Peter S., 148

Davis, Richard, 132
Davis, Rita, 150
Davis, Robin, 166
Davis, Roger, 131, 145
Davis, Sammy, Jr., 219
Davis, Tom, 143
Davis, Walt, 118, 135, 149
Davison, Bruce, 41
Davison, Donn, 139
Davlaeminck, Laurent, 192
Dawson, Anthony, 205
Dawson, Beatrice, 210
Dawson, Rico, 36
Day, Dennis, 219
Day, Doris, 38, 219
Day, John, 112
Day, Laraine, 219
Day for Night, 161
Day the Lord Got Busted, The, 142
Dayan, Assef, 219
Daydreamer, The, 207
Dayton, Lyman D., 149, 150
De Angeles, Nato, 167
De Azevedo, Lex, 150
de Barnardi, Piero, 210
De Bell, Kristine, 138
de Berg, Jean, 128
de Bont, Jan, 212
De Bosio, Gianfranco, 172
De Broin, Michel, 207
De Brora, Philippe, 210
de Broux, Lee, 30
De Carlo, Yvonne, 219
De Casablanca, Denise, 213
de Diego, Bill, 132
De Fore, Don, 219
de Forest, Lee, 161
de Goguel, Constantin, 124, 201, 206, 214
De Haven, Gloria, 219
de Havilland, Olivia, 160, 219
de Jesus, Luici, 126
De Keyser, David, 124
De Kova, Frank, 149
De La Croix, Raven, 146
de la Fouchardiere, Georges, 206
De La Pena, Gilbert, 134, 148
de Lamothe, Francois, 203
de Lani, Glorya, 147
De Laurentiis, Dino, 116
De Laurentiis, Federico, 116
De Leeuwe, Hannah, 212
De Luise, Dom, 219
De Marco, Anthony, 134
De Martino, Alberto, 212
De Mejo, Carlo, 202
de Neuve, Danielle, 126, 142
de Neuve, Renee, 142
De Niro, Robert, 219
De Oliveira, Lucia, 204
de Pablo, Luis, 212
de Plata, Manitas, 202
De Plume, Norm, 149
de Ravet, Ward, 214
de Renzy, Alex, 137
de Rodas, Lorenzo, 210
De Rossi, Gianetto, 205
De Roubaix, Francois, 208
De Sade, Ana, 66
de Sade, Marquis, 213
de Sales, Francis, 143
de Santis, Pasqualino, 212
De Vargas, Val, 141
De Vito, Danny, 154
Deadly Hero, 17
Dean, Isabel, 210
Dean, Jimmy, 219
Dean, Larry, 146
Dean, Ron, 145
DeAngelo, Phillip, 139
DeAntonio, Emile, 137
Dear, William, 130
Dear Pam, 138, 140
Deas, Henry, 107
Deason, Ted, 202
Death Collector, 148
Death Is Not the End, 132
Death Journey, 136
Death Machines, 140
Death of a Stranger, 208
Death Play, 144
Death Riders, 140
DeBell, Kristine, 138
DeBenning, Burr, 74
Decae, Henri, 210
DeCarlo, Louise, 44
DeCarlo, Yvonne, 212
DeCaro, Lucio, 213
DeCastro Sisters, 133
DeCeco, Franklin, 132, 148, 149
Decker, Geraldine, 44
DeClara, Patrizia, 188
DeCloss, James, 44
Deconinck, Rick, 202
Deconinck, Romain, 214
Decugis, Cecile, 191

Dedet, Yann, 192
Dee, Buffy, 141
Dee, Frances, 219
Dee, Joey, 219
Dee, Ruby, 135, 219
Dee, Sandra, 219
Deeds, Maria, 31
Deeley, Heather, 205
Deeley, Michael, 180
Deep Jaws, 135
Deep Red, 208
Deer, Bambi, 148
Deering, Elizabeth, 129
DeFelice, Ermelinda, 162
DeGregorio, Eduardo, 214
DeHat, Phillip, 141
DeHaven, Gloria, 40
Dehn, Paul, 233
Dehner, John, 148, 150
DeJesus, Louie, 149
del Amo, Tablo G., 212
del Pierre, Dominique, 203
Del Pozo, Angel, 208
Del Prete, Duilio, 210, 213
Del Rio, Dolores, 133, 219
Del Rio, Martha, 206
Del Rio, Pancho, 201
Del Rio, Vanessa, 132, 136, 140, 148, 214
DeLacroux, Yvonne, 206
Delegall, Robert W., 133
DeLeon, Leon, 149
Delerue, Georges, 201, 214
Dell, Charlie, 140
Dell, Gabriel, 219
Dell, Perry, 135
della Sorte, Joseph, 127
Delon, Alain, 201, 210, 219
Delor, Suzanne, 135
Deluca, Claudio, 192
DeLuca, Frank, 192
DeLuca, Rudy, 48
DeLuise, Dom, 48, 49
DeMaal, Theo, 191
Demare, Maria Jose, 207
Demarest, William, 219
Demazis, Orane, 165
DeMille, Cecil B., 160
DeMirjian, Denise, 89
Demme, Jonathan, 148
Demon Witch Child, 208
Demons of the Mind, 201
Dempsey, Jerome, 102
Dempsey, Sandy, 149
Deneuve, Catherine, 201, 219
Denham, Maurice, 197
DeNiro, Robert, 6, 8, 9, 104, 105, 161
Denis, Jacques, 214
Denison, Michael, 219
Denizot, Gerard, 203
Denner, Charles, 212, 219
Dennis, Alfred, 72
Dennis, Mark, 114
Dennis, Sandy, 148, 161, 219
Denny, Denise, 144
Denny, Leonard, 144
Denny, Phyllis, 144
Dentie, Gino, 144
Denver, Bob, 144
Denyer, Jan, 124
Denyer, Peter, 140
DePalma, Brian, 70, 98
DePalma, Cameron, 98
Depardieu, Gerard, 204, 208, 212, 213
DePina, Manuel, 68
DePriest, Ed, 205
dePriest, James E., 150
Derek, John, 219
DeRita, Massimo, 202
Dern, Bruce, 24, 25, 40, 219
Derobe, Alain, 207
DeRome, Peter, 147
Dersu Uzala, 154, 161
des Olbes, Claude, 209
DeSade, Ana, 67
Desado, Pat, 126
DeSantis, Tony, 78
Desanzo, Juan Carlos, 207
DeSegonzac, Edouard, 203
Deshayes, Anne-Marie, 165
DeShields, Jack, 92
Desiree, 148
Desjonqueres, Guislaine, 205
Deslauriers, Nicole, 92
Desmouceaux, Geory, 192
Desny, Ivan, 202
Dester, Tony, 126
Destroying Angel, The, 147
Detrick, Bruce, 130
Detroit, N., 145
Devane, William, 24, 25, 92, 93
DeVarona, Joanna, 147
Devenish, Ross, 175
Devil within Her, 167
Devil Woman, 213
DeVilliers, Dirk, 209

Devine, Andy, 219
DeVito, Danny, 154
DeVito, Ralph, 148
Devlaeminck, Francis, 192
Devlin, Don, 44
Devlin, John, 18
Devlin, Susan, 149
Devlon, Joan, 147
Devonshire, Felicity, 201, 206
Devore, Dorothy, 233
DeVorzon, Barry, 133
Devos, Emile, 205
Dewaere, Patrick, 203
Dewar, Aubrey, 211
Dewhurst, Colleen, 219
DeWitt, Jack, 66, 131
DeWolfe, 205
Dexter, Alan D., 128
Dexter, Anthony, 219
Dexter, Brad, 134
Deyell, Dave, 186
Dhiegh, Khigh, 219
Dia, Claire, 128, 148
Diagne, Fatim, 211
Diamond, Arnold, 210
Diamond, Reed, 107
Diana, Lady, 135
Diary of Anne Frank, The, 161
Diax, Romy, 213
Diaz, Vic, 146
Dibango, Manu, 133, 135
Diberti, Luigi, 164
DiCenzo, George, 127
Dick Deadeye, 209
Dickinson, Angie, 219
Didion, Joan, 111
Diehl, Candy Clifford, 146
Dietrich, Carrie, 137
Dietrich, Marlene, 219
Digangi, Ciro James, 233
Digart, Uschi, 144
DiGeronimo, Bruno, 206
Diller, Phyllis, 219
Dillman, Bradford, 108, 219
Dillon, Carmen, 60
Dillon, Melinda, 122, 123
Dillon, Rick, 144
Dimitri, Nick, 147
Dimmick, Walter, 141
Dior, Frenchie, 144
DiOrio, Piero, 162
Dirty Hands, 212
Dirty Knights' Work, 146
Discreet Charm of the Bourgeoisie, The, 161
Dishy, Bob, 62
Disney, Walt, 160
Disraeli, 160
DiStefano, Tony, 145
Dittrich, Scott, 150
Diversions, 205
Divine Lady, The, 160
Divine Obsession, The, 126
Divorcee, The, 160
Dixie, 128
Dixie Dynamite, 136
Dixon, Ivan, 86
Dixon, McIntyre, 82
Dixon, Richard M., 130, 139
Dlugolecka, Graznya, 213
Dmytryk, Edward, 139
Dobbins, Bennie, 22
Dobbins, Gene, 131
Dobbs, Heidi, 126, 135
Dobson, Kevin, 56
Dobson, Tamara, 77, 219
Dodd, Barbara, 137
Dodds, Mike, 213
Doff, Neel, 212
Dohanos, Peter, 16
Dohrn, Bernardine, 137
Doll, Dora, 203
Domburg, Andrea, 212
Domergue, Faith, 219
Dominatia, 150
Domination Blue, 140
Dominatrix Without Mercy, 132
D'On Thompson, Pamela, 149
Donaggio, Pino, 98
Donahue, Troy, 219
Donald, Val, 175
Donat, Robert, 160
Donnell, Jeff, 219
Donnelly, Budd, 135
Donnelly, Ruth, 219
Donnelly, Terry, 12, 30
Donner, Bob, 23
Donner, Richard, 60
Donno, Eddy, 44
Donovan, Casey, 137
Donovan, Elaine, 211
Don't Open the Window, 205
Doohan, Anita, 40
Doomwatch, 201
DoQui, Robert, 141
Doran, Johnny, 141

Dore, Nancy, 138
Dorf, Gary, 133
Dorn, Dody, 143
Dors, Diana, 204, 219
D'Orsay, Fifi, 219
Dorsey, Joe, 135
Dorsky, Nathaniel, 137
Dorsman, Judith, 140
Double Exposure Of Holly, The, 145
Double Life, A, 160
Doubleday, Frank, 131, 148
Doucette, John, 148
Doughty, Richard, 43
Douglas, Damon, 76, 137, 144
Douglas, Kirk, 219
Douglas, Melvyn, 42, 161, 219
Douglas, Michael, 154, 219
Douglas, Mike, 69
Douglass, Charles, 150
Dourif, Brad, 154, 155, 219
Douy, Max, 206
Dova, Ben, 62
Dow, R. A., 141
Dowling, Ed, 145
Down, Lesley Ann, 199, 219
Down, Maurice, 146
Downes, Anson, 98
Downey, Cheryl, 34, 106
Down-in-the-Hole Gang, The, 212
Doyle, David, 134
Doyle, Terry, 207
Dr. Black Mr. Hyde, 127
Dr. Jekyll and Mr. Hyde, 160
Dr. Tarr's Torture Dungeon, 203
Drady, Curt, 135
Dragon, Dennis, 142
Dragonfly, 16
Dragons Never Die, 212
Drake, Allan, 77
Drake, Betsy, 219
Drake, Charles, 219
Drake, Dick, 30
Drake, Marcie, 133
Drake, Miller, 142
Dreaded Mr. Twister, The, 150
Dream City, 214
Dreghorn, Lea, 194
Dresdel, Sonia, 233
Dressler, Marie, 160
Drew, Ellen, 219
Drew, Gene, 133
Drexel, Ruth, 191
Dreyfuss, Richard, 130, 219
Driscoll, Charles, 206
Driscoll, Bobby, 160
Driscoll, Robert Miller, 44
Drivas, Robert, 148, 219
Drive-In, 136
Dru, Joanne, 219
Drube, Diana, 147
Drum, 143
Druon, Maurice, 88
Dubbins, Don, 219
Dubin, Charles S., 143
Dubois, Marie, 204
Dubs, Arthur P., 150
Dubus, Marie Sophie, 202
Duce, Jerri, 52
Duce, Joy, 52
Duchaussoy, Michel, 201
Duchess and the Dirtwater Fox, The, 22
Ducugis, Cecile, 213
Duel in the Tiger Den, 209
Duell, William, 154, 155
Duering, Carl, 124
Duerrenmatt, Friedrich, 182
Duff, Howard, 219
Duffell, Peter, 201
Duff-MacCormick, Cara, 18
Dufilho, Jacques, 166
Dugan, Dennis, 44, 77
Dugan, Michael, 132
Dugger, Florrie, 84, 85
Duke, Bill, 86
Duke, Patty, 160, 161, 219
Dullea, Keir, 219
Dumont, Robert, 203
Dunaway, Faye, 7, 102, 103, 124, 125, 161, 219
Duncan, Sandy, 219
Dunham, Rosemarie, 196, 202
Dunn, James, 160
Dunn, Liam, 48, 126, 233
Dunne, Irene, 219
Dunne, Joe, 124
Dunne, John Gregory, 110
Dunne, Murphy, 62
Dunning, John, 144
Dunnock, Mildred, 16, 219
Dupre, John Leslie, 126, 132, 137, 148, 149

Dupuis, Jean L., 207
Durante, Jimmy, 219
Durbin, Deanna, 160, 219
Durfee, Ross, 107
Durning, Charles, 32, 44, 220
Durren, John, 133, 135, 143
Dussollier, Andre, 213, 220
Duthie, Michael, 197
Duvall, Robert, 94, 95, 102, 103, 220
Duvall, Shelly, 52
Duverge, Dominique, 204
Dvorak, Ann, 220
Dvorjetzki, Vladislav, 213
Dyall, Valentine, 194
Dyke, Thomas L., 130
Dynarski, Gene, 18
Eagle, Dexter, 136
Eagle, Jeff, 148
Earl, Thomas, 145
Earnshaw, Catherine, 145
Easley, Larry, 142
East, Everett, 210
East, Todd, 145
East of Eden, 161
Eastman, Gordon, 128
Easton, Joyce, 133
Easton, Robert, 220
Eastwood, Clint, 6, 46, 47, 108, 109, 220
Eat My Dust, 135
Eaton, Marion, 132
Eaton, Roberta, 144
Eaton, Shirley, 220
Eaton, Wallas, 212
Ebeling, George, 31
Ebert, Michael, 135
Ebony Ivory And Jade, 140
Ebsen, Buddy, 220
Echoes of a Summer, 134
Echols, Kermit, 135
Eckemyr, Agneta, 220
Eddins, Beverly, 135
Eddins, Rebecca, 135
Eddy, Duane, 136
Edelman, Louis F., 233
Eden, Barbara, 220
Edgerton, Earle, 127
Edmonds, Don, 131
Edsley, Larry, 132
Edvard Munch, 211
Edwards, Blake, 199
Edwards, Elizabeth, 143
Edwards, Eric, 126, 130, 131, 134, 136, 140, 146, 148, 149, 205
Edwards, Patty, 132
Edwards, Paul, 134
Edwards, Vince, 220
Effertz, Henry, 136
Efron, Marshall, 137, 139
Efros, Mel, 62
Egan, Michael, 12
Egan, Richard, 220
Egan, Ward, 136
Egerton, Mark, 140
Eggar, Samantha, 94, 95, 220
Eggericks, Marianne, 202
Ehlers, Corky, 54
Ehrenfreund, Heinz, 174
8 1/2, 161
Eisenman, Allan, 107
Ekberg, Anita, 220
Ekland, Britt, 210, 220
Ekman, Gosta, 178
El Gran Combo, 133
Elam, Jack, 131, 139, 149
Elcar, Dana, 20, 21, 74, 137
Elder, Lonne, III, 147
Elder, Patty, 107
Elene, Susie, 137
Elerick, John, 40
Eleven, Stan, 135
Elfers, Konrad, 201
Elia, Bob, 202
Elic, Josip, 154, 155
Elion, Lawrence, 207
Eliot, Nick, 131
Eliza's Horoscope, 213
Elizondo, Hector, 220
Elk, Lois Red, 148
Elkin, Stanley, 96
Ell, Ralph, 126, 145
Ellie, Francis, 148
Elliot, Robert, 136
Elliott, Tamara, 147
Elliott, Denholm, 124, 170, 214, 220
Elliott, Patricia, 31
Elliott, Rosalind, 206
Elliott, Ross, 128
Elliott, Sam, 55, 151
Elliotte, Herb, 145
Elliotts, Paul, 214
Ellis, Tony, 97
Ellison, Harlan, 139
Elmer Gantry, 161
Elmi, Nicole, 204

Elsom, Isobel, 220
Elster, J. G., 203
Elvera, 126
Ely, Ron, 220
Emanuelle, 213
Embryo, 40
Emerson, Faye, 220
Emge, David, 145
Emhardt, Robert, 96
Emilienne & Nicole, 209
Emmanuelle—The Joys of a Woman, 202
Emmet, Jesse, 127
Emmich, Clifford, 133
Enberg, Dick, 64, 107
End of the Game, 182
Endemann, Gernot, 197
Enforcer, The, 108
Engesser, William, 69
Engle, Harrison, 146
English, Louise, 84
Englund, Robert, 22
Enke, Olivia, 132
Enrico, Robert, 206, 208
Enriquez, Luis, 145
Enserro, Michael, 220
Erdman, Richard, 220
Erhart, Tom, 112, 114
Eric, Martin, 150
Erice, Victor, 212
Erickson, Leif, 220
Ericson, John, 140, 220
Ericson, Karen, 140
Ernst, Frank, 197
Escape from Angola, 200
Escobedo, Jaime, 28
Estormes, Nate, 18
Esky, Mike, 147
Esmond, Carl, 220
Espelin, Maury, 144
Esposito, Phil, 126
Esser, Carl, 126
Esterhazy, Andrea, 70
Estrada, Erik, 134
Estrin, Robert L., 106
Eubank, Shari, 149
Eunson, Dale, 148
Evans, Art, 14, 15
Evans, Dale, 220
Evans, Dame Edith, 194, 233
Evans, Gene, 220
Evans, Maurice, 220
Evans, Nigel, 201
Evans, Paul L., 213
Evans, Robert, 92
Evans, Warren, 134
Everett, Chad, 220
Everson, John, 78
Every, Eve, 145
Everyday, 144
Evigan, Greg, 147
Evil in the Deep, 144
Ewell, Tom, 220
Execution Squad, 213
Exit the Dragon Enter the Tiger, 201
Expose Me Lovely, 130
Exton, Clive, 201
Eymesz, Thea, 203, 208
Eymon, Florence, 211
Fabares, Shelley, 220
Faber, Peter, 212
Faber, Ron, 206
Fabian, 220
Fabian, Francoise, 168
Fabiankovich, Robert, 203
Fabray, Nanette, 220
Fabre, Dominique, 204
Fabrega, Christine, 210
Fabrizi, Franco, 213
Face to Face, 178
Fachelday, Gisela, 208
Fairbairn, Douglas, 183
Fairbanks, Douglas, 160
Fairbanks, Douglas, Jr., 220
Fairchild, Alice, 126
Fairchild, June, 136
Fairchild, Margaret, 135
Faithfull, Marianne, 133
Fajardo, Eduardo, 209
Faking of the President, The, 139
Falk, Camilla, 211
Falk, Peter, 50, 51, 120, 121, 220
Family Plot, 24
Fang, Peter, 213
Fania All Stars, 133
Fankboner, Sarah, 118
Fansett, Michele, 207
Fantasex, 136
Farentino, James, 220
Fargas, Antonio, 12, 86
Fargo, Jim, 46, 108
Farhat, Suhaila, 126
Farley, Elizabeth, 144
Farley, Morgan, 104, 114
Farlow, Wayne A., 24, 68
Farmer, Frank, 145
Farmer, Mimsy, 206, 210
Farmer, Reginald, 86

Farmer's Daughter, The, 160
Farmiloe, Sally, 211
Farr, Derek, 220
Farr, Felicia, 220
Farrar, Robert, 140
Farrell, Charles, 220
Farrell, Sharon, 129
Farrow, Mia, 220
Fasana, Alberto, 138
Fassbinder, Rainer Werner, 203, 208
Fast, Alvin L., 132, 147
Faulk, John Henry, 14
Faulkner, Graham, 220
Faulkner, Max, 146
Faulkner, Stephanie, 127, 136, 141
Faull, Prue, 211
Favrod, Charles-Henri, 211
Fawcett, Charles, 206
Fawcett-Majors, Farrah, 58, 59, 152
Faye, Alice, 220
Faye, Joey, 82
Fear or Fantasy, 128
Fears, Tom, 107
Fegte, Ernst, 233
Fehn, Kathy, 147
Fei, Lung, 201, 202
Feigenbaum, Bill, 127
Feinberg, Ron, 139
Feinstein, Alan, 148
Feld, Fritz, 48
Felder, Michael, 140
Feldman, Edward S., 107
Feldman, Marty, 48, 49, 209
Feldman, Richard, 107
Feldon, Barbara, 10, 220
Feldshuh, David, 147
Felicia, 214
Fell, Norman, 150
Fellen, Ricky, 86
Fellous, Roger, 214
Fellows, Don, 144, 201
Fellows, Edith, 220
Felsen, Milt, 144
Female Chauvinists, 144
Females for Hire, 212
Femmes De Sade, 137
Fendel, Rosemarie, 214
Fendors, Lan, 154
Fenech, Edwige, 207
Fenemore, Hilda, 210
Fennell, Michael, 86
Fenwick, Moya, 212
Ferguson, Perry, 118
Ferjac, Anouk, 208
Ferova, Tanya, 213
Ferrari, Mario, 172
Ferrel, Pablo, 210
Ferrell, Conchata, 102
Ferrell, Phil, 136
Ferrer, Jose, 62, 124, 160, 208, 220
Ferrer, Mel, 209, 220
Ferrer, Nino, 209
Ferreri, Marco, 201, 208
Ferriol, Caroline, 133
Ferris, Barbara, 220
Ferro, Talya, 133
Ferro, Turi, 206
Ferry, Christian, 116
Ferzetti, Gabriele, 88, 182, 220
Fetterman, Richard, 43
Feury, Peggy, 97, 104, 128
Fidenco, Nico, 213
Fiedel, Bard, 17
Fiedler, John, 118
Field, Angela, 144
Field, Sally, 22, 220
Field, Walter, 233
Fielding, Jerry, 28, 46, 108
Fields, Freddie, 26
Fields, Vanetta, 110
Fighting Mad, 148
Figueroa, Ruben, 220
Fillipo, Lou, 100
Fimple, Dennis, 22, 116, 131
Finch, Peter, 102, 103, 161, 202
Finder, Ignacio, 207
Findhorn, 210
Findlay, Michael, 128
Findley, Roberta, 141
Fine, Mort, 97
Finely, Spring, 149
Fink, Harry Julian, 108
Fink, Martin, 154
Fink, Michael, 140
Fink, R. M., 108
Finklestein, Bruce, 138
Finley, Greg, 131
Finn, Lila, 143
Finnegan, John, 114, 129
Finnell, Mike, 142
Finney, Albert, 187, 220
Finney, Shirley Jo, 131, 134
Fiore, Elena, 162
Firestone, Eddie, 20

Firestone, Scott, 28
First Nudie Musical, The, 131
Fischer, Bruce M., 150
Fischer, Corey John, 132
Fish, Hamilton, 87
Fishel, Doug, Jr., 31
Fisher, Eddie, 220
Fisher, Maryanne, 137
Fisk, Jack, 98, 134
Fitch, Louise, 127
Fitzgerald, Barry, 160
Fitzgerald, F. Scott, 104
Fitzgerald, Geraldine, 134, 220
Fitzgerald, Walter, 233
Fitzsimmons, Tom, 68
Flagg, Fannie, 22
Flaherty, Joseph X., 96
Flaiano, Ennio, 201
Flamant, Georges, 206
Flambe, 149
Flami, Golde, 207
Flannery, Susan, 143, 220
Flash and Firecat, 145
Flasher, The, 135
Flavin, James, 220, 234
Flaxman, Harvey, 135
Flecks, Harry, 130, 145
Fleischer, Richard, 196
Fleming, Cynthia, 130
Fleming, Lone, 208
Fleming, Rhonda, 220
Fleming, Robert, 133
Fleming, Stu, 110
Fleming, Victor, 160
Flemyng, Robert, 220
Fletcher, Dexter, 84
Fletcher, Louise, 54, 155, 157, 161, 220
Flippin, Lucy Lee, 82
Flocker, James T., 132
Florence, Joe, 108
Flower, George, 150
Flower, Joe, 136
Flower with the Deadly Sting, The, 210
Flowers, Wayland, 77
Floyd, Johnny Big, 201
Fluellen, Joel, 36
Flyn, Archie, 148
Flynn, Patrick, 212
Foa, Arnolda, 88
Foch, Nina, 220
Folsey, George, Jr., 38, 77, 141
Fonda, Henry, 56, 57, 220
Fonda, Jane, 161, 207, 220
Fonda, Peter, 80, 81, 148, 220
Fondato, Marc, 214
Fondato, Marcello, 206
Fong, Benson, 139
Fontaine, Flame, 140
Fontaine, Joan, 160, 220
Fontana, Rocco, 206
Fontelieu, Stocker, 70
Food of the Gods, The, 54
For Me and My Gal, 39
For Whom the Bell Tolls, 160
Foran, Dick, 220
Forbes, Bryan, 194
Forbes, Marion, 150
Forbidden Games, 160
Ford, Aleksander, 209
Ford, Ann, 58
Ford, Derek, 205, 213
Ford, Glenn, 56, 220
Ford, John, 160
Ford, Paul, 234
Ford, Valerie, 205
Foree, Ken, 36
Foremost, Sally, 132
Forest, Frank, 234
Forest, Lee, 149
Forest, Mark, 220
Forest, Michael, 204
Forman, Milos, 154, 161, 208
Forrest, Frederic, 34
Forrest, John, 210
Forrest, Steve, 220
Forster, Robert, 220
Forsyth, Ed, 149
Forsythe, John, 220
Forte, Fabian, 142
Fortes, Fernando, 126
Fortune Cookie, The, 161
Forward, Robert, 134
Fosse, Bob, 161
Foster, Clay, 150
Foster, Jodie, 8, 9, 84, 134, 152, 220
Foster, Meg, 141
Foster, Norman, 234
Foster, Pat, 205
Foster, Stan, 144
Four Deuces, The, 201
Fourastie, Angela, 205
Fourteen and Under, 204

Fowler, Buck, 143
Fowley, Douglas V., 76
Fox and His Friends, 203
Fox, Charles, 107
Fox, Edward, 220
Fox, James, 220
Fox, John J., 135, 148
Fox, Mickey, 135
Foxe, Fanne, 146
Foxworth, Robert, 141
Foxx, Redd, 77, 220
Fraas, Gro, 211
Frade, Jose, 209
Fraey, Susanka, 211
Fraisse, Robert, 202
Fraizer, Quin, 139
Fraker, William A., 26, 69, 148, 154
Frame, Elton, 210
Francesco, 26
Franciosa, Anthony, 220
Francis, Anne, 220
Francis, Arlene, 220
Francis, Connie, 220
Francis, Derek, 214
Francis, Nina, 211
Franciscus, James, 220
Francks, Don, 220
Franco, Gino, 148
Frangipane, Ron, 148
Frank, Ben, 135
Frank, Melvin, 22
Franken, Al, 143
Frankland, Peter, 148
Franklin, Alberta, 204
Franklin, C. Lester, 201
Franklin, Dan, 86
Franklin, Harry, Sr., 147
Franklin, Julia, 126, 130
Franklin, Pamela, 54, 220
Franklin, Steve, 34
Franklin, Valerie, 145
Franklyn, Fred, 76
Frankovich, M. J., 72, 76
Franks, Michelle, 136
Frann, Mary, 145
Franz, Arthur, 220
Franz, Eduard, 220
Fraser, Helen, 202
Fraser, Hugh, 78
Fraser, Karen, 149
Fraser, Mitzi, 137
Fraticelli, Franco, 164
Frawley, James, 62
Frazer, Shelagh, 201
Frazier, Harry, 135
Frazier, Joe, 100
Frazier, Sheila, 220
Frederick, Lynne, 124, 125
Frederickson, Mary Carole, 139
Fredricks, B. Anthony, 138
Free Soul, A, 160
Free, Stan, 145
Freed, Gordon, 135
Freeman, Al, Jr., 135, 220
Freeman, Barbara, 144
Freeman, Fred, 62
Freeman, Mona, 220
Freeman, Paul, 201
Freewheelin', 150
French, Arthur, 86
French, Bruce, 106
French, Lola, 140
French, Rita, 135
French Connection, The, 161
French Heat, 205
French Provincial, 165
Fresson, Bernard, 42
Freud, Stephen, 150
Frey, Leonard, 220
Fried, Gerald, 134, 210
Friedan, Bud, 38
Friedkin, William, 161
Friedland, Alice, 129
Friedmann, Anne, 210
Friedrich, John, 89
Frimel, Rude, 114
Froemke, Susan, 130
Frohlich, Sig, 44
Frohman, Melvyn, 129
From beyond the Grave, 204
From Here to Eternity, 161
From Noon Till Three, 76
Frome, Milton, 118
Fromer, Ben, 86
Front, The, 82
Frontiere, Dominic, 143
Frost, David, 14, 194
Frost, Jean Sarah, 130, 144
Frost, Lee, 136
Fruchtman, Lisa, 210
Frye, Virgil, 34, 133
Fryer, Robert, 124
Fu Sheng, Alexander, 210
Fuchs, Leo L., 203
Fugard, Athol, 175
Fujimoto, Tak, 127, 142
Fujioka, John, 80
Fujita, John, 205
Fukuda, Jun, 205

Fulci, L., 211
Fuller, M. Wayne, 129
Fuller, Penny, 18, 19
Fuller, Robert, 131
Fulton, Jessie Lee, 136
Funk, 150
Funny Girl, 161
Furie, Sidney J., 128
Furlong, John, 18
Furneaux, Yvonne, 220
Furrer, Urs B., 31, 147
Furth, George, 77
Futch, Lori, 69
Futureworld, 80
Gabel, Martin, 220
Gabin, Jean, 210, 234
Gable, Christopher, 194
Gable, Clark, 39, 160
Gable and Lombard, 128
Gabor, Eva, 220
Gabor, Zsa Zsa, 220
Gabriel, Francois, 206
Gabriel, Larry, 129, 134
Gage, Joe, 131
Gage, Robert, 144
Gagnon, Ginny, 64
Gaillard, 206
Gaillard, Jacques, 212
Gaines, Charles, 22
Galbo, Christina, 205
Gale, Eddra, 137
Gale, George, 200
Gale, Scott, 150
Galfas, Timothy, 129
Galik, Denise, 12
Gall, Carl, 207
Galland, Philippe, 165
Gallard, Rhonda, 128
Gallardo, Cesar, 140
Galleani, Eli, 205
Gallegly, Karlene, 44
Galli, Hall, 149
Gallili, Hal, 78
Gallitti, Alberto, 172, 201
Gallo, Fred T., 50, 100
Gallo, Maria Rosa, 207
Gallo, Mario, 116
Gallo, Neil, 148
Galvin, Frank, 149
Galvonie, Milan, 206
Gam, Martha, 207
Gam, Rita, 220
Gambina, Jimmy, 100
Gambino, Rikki, 132
Gamble, Duncan, 137
Gammell, Robin, 26
Gammon, James, 133, 138
Ganibalova, Valentina Ganilae, 207
Ganis, Glenda, 106
Ganis, Sidney, 18
Ganne, Madeleine, 203
Ganz, Bruno, 191, 198
Garage Sale, 150
Garber, Victor, 221
Garbo, Greta, 38, 161, 221
Garbo, Ingrid, 202
Garbuglia, Mario, 182
Garcia, Ginette, 209
Garcia, Margarita, 112
Garcia, Ronald, 133
Garcin, Ginette, 184
Garcin, Henri, 203, 209
Garden, Eva, 214
Garden of the Finzi-Continis, The, 161
Gardenia, Vincent, 221
Gardiner, Reginald, 221
Gardner, Arthur, 69
Gardner, Ava, 207, 221
Gardner, Cecilia, 145
Garfield, Alan, 41
Garfield, Allen, 41, 127, 128, 208, 221
Garfield, Brian, 23
Garfield, Julie, 82
Gargonne, Jean, 192
Garko, Gianni, 210
Garland, Beverly, 221
Garland, Judy, 39, 160
Garling, Kim, 148
Garner, James, 221
Garner, Peggy Ann, 160, 221
Garr, Teri, 40, 221
Garrani, Ivo, 145
Garrett, Betty, 221
Garrett, Donna, 143
Garrett, Hank, 17
Garrison, Sean, 221
Garsin, Mort, 132
Garson, Greer, 160, 221
Gartner, Sandra, 144
Gary, Dean, 150
Gary, Lorraine, 86
Gasc, Christian, 165
Gasgarth, Gary, 134
Gaslight, 160
Gaslini, Giorgio, 208
Gasser, Yves, 214
Gassman, Vittorio, 201, 214, 221
Gast, Leon, 133

Gate of Hell, 161
Gates, Andrew, 31
Gates, David, 31
Gates, Stephanie, 144
Gatlin, Jerry, 22
Gator, 69
Gatti, Marcello, 172
Gaunt, Michael, 214
Gau-uan, Rick, 139
Gavigan, Gerry, 176
Gavin, Amanda, 89
Gavin, John, 221
Gavin, Mary, 146
Gay, John, 88
Gay, Undis T., 210
Gaybis, Anne, 135
Gayle, Monica, 131
Gayles, Belinda, 138
Gaynes, George, 44, 114
Gaynor, Janet, 160, 221
Gaynor, Mitzi, 221
Gazzaniga, Don, 63
Gazzara, Ben, 124, 125,
    129, 210, 221
Gee, Timothy, 194
Geer, Will, 143, 207, 221
Geeson, Judy, 201, 221
Gegauff, Danielle, 206
Gegauff, Paul, 206
Gehret, Jean, 206
Gehring, Ted, 114
Geisinger, Elliot, 214
Gelb, Susan, 131
Gelfman, Samuel W., 142
Gelin, Xavier, 168
Gellis, Henry, 190
Gelman, Larry, 138, 143,
    145
Gemser, Laura, 124, 125
General Idi Amin Dada, 211
Genn, Leo, 209, 221
Gennaro, Gino, 82
Genoves, Andre, 206
Gentleman's Agreement,
    160
Gentry, Bobbie, 45
Geodopoulis, 132
George, Chief Dan, 46, 190,
    221
George, Christopher, 56,
    135, 136
George, Nathan, 154, 155
George, Nicholas, 210
George, Susan, 143
Gerardi, Robert, 182
Geray, Linda, 41
Gerchunoff, Alberto, 207
Gerdon, Melody, 136
Gere, Richard, 137
Germi, Pietro, 210
Gershe, Leonard, 38
Gershwin, Jerry, 32
Get Mean, 206
Getchell, Robert, 122
Getting Together, 150
Ghio, Adrian, 207
Gholson, Julie, 221
Ghostley, Alice, 69
Ghyka, Roderick, 126
Giacobetti, Francis, 202
Giambellua, Joseph C., 100
Gianini, Michelangelo, 135
Giannetti, Joe, 147
Giannini, Giancarlo, 162,
    163, 213, 221
Giant, 161
Gibbs, Alan, 114
Gibbs, Anthony, 176
Gibbs, Sheila Shand, 94
Gibson, Mary Ann, 118
Gibson, Sasha, 129
Gibson, Steve, 128
Gidekel, Karrin, 144
Gielgud, John, 221
Gierasch, Stefan, 98, 112
Gifford, Alan, 144
Gifford, Frank, 107
Gigi, 161
Gignoux, Hubert, 184
Gil, Rosemarie, 213
Gilbert, Brian, 124
Gilbert, Christopher, 205
Gilbert, Herschell Burke,
    128
Gilbert, Joseph, 213
Gilbert, Lou, 92
Gilbert, Ray, 234
Gilbert and Sullivan, 209
Gilford, Jack, 44
Gill, Bob, 145
Gill, Brenda, 126
Gill, William, 120
Gillette, Ruth, 118
Gilliam, Burton, 69
Gilliam, Stu, 127
Gillian, Jenn, 206
Gillies, Max, 139
Gilligan, Mike, 137
Gilliland, Richard, 22
Gillin, Linda, 142
Gillis, Anne, 221
Gillis, Don, 207
Gillis, Jamie, 128, 129,

132, 134, 135, 137,
    141, 142, 145, 146,
    148
Gillmore, Margalo, 221
Gilman, Sam, 34
Gilmore, Virginia, 221
Gilmore, William S., Jr., 68
Gilroy, Frank D., 76
Gimpera, Teresa, 212
Gingold, Hermione, 221
Ginty, Robert, 107
Giovanina, 126
Giovanni, Jose, 210
Girard, Andre, 206
Girardot, Annie, 201, 205,
    213
Giraudeau, Bernard, 210
Girdler, William, 135, 146
Girl from Starship Venus,
    The, 213
Girl from the Red Cabaret,
    The, 209
Girls and the Love Games,
    202
Girls in Trouble, 201
Girney, Alan L., 200
Girotti, Massimo, 202
Gish, Lillian, 161, 221
Gist, Rod, 143
Gitchell, Gary, 136
Gittes, Harry, 44
Gittings, Richard, 128
Giusti, Paolo, 212
Gladys Knight and The Pips,
    106
Glasner, Christine, 203
Glass, Seamon, 44
Glassberg, Peter, 100
Glattes, Wolfgang, 201
Gleason, Jackie, 221
Gleason, Paul X., 134
Gleason, Regina, 137
Gleeson, Redmond, 106
Glen, Scott, 148
Glenn, Pierre-William, 192
Glick, Michael S., 40
Glick, Phyllis, 137
Glickler, Paul, 142
Glickman, Paul, 148
Glitter Band, The, 140
Glitters, Goldie, 150
Globus, Yuram, 201
Glouner, Richard C., 143
Glover, Brian, 146
Glover, Geoffrey, 205
Go for It, 142
Gobbi, Sergio, 204
God Told Me To, 148
Goddard, Claude, 135, 142
Goddard, Paulette, 221
Godfather, The, 161
Godfather Part II, The, 161
Godfather Squad, The, 206
Godwin, Frank, 201
Godzilla vs. Megalon, 205
Goetman, Gerard, 212
Goetz, Peter, 147
Goin' Home, 150
Going My Way, 160
Golan, Menachem, 201
Gold, Harry, 98
Gold, Ron, 132
Goldberg, Alan B., 148
Goldberg, Leonard, 137
Goldblatt, Harold, 202
Goldblum, Jeff, 12, 63
Goldfarb, Philip, 8
Goldin, Marilyn, 43, 165
Golding, Bill, 97
Golding, Jerry, 132
Goldman, Bo, 154, 182
Goldman, Danny, 34
Goldman, James, 170
Goldman, Lorry, 143
Goldman, Michael F., 135
Goldman, Philippe, 192
Goldman, Ronald K., 145
Goldman, Steve, 129
Goldman, William, 18, 92
Goldoni, Lelia, 137
Goldsboro, Bobby, 69
Goldsmith, Jerry, 23, 32,
    58, 60, 210
Goldstein, Al, 126, 127
Goldstein, David, 144
Goldstein, William, 36, 77
Goldstone, James, 68
Goldstraw, Lawrence, 213
Golfier, Richard, 192
Gomes, Panchito, 208
Gomez, Fernando Fernan,
    212
"Gone to Texas", 46
Gone With The Wind, 160
Gonsky, Paul, 133
Gonzales, George, 28
Gonzales-Gonzalez, Pedro,
    221
Good Earth, The, 160
Goodbye, Mr. Chips, 160
Goodbye, Norma Jean, 130
Goodbye Bruce Lee: His Last
    Game of Death, 201

Goodliffe, Michael, 214,
    234
Goodman, Al, 129
Goodman, Dan, 149
Goodman, David Zelag, 58
Goodman, George, 213
Goodman, Terence, 45
Goodnoff, Irv, 131
Goodrum, Kevin, 132
Gora, Claudio, 189
Gordon, Bert I., 54
Gordon, Carl, 36
Gordon, Donna, 129
Gordon, Gale, 221
Gordon, Hannah, 206
Gordon, Jack, 127
Gordon, Kelly, 144
Gordon, Leo, 131
Gordon, Robert, 127, 141
Gordon, Ruth, 62, 161,
    221
Gordon, Tom, 144
Gordy, Berry, 36
Gori, Mario Cecchi, 202,
    206
Goring, Marius, 221
Gorman, Cliff, 221
Gorski, Alexandra, 203
Gortner, Marjoe, 54, 133,
    221
Gorwitz, Jeremiah, 127
Gossett, Lou, 134, 141,
    221
Goth, Ray, 112
Gottfried, Howard, 102
Gottlieb, Carl, 142
Gottlieb, David, 142
Gottlieb, F. G., 202
Gotz, Karin, 202
Gough, Lloyd, 82
Gould, Elliott, 44, 127,
    130, 221
Gould, Harold, 48, 49, 62,
    64
Gould, Lea, 142
Gould, Sara Jane, 114
Gould, Sid, 22
Goulet, Robert, 221
Goya, Tito, 92
Grace, Bud, 141
Grace, Carol, 120
Graduate, The, 161
Graham, Barbara, 127
Graham, Gerrit, 63, 133,
    142, 143
Graham, Herb, 131
Graham, Juliet, 136, 138
Graham, Margaret, 129
Graham, Michael, 214
Graham, William A., 147
Grahame, Gloria, 146, 160,
    221
Grainer, Ron, 167, 210
Grainger, J. Edmund, 88
Granberry, Donald, 131
Grand, Barbara, 127
Grand, Richard, 127
Grand Hotel, 38, 160
Grande, Nico II, 204
Granel, Stephanie, 192
Granger, Farley, 221
Granger, Stewart, 221
Grant, Andrew, 213
Grant, Arthur, 201
Grant, Barra, 41
Grant, Cary, 161, 221
Grant, Cy, 209
Grant, Frank, 145
Grant, Heather, 149
Grant, Kathryn, 221
Grant, Lee, 124, 125, 159,
    161, 221
Grant, Peter, 213
Grant, Sarina C., 36, 86
Granville, Bonita, 221
Granville, Rene, 129
Grapes of Wrath, The, 160
Gratz, Humphrey, 52
Grau, Jorge, 205
Grauman, Sid, 146
Graunberger-Richebe, 206
Graver, Gary, 136
Graves, Peter, 142, 194,
    221
Gravina, Carla, 168
Gray, Charles, 94
Gray, Coleen, 221
Gray, Dobie, 127
Gray, Fred, 137
Grayson, Claudine, 131
Grayson, Kathryn, 221
Graystone, Gerald, 140
Great Adventure, The, 214
Great, Don, 132, 214
Great Lie, The, 160
Great Scout and Cathouse
    Thursday, The, 139
Great Texas Dynamite
    Chase, The, 144
Great Ziegfeld, The, 160
Greatest Show on Earth,
    The, 160
Green, Bill, 18

Green, Bud, 136
Green, Grant, 148
Green, H. F., 149
Green, Utah, 148
Greenberg, Adam, 205
Greenberg, Barry, 137
Greenberg, Harold, 186
Greenberg, Jerry, 34
Greene, Angela, 80
Greene, Danford B., 148
Greene, Ellen, 12, 13
Greene, James, 34
Greene, Leon, 78, 94
Greene, Loretta, 14
Greene, Lorne, 221
Greene, Michael, 44
Greene, Reuben, 120
Greene, Richard, 221
Greene, Robert, 136
Greenhut, Robert, 82
Greenspun, Janie, 210
Grenstreet, Cindy, 149
Greenwald, Ted, 137
Greenwood, Joan, 221
Greer, Bill, 126
Greer, Dan, 149, 150
Greer, Jane, 221
Greer, Michael, 221
Grefe, William, 141
Gregg, Virginia, 137
Gregory, Gillian, 84
Gregory, John, 150
Greif, George, 44
Gremillion, Barry, 136
Grey, Christian, 114
Grey, Joel, 52, 53, 94, 95,
    161, 221
Grey, Virginia, 221
Grey Gardens, 130
Grezel, Sylvie, 192
Gribble, Bernard, 40, 174
Griem, Helmut, 124, 221
Grier, Pam, 143
Grier, Rosey, 144
Gries, Tom, 32
Griffin, D. W., 149
Griffin, Jack, 128
Griffith, Andy, 221
Griffith, Charles B., 135
Griffith, Cindi, 190
Griffith, D. W., 160
Griffith, Eva, 140
Griffith, Grover, 132
Griffith, Hugh, 161, 195,
    221
Griffith, Kenneth, 131, 204
Griffith, Melanie, 221
Grill, Alexander, 214
Grimaldi, Hugo, 201
Grimaud, Martine, 206
Grimes, Gary, 64, 65, 221
Grimes, Stephen, 50
Grimes, Tammy, 221
Grinko, Nikolai, 213
Grisman, David, 135
Gritzus, Ionas, 207
Grizzard, George, 221
Grizzly, 135
Grodin, Charles, 116, 221
Grody, Kathryn, 44
Groh, David, 107, 221
Groome, Malcolm, 150
Gross, Gene, 102
Gross, Josef, 209
Grossman, Amy, 18
Grossman, Steve, 148
Grover, Cindy, 102
Grover, Stanley, 102
Grow, Ronald R., 64
Gruenberg, Axel, 127
Grundy, Guy, 150
Grusin, Dave, 50
Guardian of the Wilderness,
    150
Guardino, Harry, 74, 108,
    221
Guardino, Jerome, 89
Guarnieri, Ennio, 182, 188
Guash, Sara, 210
Guenette, Robert, 142, 149
Guenol, Zelmar, 207
Guerin, Nathalie, 206
Guernica, 206, 207
Guerrini, Orso Maria, 88
Guerritore, Monica, 210
Guess Who's Coming to
    Dinner, 161
Gueye, Doudou, 211
Gueye, Makhouredia, 211
Guffray, Pierre, 42
Guidice, Don, 44
Guido, Alberti, 208
Guillemin, Claudine, 208
Guillemot, Anges, 184
Guillermin, John, 116
Guinness, Alec, 50, 161,
    221
Guiomar, Julien, 165
Gulassa, Anthony, 144
Gulpili, David, 212
Gumball Rally, The, 143
Gums, 149
Gun Down, 23

Gunn, Moses, 221
Gunzburg, Roy, 30
Gus, 64, 65
Guss, Louis, 114
Gustavson, Lanny, 134
Guth, Raymond, 62
Guthridge, John, 172
Guthrie, Woody, 122
Gutman, James, 149
Gutschwager, Helo, 191
Guy, Jack, 214
Guy, Rory, 129
Gwenn, Edmund, 160
Gwillim, David, 221
Gwynne, Michael C., 63,
    234
Gwynne, Peter, 140
Habif, Jim, 144
Hacker, Philip J., 149
Hackett, Buddy, 221
Hackett, Henry, 124
Hackett, Joan, 141, 221
Hackett, John, 44
Hackman, Gene, 7, 161,
    221
Haddah, Jelah, 211
Haddit, Gloria, 142
Haddon, Dayle, 209, 210,
    221
Haddrick, Roy, 140
Hafferkamp, Jack, 145
Hagan, Anna, 190
Hagegard, Anne, 178
Hagen, Erica, 41
Haggard, Mark, 131, 136
Haggerty, Dan, 127, 148
Haggerty, H. B., 201
Hagle, Roy David, 133
Hagman, Larry, 41, 62, 221
Hagopian, Ruth, 150
Hahn, Archie, 142
Hahn, Gisela, 203
Hahn, Jess, 206, 207
Hahn, Rob, 134
Haig, Sid, 68
Haigh, Kenneth, 170, 171
Haims, Eric, 145
Haims, Shelley, 145
Haines, Brian, 130
Hairston, Jester, 36
Hajer, Grethe, 211
Haji, 129, 132
Halberg, Garry, 116
Hale, Barbara, 221
Hale, Georgina, 124
Hale, Ron, 18
Hale, Scott, 72
Haley, Jackie Earle, 28
Haley, Michael, 22
Halfon, Samy, 204
Hall, Albert P., 14
Hall, Brian, 146
Hall, Conrad, 92
Hall, Derry, 214
Hall, Joanna, 80
Hall, Mark Edward, 150
Hall, Rene, 131
Hall, Terri, 126, 127, 132,
    136, 137, 138, 141,
    145, 148, 149
Hall, Tony, 207
Hallam, John, 146
Hallberg, William, 45
Haller, Michael, 122
Hallsey, Lottie, 126
Halmi, Robert, 127
Halop, Billy, 234
Halpin, Luke, 141
Halsey, Richard, 12, 100
Halstead, Robin, 124
Hambleton, Duffy, 133
Hambling, Gerry, 84, 172
Hamburg, Wendell, 144
Hamel, Veronica, 142
Hamilton, Colin, 44, 107
Hamilton, George, 221
Hamilton, Judith, 128
Hamilton, Lynn, 14
Hamilton, Margaret, 221
Hamilton, Neil, 221
Hamilton, Warren, Jr., 135
Hamlet, 160
Hammer, Theodore S., 150
Hamon, Lucienne, 207
Hamowy, Cynthia, 86
Hampshire, Susan, 221
Hampton, James, 30
Hampton, Paul, 141
Hampton, Roger, 114
Hanack, Sigrid, 201
Hancock, John, 137
Hanft, Helen, 12
Hankerson, Barry, 106
Hanley, Jenny, 206
Hannemann, Walter, 107
Hansel, Arthur, 203
Hansen, Heidi, 213
Hansome, Rhonda, 150
Hanson, Jacque, 140
Hanson, Preston, 130
Happy Housewives, The,
    214
Hard Candy, 149

244

Hard Woman, 213
Hardin, Sherry, 150
Hardin, Ty, 221
Harding, Ann, 222
Harding, Malcolm, 34
Hardy, Brian, 84
Hardy, Diana, 145
Hardy, Robert, 201
Hare, The, 144
Harewood, Dorian, 133, 222
Hargreaves, John, 212
Harkey, Mary S., 131
Harman, Mildred, 31
Harnois, Beatrice, 206, 214
Harper, Donn, 150
Harper, Jessica, 130
Harper, Robert, 129
Harper, Valerie, 222
Harrington, Pat, 222
Harris, Alan, 145
Harris, Barbara, 24, 25, 222
Harris, Burtt, 92, 97
Harris, Chris, 78
Harris, Crystal, 149
Harris, John, 130
Harris, Julie, 124, 125, 194, 222
Harris, Julius, 116
Harris, Lawrence, 144
Harris, Leonard, 8, 9
Harris, Linda, 145
Harris, Lynn, 149, 150
Harris, Martin, 212
Harris, Michael, 145
Harris, Paul, 149
Harris, Richard, 28, 66, 67, 134, 170, 171, 222
Harris, Roger, 175
Harris, Rosemary, 222
Harrison, Gregory, 129
Harrison, Hal, Jr., 149, 150
Harrison, Mare, 146
Harrison, Noel, 222
Harrison, Phillip, 78
Harrison, Rex, 161, 222
Harrison, Simon, 131
Harrison, Tony, 207
Harrison, Vangie, 78
Harry, 146
Harry and Tonto, 161
Harry and Walter Go to New York, 44
Hart, Diane Lee, 138, 142
Hart, Erica, 132
Hart, Harvey, 183
Hart, Helena, 183
Hart, Jacob, 136
Hartig, Will, 146
Hartman, David, 222
Hartman, Elizabeth, 222
Hartwig, Wolf C., 203, 204
Harvey, 160
Harvey, Laurence, 141
Harwood, Bo, 129
Harz, Claude, 212
Hashimoto, Richard, 56, 86, 129
Haskell, Jimmie, 26
Hasle, Berit Rytter, 211
Hasselhoff, David, 137
Hassett, Marilyn, 107, 190
Hastings, Bob, 10
Hatch, Tony, 209
Hatcher, Harley, 142
Hau, Joanna, 148
Hauben, Lawrence, 154
Haucke, Gert, 203
Hauer, Rutger, 212
Hausman, Michael, 120
Haven, Annette, 126, 130, 135, 137, 145, 146, 147, 148, 149
Haver, June, 222
Havoc, June, 222
Hawker, John, 133
Hawkins, Odie, 150
Hawks, Howard, 161
Hawmps, 30
Hawn, Goldie, 22, 161, 222
Haworth, Ted, 176
Hayakawa, Mie, 211
Hayase, Astrid, 138
Hayashi, Yutaka, 205
Hayden, Linda, 202, 222
Hayden, Sterling, 222
Hayers, Sidney, 201, 204
Hayes, Alfred, 207
Hayes, Helen, 160, 161, 222
Hayes, Isaac, 222
Hayes, John, 118, 140
Hayes, Margaret, 222
Hayes, Sylvia, 106
Hayman, Lillian, 143
Haymer, John, 201
Haynes, Cal, 127
Haynes, Hilda, 134
Hayter, James, 210
Hayward, Sondra, 136
Hayward, Susan, 161
Hayworth, Rita, 222

Hazard, Al, 146
Haze, Stan, 76
He Is My Brother, 139
Head, Edith, 20, 24, 128
Headmaster, 142
Hearn, Maryann, 135
Hearne, Catherine, 30
Heath, Scott, 131
Heathcote, Thomas, 146
Heatherton, Joey, 222
Hebert, Mona, 138
Heckart, Eileen, 90, 161, 222
Hedison, David, 222
Hedrich, Dagmar, 204
Heffernan, John, 148
Heffley, Wayne, 116
Heffron, Richard T., 80, 134
Heflin, Marta, 110
Heflin, Van, 160
Hefty, Neal, 40
Heiden, Janice, 136
Heilbron, Lorna, 207
Heim, Alan, 102
Heinz, Carl, 204
Heinz, Gerhard, 203
Heiress, The, 160
Helena, 210
Heller, Paul, 133, 134, 139, 146
Hellwig, Juergen, 149
Helmond, Katherine, 24, 137
Help Me. . .I'm Possessed, 126
Helpern, David, Jr., 149
Heltau, Michael, 205
Hemingway, Margaux, 26, 27
Hemingway, Mariel, 26, 27
Hemmings, David, 208, 222
Hempel, Anouska, 210
Hemphill, Simpson, 45
Hemple, Stuart, 128
Henabery, Joseph, 234
Henderson, Bill, 41
Henderson, Don, 124
Henderson, Marcia, 222
Hendrix, Wanda, 222
Hendry, Gloria, 222
Hendry, Marsh, 149
Hennesy, Dale, 116
Henreid, Paul, 222
Henriau, Marie, 198, 208
Henriksen, Lance, 97, 146
Henry, Buck, 180, 222
Henry, Mike, 126, 127
Henson, Gladys, 210
Henson, Nicky, 210
Hentz, Pierre, 203
Hepburn, Audrey, 161, 170, 171, 222
Hepburn, Katharine, 38, 160, 161, 222
Hepton, Bernard, 124, 125
Her Family Jewels, 201
Herbert, Andrew, 135
Herbert, Jean, 184
Herbert, Percy, 201
Herbst, Cynthia, 18
Herd, Richard, 18
Herdan, Earle, 142
Herdegen, Leszek, 206
Herigstadt, Gordon, 135
Herlitzka, Roberto, 162
Herman, Alan, 17
Hermann, Irm, 208
Hermes, Leonard, 149
Hernandez, Andy, 149
Hernandez, Sosimo, 77
Herndon, Walter Scott, 31, 41, 137, 147
Heroux, Claude, 186
Herr, Bianca, 146
Herrera, Anthony, 57
Herrerra, Regino, 66
Herrgott, Francis, 203
Herring, Pembroke J., 122
Herrmann, Bernard, 8, 70
Herron, J. Barry, 131
Hershey, Barbara, 23, 146, 214
Hersholt, Jean, 160
Hertelendy, Hanna, 107
Hertzberg, Michael, 48
Herzfeld, John, 142
Hesseman, Howard, 62, 133, 143
Heston, Charlton, 7, 23, 56, 57, 107, 146, 161, 222
Hewson, Sherrie, 194
Heyman, Barton, 137
Heyns, Thys, 200
Heywood, Anne, 222
Heywood, Chris, 139
Hibler, Christopher, 64
Hice, Fred, 107
Hickey, William, 120
Hickman, Darryl, 102, 222
Hickman, Dwayne, 222
Hickman, Gail Morgan, 108

Hickox, Douglas, 131
Hickox, S. Bryan, 77
Hicks, Carolyn, 213
Hidalgo, Ginamaria, 207
Hietala, Kathleen, 131
Higgins, Anthony, 124
Higgins, Colin, 112
Higgins, Fran, 141
Higgins, Michael, 144
High Noon, 160
High School Honies, 144
High Society, 39
High Velocity, 210
Highway Hookers, 130
Hilbeck, Fernando, 205
Hilden, Joanna, 145
Hilditch, Robert, 140, 212
Hilkene, Michael, 133
Hill, Arthur, 80, 222
Hill, Bernard, 146
Hill, Bill, 124
Hill, Dennis, 52
Hill, George Roy, 161
Hill, Graham, 202
Hill, James, 211
Hill, John, 94, 140
Hill, Steven, 222
Hill, Terence, 206, 222
Hiller, Arthur, 20, 112
Hiller, Wendy, 124, 161, 222
Hiller, Wolfgang, 203
Hillman, Rebecca, 144
Hills, Gillian, 201
Hilton, George, 210
Hilton, Kathy, 144, 149
Hilton, Nikki, 150
Hindgrind, Harold, 140, 149
Hindle, Art, 143
Hiney, William, 110
Hingle, Pat, 222
Hinz, Don, 133
Hinz, Michael, 202, 204
Hinz, Terry, 107
Hiona, Sam, 133
Hipp, Paul, 140
Hippe, Laura, 58
Hirsch, Paul, 70, 98
Hirschfeld, Gerald, 107
Hirschfeld, Jerry, 16
Hirsh, Tina, 135
Hirtz, Dagmar, 182
Hitchcock, Alfred, 24
Hitchcock, Jane, 114, 115
Hivley, Jack B., 127
Ho, Linda, 206
Ho, Yu Ming, 209
Hobgood, Eugene, 120
Hofbauer, Ernst, 204
Hoffman, Basil, 18
Hoffman, Cary, 143
Hoffman, Dustin, 6, 18, 19, 92, 93, 222
Hoffman, Jerry, 131
Hoffman, Lee, 203
Hoffman, Marriane, 212
Hoffman, Robert W., 148, 208
Hoffman, Tom, 146
Hohoff, Christian, 203
Holbrook, Gerald, 150
Holbrook, Hal, 18, 56, 222
Holbrook, John, 190
Holden, William, 102, 103, 161, 222
Holder, Geoffrey, 68
Holder, Peter, 84
Holder, Roy, 146
Holder, Wilbert, 213
Holdridge, Lee, 131, 150
Holes, The, 212
Holiday, Bonnie, 126, 135
Holiday, Fillip, 144
Holland, Hilary, 180
Hollander, Jack, 100, 144
Holliday, Judy, 160
Holliday, Polly, 18
Holliman, Earl, 222
Hollingsworth, 140
Holloman, Bridget, 145
Holloway, Stanley, 213, 222
Holloway, Sterling, 132
Hollywood, Peter, 150
Hollywood High, 150
Hollywood on Trial, 149
Hollywood She-Wolves, 138
Holm, Celeste, 89, 160, 222
Holm, Cynthia, 150
Holm, Ian, 170, 197
Holmes, Christopher, 86
Holmes, John C., 131, 132, 138, 140, 142, 144, 145, 147, 148, 149
Holmes, Richard, 78
Holmes, Rupert, 144
Holmes, Stacy, 135
Holokan, John, 135
Holscher, Heinz, 203
Holtzman, Jack, 144
Holtzman, Mark, 18
Holzman, Alan, 134

Homeier, Skip, 127, 222
Homer, Raymond P., 214
Homolka, Oscar, 222
Honeypie, 127
Honjo, Mari, 139
Hood, Don, 70
Hooks, Robert, 222
Hooper, Charles, 128
Hooper, Geraldine, 206
Hooten, Peter, 136
Hoover, Phil, 150
Hope, Bob, 160, 161, 222
Hopkins, Allan, 97
Hopkins, Bo, 143
Hopkins, Jay Allan, 102
Hopkins, Robert, 137
Hopper, Dennis, 212, 222
Hordern, Michael, 194, 201
Horger, Jack, 177
Horger, John C., 143
Horn, Isabelle, 106
Horn, Tyler, 149
Hornblow, Arthur, Jr., 234
Horne, Lena, 222
Horner, Harry, 44
Horowitz, Jimmy, 209
Horror Rises from the Tomb, 205
Horsburgh, Mike, 146
Horsfall, Bernard, 197
Horton, Cynthia, 204
Horton, Louisa, 68
Horton, Robert, 222
Horton, Suzanne, 134
Horulu, Kemal, 205
Hoskins, Bob, 130
Hossein, Robert, 203
Hot and Heavy, 135
Hot Nasties, 147
Hot Potato, 132, 133
Hot Shots, 145
Hot Summer in the City, 144
Hotchkis, Joan, 45, 134
Hoty, Dee, 44
Houck, Joy, Jr., 131
Houghton, Katharine, 222
House, Ashley, 94
House of Exorcism, 209
House of Psychotic Women, 210
Houseman, John, 74, 161, 222
Houser, Jerry, 222
Houston, Donald, 124, 222
Houston, Thelma, 36
Houwer, Bob, 212
Hovannes, Vahagn, 130
Hoven, Adrian, 201, 203
Hovey, Tim, 222
How Funny Can Sex Be?, 213
How Green Was My Valley, 160
Howard, Arthur, 210
Howard, Clint, 135
Howard, Cy, 40
Howard, Frances, 234
Howard, Harry, 14
Howard, John C., 20, 48
Howard, Ken, 222
Howard, Rance, 135
Howard, Ron, 72, 73, 135, 222
Howard, Sandy, 40, 66, 131, 134
Howard, Trevor, 210, 222
Howarth, Anthony, 213
Howe, James Wong, 234
Howell, Edward, 139
Howell, Hoke, 76
Howell, Russ, 150
Howells, Ursula, 222
Howerton, Charles, 135
Howes, Sally Ann, 222
Hoy, Bub, 22
Hsu, Herman, 201
Hsu, Victor, 133
Hubacher, Edy, 182
Hubbard, Janet, 36
Huber, Arthur Paul, 203
Huber, Hezzo, 191
Hubert, Jacques, 190
Hubert, Lynn, 130
Hubert, Roger, 206
Hubert-Trimbal, Mela, 97
Huckabee, Cooper, 138
Hud, 161
Huddleston, David, 32
Hudson, Rock, 40, 222
Huegli, Willy, 182
Huff, Tom, 107
Huffaker, Clair, 203
Hugh, Soto Joe, 129
Hughes, Barnard, 222
Hughes, Howard, 235
Hughes, Kathleen, 222
Hughes, Ken, 206
Hughes, Leslie, 150
Hugo, Michel, 45
Hugo the Hippo, 127
Hulette, Don, 139
Hull, Eve, 145

Hull, Josephine, 160
Human Tornado, The, 147
Hume, Alan, 146, 204, 209
Hume, Edward, 107
Humphree, Suzy, 150
Humpoletz, Paul, 124
Hung, Chang, 213
Hunnicutt, Arthur, 222
Hunnicutt, Gayle, 222
Hunsperger, Rudolf, 182
Hunt, Amber, 137
Hunt, Laura, 136
Hunt, Marsha, 222
Hunt, Paul, 145
Hunt, Peter, 197
Hunted, The, 202
Hunter, Bill, 212
Hunter, David, 131
Hunter, Ian, 222
Hunter, Jim, 186
Hunter, Kim, 160, 222
Hunter, Tab, 222
Hunter, Tanna, 130
Huppert, Isabelle, 209
Hurkos, Peter, 142
Hurley, Gerard, 139
Hurst, Gordon, 112, 114, 136
Hurst, Jeffrey, 136, 142, 145, 146, 148, 149, 214
Hurst, Rick, 143
Husong, Robert, 144
Hussey, Ruth, 222
Huster, Francis, 198
Hustler Squad, 140
Iluston, Angelica, 68, 104
Huston, John, 160, 222
Huston, Walter, 160
Hutchins, Will, 145
Hutton, Betty, 222
Hutton, Lauren, 69, 222
Hutton, Linda, 180
Hutton, Robert, 222
Hyams, Peter, 126
Hyde-White, Wilfrid, 222
Hyer, Martha, 222
Hylands, Scott, 89
Hynes, Richard, 150
Hyry, David, 130
I Want to Live, 161
I Will, I Will . . . for Now, 130
I Will, I Will . . . for Now, 130
Iannacci, Enzo, 162
Igawa, Hasashi, 211
Igus, Darrow, 86
Illescas, Charles, 203
Ilsa, Harem Keeper of the Oil Sheiks, 130, 131
Image, The, 128
Imi, Tony, 194
Immoral Tales, 204, 205
In Old Chicago, 160
In Search of Bigfoot, 140
In Search of Noah's Ark, 141
In the Heat of the Night, 161
Inagaki, Shun, 211
Incredible Sarah, The, 196
Incredible Torture Show, The, 149
"Indians", 52
Inescort, Frieda, 234, 235
Infanti, Angelo, 213
Infascelli, Roberto, 203
Infidel, The, 132
Informer, The, 160
Ingels, Marty, 222
Inkpen, Ron, 140
Inman, Walter, 129
Inn, Frank, 30
Inserts, 130
Inside Marilyn Chambers, 130
Inside Out, 201
Intimate Playmates, The, 201
Invasion of the Blood Farmers, 139
Investigation of a Citizen above Suspicion, 161
Iocouvozzi, Kim, 141
Iovieno, Frank, 130
Ipale, Aharon, 172
Ippolito, Ciro, 206
Ireland, Jill, 32, 33, 76, 203
Ireland, John, 141, 209, 222
Ireland, John, Jr., 137
Irons, Stanley, 137
Irving, Amy, 98
Irving, David, 144
Irving, George S., 17, 150
Irving, Holly, 107
Isacksen, Pete, 135
Isbell, Jack, 136
Isle, Evans, 132
Isnardon, Robert, 210
Israel, Neil, 143

It Happened One Night, 160
It Is Raining on Santiago, 213
It Seemed Like a Good Idea at the Time, 212
Ito, Robert, 57, 63
It's Showtime, 134, 135
Ives, Burl, 127, 150, 161, 222
Iyllia, Moses, 140
J. D.'s Revenge, 141
Jabbar, Kareem Abdul, 201
Jack and the Beanstalk, 127
Jackson, Anne, 223
Jackson, Carson, 130
Jackson, David E., 132
Jackson, Glenda, 160, 161, 196, 223
Jackson, J. J., 86
Jackson, Jamie Smith, 18
Jackson, Jay, 144
Jackson, Joanie, 142
Jackson, Leonard, 86
Jackson, Lynne, 126
Jackson, Mary, 142
Jackson, Michael, 84
Jackson, Robert, 144
Jackson County Jail, 133
Jaco, Cindy, 136
Jacobi, Lou, 12, 223
Jacobs, Jon Ian, 127
Jacobsen, Ulla, 203
Jacoby, Scott, 223
Jacque, Christian, 203
Jaeckel, Richard, 135, 141, 223
Jaeger, Frederick, 94, 124
Jaffa, Melissa, 139
Jaffe, Sam, 223
Jaffe, Stanley R., 28
Jaffer, Melissa, 140
Jagger, Dean, 160, 223
Jakubisko, Juri, 204
Jaloma, Ramiro, 89
James, Anthony, 90, 91
James, Brion, 44, 114
James, Clifton, 112, 223
James, Fred, 137
James, Godfrey, 209
James, Ken, 186
James, Marilyn, 136
James, Michael, 132
James, Sidney, 235
James, Terry, 134
James Dean, The First American Teenager, 150
Jameson, Joyce, 147
Jamieson, Kevin, 138
Jamison, Peter, 135
Jan, Yee, 209
Jandl, Ivan, 160
Janes, Ellen, 44
Janett, George, 203
Janis, Conrad, 22
Jannings, Emil, 160
Jansen, Pierre, 212
Janson, Horst, 197
Janssen, David, 107, 223
Janssen, Kitty, 214
Janssen, Rex, 30
Jardin, Pascal, 208
Jarman, Claude, Jr., 160, 223
Jarre, Maurice, 104, 197, 207
Jarrell, Emanual, 147
Jarto, Gro, 211
Jason, Harvey, 143
Jason, Mitchell, 102
Jason, Rick, 128, 223
Jasper, Zina, 144
Jaubert, Maurice, 192
Javal, Bertrand, 184
Javet, Francoise, 210
Jawdokimov, Alex, 97
Jaws of Death, The, 141
Jean, Gloria, 223
Jean, Rozaa, 14
Jeanine, Sonja, 147
Jee, Victoria, 126
Jefferson, Mike, 130, 136, 150
Jefferson, Roy, 145
Jeffreys, Anne, 223
Jeffreys, Bruce, 148
Jeffries, Lionel, 201, 223
Jeffries, Michael, 136, 214
Jeffries, Philip M., 45, 74
Jeffries, Ray, 134
Jemma, Ottavio, 206, 210
Jendly, Roger, 214
Jenkins, Albin, 84
Jenkins, George, 18
Jenkins, Paul, 102
Jenkmson, Chris, 124
Jennings, Claudia, 144
Jennings, Fabian, 207
Jennings, Georgette, 146
Jennings, Jean, 145
Jens, Sarah Lee, 145

Jensen, Jean, 136
Jensen, Peter, 190
Jensen, Raylan, 141, 142, 148
Jenson, Roy, 22, 32
Jergens, Adele, 223
Jernigan, Rebecca, 45
Jessel, George, 223
Jesserer, Gertraud, 205
Jessie, DeWayne, 36, 86, 133
Jessie's Girls, 135
Jessup, Bob, 143
Jessup, Carrie, 136
Jessup, Robert, 136
Jeter, James, 62, 122
Jewish Gauchos, The, 207
Jillson, Joyce, 145
Jim—The World's Greatest, 129
Jive Turkey, 149
Job, Enrico, 162, 164
Jobes, Marigray, 145
Joe Panther, 148
Joffe, Charles, 82
Johansson, Ulf, 178, 179
Johari, Azizi, 129
John, Alexander, 146
John, Carl, 129
John, Elton, 150
John, Jonathan, 205
Johnigarn, Tom, 147
Johnny Belinda, 160
Johnny Eager, 160
Johns, Anne, 148
Johns, Glynis, 223
Johnson, Angelica, 214
Johnson, Arnold, 106
Johnson, Ben, 32, 161
Johnson, Bernard, 36
Johnson, Celia, 223
Johnson, Charles, 150
Johnson, Dennis, 145
Johnson, Don, 139
Johnson, Dorothy M., 66
Johnson, Duke, 144
Johnson, Georgann, 82
Johnson, George Clayton, 58
Johnson, Glen, 142
Johnson, Hans, 126, 127, 144
Johnson, Horace, 148
Johnson, James, 148
Johnson, Joseph Ray, 135
Johnson, Joshua, 139
Johnson, Julie Ann, 114
Johnson, Ken, 139
Johnson, Kyle, 145
Johnson, Lamont, 26
Johnson, Laurie, 211
Johnson, Page, 223
Johnson, Rafer, 223
Johnson, Randi, 210
Johnson, Richard, 203, 204, 223
Johnson, Richmond, 144
Johnson, Sandy, 107
Johnson, Terri, 149
Johnson, Van, 223
Johnstone, Anna Hill, 97, 104
Johnstone, Jane Anne, 136
Jolley, Stan, 143
Jolley, Vic, 136
Jonah, 214
Jonah Who Will Be 25 in the Year 2000, 214
Jones, Abel, 136
Jones, Alan, 199
Jones, Anissa, 235
Jones, Carolyn, 223
Jones, Christopher, 223
Jones, Dean, 118, 119, 223
Jones, Dennis, 133
Jones, Freddie, 140
Jones, Hank, 118
Jones, Isaac L., 134
Jones, J. J., 136
Jones, Jack, 223
Jones, James Earl, 17, 36, 37, 68, 134, 223
Jones, Jeff, 137
Jones, Jennifer, 160, 223
Jones, Jerry, 147
Jones, Jocelyn, 144
Jones, John Paul, 213
Jones, Ken, 150
Jones, Kentucky, 144
Jones, L. Q., 41, 139
Jones, Larry, 145
Jones, Lauren, 86
Jones, Marianne, 190
Jones, Mark, 213
Jones, Miguel, 126
Jones, Mike, 149
Jones, Pamela, 148
Jones, Paul, 201
Jones, Robert, 122
Jones, Shirley, 161, 223
Jones, Sonny, 76

Jones, Tom, 199, 223
Jones, Tom Lee, 133, 213
Jones-Moreland, Betsy, 104, 128
Jordan, Chris, 140, 148
Jordan, Jennifer, 128, 136, 140, 141, 148
Jordan, Patrick, 194
Jordan, Richard, 58, 59, 223
Jorge, Hugo, 210
Jory, Victor, 223
Joseph, Allen, 92
Joseph, Robert L., 134
Josephson, Erland, 178
Josephson, Les, 114
Joshua, 150
Joston, Darwin, 148
Jourdan, Louis, 223
Journey into Fear, 213
Journey to Matecumbe, A, 141
Jouvet, Maurice, 207
Joy, Marilyn, 131
Joy of Letting Go, The, 150
Joyce, Vern, 131
Joyner, Tom, 36
Jozefson, Jac, Jr., 89
Jubert, Alice, 141
Judd, Dino, 114
Judd, Edward, 196, 201
Judd, Robb, 207
Judge and His Hangman, The, 182
Judgment at Nuremberg, 161
Judgement Day, 143
Julia, Raul, 143
Julia: Innocence Once Removed, 203
Julian, Marcel, 208
Juliano, Joseph R., 204
Julio, Montserrat, 170
Jung, Tsao Shao, 201
Jurado, Katy, 223
Jurgens, Curt, 212
Jurgenson, Albert, 198
Jurihara, Komaki, 211
Jurwich, Don, 144
Jusid, Juan Jose, 207
Justice, Susan, 146
Justin, Larry, 144
Justine de Sade, 213
Justis, Jack, 140, 148, 149
Jutt, John, 139
Jympson, John, 174, 196
K. B., 128
Kaailewis, Bernie, 140
Kaden, Rolf, 191
Kaftel, Sue, 144
Kahane, B. B., 161
Kahane, Roger, 201
Kahn, Jonathan, 176, 177
Kahn, Madeline, 40, 223
Kahn, Michael, 66
Kahn, Sheldon, 120, 139, 154
Kakefuda, Masahiro, 211
Kalbus, Terri, 150
Kalis, Murray, 144
Kallaniotes, Helena, 22
Kamen, Michael, 97
Kamen, Milt, 20, 41
Kane, Art, 128
Kane, Byron, 199
Kane, Carol, 44, 223
Kane, Jackson D., 180
Kang, Kam, 202
Kang, Philip, 213
Kanokogi, Ryoki, 97
Kanter, Igo, 133, 147
Kanter, Joseph, 136
Kaplan, Elliot, 54
Kaplan, J. S., 148
Kaplan, Jonathan, 142
Kaplan, Mike, 52
Kaplan, Murray M., 144
Kaplan, Ohad, 209
Kaplan, Robert J., 149
Kapp, Joe, 107
Kaprall, Bo, 143
Kaquitts, Frank, 52
Karalexis, Serafim, 206
Karate: One by One, 203
Karen, Candy, 148
Karen, James, 18
Karlen, John, 143
Karlin, Fred, 14, 137, 148
Karlin, Miriam, 209
Karlowa, Elma, 174
Karnes, 128
Karns, Jason, 145
Karp, Michael, 145
Karp, Sherril, 149
Karpen, Earl, 135
Karrin, Bonnie, 137
Karsmakers, Pierre, 145
Karzakian, Chuck, 139
Kaseki, 211
Kasem, Casey, 142
Kasper, Holger, 132
Kastner, Elliott, 32, 34, 68
Kasznar, Kurt, 223

Kato, Goh, 211
Katon, Rosanne, 140, 149
Katt, William, 98
Katz, Sidney, 129
Katz, Stephen M., 89, 127, 138
Katz, Zulema, 207
Kauer, Gene, 150
Kaufman, Christine, 223
Kaufman, Joseph, 148
Kaufman, Lloyd, 100, 126
Kaufman, Michael, 201
Kaufman, Phil, 46
Kaufman, Robert, 44
Kawalerowicz, Jerzy, 206
Kawase, Kiroyuki, 205
Kaye, Bernard, 124
Kaye, Celia, 148
Kaye, Danny, 161, 223
Kaye, Stubby, 223
Kaye, William, 144
Kayoonwong, Anuson, 133
Kazan, Elia, 104, 160, 161
Kazanjian, Howard G., 24
Kazann, Zitto, 134
Keach, James, 142, 144
Keach, Stacy, 145, 148, 150, 223
Keams, Geraldine, 46
Kean, Ras, 130, 137, 144, 149, 150
Keast, Breant, 148
Keating, Kevin, 133
Keaton, Buster, 161
Keaton, Diane, 44, 130, 223
Keats, Steven, 131, 143
Kedrova, Lila, 42, 161, 204, 213, 223
Kee, Regan, 136
Keehne, Chuck, 10
Keel, Howard, 223
Keeler, Ruby, 223
Keen, Geoffrey, 201
Keen, Noah, 128
Keetje Tippel, 212
Keffer, John, 31
Kehlau, Marianne, 203
Kehoe, Jack, 86
Kehoe, Pat, 116
Keitel, Harvey, 8, 9, 41, 52, 53
Keith, Brian, 114, 115, 148, 223
Kellaway, Roger, 134
Kelleher, Ed, 128, 130
Keller, Frank P., 41
Keller, Marthe, 92, 93
Kellerman, Sally, 62, 223
Kellett, Bob, 211
Kellin, Mike, 12, 148
Kellogg, D. A., 89
Kelly, David, 97, 135
Kelly, Duke, 144
Kelly, Gene, 38, 39, 160, 223
Kelly, Grace, 39, 161, 223
Kelly, Jack, 223
Kelly, Jim, 132, 133
Kelly, M. G., 110
Kelly, Nancy, 223
Kelly, Norman, 130
Kelly, Patsy, 223
Kelly, Paula, 143
Kelly, Scott, 144
Kelly, Sharon, 131
Kelly, Tim, 129
Kelton, Richard, 139
Kemeny, John, 190
Kemmerling, Warren J., 24, 135
Kemp, Bill, 136
Kemp, Jeremy, 94, 211, 223
Kemp, Sally, 128
Kemper, Victor J., 104, 120
Kempke, Helga, 203
Kemplen, Willy, 146
Kendall, Suzy, 208
Kendrick, Henry, 30
Kenneally, Phil, 44
Kennedy, Arthur, 205, 223
Kennedy, Burt, 148
Kennedy, George, 161, 223
Kennedy, Jayne, 149
Kennedy, Sarah, 145
Kennedy, Simon, 210
Kenner, Warren, 147
Kenney, Bill, 43, 143, 150
Kenney, Sean, 144
Kenny, Ken, 154
Kenny, William, 98
Kenny & Co., 150
Kensitt, Patsy, 206, 207
Kent, Jean, 197
Kent, Jose, 143
Kent, Roberta, 143
Kent, Tim, 147
Kentucky, 160
Kenyon, Tom, 149
Kenyon, Tony, 205
Kercheval, Ken, 102
Kerley, Bruce, 132

Kernan, Thomas, 139
Kerr, Barry, 135
Kerr, Deborah, 223
Kerr, John, 134, 223
Kershner, Irvin, 66
Keryan, Nathalie, 213
Kerylene, Anne, 208
Kesey, Ken, 154
Kesner, Jillian, 136
Kester, Jim, 138
Key, Janet, 167
Key, Ted, 64
Key Largo, 160
Keyes, Burt, 127
Keyes, Johnnie, 130, 137, 142
Khambatta, Persis, 223
Kidder, Margot, 223
Kiel, Richard, 112, 145
Kier, Udo, 223
Kiezlich, Gunther, 204
Kikoine, Gerard, 210
Kiley, Richard, 223
Kilian, Victor, 223
Killer Inside Me, The, 148
Killing Machine, The, 202
Killing of a Chinese Bookie, The, 129
Kim, Evan, 137
Kimball, Bruce, 106
Kimbrough, Charles, 82
Kimmel, Bruce, 131, 136
Kimmel, Kathryn, 131
Kimmins, Kenneth, 102
Kincaid, Aron, 128, 142, 223
Kincaid, Jason, 129
King, Alan, 223
King, Amos, 31
King, Clyde, 110
King, Dave, 78
King, Mabel, 36
King, Meegan, 140
King, Perry, 26, 27
King, Stephen, 98
King, Tony, 133
King, W. Geoffrey, 140
King, Woodie, 140
King, Zalman, 145
King and I, The, 161
King Kong, 116
Kingfish Caper, The, 209
Kingi, Henry, 86
Kinky Ladies of Bourbon Street, 214
Kino, Lloyd, 57, 104
Kinoy, Ernest, 14
Kinski, Klaus, 201
Kinski, Nastassja, 214
Kinsky, Eva, 204
Kinsley, Colleen, 139
Kirby, B., Jr., 137
Kirby, Bruce, 127
Kirby, George, 118
Kirby, John, 127, 131
Kirk, Howard, 133
Kirk, Tommy, 144
Kirkby, Michael, 84
Kirkland, Geoffrey, 84
Kirkland, Sally, 106, 110
Kirkpatrick, David, 144
Kirkpatrick, Peggy, 140
Kirkwood, Gene, 100
Kirtman, Leonard, 127
Kiser, Virginia, 144
Kishi, Keiko, 211
Kiss of the Tarantula, 135
Kiss Today Goodbye, 140
Kissinger, Charles, 135
Kit, Hong Ying, 212
Kitt, Eartha, 223
Kitty Foyle, 160
Klate, Seymour, 134
Klauber, Gertan, 94
Klein, Danny, 120
Klein, I. W., 82
Kleinberg, Elaine, 144
Kleiser, Randall, 145
Klemperer, Werner, 223
Kline, Richard H., 40, 116
Kling, Buddy, 144
Klinger, Michael, 197, 202
Klingman, Lynzee, 154
Klopp, Julia, 141
Kluck, Wilburn, 146
Klugman, Jack, 107, 223
Klugman, Lynn, 102
Klunis, Tom, 97
Klute, 161
Knapp, Charles, 41
Knapp, Douglas, 131, 148
Knapp, Max, 203
Knight, Davidson, 84
Knight, Don, 141, 143
Knight, Edward, 137
Knight, Esmond, 170, 223
Knight, Fuzzy, 235
Knight, Gladys, 106
Knight, June, 38
Knight, Marcie, 144
Knight, Norma, 132
Knight, Shirley, 223
Knopf, Marty, 150

Knotts, Don, 10, 11, 64, 65
Knowles, Patric, 223
Knox, Alexander, 223
Knox, Catherine, 31
Knox, Elyse, 223
Knuth, Klaus, 203
Kobayashi, Masaki, 211
Koch, Howard W., Jr., 92
Koenekamp, Fred, 40
Koenig, Klaus, 182
Koff, David, 213
Kogan, Milt, 127
Kohlberg, Jeff, 144
Kohner, Pancho, 74
Kohner, Susan, 223
Kokubo, Christina, 56
Kolldehoff, Rene, 197
Kondo, Hiroshi, 211
Kong, 116
Konrad, Dorothy, 80
Konwicki, Tadeusz, 206
Koon, Bob, 144
Kopperl, Helga, 150
Koppit, Arthur, 52
Korda, David, 139
Korkes, Jon, 107
Korman, Harvey, 223
Korshak, Harry, 128
Kort, Dennis, 62, 144
Korty, John, 96
Korvin, Charles, 201, 223
Koscina, Sylva, 209
Koski, Bill, 207
Kosleck, Martin, 223
Koslo, Paul, 124, 125
Koslow, Ron, 55
Koss, Alan, 148
Kostal, Irwin, 207
Koster, Robert, 80
Kotler, Oded, 205
Kotto, Yaphet, 143, 150, 223
Kouyama, Shigeru, 211
Kovacs, Laszlo, 44, 114, 137
Kove, Martin, 201
Kral, James, 150
Kramer, John, 135
Kramer, Remi, 210
Krasny, Paul, 148
Kreiger, Nick, 70
Krimn, Ricki, 148
Krem, Viji, 149
Kress, Carl, 143
Kress, Harold F., 69
Kreuger, Kurt, 223
Krigbaum, Carolyn, 102
Krigbaum, Mark, 139
Kristel, Sylvia, 202, 203
Kristen, Lidia, 36
Kristiansen, Erik, 211
Kristofferson, Kris, 110, 111, 134, 176, 177, 223
Kroeger, Wolf, 186
Kronen, Ben, 141
Kruger, Hardy, 208, 223
Krugman, Saul, 142
Krupnick, Jack, 129
Kruschen, Jack, 150
Kruse, John, 204
Kuang, I, 210
Kuan-tai, Chen, 210
Kuby, Bernard, 136
Kullers, John Red, 129
Kung Fu Master: Bruce Lee Style, 213
Kung, Kam, 203
Kuntsmann, Doris, 223
Kurata, Yasuai, 203
Kurgens, Curt, 212
Kurtzo, Joe, Jr., 133
Kusatsu, Clyde, 56
Kusley, Mike, 76
Kuumba, 147
Kuveiller, Luigi, 208
Kwan, Nancy, 146, 223
Kwouk, Burt, 199
Kyle, David, 140
Kyriazi, Jerrie, 139
Kyriazi, Paul, 139
La Chienne, 206
La Due, Joe, 134
La Foret, Marie, 208
La Habana, Joaquin, 148
La Monde, Pauline, 210
La Strada, 161
La Vierge et L'Amureaux, 205
Labello, Vincenzo, 172
Labounty, Steve, 139
Labourier, Dominique, 214
Labrot, Paula, 126
Lacey Bodine, 142
Lacher, Taylor, 150
Lackey, Brad, 145
Lackey, Douglas, 150
Lacy, Cary, 130
Lacy, Jerry, 223
Lacy, Tom, 68
Ladd, David, 144
Ladd, Diane, 40, 223
Ladebo, Ladi, 135

Lado, Aldo, 210
Lae, Foxy, 146
LaFountaine, George, 107
Lagache, Frederic, 202
Lai, Francis, 201, 202, 205, 208
Lai, Sung, 202
Laine, Jimmy, 210
Laing, C. J., 132, 134, 140, 145, 148, 149
Lake, Chelsea, 148
Lake, Michael, 212
Lamarr, Hedy, 223
Lamas, Fernando, 39, 223
Lamb, Gil, 223
Lambert, Dennis, 143
Lambert, Mel, 154
Lambert, Michael, 207
Lambert, Paul, 18, 133
Lambert, Robert, 142
Lamm, Karen, 134
Lamont, Peter, 94, 201
Lamour, Dorothy, 224
Lamour, Penelope, 214
Lampson, Mary, 137
Lancaster, Bill, 28
Lancaster, Burt, 52, 53, 161, 172, 173, 212, 224
Lancaster, Stuart, 130
Lancaster, William, 172
Lanchbury, Karl, 207
Lanchester, Elsa, 50, 51, 224
Land, Geoffrey, 135, 140
Landau, Martin, 224
Landham, Sonny, 136, 145, 149
Landon, Michael, 224
Landon, Patricia, 135
Lane, Abbe, 224
Lane, Dick, 118
Lane, Fran, 128
Lane, Lena, 207
Lang, Christa, 114
Lang, Fritz, 235
Lang, Helen, 137
Lang, Jennings, 68
Lang, Lee Fung, 201
Lang, Robert, 197
Langan, Glenn, 224
Lange, Hope, 224
Lange, Jessica, 116, 117, 224
Langford, Bonita, 84
Langhorne, Bruce, 22, 148
Langley, Barry, 214
Langley, Peter, 183
Langton, David, 196
Langton, Diane, 146
Langton, Paul, 224
Lankford, Kim, 44
Lanoux, Victor, 184, 185, 209, 210
Lansac, Frederic, 214
Lansbury, Angela, 224
Lansbury, Edgar, 141
Lansing, Robert, 89, 224
Lanteau, William, 76
Laperrousaz, Pascal, 201
Laplace, Victor, 207
LaPouf, Pierre, 138
Laretei, Kabi, 178
Larimer, Linda, 136
Larimer, Robert, 127
Larner, Stevan, 90
LaRossa, Adrienne, 211
Larouette-Debelmas, Chantal, 203
Larranga, Fernando, 210
Larraz, Joseph, 207
Larsen, Fred N., 52
Larsen, Keith, 141
Larsen, Tambi, 46
Larson, Darroll, 80
Larussa, Adrienne, 180
Lary, Lem, 144
Las Vegas Lady, 131
LaSalle, Martin, 203
Lash, Bob, 144
Lashly, James, 142
Laskey, Jesse, Jr., 174
Laskos, Andrew, 127
Lasky, Zane, 132
Lassick, Sydney, 98, 154
Last Affair, The, 145
Last Castle, The, 134
Last Chance for a Born Loser, 222
Last Hard Men, The, 23
Last Picture Show, The, 161
Last Stop on the Night Train, 132
Last Tycoon, The, 104
Last Woman, The, 208
Laszlo, Andrew, 135
Laszlo, Ernest, 58
Lathrop, Philip, 68
Latimer, Cherie, 131, 201
Latimore, Frank, 18
Lattuada, Alberto, 206
Laughton, Charles, 160

Lauldi, Antonella, 204
Laumer, Keith, 126
Launer, S. John, 128
Laurel, Stan, 161
Laurence, Caroline, 202
Laurence, John, 138
Laurent, Cynthia, 149
Laurent, Jacqueline, 202
Laurie, Piper, 98, 99, 224
Lauter, Ed, 24, 25, 32, 116
Lavi, Efrat, 205, 209
Lavia, Gabriele, 208
Lavie, Raul, 207
LaVigne, Robert, 137
Law, John Philip, 211, 224
Lawford, Peter, 224
Lawless, John, 129
Lawlor, John, 133
Lawrence, Barbara, 224
Lawrence, Carol, 224
Lawrence, Dick, 76
Lawrence, Elliot, 102
Lawrence, Gail, 137
Lawrence, John, 138
Lawrence, Ken, 133
Lawrence, Marc, 92
Lawrence, Tom, 44
Lawrence of Arabia, 161
Laws, Sam, 36, 148
Lawson, Leigh, 224
Lawson, Richard, 129
Lawton, John, 139
Layman, Debora, 136
Lazareno, Norma, 210
Lazarus, Paul N., III, 80
Le Magnifique, 210
Le Person, Paul, 205
Leach, Britt, 133
Leachman, Cloris, 161, 224
Leadbelly, 14
Leaders, Bonnie, 52
Lean, David, 161
Lear, Evelyn, 52
Leary, Margaret, 31
Lebor, Stanley, 167
LeBron, Larry, 127
Lebrun, Francoise, 165
Lec, Alex Tang, 213
LeClair, Michael, 137
Ledding, Ed, 74, 110
Leder, Paul, 147
Leder, Reuben, 147
Lederer, Charles, 235
Lederer, Francis, 224
Lee, Bruce, 201
Lee, Chen, 201
Lee, Christopher, 214, 224
Lee, Dana, 80
Lee, Dixie, 134
Lee, Eric, 139
Lee, Gerald, 132
Lee, Glade, 149
Lee, Gracia, 107
Lee, Jennifer, 22
Lee, John, 84
Lee, Judy, 211
Lee, Kay, 154
Lee, Margaret, 188, 206
Lee, Michelle, 224
Lee, Patricia, 126, 132, 144, 149
Lee, Sanford, 136
Lee, Susie Sung, 150
Lee, Tony, 131
Leeming, Peter, 194
Leferiere, Catherine, 202
Lefevre, Rene, 128
Legacy, 134
Legend of Bigfoot, The, 126
Leggatt, Alison, 94
Legrand, Michel, 45, 128
Lehman, Ernest, 24
Lehman, Eunice, 31
Lehmann, Ted, 36
Lehne, John, 24, 122, 128
Leibman, Ron, 40, 224
Leigh, Heather, 147
Leigh, Janet, 224
Leigh, Vivien, 160
Leighton, Margaret, 146, 204, 235
Leighton, Michael W., 148
Leiterman, Richard, 207
Lemaire, Gerard, 203
Lembeck, Harvey, 224
Lemieuvre, Richard, 206
Lemm, Stanislas, 213
Lemmon, Jack, 96, 160, 161, 224
Lemole, Lisa, 136
Lendi, Georges, 184
Leningrad Kirov Ballet, The, 207
Lennon, John, 150
Lennox, Doug, 186
Lenska, Rula, 206
Lenz, Kay, 139, 143
Lenz, Richard, 72
Lenz, Rick, 224
Lenzi, Umberto, 208
Leonard, Gloria, 137, 149, 150
Leonard, Joel, 132

Leonard, Sheldon, 224
Leone, Alfred, 209
Leone, Kathy, 209
Leonetti, Tony, 144
Leoning, John, 106
Leperier, Diana, 213
Lerner, Irving, 134
Lerner, Michael, 74
Lerner, Richard, 137
LeRoux, Maurice, 204
LeRoy, Gloria, 141
Leroy, Philippe, 224
Les Gaspards, 212
Lcs Nympho Teens, 149
Les Suspects, 206
Leslie, Bethel, 224
Leslie, Joan, 224
Leslie, John, 137, 140, 143, 144, 145
Leslie, Karen, 144
Leslie, Lisa, 106
Lester, Mark L., 133, 224
Lester, Richard, 78, 170
Letivsky, Al, 145
Letizia, Jodi, 100
Let's Talk about Men, 188
Letterman, Ron, 144
Leung, Chow Fook, 201
Lev, Martin, 84
Levene, Sam, 137, 148, 224
Levene, Terry, 211
Leventhal, Harold, 122
Levesque, Michel, 133, 142, 146
Levey, William A., 145
Levin, Sidney, 82, 147
Levine, Robert, 97
Levinson, Arthur, 18, 41
Levinson, Barry, 48
Levy, Jules V., 69
Lewin, Albert E., 130
Lewin, Michel, 206
Lewis, Diana, 100, 101
Lowis, Edward, 207
Lewis, Fiona, 143
Lewis, Geoffrey, 66
Lewis, Hedgemon, 114
Lewis, James P., 207
Lewis, Jerry, 224
Lewis, Linda, 209
Lewis, Michael, 207
Lewis, Morton, 213
Lewis, Shaker, 210
Lewiston, Denis C., 174
Leye, Thierno, 211
Li, Bruce, 201
Liagade, Ana, 211
Liang, Bruce, 206
Liberman, Robert, 17
Liberty, 136
Lichterman, Marvin, 82
Lichtig, Scott, 55
Lieberman, Jeff, 141
Lieberson, Sandy, 150
Liebske, Wieland, 182
Lieh, Lo, 205, 210
Life of Emile Zola, The, 160
Life Size, 207
Lifeguard, 55
Lifschutz, Joel, 210
Ligon, Tom, 224
Lilies of the Field, 161
Lillie, Beatrice, 224
L'image, 128
Lincoln, Abbey, 224
Lincoln, Fred, 132, 148, 149
Lincoln, Steve, 145
Linda, 202
Lindberg, Sven, 178
Lindfors, Viveca, 224
Lindsay, Lara, 58
Lindsey, Gene, 18
Line, Helga, 205
Ling, Suzanne, 135, 146
Link, Andre, 141
Link, John F. II, 22
Linkers, Eduard, 191
Linson, Art, 86
Linson, John, 86
Linville, Joanne, 110, 128
Lion, Mickey, 209
Lion in Winter, The, 161
Lionelli, Alberto, 213
Lions, Wendy, 137
Lipkind, David, 205
Lipman, Jerzy, 209
Lipstick, 26
Lipton, Michael, 102
Liquid Lips, 142
Lisi, Virna, 204, 224
Lister, James, 205
Liston, Melba, 14
Lithgow, John, 70, 71
Litsky, Barbara, 18
Little, Cleavon, 224
Little, Ken A., 144
Little Angel Puss, 126
Littleton, Caro, 134
Littleton, Emmett, 139
Litto, George, 70, 136
Litvinoff, Si, 180

Livadas, Telly, 209
Livermore, John, 214
Livesey, Robert, 235
Living Dead at Manchester Morgue, The, 205
Livingston, Mark, 128
Liza, 201
Llewelyn, Doug, 18
Lloyd, Christopher, 154
Lloyd, David, 129
Lloyd, Frank, 160
Lloyd, Harold, 160
Lloyd, Jan, 142
Lloyd, Jeremy, 210
Lloyd, John, 68
Lloyd, Kathleen, 34, 35
Lloyd, Kevin, 146
Lloyd, Michael, 138
Lloyd, Sue, 211, 214
Lo Presti, Giuseppe, 206
Lobdell, Felix, 145
Lober, Joy, 126
LoBianco, Tony, 148, 207
Locke, Gary, 176, 177
Locke, Henry, 137
Locke, Sondra, 46, 224
Locke, Terence, 130
Lockhart, June, 224
Lockmiller, Richard, 133
Lockwood, Alexander, 24
Lockwood, Gary, 146, 224
Lockwood, Margaret, 194, 224
Logan, Bruce, 133, 140
Logan, Robert, 150
Logan's Run, 58
Lohmann, Paul, 52
Lohner, Helmut, 205
Loiseleux, Jacques, 209
Lollipop Palace, 144
Lollobrigida, Gina, 224
Lom, Herbert, 199, 224
Lombard, Michael, 102
London, Julie, 224
Lone, John, 116
Lonero, Mimita, 204
Long, Anni, 132
Long, Keny, 116
Long, Nate, 147
Long, Steven, 126
Long, Will, 45
Long Night, The, 140
Longo, Tiziano, 205
Lonmann, Paul, 48
Lonsdale, Michel, 202, 206, 214
Lookinland, Todd, 207
Loomis, Nancy, 148
Loose, William, 146
Lopez, Perry, 224
Lopez, Rafael, 134
Lopez-Pineda, Humberto, 66
Lord, Jack, 224
Lord, Robert, 235
Loren, Sophia, 161, 224
Lorena, Liza, 140
Loria, Edith, 208
Loros, George, 20
Lorys, Diana, 210
Lost Weekend, The, 160
Lottman, Evan, 43
Loudermilk, Sherman, 143
Lougene, Carmel, 44
Lough, James, 137
Louie, Bill, 211
Louise, Tina, 224
Lourie, Eugene, 90
Love, Bessie, 78
Love, Candy, 126, 148
Love, Lucretia, 211
Love and Other Crimes, 96
Love Comes Quietly, 214
Love Doll, 207
Love Games, 205
Love in Strange Places, 149
Love Mates, The, 201
Love Me or Leave Me, 38
Love Me Strangely, 204
Love Slaves, 144
Lovelace, Leo, 130
Lovelace, Linda, 224
Lovell, Capt. James, 180
Lovell, Pedro, 100
Lovelock, Ray, 205
Lovemore, Linda, 130, 134
Lovern, Bruce, 150
Lovers and Other Relatives, 210
Loves and Times of Scaramouche, The, 204
Lovett, Robert, 97
Loving Cousins, 195
Lowe, Arthur, 210
Lowe, John, 139
Lowe, Sammy, 129
Lowe, Skip, 132
Lowell, Sandra, 138
Lowenadler, Holger, 213
Lowenthal, Wolfe, 206
Lower, Tony, 212
Lowry, Judith, 235
Lowry, Lynn, 141, 148
Lowry, Murray, 190

Loy, Myrna, 134, 224
Lubitsch, Ernst, 160
Lucas, Marcia, 8
Lucatorto, Tony, 129
Lucero, Claudio, 207
Lucero, Enrique, 66, 67
Luchini, Fabrice, 204
Luciano, Michael, 133, 147
Lucidi, Maurizio, 145, 202
Lucidi, Renzo, 206
Lucien, Antoinette Zoe, 205
Lucioni, Jose, 203
Lucisano, Fulvio, 206
Luckey, W. L., 135
Luckinbill, Laurence, 137
Lucking, Bill, 31, 66
Ludden, Allen, 80
Ludmila, 144
Ludwig, Salem, 97
Luhr, Peter, 191
Lukas, Karl, 107, 118, 127
Lukas, Paul, 160
Lukaszewicz, Olgierd, 213
Lukather, Bill, 150
Luke, Jorge, 66
Lukschy, Wolfgang, 201
Lulli, Piero, 201
Lumet, Sidney, 102
Lumiere, 198
Lumont, Roger, 206
Lun, Lo, 209
Luna, Barbara, 145
Lund, Art, 137
Lund, John, 224
Lundgren, Siv, 178
Lundin, Richard, 30
Lundin, Victor, 132
Lung, Alex, 212
Lung, Kin, 203, 205
Lung, Lee Hsiao, 209
Lung, Ti, 210
Lupino, Ida, 54, 224
Lupo, Michele, 207
Luppi, Gustavo, 207
Luscious Lickers, The, 149
Lust for Life, 161
Luthardt, Robert, 26
Lutter, Alfred W., 28
Lutz, Rick, 126, 132, 144
Lydon, James, 134, 224
Lyke, Lisa, 107
Lyn, Ann, 211
Lynas, Jeffrey, 186
Lynch, Jimmy, 147
Lynch, Richard, 129, 148
Lynch, Sean, 209
Lynde, Paul, 127, 224
Lynley, Carol, 201, 224
Lynn, Jeffrey, 224
Lyon, Alexandra, 144
Lyon, Sue, 224
Lyon, Turk, 126, 128, 143, 148
Lyons, Robert F., 224
Lyons, Stuart, 194
Lyssy, Rolf, 203
Lyttle, Joseph, 144
Lytton, Debbie, 134
Ma, Wu, 202
Maas, Sybil, 184
Mabinda, Tom, 200
Mabry, Moss, 72, 76, 116
Macari, Ruggero, 201
MacArthur, James, 224
Maccari, Ruggero, 213
Macclone, Aldo, 204
MacDonald, Pirie, 102
MacDonald, Richard, 92
Macey, Elizabeth, 122
MacGinnis, Niall, 224
MacGraw, Ali, 224
Machat, Martin J., 150
MacKay, Jeff, 18
MacKay, John, 97
Mackenzie, Patch, 130
Macklin, David, 141
MacLaine, Shirley, 224
MacLean, Alistair, 32, 202
MacLean, Peter, 141
MacLeod, Robert, 60
MacMahon, Aline, 224
MacMurray, Fred, 224
MacNamara, Ed, 183
Macnee, Patrick, 224
MacPherson, Patricia, 210
MacRae, Bruce, 147
MacRae, Gordon, 224
Macreading, James, 145
Macready, Michael, 142
Mad Dog, 212
Madaris, Robert, 141
Madden, Dave, 135
Madden, Joe, 12
Madigan, Helen, 131, 135
Madison, Guy, 224
Maeder, Fritz, 203
Maeterlinck, Maurice, 207
Mafela, Joe, 200
Magder, Zale, 183
Magee, Patrick, 224
Magnani, Anna, 161
Magro, Anthony, 148
Mahal, Taj, 147

Maharaj, Ralph, 213
Maharis, George, 224
Mahon, Anthony, 129
Mahoney, Jock, 147, 224
Maier, Brigitte, 128
Main, David, 212
Maistre, Francois, 212
Maitland, Marne, 199, 202
Maitresse, 213
Maiuri, Dino, 202
Makee, Blaidsell, 144
Makin, Harry, 212
Making of a Lady, The, 203
Malden, Karl, 160, 224
Male of the Century, 208
Malkin, Barry, 16
Malley, Bill, 96
Malone, Dorothy, 161, 224
Man and a Woman, A, 161
Man Called Horse, A, 66
Man for All Seasons, A, 161
Man Who Fell to Earth, The, 180
Manasse, George, 141
Mancini, Carla, 213
Mancini, Henry, 20, 96, 112, 199
Mancini, Ric, 114
Mandel, John, 176
Mandel, Tommy, 17
Mandell, Mitch, 145
Manes, Stephen, 41
Manferdini, Carole, 12
Manfredi, Nino, 188
Mangano, Silvana, 212
Mangine, Joseph, 141
Manicottale, Luigi, 214
Manicurist, The, 140
Mankiewicz, Joseph L., 160
Mankiewicz, Tom, 41
Manmak, Trevor, 136
Mann, Aaron, 144
Mann, Alex, 150
Mann, Burch, 141
Mann, Claude, 165
Mann, Daniel, 213
Mann, David, 186
Mann, Delbert, 31, 161
Mann, Edward, 148
Mann, Kurt, 224
Mann, Larry D., 140, 149
Mann, P. L., 126
Mann, Stanley, 131, 186
Mann, Ted, 55
Mannequin, 210
Manni, Entore, 145
Manning, Joan, 126
Manning, Ruth, 140
Mannini, Elena, 208
Mannino, Anthony, 18
Mannix, Julie, 143
Manno, Dana, 14
Manno, Franco, 212
Mansbridge, John B., 10, 64, 118, 141
Mansfield, Elizabeth, 194
Mansion of the Doomed, 146
Manson, Alan, 14
Manson, Maurice, 114
Manson Massacre, The, 144
Mantania, Clelia, 206
Mantee, Paul, 20
Manuel, Richard, 213
Marais, Jean, 224
Maranne, Andre, 199
Marasco, Robert, 90
Marathon Man, 92
Marc, Sebastien, 192
Marcel, Terry, 133, 196
March, Fredric, 160
March, Marvin, 126
Marchal, Robin, 124
Marchall, Isabelle, 213
Marchand, Andree, 211
Marchand, Corrine, 201
Marchent, Rafaello R., 211
Marchini, Mike, 139
Marchini, Ron, 139
Marciano, Francesca, 162
Marcovicci, Andrea, 82, 153
Marcus, Irwin, 18
Marcus, Lawrence B., 96
Marcus, Wade, 148
Mareze, Janie, 206
Marfield, Dwight, 154
Margallo, Juan, 212
Margo, 128, 224
Margold, William, 138, 144, 149
Margolin, Alan C., 149
Margolin, Janet, 224
Margolin, Stuart, 62, 80
Margulies, David, 82
Margulies, Ed, 134
Margulies, Michael, 134
Maria, Bella, 143
Maria, Sylvia, 210
Mariani, Mario, 213
Marielle, Jean-Pierre, 208, 209

Marin, Jacques, 92, 203, 224
Marino, Art, 131
Marino, Benny, 129
Mariscal, Alberto, 66
Mark, Robert, 213
Markham, Monte, 56
Markland, Ted, 148, 154
Markley, Edward, 143, 150
Markowitz, Murray, 207
Marks, Arthur, 141, 150
Marks, Guy, 126
Marks, Marianne, 146
Marks, Maurice, 28
Marks, Richard, 104
Marley, John, 20
Marlino, Julia, 147
Marlon, Leah, 205
Marlow, Alan, 126, 150
Marlow, Judy, 146
Marlow, Nancy, 139
Marlowe, Hugh, 224
Marlowe, Scott, 213
Maroff, Robert, 145
Marquand, Serge, 202
Marquette, Jacques, 90
Marquis, Andre, 208
Marquise of O . . ., The, 191
Marriage and Other Four Letter Words, 129
Mars, Betty, 209
Marsani, Claudia, 212
Marsh, Julian, 150
Marsh, Ray, 148
Marshall, Alan, 84
Marshall, Brenda, 224
Marshall, E. G., 224
Marshall, Ed, 128, 136, 138, 214
Marshall, Edward, 114, 133, 146
Marshall, Frank, 114
Marshall, Norman Thomas, 137
Marshall, Tom, 204
Marshall, William, 224
Martel, William, 137
Martellanz, Pietro, 145
Martens, Michel, 209
Martin, Ann, 45
Martin, Dean, 224
Martin, Derek, 205
Martin, Don, 201
Martin, D'Urville, 136, 148
Martin, Eugenio, 209
Martin, Greg, 18
Martin, Jean, 210
Martin, Karen, 207
Martin, Mary, 224
Martin, Nan, 133
Martin, Perry, 30
Martin, Sally, 145
Martin, Strother, 139, 224
Martin, Todd, 96
Martin, Tony, 224
Martinelli, John, 40
Martinez, A., 127, 148
Martinez, Jimmy, 143
Martinez, Joaquin, 139
Martinez, Leo, 140
Martini, Nino, 235
Martino, Lucio, 209
Martino, Sergio, 195, 209, 210
Martinson, Leslie, 200
Marty, 161
Martyr, The, 209
Marvin, Lee, 139, 161, 197, 225
Marx, Brett, 28
Marx, Groucho, 225
Marx, Ivan, 126
Marx Brothers, The, 39
Mary Poppins, 161
Masak, Ron, 145
Mascia, Tony, 180
Maser, Bob, 150
M*A*S*H*D, 136
Maslansky, Paul, 207
Masolini, Joseph, 134
Mason, Bob, 128
Mason, Eric, 135
Mason, Hilary, 167
Mason, James, 124, 201, 225
Mason, Jennifer, 140, 148
Mason, Marsha, 225
Mason, Pamela, 225
Massacre at Central High, 144
Massage Parlor Wife, 206
Massen, Osa, 225
Massey, Daniel, 196, 225
Massey, Jamila, 97
Massey, Raymond, 225
Massot, Joe, 213
Masters, Sharon, 104
Masterson, Peter, 225
Masterson, Willy, 150
Mastroianni, Marcello, 168, 189, 201, 225

Mastroianni, Ruggero, 212
Masucci, Jerry, 133
Masur, Richard, 89
Matelli, Dante, 208
Mateos, Julian, 208
Mather, Jack, 112
Mathews, Paul, 150
Mathews, Robert, 142, 147
Matlock, Norman, 8, 43
Matsumoto, Isao, 202
Matsumoto, Robert, 130
Matter of Time, A, 88
Mattes, Eva, 208
Matthau, Walter, 6, 28, 29, 160, 161, 225
Matthews, Stephanie, 131
Mattone, Claudio, 195
Mature, Victor, 225
Mauri, Glauco, 208
Mauro, Frank, 128
Maury, Alain, 210
Maury, Derrel, 140, 144
Maury, Edy, 210
Maury, M. D., 136
Max, Ultra, 132
Maxine, Ultra, 148
Maxwell, Casey, 137
Maxwell, Jody, 130
Maxwell, Len, 127
May, Alexander, 214
May, April, 150
May, Elaine, 120, 225
May, Harry, 141
May, Jack, 94
May, Melba, 145
Maybach, Christiane, 203
Maybrook, Jenny, 107
Mayehoff, Eddie, 225
Mayer, Karin, 210
Mayer, Louis B., 160
Mayer, Manuela, 191
Mayer, Yolanda, 44
Mayersberg, Paul, 180
Mayfield, Curtis, 133
Mayfield, Julian, 140
Mayhew, Robbie, 136
Maynard, Bill, 170
Maynard, Mimi, 30
Mayo, Howard Tobar, 145, 149
Mayron, Melanie, 86, 128
Maysles, Albert, 130
Maysles, David, 130
Maysles Brothers, 130
Mayuga, Christie, 140
Mazik, Betty, 123
Mazursky, Paul, 12, 110
McAdams, Jack, 134
McBain, Suzanne, 141, 149
McBride, Joe, 142
McBride, Lilyan, 130, 134, 137
McBroom, Marcia, 36
McCabe, Cathy, 142
McCall, Joan, 135
McCallum, David, 209, 225
McCallum, Robert, 128
McCambridge, Mercedes, 160, 225
McCann, Chuck, 48
McCann, Dan, 150
McCardle, Mickey, 20
McCarey, Leo, 160
McCarthy, Ann, 80
McCarthy, Dan, 134
McCarthy, Kevin, 52, 225
McCarthy, Neil, 146
McCarthy, Todd, 142
McCartney, Paul, 150
McCarty, Charlie, 147
McCaskill, Patricia, 150
McCauley, Danny, 104
McCauley, John, 132
McCauley, William, 212
McClory, Sean, 225
McCloskey, Michael, 133
McClung, Susan, 31
McClure, Doug, 201, 209, 225
McClurg, Bob, 143
McCombie, J. A. S., 144
McCormick, Maureen, 149
McCormick, Pat, 52, 118, 119
McCowan, George, 190
McCowen, Alec, 225
McCoy, Boots, 145
McCoy, Tim, 126, 145
McCrea, Joel, 131, 225
McCrory, Thomas B., 143
McCullough, Jim, Jr., 131
McCurry, John, 36
McCuster, Mary, 143
McDaniel, George, 134
McDaniel, Hattie, 160
McDermott, Della, 124
McDermott, Garry, 124
McDermott, Hugh, 225
McDevitt, Ruth, 235
McDonald, David, 137
McDonald, George S., 130, 132

McDowall, Roddy, 40, 127, 225
McDowell, Malcolm, 124, 125, 225
McElroy, Hal, 139
McElroy, Jim, 139
McEnery, Peter, 225
McEveety, Joe, 10
McEveety, Vincent, 64, 141
McEwan, Geraldine, 210
McFadden, Tom Lee, 137
McGavin, Darren, 10, 11, 225
McGhee, Bill, 136
McGiffert, David, 116
McGill, Felix, 139
McGinnis, Carol, 127, 128
McGlurg, Edie, 98
McGoohan, Patrick, 112, 113
McGovern, Terrance, 206
McGrath, Thomas J., 17
McGraw, Charles, 148
McGreevey, Michael, 118
McGrew, Rod, 86
McGrew, Steven, 150
McGuane, Thomas, 34
McGuire, Biff, 56, 225
McGuire, Debora, 144
McGuire, Dorothy, 225
McGuire, Mark, 137
McGuire, Stephen, 144
McHaley, Kathy, 136
McHattie, Stephen, 143
McIntire, Mark, 148
McIntire, Tim, 139, 143, 148
McKay, Gardner, 225
McKay, Scott, 82
McKee, John R., 36
McKee, Lonette, 133
McKee, Vivienne, 194
McKenna, Virginia, 225
McKenzie, Bleu, 149
McKern, Leo, 60
McKinney, Bill, 46, 72, 142
McKnight, David, 141
McKone, Vivienne, 84
McKuen, Rod, 225
McLaglen, Andrew V., 23
McLaglen, Victor, 160
McLain, Karen, 129
McLane, Robert, 146
McLaughlin, Lee, 112
McLean, Dwayne, 186
McLean, Peter, 141
McLerie, Allyn Ann, 18, 225
McLey, David, 186
McLiam, John, 34
McMahon, Phyllis, 167
McManus, Mark, 18
McMartin, John, 18
McMullin, Robert, 190
McMurray, Sam, 82
McNab, John, 202
McNair, Barbara, 225
McNally, Edward, 107
McNally, Stephen, 225
McNally, Terrence, 78
McNamara, Connie, 133
McNamara, Cornelia, 133
McNamara, Ed, 112
McNamara, Maggie, 225
McNamara, Patrick, 70, 82
McNamara, Rosemary, 129
McNight, Sharon, 145
McPeak, Sandy, 45
McQueen, Armelia, 133
McQueen, Butterfly, 225
McQueen, Steve, 225
McRae, Alan, 136, 183, 186
McRae, Frank, 106
McRoberts, Briony, 199
McShane, Ian, 213
Mead, Kevin, 150
Meador, Dale, 145
Meadows, Audrey, 225
Meadows, Jane, 77, 225
Mean Frank and Crazy Tony, 207
Mean Johnny Barrows, 127
Means, Ken, 150
Measless, David, 134
Medalis, Joseph G., 114
Medford, Gloria Jane, 145
Medford, Kay, 225
Medioli, Enrico, 212
Medwin, Michael, 225
Meeker, Ralph, 54, 214, 225
Meekunsut, Somejai, 133
Mehdi, 203
Mehoff, Jack, 132
Meier, Petra, 191
Meillon, John, 139, 140
Meineke, Eva Marie, 214
Meisner, Guenter, 124, 201
Meisner, Sanford, 120
Meissner, Siegfried, 203
Mejovsek, Damir, 204
Melato, Mariangela, 172, 206, 207, 213

Meleleu, Ron, 84
Melendez, Bill, 209
Melendez, Steven, 209
Mell, Marisa, 225
Melle, Gil, 40
Mellis, Tawm, 128
Melnick, Dan, 38
Melvin, Murray, 197, 210
Memmoli, George, 100, 133
Memory of Justice, The, 87
Menchine, Ron, 18
Mendem, Mary, 128, 214
Mendoza-Nava, Jaime, 131, 139
Meniconi, Enzo, 208
Menten, Dale, 55, 147
Mercer, Johnny, 235
Mercier, Chantal, 192
Mercier, Michele, 203
Mercouri, Melina, 225
Meredith, Burgess, 90, 100, 101, 225
Meredith, Jo Anne, 141
Meredith, Lee, 225
Meril, Macha, 208
Merino, Mike, 135
Merisi, Pipo, 203
Merkel, Una, 225
Merman, Ethel, 225
Merrill, Bob, 20
Merrill, Dina, 225
Merrill, Gary, 225
Merry Go Round, 205
Merry Widow, The, 39
Merson, Marc, 14
Mervyn, William, 210
Messinger, Mike, 128
Metcalfe, Charlie, 139
Metcalfe, Ken, 140
Mettey, Lynnette, 63
Metz, Rex, 129
Metzger, Ed, 86
Metzger, Radley, 128
Metzler, Fred L., 161
Meurisse, Paul, 206
Meurisse, Theo, 201
Meyer, Nicholas, 94
Meyer, Russ, 146
Meyers, Ross, 146
Meziere, Myriam, 214
Miano, Robert, 96
Michaels, David E., 144
Michaels, Drew, 128
Michaels, Greg, 58
Michaels, Joel B., 89
Michaels, Richard, 132
Michaels, Steve, 136
Michell, Keith, 142, 161
Michelle, Vicki, 206
Michlin, Barry, 143
Middleton, Burr, 130
Middleton, Jonas, 145
Middleton, Malcolm, 84
Midnight Cowboy, 161
Midnight Desires, 134
Midnight Pleasures, 214
Midway, 56
Miers, Greg, 131
Mifune, Toshiro, 56, 225
Migicovsky, Alan, 141
Migliano, Bob, 126, 135
Migliette, Bob, 146
Mikael, Ludmilla, 204
Mikey & Nicky, 120
Mikita, Mori, 205
Mikolajewska, Krystyna, 206
Mikuriya, Katsutoschi, 201
Milam, Bob, 154
Milana, Vincent, 89, 114
Mildred Pierce, 160
Miles, Joanna, 139
Miles, Kevin, 139
Miles, Sarah, 176, 177, 225
Miles, Sylvia, 139, 225
Miles, Vera, 225
Milestone, Lewis, 160
Milian, Thomas, 211
Milkis, Edward K., 112
Milland, Ray, 104, 105, 160, 225
Miller, Allan, 107, 122, 137
Miller, Ann, 225
Miller, Burton, 68
Miller, Carrie, 104
Miller, Cheryl, 150
Miller, David, 89
Miller, Dick, 142, 143
Miller, Ira, 133, 143
Miller, Jason, 225
Miller, Kathleen, 22, 148
Miller, Linda, 16
Miller, Marvin, 225
Miller, Michael B., 16, 82, 133
Miller, Norma, 133
Miller, Richard Drout, 63
Miller, Robin, 209
Miller, Roland, 149
Miller, Ron, 10, 64, 118, 140, 141
Miller, Sharon Joy, 145
Miller, Stanley, 207

Miller, Thomas L., 112
Miller, Warren, 107
Miller, William F., 140
Milliken, Billy, 136
Millington, Jim, 207
Millman, Jack, 135
Millo, Don, 126
Mills, Barbara, 149
Mills, Brooke, 107
Mills, Edwin, 41
Mills, Hayley, 161, 201, 209, 225
Mills, Jerry, 142
Mills, John, 146, 161, 203, 225
Mills, Larry L., 143
Mills, Sarah, 148
Milner, Martin, 225
Milt, Victor C., 129
Mimieux, Amparo, 133
Mimieux, Yvette, 133, 213, 225
Min and Bill, 160
Mina, Nika, 131
Minardos, Nico, 133
Mineo, Sal, 235
Minford, Sally, 211
Ming, Ack, 210
Ming, Chen S., 213
Ming, Paul, 206
Mingay, David, 211
Minguillon, Margarita, 170
Minnelli, Liza, 6, 88, 161, 225
Minnelli, Vincente, 88, 161
Miou-Miou, 214
Mira, Tina, 145
Miracle On 34th Street, 160
Miracle Worker, The, 161
Miranda, Isa, 206, 225
Mirisch, Walter, 56
Mishima, Yukio, 176
Mishko, Ernie, 44
Mislaid Genie, The, 145
Mislove, Michael, 143
Miss Nude America, 145
Missouri Breaks, The, 34
Mister Roberts, 161
Misty, 148
Mitchel, J. W., 129
Mitchel, Artie, 130, 132, 145
Mitchell, Cameron, 225
Mitchell, Charlotte, 129
Mitchell, Craig, 129
Mitchell, George Alfred, 160
Mitchell, Gordon, 201, 206
Mitchell, James, 80, 126, 130, 132, 145, 225
Mitchell, Keith, 129
Mitchell, Lundee, 136
Mitchell, Paula, 130
Mitchell, Sharon, 140
Mitchell, Thomas, 160
Mitchell, Yvonne, 196, 201
Mitchum, Christopher, 23
Mitchum, James, 134, .225
Mitchum, John, 106, 108
Mitchum, Robert, 56, 104, 105, 225
Mittermayer, Alois, 203
Miyamoto, Kenny, 148
Mlodzik, Ronald, 141
Mnouchkine, Alexandre, 210
Moctezuma, Juan L., 203
Modlin, Elmer, 124
Mohr, Hanro, 200
Molenkamp, Onno, 214
Molinaro, Edouard, 214
Molle, Jean-Gabriel, 203
Moller, Heidi, 191
Mollicone, Henry, 129
Molloy, Mike, 212
Molloy, William, 133
Momo, Alessandro, 201, 210
Monahan, Stevie, 150
Monash, Paul, 98
Moncado, Santiago, 213
Mondy, Pierre, 214
Monet, Monica, 208
Money, Constance, 137
Money, The, 137
Monicelli, Mario, 210
Monkey Hustle, The, 150
Monod, Jacques, 42, 210
Monod, Veronique, 214
Monsarrat, Nicholas, 202
Monsieur Vincent, 160
Montalban, Ricardo, 148, 225
Montana, Lenny, 129
Montand, Yves, 204, 225
Montgomery, Belinda J., 186, 225
Montgomery, Diane, 132
Montgomery, Elizabeth, 225
Montgomery, George, 225
Montgomery, John, 149
Montgomery, Lee H., 90, 91, 149, 150

Montgomery, Michael, 147
Montgomery, Robert, 225
Monti, Carlotta, 20
Montoro, Edward L., 135, 139, 204
Moo, San, 201
Moody, Lynne, 127
Moody, Titus, 138
Moody, William, 149
Moon, Horace, 126
Moon, Keith, 225
Moon, Marsha, 131
Mooney, William, 97
Moor, Bill, 225
Moore, Alvy, 199
Moore, Archie, 32, 33
Moore, Constance, 225
Moore, Dejah, 136
Moore, Dick, 225
Moore, Dorothy, 209
Moore, Edward J., 18
Moore, G. T., and Susha, 213
Moore, Ivanna, 137
Moore, John, 88, 167
Moore, Kenneth, 225
Moore, Kieron, 225
Moore, Kitty, 149
Moore, Lee Gordon, 114
Moore, Mary Tyler, 225
Moore, Millie, 144, 148
Moore, Norma, 140
Moore, Paula, 206
Moore, Randy, 148
Moore, Robert, 50
Moore, Roger, 145, 197, 225
Moore, Rudy Ray, 147, 150
Moore, Sherry, 44
Moore, Terry, 225
Moorman, Elizabeth, 213
Mora, Philippe, 212
Morales, Hector, 76
Mordini, Gino, 212
More, Kenneth, 194, 226
More the Merrier, The, 160
Moreau, Jeanne, 104, 105, 165, 198, 226
Moreau, Jim, 140
Morell, Andre, 194
Moreno, Jorge, 116
Moreno, Jose Elias, 210
Moreno, Juan, 124
Moreno, Rita, 7, 78, 79, 161, 226
Moretti, Michele, 165
Moreux, Jean-Pierre, 203
Morgan, Alexandra, 131
Morgan, Debbi, 150
Morgan, Dennis, 226
Morgan, Gary, 58
Morgan, Harry (Henry), 72, 226
Morgan, Jack, 149
Morgan, Jeffrey, 205
Morgan, Michele, 226
Morgan, Mimi, 137
Morgan, Read, 44, 142
Morgan, Robert W., 68, 140
Morgan, Ruth, 130
Morgan, Tracy, 142
Morgan, William Jr., 31
Moriarty, Michael, 226
Morison, Patricia, 226
Morita, Pat, 57
Morita, Louisa, 154
Morley, Robert, 127, 207, 226
Morley, Ruth, 8, 16, 82
Morning, Noon and Night, 131
Morning Glory, 160.
Morrall, Adrian, 89
Morricone, Ennio, 172, 208
Morrill, John Arthur, 139
Morris, Bea, 149
Morris, Garrett, 86
Morris, Greg, 135, 226
Morris, Howard, 226
Morris, John, 48
Morris, Oswald, 94
Morris, Reginald, 54, 190
Morris, Yvette, 129
Morris-Adams, Richard, 202
Morrison, Ernie, 129
Morrison, Glenn, 137
Morrison, Robert L., 148
Morriss, Frank E., 45
Morrow, Vic, 28, 29, 141, 226
Morse, Robert, 226
Morse, Terry, Jr., 66, 131
Morshower, Glenn, 136
Mortiz, Louisa, 142
Morton, Paula, 140
Moschin, Gastone, 210
Moses, 172
Mosley, Robert E., 22
Mosley, Roger E., 14, 15, 134
Moss, Arnold, 226
Moss, Delbert, 132
Moss, J. H., 140

Moss, Jenny, 211
Mostel, Zero, 82, 213, 226
Moston, Murray, 82
Mother, Jugs & Speed, 41
Moulin, Jean-Pierre, 208
Moussou, George, 133
Moutoussamy, Laure, 206
Moving Violation, 143
Moye, Norma, 133
Moyer, Richard, 136
Mozart, 178
Mr. Deeds Goes to Town, 160
Mrs. Miniver, 160
MS. Don Juan, 160
Mu To, Kung, 210
Mubarak, Antar, 86
Mud, 140
Mudd, Victoria, 210
Mueller, Federico, 206
Muir, David, 175
Muller, Marion, 191
Mulligan, Richard, 62, 226
Mullins, Michael, 138
Munger, Chris, 135
Muni, Paul, 160
Munro, Caroline, 167, 209
Murder by Death, 50
Murder on the Orient Express, 161
Murdock, Frank, 126
Murdock, Jack, 143
Murphy, Charles Thomas, 114
Murphy, George, 160, 226
Murphy, Michael, 82, 83
Murphy, Paul, 84, 85
Murphy, Robin, 144
Murray, Charlie, 44
Murray, Christopher, 18
Murray, David, 207
Murray, Don, 17, 226
Murray, Graeme, 54
Murray, Ken, 226
Murtaugh, James, 18
Musante, Tony, 226
Muse, Clarence, 86
Music, Lorenzo, 114
Musson, Bernard, 203
Mustain, Dayle, 143
Mustang Country, 131
Mustin, Burt, 150
Musumeci, Tuccio, 206
Muthers, The, 149
Muti, Ornella, 208
Mutiny on the Bounty, 160
Muxeneder, Franz, 174
Muytten, Bruno, 165
My Erotic Fantasies, 142
My Fair Lady, 161
My Friends, 210
My Michael, 205
My Name Is Legend, 144
My Uncle, 161
Myers, Charles A., 122
Myers, David, 142
Myers, James T., 90
Myers, Sheri, 137
Myers, Stanley, 202
Myerson, Alan, 134
Myhers, John, 118
Myrow, Fred, 129, 150
Mysterious Monsters, The, 142

Nadasi, Mia, 167
Nadeau, Ray, 107
Nadelman, Jess, 18, 107
Nader, George, 226
Nadiuska, 211
Nagai, Toru, 97
Nagy, Harry, 139
Nagy, Ivan, 17, 134
Nahan, Stu, 64
Nahay, Michael, 144
Nail, Joanne, 143
Nakajima, Yoshio, 202, 211
Nakajima, Yutaka, 202
Nakaraj, Punchong, 133
Nakatani, Ichiro, 211
Nakauchi, Al, 148
Naked Afternoon, 148
Nam, Lee Tse, 201
Nanjo, Tatsuya, 211
Napier, Alan, 226
Narita, Richard, 50, 137
Naschy, Paul, 205, 210
Nash, Mary, 235
Nash, N. Richard, 16
Nashville Girl, 131
Nassivera, Joe, 137
Nathan, Glen, 131
Nathan, Richard, 135
Nathan, Stephen, 131
National Velvet, 126, 160
Natividad, Francesca, 146
Natwick, Mildred, 226
Naughton, Bill, 206
Naughton, Harry, 44
Naughton, James, 226
Naughty School Girls, 144
Naylor, Cal, 128
Neal, George, 139
Neal, Patricia, 161, 226

Nebiolo, Carlo, 210
Needham, Hal, 114, 126, 133
Neel, Phil, 129
Neely, Richard, 212
Neff, Hildegarde, 226
Neil, Bob, 58
Neilson, John, 142
Neill, Carlo, 203
Nelson, Albert, 180
Nelson, Argyle, 55, 128
Nelson, Barry, 226
Nelson, Christine, 107
Nelson, David, 226
Nelson, Don, 10, 64
Nelson, Ed, 56
Nelson, Erik, 89
Nelson, Gene, 226
Nelson, Harriet Hilliard, 226
Nelson, Lori, 226
Nelson, Nancy, 147
Nelson, Ralph, 40
Nelson, Rick, 226
Nelson, Ron, 138
Nelson, Terry, 147
Nennesy, Dale, 58
Neogy, Chiitra, 129
Nero, Franco, 202
Neron, Claude, 204
Nesbitt, Cathleen, 24, 226
Nethery, Miriam Byrd, 114
Nettleton, Lois, 134
Network, 102, 161
Netzer, Anton, 182
Neufeld, Mace, 60
Neumann, Kurt, 116
Nevedomsky, Leonid, 207
Never Too Young to Rock, 140
Nevouras, Takis, 133
Newhart, Bob, 226
Newkirk, Dorothy, 149
Newkirk, Loren, 133
Newley, Anthony, 212, 226
Newman, Alexander, 147
Newman, Barry, 226
Newman, Dorothy, 34
Newman, Eve, 107
Newman, Larraine, 143
Newman, Paul, 6, 52, 53, 226
Newman, Scott, 226
Newman, Stephen D., 97
Newman, William, 141
Newmar, Julie, 226
Newsom, Lee, 136
Newton, David, 150
Next Man, The, 97
Next Stop, Greenwich Village, 12
Ngobeni, Mackson, 200
Niamg, Miriam, 211
Nibley, Christopher Sloan, III, 150
Nicholas, Paul, 226
Nicholls, Allan, 52
Nicholls, Anthony, 60
Nichols, Barbara, 235
Nichols, James, 148
Nichols, Mike, 161, 226
Nichols, Paul, 141
Nichols, Wade, 131, 148
Nicholson, Jack, 6, 34, 35, 140, 154, 155, 156, 161, 226
Nicholson, Laura, 145
Nicholson, Sarah, 129, 148
Nickelodeon, 114
Nickerson, Jimmy, 44
Nicol, Alex, 145, 147, 226
Nicolai, Bruno, 201
Nicoletta, John, 43
Nicolodi, Daria, 208
Nielsen, Betty, 129, 214
Nielsen, Leslie, 146, 226
Nielson, Noreen, 18
Night at the Opera, A, 39
Night Caller, 128
Night Child, 204
Night of the Spanish Fly, 148
Night Pleasures, 214
Nights of Cabiria, The, 161
Nine Lives of a Wet Pussycat, 210
Nitzsche, Jack, 154
Niven, David, 10, 11, 50, 51, 161, 226
Niven, Kip, 68
Nizet, Charles, 126
No Deposit, No Return, 10
No Way Back, 137
No Way Out, 137
Noah, 138
Nobel, Thom, 201
Noble, James, 16, 144
Noble, Nancy, 133
Nofles, Irene, 147
Noiret, Philippe, 208, 210, 212
Nolan, Jeanette, 139
Nolan, Lloyd, 226
Nolan, William F., 58, 90

Nolte, Nick, 226
None but the Lonely Heart,
160
Noonan, John Ford, 12
Norman . . . Is That You?,
77
Norman, Madie, 148
Norman, Robert, 136
Norris, Christopher, 135,
226
Norris, Jim, 97
Norris, Patricia, 34
Norris, William, 145
North, Alex, 213
North, Heather, 226
North, Noelle, 98, 145
North, Sheree, 72, 226
North of the Sun, 128
Northrup, Harry, 8, 148
*Northville Cemetery
Massacre, The,* 130
Norton, Ken, 143, 226
Norton, Rosanna, 98
Norton, William, 69, 143
Norville, Herbert, 84
Nosseck, Noel, 127
Notorianni, Pietro, 188
Nottage, Douglas, 124
Nouwen, Delphie, 204
Nova, Eddie, 140
Nova, Ludmilla, 194
Novack, Sheely, 134
Novak, Allen, 138
Novak, Harry, 132
Novak, Kim, 226
Novelli, Mario, 206
Novices, The, 205
Novikoff, Rashel, 12
Nownes, James E., 137
Noyes, Joanna, 186
Nubarr, Alex, 210
Nuchtern, Simon, 211
Nugent, Elliott, 226
Nulli, Al, 148
Nussbaum, Raphael, 132
Nute, Don, 226
Nutter, Mayf, 22
Nuyen, France, 226
Nykvist, Sven, 42, 178
Oates, Simon, 201
Oates, Warren, 136, 143,
226
Ober, Arlon, 145
Oberon, Merle, 226
Obori, Sanae, 211
O'Brian, Hugh, 72, 226
O'Brien, Clay, 226
O'Brien, Edmond, 161, 226
O'Brien, Margaret, 160,
226
O'Brien, Pat, 226
O'Brien, Richard, 118
O'Brien, Seamus, 149
Obsession, 70
O'Casey, Ronan, 145
Occhini, Ilaria, 210
O'Connell, Arthur, 226
O'Connell, James, 114
O'Connor, Carroll, 226
O'Connor, Donald, 226
O'Connor, Glynnis, 45, 137,
226
O'Connor, John, 142
O'Connor, Joseph, 201
O'Dare, Kathy, 135
Ode to Billy Joe, 45
O'Dell, Denis, 78, 170
Odell, Valerie, 14
O'Donovan, Edwin, 154
O'Flaherty, Joe, 143
Ogawa, Mayimi, 211
Ogden, David, 137
Ogen, Kathrin, 213
Ogier, Bulle, 213, 214
O'Grady, Lanie, 137, 144
Oh! Alfie, 206
O'Halloran, Jack, 116
O'Hanlon, George, 100, 226
O'Hara, Maureen, 226
O'Hara, Shirley, 100
O'Hare, Rosie, 126
Ohashi, Takashi, 210
O'Henry, Marie, 127
O'Herlihy, Dan, 226
Ohotnikoff, Catherine, 203
Ohta, Bennett, 56
Okazaki, Kouzo, 211
Okun, Charles, 40
Okuneff, Gerry, 107
Oland, Inger-Berit, 211
Old Arizona, 160
Old Gun, The, 208
O'Leary, Jack, 112, 133
O'Leary, John, 18
Olimpia, 214
Oliver!, 161
Oliver, Greg, 36
Oliver, Kevin, 150
Oliver, Rochelle, 12
Olivier, Laurence, 92, 93,
94, 160, 226
Oliverio, Nino, 88
O'Loughlin, Gerald S., 226

Olsen, Rolf, 212
Olson, Nancy, 226
Olusola, Elsie, 135
O'Malley, David, 148, 150
O'Malley, J. Pat, 143
O'Malley, Kathleen, 72
O'Malley, Rex, 236
O'Mara, Kate, 201
Omen, The, 60
On the Waterfront, 161
Once upon a Girl, 144
Onching, Kachain, 133
One Chance to Win, 145
*One Flew over the Cuckoo's
Nest,* 154, 156, 157,
161
One of a Kind, 135
One Summer Love, 16
O'Neal, Griffin, 114
O'Neal, Patricia, 114
O'Neal, Patrick, 226
O'Neal, Ron, 226
O'Neal, Ryan, 114, 115,
226
O'Neal, Tatum, 6, 28, 29,
114, 115, 161, 226
O'Neal, Tricia, 226
O'Neil, Robert Vincent, 208
O'Neil, Tom, 109
O'Neil, Tricia, 143, 226
O'Neill, Dick, 74
O'Neill, Jennifer, 226
Onymous, Ann, 149
Opel, Bob, 150
*Opening of Misty Beethoven,
The,* 137
Ophuls, Marcel, 87
Oppenheimer, Peer J., 131
Orano, Alessio, 209
Orchard, Julian, 194
Orchid, Black, 144
Oreos, The, 110
Orgolini, Arnold H., 40
Orlando, Orazio, 210
Orlando, Tony, 111
Ornadel, Cyril, 210
Ornitz, Arthur, 12
Orsatti, Ernie, 131
Orsini, Umberto, 202, 204
Orson, Elen, 127
Orson, Janice, 127
Ortiz, Joe, 132
Ortolani, Riz, 207
Osborne, Debbie, 144
Osborne, Holmes, 136
Oscarsson, Per, 214
Osceola, Gem Thorpe, 148
Osco, William, 138
Osmond, Cliff, 148, 150
Osmond, Jimmy, 127
Osmond, Marie, 127
Ossorio, Amando, 208
O'Steen, Sam, 133
Osterhout, David R., 143,
148
O'Sullivan, Maureen, 135,
226
Osuna, Jess, 18
Other Side, The, 214
*Other Side of the
Underneath, The,* 211
Otis, James, 16
O'Toole, Peter, 226
O'Toole, Stanley, 94
Ottenheimer, Albert M., 82
Oudry, Pierre, 209
Outlaw Josey Wales, The,
46
Overly, Michael, Band, 143
Owen, Cliff, 210
Owen, Reginald, 226
Owens, Carol Jean, 141
Owens, Fred, 146
Ozanne, Christine, 210
Ozeray, Madeline, 208
Pacewiez, Lidia, 213
Pacino, Al, 6, 226
Paco, 208
Pacome, Maria, 207
Padalewski, Erich, 94, 174
Page, Anthony, 187
Page, Geraldine, 226
Page, Jimmy, 213
Paget, Debra, 227
Pagni, Eros, 164, 208
Pai Pow, Jason, 206
Paige, Janis, 227
Pakula, Alan J., 18
Pal, Laszlo, 147
Palacios, Richard, 205
Palance, Holly, 60
Palance, Jack, 201, 214,
227
Palavicini, Fernando, 210
Palevsky, Max, 87
Palladino, Roy, 145
Pallottini, Riccardo, 213
Palmer, Betsy, 227
Palmer, Carla, 136
Palmer, Gregg, 72, 227
Palmer, Keith, 167
Palmer, Lilli, 227
Palmer, Maria, 227

Palmer, Norman, 118
Palmer, Renzo, 202
Palmi, Doriglia, 162
Paluzzi, Luciana, 188
Pampanini, Silvana, 227
Panama, Norman, 130
Panama Red, 149
Pant, Lou, 138
Pantin, Raoul, 213
Panzer, William N., 148
Papamichael, Phedon, 129
Papas, Irene, 172, 173,
206, 227
Papathanassiou, Vangelis,
174
Paper Chase, The, 161
Paper Moon, 161
Pappe, Stuart H., 143
Paquis, Gerard, 197
Paredes, Daniel, 86
Parenti, Mauro, 211, 213
Parenzo, Allessandro, 210
Parfrey, Woodrow, 22, 46
Pariante, Roberto, 204
Paris, Henry, 137
Paris, Renee, 82
Pariser, Alfred, 141, 186
Parker, Alan, 84
Parker, Carl, 128
Parker, Carole, 201
Parker, Earl, 142
Parker, Eleanor, 227
Parker, Fess, 227
Parker, Jean, 227
Parker, Kathleen, 100
Parker, Michael, 134
Parker, Morrie, 144
Parker, Roger, 143
Parker, Suzy, 227
Parker, Tom, 144
Parker, Willard, 227
Parkes, James R., 107, 134
Parkes, Walter, 145
Parkins, Barbara, 197, 227
Parkinson, Robin, 206
Parks, Andrew, 20, 136
Parks, Gordon, 14
Parks, Michael, 23
Parks, Trina, 149
Parradine, J. P., 138
Parris, Hamilton, 213
Parrondo, Gil, 209
Parry, Harvey, 143
Parson, Michael J., 210
Parsons, Clive, 130
Parsons, Estelle, 161, 227
Parsons, Ned, 30
Parsons, Pamela, 146
Part, Brian, 31
Part 2 Sounder, 147
Partnow, Elaine, 114
Pasarell, Ursula, 134, 136
Pascual, Jimmy L., 212,
213
Pascual, Tommy L., 213
Passer, Ivan, 174
Pastore, Louis, 129
Pat and Mike, 38
Pataki, Michael, 146
Patch of Blue, A, 161
Pate, Johnny, 127
Pate, Michael, 212
Patrick, Alain, 143, 149
Patrick, Dennis, 227
Patrick, Nigel, 227
Patrizi, Stefano, 212
Pattee, Rowena, 210
Patterson, George, 148
Patterson, Lee, 227
Patterson, Neva, 18
Pattison, Roy, 124
Patton, 161
Patty, 129
Patucchi, Daniele, 206
Paul, Andrew, 84
Paul, John, 201
Paull, Morgan, 23
Paulo, Kathy, 139
Paulsen, Albert, 97
Pavan, Marisa, 227
Pavlova, Nadia, 207
Pawloski, Piotr, 206
Paxinou, Katina, 160
Payne, Carolyn, 142
Payne, George, 140
Pea, Alfredo, 195
Peach, Mary, 227
Peach, Melba, 143
Peake, Don, 126, 143
Peaker, E. J., 201
Pearcy, Patricia, 141
Pearson, Beatrice, 227
Pearson, Richard, 207
Pecas, Max, 214
Peck, Gregory, 7, 60, 61,
161, 227
Peckham, Ruth, 207
Pedersen, Katja, 211
Pedler, Dr. Kit, 201
Peeper, 126
Peerce, Larry, 107
Peerce, Sander, 107
Peete, Bob, 136

Peeters, Barbara, 135
Peizer, Hazel, 211
Pelegri, Pierre, 206
Pelham, Trisha, 129
Pelle, Shirley, 200
Pellegrini, Ines, 206
Pellow, Cliff, 22
Pelluttier, David, 212
Pena, Luz Maria, 139
Pendleton, David, 120
Penn, Arthur, 34
Pennacchini, Robert, 175
Pennington, Marla, 129
Pennock, Chris, 144
Pentecost, George, 18
Penz, Alena, 214
Penzer, Jean, 168
People of the Wind, 213
Peoples, David, 150
Peoples, Melvina, 138
Peppard, George, 227
Pepper, Florence, 18
Pepper, Keith, 190
Pepperman, Paul, 129, 150
Peralta, Stacy, 150
Peralto, Goyo, 205
Percy, Graham, 127
Perez, Lazaro, 143
Perez, Tony, 140
Perilli, Frank Ray, 146
Perkin, Robert, 146
Perkins, Anthony, 227
Perkins, Harold, 140
Perkins, Jack, 114
Perkins, Kent, 136
Perkins, Millie, 128
Perl, F. C., 145
Perla, B. J., 43
Perles, Nadine, 210
Perondo, Gil, 170
Perreau, Gigi, 227
Perrin, Francis, 201
Perrine, Valerie, 20, 21,
227
Perrot, Francois, 212
Perry, John Bennett, 26
Perry, Peter, 150
Perry, Steve, 100
Perschy, Maria, 210
Persky, Marilyn, 82
Persoff, Nehemiah, 124
Persson, Jorgen, 214
Pesci, Joseph, 148
Peters, Barry, 209
Peters, Bernadette, 20, 48,
49, 134, 227
Peters, Brock, 107, 227
Peters, Deedy, 126
Peters, Gus, 133
Peters, Jean, 227
Peters, Jon, 110
Peters, Timothy, 206
Peters, Werner, 213
Petersen, Stewart, 149
Peterson, Con, 145
Peterson, Diane, 97
Peterson, Robert Raymond,
129
Petitdidier, Denise, 166
Petitot, George, 202
Petranto, Russ, 102
Petrie, Daniel, 55
Petroff, Robert, 146
Petrov, Andrei, 207
Pettet, Joanna, 141, 227
Peyleron, Michel, 208, 209
Peyrot, Yves, 214
Peyser, Penny, 18
Phaedre, 139, 142
Pharaoh, 206
Phelps, Stuart W., 131
Philadelphia Story, The,
160
Philippe, Andre, 130
Phillips, Alex, Jr., 139
Phillips, Bob, 127
Phillips, Colin, 132
Phillips, Don, 86
Phillips, Frank, 10, 64, 118,
141
Phillips, John, 180
Phillips, Julia, 8, 62
Phillips, Leslie, 211
Phillips, MacKenzie, 227
Phillips, Michael, 8, 62
Phillips, Michelle, 227
Phillips, Robert, 126, 129
Phipps, Max, 19
Piacente, Carol, 144
Piazza, Ben, 28
Piazzola, Astor, 198
Picasso, Paloma, 204
Picazo, Miguel, 212
Piccioli, Gianfranco, 210
Piccioni, Piero, 164
Piccoli, Michel, 201, 204,
207, 208
Picerni, Paul, 227
Pickard, Timothy, 14
Pickens, Slim, 30, 140,
149, 227
Pickens, Slim, Band, 149

Picker, David V., 40
Pickering, Laurie, 144
Pickett, Lowell, 128
Pickett, Noel, 149
Pickford, Mary, 160, 161,
227
Picton, Don, 214
Pidgeon, Walter, 107, 227
Piece of Pleasure, A, 206
Pieplu, Claude, 42
Pierce, Bobby, 150
Pierce, Charles B., 139
Pierce, Chuck, Jr., 139
Pierce, Stack, 137
Pieri, Renau, 206
Pierson, Claude, 213
Pierson, Frank, 110
Pierson, Glenn, 139
Pike, John, Jr., 147
Pikola, Franz, 191
Pillsbury, Garth, 130
Pine, Phillip, 146, 227
Pinelli, Tullio, 210
Ping, An, 201
Pinheiro, Victor, 96
*Pink Panther Strikes Again,
The,* 199
Pink Telephone, The, 214
Pinkard, Fred, 141
Pinkney, Leon, 86
Pinoteau, Claude, 201
Pinter, Harold, 104
Pipe Dreams, 106
Pirell, David, 210
Pischinger, Herta, 174
Pisier, Marie-France, 165,
184, 185, 214
Pitavan, Veerapol, 133
Pitt, Ed, 140
Place, Mary Kay, 227
Place in the Sun, A, 160
Plaine, Alfred, 205
Planet of the Apes, 161
Plant, Robert, 213
Platt, Howard, 139
Platt, Polly, 28, 110
Platters, The, 208
Player, Susan, 138, 195
Playfair, Wendy, 140
Playten, Alice, 227
Pleasence, Angela, 207
Pleasence, Donald, 104,
146, 167, 204, 206,
213, 227
Pleasure Cruise, 136
Pleshette, Suzanne, 118,
119, 227
Plessis, Pierre, 184
Plotnick, Stanley, 17
Pluhar, Erika, 205, 213
Plummer, Christopher, 227
Pochath, Werner, 131
Podany, Olinka, 205
Podesta, Rosana, 227
Poe, Al, 128
Poessiger, Jack, 136
Pohlmann, Eric, 210
Poinareff, Michel, 26
Pointer, Priscilla, 98, 114
Pointer Sisters, 86
Poire, Alain, 168, 201,
205, 207, 214
Poirier, Henri, 213
Poisson, Odile, 209
Poitier, Sidney, 161, 227
Polakof, James, 139
Poli, Fernando, 195
Polito, Gene, 134
Polito, Lina, 164, 206, 227
Politti, Luis, 207
Poll, Lee, 176
Poll, Martin, 176
Pollack, Bernard, 102
Pollard, Michael J., 227
Pollock, David, 28, 129
Pollock, Larry, 129
Pollock, Nancy R., 144
Pom Pom Girls, The, 149
Pomerantz, Jacob, 145
Pompian, Paul, 149
Pons, Lily, 236
Ponti, Carlo, 195
Pony Express Rider, 149
Pool, William, 70
Poole, Robert Dale, 150
Poole, Roy, 102
Poor White Trash: Part 2,
140
Pope, Georgette, 131
Pope, Kim, 126, 130, 131,
145
Poplin, Jack, 63
Popov, Oleg, 207
Popovich, Michael, 143
Porat, Orna, 209
Porcheral, J., 206
Porel, Marc, 206
Portal, Michel, 214
Porter, Eric, 211, 227
Porter, Joan, 82
Porter, Rand, 144
Posey, Curtis, 136

Posse from Heaven, 146
Potter, Brien, 143
Potter, Jessica, 135
Pottle, Harry, 206
Poulson, Hans, 210
Powell, Don, 213
Powell, Eleanor, 39, 227
Powell, Jane, 227
Powell, Karen, 44
Powell, Robert, 227
Powell, William, 134, 227
Power, Richard, 134
Powers, Mala, 227
Powers, Stefanie, 212
Prachtel, Volker, 191
Praise, Ian, 131
Pratt, Anthony, 202
Pratt, Charles A., 63
Pratt, Judson, 134
Pravda, George, 97
Prechtel, Volker, 174
Premonition, The, 129
Prentiss, Chris, 150
Prentiss, Paula, 227
Presboist, Paul, 207
Prescot, Cynthia, 130
Presidential Peepers, The,
   130
Presle, Micheline, 227
Presley, Elvis, 227
Presnell, Harve, 227
Pressman, Michael, 144
Preston, Earl, 183
Preston, J. A., 107
Preston, Paul, 141
Preston, Robert, 227
Preston, Ward, 40
Prestwood, Robert, 136
Prete, Giancarlo, 202, 204
Prevet, Ray, 214
Prevost, Francoise, 214
Price, Alan, 206
Price, Jesse, 133
Price, Paul B., 78
Price, Stanley, 167, 197
Price, Vincent, 213, 227
Prickett, Maudie, 236
Priest, Dan, 132
Priestley, Tom, 124, 187
Prime of Miss Jean Brodie,
   The, 161
Prince, Robert, 141
Prince, Ron, 133, 143
Prince, William, 24, 102,
   227
Principal, Victoria, 130,
   134, 227
Prine, Andrew, 127, 135,
   139
Pringle, Joan, 141
Pritchett, Melissa, 139
Private Life of Henry VIII,
   The, 160
Proclemer, Anna, 88
Proctor, Phil, 143
Proietti, Luigi, 206
Project: Kill, 146
Prophet, The, 214
Proslier, Jean-Marie, 208
Prouse, Peter, 180
Proval, David, 44
Provine, Dorothy, 227
Prowse, Juliet, 227
Prus, Boleslaw, 206
Pryce, Jonathan, 124, 125
Pryor, Nicholas, 143
Pryor, Richard, 36, 86,
   112, 113, 126, 227
Pulford, Don, 134
Puppo, Ramon, 145
Puppo, Romano, 202, 204
Purcell, Evelyn, 148
Purcell, Lee, 227
Purcell, Noel, 227
Purcell, Pat, 45
Purdom, Edmund, 204, 227
Purl, Linda, 20
Pursall, David, 201
Putnam, George, 64, 65
Puttnam, David, 84, 150
Pye, Alonzo, 144
Pyke, Hy, 131, 132
Pyle, Denver, 30, 52, 148,
   150
Quade, John, 23, 63
Quaid, Randy, 34, 122, 123
Qualtinger, Helmut, 182
Quayle, Anna, 94
Quayle, Anthony, 172, 173,
   227
Querejeta, Elias, 212
Quiet Man, The, 160
Quilligan, Veronica, 170
Quine, Richard, 227
Quinlan, Kathleen, 55
Quinn, Anthony, 160, 161,
   227
Quinn, Barbara, 141
Quinn, Louis, 18
Quong, Rose, 213
Qvale, Kjell, 133
Raab, Kurt, 208
Raben, Peer, 203

Rabier, Jean, 206, 212
Racette, Frannie, 198
Racimo, Victoria, 210
Radd, Ronald, 236
Radnitz, Robert B., 31, 147
Rafelson, Bob, 22
Rafelson, Toby Carr, 22
Rafferty, Frances, 227
Raffill, Stewart, 150
Raffin, Deborah, 148, 227
Rafner, Lee, 141
Raft, George, 227
Ragin, John S., 143
Ragland, Robert O., 135,
   146, 149
Ragsdale, Linda Sue, 146
Rainbird Pattern, 24
Rainer, Luise, 160
Raines, Ella, 227
Rainey, Ford, 150
Rains, Darby Lloyd, 130,
   141, 205
Raksin, Rudy, 142
Ralls, Debra, 147
Ralph, Brian, 124
Ralston, Jane, 131
Ram, Brenda, 149
Ramati, Alexander, 209
Ramer, Henry, 212
Ramirez, Monika, 127, 148
Ramos, Travador, 201
Rampling, Charlotte, 202,
   227
Ramrog, Joe, 82
Ramsay, John, 107
Ramsay, Remak, 82
Ramsay, Robin, 212
Ramsey, Eileen, 121
Ramsey, Logan, 227
Randall, Charles, 97
Randall, Marilyn, 120, 121
Randall, Tony, 227
Randell, Ron, 227
Randolph, John, 116
Random, Robert, 141
Ranieri, Massimo, 201
Rankin, Dugald, 206
Rankin, Gilman, 148
Ransohoff, Martin, 112
Rape Killer, The, 209
Rape of Innocence, 209
Rapisarda, Sara, 164
Rapp, Nell, 142
Rapp, Paul, 142
Rapstead, Jean, 144
Rasback, John, 139
Rashomon, 160
Rasmussen, Thomas, 131
Rassam, Jean-Pierre, 211
Rassimov, Ivan, 208
Rassimov, Rada, 207
Rasulala, Thalmus, 23, 126,
   227
Rath, Earl, 126
Rattlers, 132
Rattray, Heather, 150
Ratzenberger, John, 78
Rauch, Judy, 144
Raucher, Herman, 45
Raunio, Johanna, 140
Raven, Marcia, 138
Rawi, Ousama, 206
Rawlins, David, 36
Rawlins, Lester, 148
Ray, aldo, 147, 201, 227
Ray, Radio, 148
Ray, Tony, 12
Raye, Martha, 227
Raye, Melba, 126
Rayfiel, David, 26
Raymond, Gene, 227
Raymond, Laura, 149
Raymond, Lina, 40, 107
Raynor, Sheila, 60

Reed, Donna, 161, 228
Reed, Erica, 130
Reed, Floyd, Jr., 140
Reed, Floyd, Sr., 140
Reed, Jerry, 69
Reed, Joel M., 149
Reed, Ken, 31
Reed, Lady, 147
Reed, Marshall, 142
Reed, Mona Tracy, 86
Reed, Myrtle, 194
Reed, Oliver, 90, 91, 139,
   228
Reed, Peggy, 130
Reed, Rex, 228
Reed, Tracy, 86, 137
Reems, Harry, 126, 128,
   135, 136, 145, 148,
   228
Rees, Danny, 44
Reese, Don, 126
Reeve, Geoffrey, 202
Reeves, Jack, 131
Reeves, Lisa, 138
Reeves, Roberta, 132
Reeves, Steve, 228
Reflections from a Brass
   Bed, 129
Regan, Russ, 150
Reggiani, Aldo, 189
Reggiani, Serge, 204
Regine, 94
Regis, Karen, 134
Reid, Ace, 149
Reid, Alistair, 197, 202
Reid, Elliott, 228
Reid, Kate, 183
Reigan, 205
Reiger, August, 204
Reincke, Heintz, 212
Reiner, Carl, 228
Reiner, Robert, 228
Reinhardt, Ray, 146
Reisman, Arnie, 149
Reisner, Dean, 108
Reitman, Ivan, 141
Reizner, Lou, 150
Rekofski, Rod, 207
Remick, Lee, 7, 60, 61,
   202, 228
Remsen, Bert, 44, 52, 137
Renard, Ken, 133
Renay, Liz, 126
Rendezvous with Anne, 128
Renfroe, Frank, 130
Renoir, Jean, 161, 206
Renoir, Marguerite, 206
Rescher, Gayne, 77
Resenthal, Laurence, 66
Resnick, Judith, 127
Reteria, Joe, 140
Rettig, Tommy, 228
Return of a Man Called
   Horse, The, 66
Return of the Panther, 202
Return of the Tall Blond
   Man with One Black
   Shoe, The, 205
Reuber-Staier, Eva, 194
Reul, Kevin, 84
Revenge, 204
Revenge of the
   Cheerleaders, 137
Revere, Anne, 31, 160
Revilla, Ramon, 140
Revill, Clive, 206, 228
Rey, Alejandro, 210
Rey, Fernando, 88, 124,
   162
Reyes, Patricia, 66
Reyes, Stanley J., 70
Reynders, Hanne, 214
Reynolds, Burt, 6, 69, 114,
   115, 228
Reynolds, Debbie, 228
Reynolds, Larry, 183
Reynolds, Marjorie, 228
Reynolds, Patrick, 31
Reynolds, Tyler, 130, 148
Rhoades, Barbara, 228
Rhodes, Earl, 176, 177
Rhodes, Loren, 150
Rhone, Trevor D., 137
Ribovska, Malka, 210
Riccardo, Rick, 180
Ricci, Rudy, 145
Rice, Cy, 20
Rice, Frank, 150
Rich, Irene, 228
Richard, Herschel, 136
Richard, Pierre, 205, 207,
   210
Richards, Buzz, 130
Richards, Elizabeth, 137
Richards, Jack L., 150
Richards, Jeff, 228
Richards, Joyce, 129
Richards, Kim, 10, 11, 63,
   148
Richards, Levi, 126
Richards, Marty, 128
Richards, Susan, 167
Richards, Vikki, 124

Richardson, Al, 140
Richardson, Chris, 144
Richardson, Lee, 102
Richardson, Ralph, 228
Richardson, Tony, 161
Richmond, Kim, 131
Richmond, Ralph, 129, 150
Richter, Ilse, 190
Richter, W. D., 114, 126
Rick Jr., 129
Rickles, Don, 228
Rico, Rigobert, 66
Riddle, Bill, 114
Riddle, Nelson, 38, 146
Riddle, Sam, 143
Ride a Wild Pony, 140
Rigaud, George, 205
Rigby, Jacky, 205
Rigg, Diana, 228
Riley, Doug, 183
Riley, Joseph, 90
Riley, Patrick, 150
Ring, William E., 100
Ringwald, Monika, 213
Ripple, Carleton, 114
Ripps, M. A., 140
Risi, Dino, 201, 213, 214
Rist, Robbie, 139
Ritchie, Michael, 28
Ritt, Martin, 82, 182
Ritter, John, 114, 115
Rittermann, Michael, 203
Ritz, Harry, 48
Ritz, The, 78
River Niger, The, 134
Rivera, Geraldo, 133
Rivera, Marika, 124
Rivero, Jorge, 23
Rivero, Julian, 236
Rivet, Catherine, 202
Roantree, Sean, 206
Roarke, Adam, 201
Robards, Jason, 18, 19,
   139, 161, 208, 228
Robbins, Gale, 228
Robbins, Jane Marla, 100
Robbins, Jerome, 161
Robbins, Matthew, 36
Robbins, Michael, 199
Robbins, Rainbow, 129
Robert, Yves, 168, 205,
   207
Roberts, Byron, 142
Roberts, Davis, 76, 136
Roberts, John Storm, 135
Roberts, Judith, 131, 136
Roberts, Marilyn, 128
Roberts, Meade, 129
Roberts, Morgan, 36
Roberts, Pascale, 209
Roberts, Pernell, 228
Roberts, Rachel, 187, 211,
   228
Roberts, Ralph, 228
Roberts, Randolph, 58
Roberts, Robbe, 31
Roberts, Robert L., 129
Roberts, Shorty, 144
Roberts, Tony, 228
Robertson, Cliff, 56, 70, 71,
   161, 183, 228
Robertson, Dale, 228
Robertson, Douglas, 131
Robertson, Hugh A., 213
Robertson, Suzanne C., 213
Robertson, Tim, 139
Robeson, Paul, 236
Robin and Marian, 170
Robin, Jackie, 133
Robin, Michel, 208
Robinson, Chris, 228
Robinson, David, 137
Robinson, Edward G., 161
Robinson, Hank, 127
Robinson, Harry, 201
Robinson, Ken, 147
Robinson, Roger, 228
Robles, Leticia, 139
Robson, Flora, 228
Robson, Zuleika, 204
Roche, Jean, 214
Rochefort, Jean, 168, 205,
   207, 208, 212
Rochester, 228
Rochester, Robert, 137
Rochut, Jean-Jacques, 208
Rocky, 4, 100, 161
Roddy, Rod, 146
Rodero, Jose Lopez, 170
Rodine, Alex, 44, 80
Rodnesky, Shmuel, 172
Rodriguez, Bob, 139
Rodriguez, Johnny, 131
Rodriguez, Percy, 127
Rodriguez, Robert, 134
Roe, Jack, 23, 28, 112
Roeg, Nicolas, 180
Roehm, Wolfgang, 131
Roelofs, Al, 64
Roerick, William, 148
Rogers, Charles "Buddy",
   228

Rogers, Dean, 128, 137
Rogers, Elizabeth E., 89,
   213
Rogers, Ginger, 160, 161,
   228
Rogers, Harriet, 16
Rogers, Nate, 129
Rogers, Noelle, 52, 53
Rogers, Roy, 228
Rogers, Steve, 206
Rogers, Timmie, 133
Rogers, Victor, 145
Rogers, Wayne, 228
Rogner, Richard, 191
Rogue, The, 206
Rohm, Maria, 206
Rohmer, Eric, 191
Rohmer, Patrice, 133, 137,
   143
Roitfeld, Jacques, 208
Roizman, Owen, 102
Roja, Victoria Merida, 170
Roland, Gilbert, 228
Roland, Gyl, 127
Rolike, Hank, 20, 100, 143
Rollerbabies, 141
Rolzman, Owen, 66
Roman, Candice, 144
Roman, Elsie, 140
Roman, Rex, 140
Roman, Ruth, 228
Roman Holiday, 161
Romanelli, Carla, 201
Romay, Lina, 202
Rome, Sydne, 205, 209
Rome, Tony, 148
Romer, Fred, 214
Romero, Cesar, 228
Romito, Victor, 44
Ronet, Maurice, 203
Rook, David, 211
Room at the Top, 161
Rooney, Mickey, 160, 228
Roper, John, 45
Roquemore, Cliff, 147
Roquet, Suzanne, 212
Rose, Alex, 133, 136
Rose, Jack, 22
Rose, Norman, 82
Rose Tattoo, The, 161
Rosemary's Baby, 161
Rosen, Chuck, 8
Rosenberg, Marion, 34
Rosenberg, Max J., 204
Rosenberg, Philip, 12, 102
Rosenberg, Stuart, 124
Rosenbloom, Maxie, 236
Rosenman, Howard, 133
Rosenman, Leonard, 31
Rosenthal, Daniel, 150
Rosenthal, Imre J., 184
Rosenthal, Richard, 142
Rosin, Mark, 144
Rosny, Jacques, 203
Ross, Alberta, 206
Ross, Annie, 206
Ross, Diana, 228
Ross, Gene, 140
Ross, Herbert, 94
Ross, Howard, 202
Ross, Jamie, 97
Ross, Joe E., 145
Ross, Katharine, 124, 228
Ross, Liz, 136
Ross, Lynn, 133, 201
Ross, Marc, 148
Ross, Megan, 201
Ross, Merrie Lynn, 133
Ross, Michael, 143
Ross, Ted, 36
Rossel, Franco, 206
Rossen, Steven, 146
Rossiter, Leonard, 124,
   199, 228
Rost, Leo, 209
Roter, Ted, 207
Roth, Ann, 50, 143
Roth, Gene, 236
Roth, Jeff, 150
Roth, Joe, 143
Roth, Lillian, 228
Roth, Phil, 154
Roth, Rose-Renee, 203
Roth, Toni, 182
Rothemund, Sigi, 203
Rothman, Marion, 26, 137
Rothstein, Roger M., 50
Rotter, Stephen, 34
Rotunno, Giuseppe, 164
Rougeul, Jean, 165
Rounds, David, 228
Roundtree, Richard, 228
Rouse, Graham, 140
Rouyer, Andre, 213
Rowan, Sue, 135, 145, 150
Rowand, Nada, 132
Rowe, Misty, 130
Rowe, Vern, 118
Rowen, Jennifer, 144
Rowlands, David, 129
Rowlands, Gena, 107, 228
Rowles, Kenneth F., 214
Rowse, Tim, 183

Roy, Lee, 201
Roy, Roger, 138
Royce, Rose, 86
Ruban, Al, 129
Rubbo, Michael, 201
Ruben, Denis, 134
Ruben, Joseph, 138
Rubettes, The, 140
Rubin, Benny, 118
Rubin, Glynn, 142
Rubinstein, John, 148
Rubinstein, Paulette, 150
Rucker, Christine, 212
Rucker, Reggie, 145
Ruderman, Eduardo, 207
Rudolph, Alan, 52, 127
Ruellan, Andre, 207
Ruffin, Melvin, 150
Rufus, 42, 214
Ruggiero, Gene, 208
Ruhland, Paul, 146
Ruisinger, Thomas, 97
Ruiz, Frank, 140
Rule, Frederick, 134
Rule, Janice, 228
Rum Runner, 206
Rungrat, Metta, 133
Rupert, Michael, 228
Ruschel, Beto, 210
Ruschell, Niva, 128
Rush, Barbara, 228
Rush, Roshell, 136
Rushka, 132
Ruskin, Shimen, 236
Russek, Jorge, 66
Russel, Evelyn, 135
Russel, Tony, 142
Russell, Chuck, 133
Russell, Harold, 160
Russell, Jane, 228
Russell, Jason, 132, 142
Russell, John, 228
Russell, Kurt, 228
Russell, Rosalind, 236, 237
Russell, Sheridan, 84
Russell, Shirley, 130
Russell, Theresa, 104
Russell, Tina, 130
Russo, Gianni, 201
Russo, Jodean, 128
Russo, John, 145
Rust, Donald, 139
Rustam, Mardi, 147
Rustigian, Ray, 139
Ruth, Robert, 68
Rutherford, Ann, 194, 228
Rutherford, Margaret, 161
Rutkin, Rudy, 135
Rutledge, Robin, 145
Ruud, Siv, 178
Ruymen, Ayn, 228
Ryan, John, 34, 80
Ryan, Mitchell, 197
Ryan's Daughter, 161
Rydell, Christopher, 44
Rydell, Evelyn, 44
Rydell, Mark, 44
Ryder, Eddie, 48
Ryder, W. Lewis, 131
Ryser, Otto, 182
Saad, Robert, 141
Saarinen, Eric, 135
Saba, Frank, 139
Sabato, Antonio, 212
Sabbatini, Enrico, 172
Sable, Claire, 150
Saboy, Teresa Ann, 206
Saburi, Shin, 211
Sachs, William, 139
Saderman, Alejandro, 207
Sadoff, Robert, 210
Saenz, Tony, 139
Saether, Odd Geir, 211
Safan, Craig, 144, 145
Sagnan, Ilimane, 211
Sahl, Michael, 149
Sailor Who Fell from Grace
  with the Sea, The, 176
Saint, Eva Marie, 161, 228
Sakai, Seth, 56
Sakata, Harold, 141
Salaman, Toby, 124
Salazar, Carlos, 144
Salerno, Enrico Maria, 213
Sales, Michel, 206
Salgado, Marian, 208
Salim, Peter, 18
Sallis, Peter, 196
Salmi, Albert, 228
Salsa, 133
Salsberg, Gerry, 186
Salt, Jennifer, 228
Salten, Felix, 118
Saluga, Bill, 143
Salut L'Artiste, 168
Salvani, Al, 100
Salvanini, Hareton, 210
Salvatori, Renato, 208
Samb, Seun, 211
Samie, Catherine, 207
Sammut, Jean-Pierre, 210
Sammy Somebody, 145
Samosiuk, Zygmunt, 213

Samperi, Salvatore, 210
Samples, Candy, 135
Sampson, Will, 47, 52, 53,
  154, 155
Samurai, 161
San Juan, Olga, 228
Sanchez, Jaime, 97
Sancho, Fernando, 208
Sand, Michelle, 203
Sanda, Dominique, 212
Sanda, Felicia, 147
Sande, Angel, 141
Sander, Otto, 191
Sanders, George, 160, 201
Sanders, Henry, 149
Sanders, Jack, 114
Sandifur, Virginia, 17
Sandler, Barry, 22, 128
Sands, Billy, 100
Sands, Tommy, 228
Sandstone, 132
Sanford, Donald S., 56
Sanguino, Victoria
  Hernandez, 170
Santana, Jorge Malo, 133
Santarelli, Dominique, 213
Santiago, Cirio H., 140, 149
Santini, Pierre, 206, 212
Santoni, Espartaco, 209
Santos, Angel Fernandez,
  212
Santos, Dominique, 210
Sanz, Renee, 149
Sapp, Robert, 139
Sarafian, Richard C., 97
Sarandon, Chris, 26, 27,
  228
Sarandon, Susan, 16, 228
Sarde, Philippe, 42, 165,
  201, 204, 208
Sargent, Richard, 228
Sarkisian, Mimi, 154, 155
Sarkisian, Sos, 213
Sarli, Maurice, 211
Sarno, Joe, 140, 148
Sarr, Farba, 211
Sarrazin, Michael, 143,
  204, 228
Sarver, J. D., 129
Sasaki, Katsuhiko, 205
Sasdy, Peter, 167, 201
Sasthu, Adijae, 200
Sato, Makato, 202
Sato, Masayki, 211
Sato, Orie, 211
Satz, Wayne, 143
Saulnier, Nicole, 208
Saunders, Brandi, 138, 206
Saunders, Russ, 76
Saunders, Trevor, 147
Sautet, Claude, 204
Savage, Brad, 10, 11, 107,
  134
Savage, Bunny, 144
Savage, David, 130, 140
Savalas, Telly, 201, 209,
  212, 228
Savalas, Yolanda, 141
Save the Tiger, 161
Savident, John, 146
Savina, Carlo, 205, 209
Savoy, Teresa Ann, 206
Saxon, John, 228
Saxton, David, 146
Sayonara, 161
Sbarigia, Giulio, 88
Scaccia, Mario, 206
Scardino, Don, 141
Scardino, Jean Paul, 144
Scarif, Paul, 146
Scarmaglia, Francesco, 206
Scarpelli, 189
Scarpitta, Guy, 136
Scavocini, Savro, 195
Scedi, Joe, 207
Scent of a Woman, 201
Schaaf, Edward, 146
Schaaf, Johannes, 214
Schaake, Katrin, 208
Schachel, Kim, 144
Schachinger, Erich, 191
Schaffner, Franklin J., 161
Schallert, Bill, 143
Scharf, David, 149
Schatzberg, Jerry, 43
Schedeen, Ann, 40
Scheider, Roy, 92, 228
Schell, Maria, 124, 228
Schell, Maximilian, 73, 74,
  161, 182, 228
Schell, Ronnie, 64, 118
Schellerup, Henning, 132,
  135
Schenck, George, 80
Schenck, Joseph M., 160
Schenk, Otto, 205
Scherbakov, Yevgeny, 207
Scherr, Michelle, 147
Schiavelli, Vincent, 134,
  154, 155
Schiffman, Suzanne, 192
Schifrin, Lalo, 63, 74, 124

Schild, Joel, 140
Schild, Marvin, 140
Schildkraut, Joseph, 160
Schiller, Joel, 62
Schiller, Norbert, 182
Schlageter, Alfred, 203
Schlatter, George, 77
Schlesinger, John, 92, 161
Schlesinger, Peter, 201
Schlubach, Jan, 201
Schmidt, Marlene, 147
Schmitzburger, Paul, 194
Schneck, Stephen, 201
Schneider, Harold, 22
Schneider, Maria, 205, 228
Schneider, Romy, 208, 212,
  228
Schneiderman, Jerry, 141
Schnitzer, Robert Allen, 129
Schnitzler, Arthur, 205
Schoener, Eberhard, 214
Schor, Richard, 133
Schott, Bob, 146
Schrader, Paul, 8, 70
Schreiber, Avery, 68
Schriver, Al, 135
Schroeder, Barbet, 211,
  213
Schroeder, E., 201, 214
Schubert, Karin, 213
Schuberth, Christine, 202
Schulman, Arnold, 40
Schultz, Derek, 86
Schultz, Michael, 86
Schultz, Robert E., 150
Schumacher, Joel, 86, 133
Schundler, Rudolf, 204
Schurr, S. W., 108
Schwartz, Alain, 210
Schwartz, Albert, 184
Schwartz, Bernard, 134
Schwartz, Elroy, 132
Schwartz, Howard, 80
Schwartz, Kenneth, 205
Schwarzenegger, Arnold,
  22
Schwary, Ronald L., 74, 190
Schygulla, Hanna, 208
Sciocia, Frank, 129
Scofield, Paul, 161, 228
Scoones, Mark, 206
Scoppa, Peter, 8, 82, 120
Scorchy, 147
Scorsese, Martin, 8, 142
Scott, Al, 45
Scott, Elliot, 196
Scott, Evelyne, 206
Scott, George C., 161, 228
Scott, Gordon, 133, 143,
  228
Scott, Hillary, 138
Scott, Jay, 135
Scott, Jim, 190
Scott, John, 175, 207, 212
Scott, Martha, 228
Scott, Nicole, 135
Scott, Randolph, 228
Scott, Susan, 210
Scott, Walter, 22
Scruggs, Linda, 127
Scum of the Earth, 140
Scutter, Ken, 130, 142,
  148
Seager, Lew, 140
Seagull, Barbara Hershey,
  228
Sealy, John, 214
Searle, Edmond, 201
Searle, Ronald, 209
Searles, Bucky, 138
Sears, Heather, 228
Sebastian, Beverly, 145
Sebastian, Ferd, 145
Sebastian, John, 138
Sebastian, Ray, 147
Sebastian, Tracy, 145
Seberg, Jean, 213, 228
Seck, Adboulaye, 211
Seck, Doota, 211
Secombe, Andrew, 167
Secombe, Harry, 228
Secret of Navajo Cave, 132
Secrets of the Gods, 139
Sector, David, 150
Seddon, Jack, 201
Sedrihini, Mohammed, 97
Seeman, John, 126, 140,
  142
Seeman, Roger, 149
Seerattan, Anna, 213
Segal, George, 22, 228
Segelcke, Tore, 178
Sei, Nyoya, 202
Seibel, Joel, 144
Seid, Art, 150
Seigal, Joel, 146
Seigel, Terri, 143
Seippel, Edda, 191
Seiter, Christopher, 118
Self, William, 72, 76
Self-Service Schoolgirls,
  131

Sellars, Elizabeth, 229
Sellers, Arlene, 94, 182
Sellers, Peter, 7, 50, 51,
  199, 229
Sellier, Charles E., Jr., 141,
  142, 148, 149, 150
Selnik, C. B., 206
Seltzer, David, 60
Seltzer, Walter, 23
Seltzer, Will, 137
Selwart, Tonio, 229
Sembene, Ousmane, 211
Sembera, Tricia, 145
Semple, Lorenzo, Jr., 116
Senatore, Paulo, 211
Senia, Jean-Marie, 214
Sennett, Mack, 160
Sensuous Housewife, The,
  214
Senter, Jack, 10, 70
Separate Tables, 161
Serail, 214
Serbagi, Roger Omar, 97
Serena, 126, 127, 142,
  144, 149
Seresin, Michael, 84
Sergeant York, 160
Serna, Pepe, 86, 148
Sernas, Jacques, 229
Serpe, Ralph, 143
Serrault, Michel, 212
Servais, Jean, 236
Setna, Renu, 197
Setrakian, Edward, 97
Seven Beauties, 162
Seven-Man Army, 210
Seven-Per-Cent Solution,
  The, 94
Seventh Heaven, 160
Severa, Joey, 132, 135,
  145, 146
Seward, Kathleen, 150
Sex Wish, 148
Sex with a Smile, 209
Seye, Younouss, 211
Seyler, Athene, 229
Seymour, Anne, 229
Seymour, Jane, 229
Shadow of the Hawk, 190
Shaffner, Karen, 127
Shaffner, Louis A., 127
Shafter, Artie, 131
Shagan, Steve, 124
Shaggy D.A., The, 118
Shah, Krishna, 134
Shah, R. P., 201
Shalet, Diane, 104
Shampan, Jack, 210
Shampoo, 159, 161
Shandel, Pia, 190
Shane, Forman, 149
Shanghai Joe, 201
Shapiro, Richard, 139
Sharif, Omar, 174, 229
Sharkey, Ray, 101
Sharma, Barbara, 77
Sharman, Harve, 183
Sharpe, Alex, 44
Sharpe, Cornelia, 97
Sharruff, Sam, 147
Shasad, Jamal, 97
Shatalow, Peter, 183
Shatner, William, 229
Shaughnessy, Alfred, 210
Shaver, Helen, 183
Shaw, Adriana, 89
Shaw, Bobbi, 106
Shaw, Eddie Ike, 129
Shaw, Gloria, 136
Shaw, Jimmy, 201
Shaw, Peter, 202
Shaw, Robert, 68, 170,
  171, 182, 229
Shaw, Run Run, 142, 205,
  210
Shaw, Sam, 129
Shaw, Sebastian, 229
Shaw, Stan, 36, 37, 100
Shaw Brothers, 210
Shawlee, Joan, 145, 229
Shawn, Dick, 229
Shea, Mike, 130
Shea, Shawn, 18
Shearer, Moira, 229
Shearer, Norma, 160, 229
Shee, Yen Nan, 202
Sheen, Martin, 229
Sheffield, John, 229
Sheldon, David, 135, 146
Sheldon, Lynette, 149
Sheldon, Ron, 107
Shelley, Joshua, 18, 82
Shelnut, Ed, 45
Shelton, Sloane, 18
Sheperd, Bob, 132
Shepherd, Cybill, 8, 63,
  229
Shepherd, Jack, 202
Shepherd, Richard, 96, 170
Sheppard, Gordon, 213
Sheppard, Patty, 205
Sherlick Holmes, 126
Sherman, Bobby, 139

Sherman, Don, 100
Sherman, Ellen, 203
Sherman, Jenny, 127
Sherman, Richard M., 194
Sherman, Robert B., 194
Sherman, Robert M., 34
Sherry, Bob, 130
Shevlin, Jean, 120
Shigeta, James, 56, 57
Shiloah, Yousef, 172
Shinault, Anthony, 136
Shiomi, Etsuko, 211
Shipp, John, 136
Shire, David, 18, 44
Shire, Talia, 4, 100, 101,
  229
Shirley, Peg, 127
Shock, Wilma, 135
Shoe Shine, 160
Shoji, Kyoko, 137
Shoot, 183
Shootist, The, 72
Shop on Main Street, The,
  161
Shore, Dinah, 229
Short, Charles W., 108
Shout at the Devil, 197
Showalter, Max, 229
Shrager, Sheldon, 44
Shriek of the Mutilated, 128
Shriver, Ina, 124
Shuken, Leo, 236
Shull, Richard B., 62
Shuter, Sally, 211
Siciliano, Antonio, 189
Sicilier, Maryse, 206
Sidaris, Andy, 107
Sidney, Sylvia, 148, 229
Siebert, Charles, 17
Sieff, Percy, 175
Siegel, Don, 72
Siegel, Jerome, 56
Signoret, Simone, 161, 229
Sikes, Steve, 144
Silayan, Vic, 146
Silberkleit, William B., 144
Silent Movie, 48
Silliphant, Stirling, 108
Sills, Paula, 137
Silva, Carmen, 209
Silva, Henry, 183
Silveira, Jonathan, 150
Silver, David, 58
Silver, Joe, 141
Silver, Joy, 210
Silver, Pat, 174
Silver, Ron, 141
Silver Streak, 112
Silverman, Charles, 106
Silverman, Ron, 55
Silvers, Phil, 40, 229
Silverstein, Shelley, 107
Silverstri, Alan, 127
Sim, Alastair, 236, 237
Sim, Gerald, 194
Simenon, Georges, 208
Simm, Raymond, 194
Simmons, Bob, 97
Simmons, Jean, 229
Simmons, Tim, 129
Simms, Leslie, 134
Simon, Albert J., 77
Simon, Francois, 198
Simon, Mayo, 80
Simon, Michel, 206
Simon, Neil, 50
Simon, Simone, 229
Simonds, Walter, 143
Simpson, Donald C., 142
Simpson, Gregory, 206
Simpson, O. J., 229
Sims, Tom, 150
Sin of Madelon Claudet, The,
  160
Sinatra, Frank, 39, 161,
  229
Sinclair, Jeanette, 150
Sinclair, Madge, 14, 15,
  130
Sinclaire, Lynda, 140
Sinden, Donald, 229
Singer, George M., Jr., 129
Singer, Patricia, 104
Singer, Robert, 90
Singh, Parkie, 150
Singleton, Ralph, 82, 102
Sinutko, Shane, 118, 119
Sip the Wine, 132
Sirisombat, Urai, 133
Sisk, Jan, 130
Sisney, Bobbi, 144
Sisson, Rosemary Anne,
  140
Sister Street Fighter, 211
Sisti, Giancarlo, 206
Sistrunk, Otis, 86
Sixteen, 205
Skala, Lilia, 17
Skall, William V., 236
Skeggs, Roy, 214
Skelton, Red, 229
Skene, Gordon, 150
Skidd, Andrew, 207

Skinner, Keith, 194
Skinner, Marie Antoinette, 150
Skinner, Peter, 150
Skippy, 160
Skirball, Jack H., 88
Skjetre, Gunnar, 211
Sklar, William D., 129
Skloot, Mike, 129
Skolmen, Ada, 211
Sky Riders, 131
Slade, Linda, 206
Slaney, Mike, 86
Slap, The, 201
Slate, Henry, 118
Slater, Derrick, 214
Slater, John J., 82
Slavin, Martin, 144
Sleepy Hollow, 128
Slezak, Walter, 229
Slinger, Penny, 211
Slipper and the Rose, The, 194
Sloate, Gretchen, 89
Slocombe, Douglas, 176, 210
Slott, Gene, 89, 127
Slumber Party '57, 145
Smafwitz, Henry, 129
Small, Marya, 154, 155
Small, Michael, 92
Small Change, 192
Small Town in Texas, A, 143
Smalls, Charlie, 143
Smallwood, Joseph, 201
Smeaton, Bruce, 139
Smedley-Aston, Brian, 141
Smight, Jack, 56
Smile Orange, 137
Smiley, Pril, 129
Smith, A. Z., 30
Smith, Alexis, 229
Smith, Allen E., 108
Smith, Billy Ray, 108
Smith, Charlie Martin, 10, 11
Smith, Cynthia, 30
Smith, Delos V., Jr., 112, 154, 155
Smith, Derek, 206
Smith, Duchyll, 150
Smith, Dwan, 133
Smith, Earl E., 139
Smith, Emton, 136
Smith, Greg, 140
Smith, Hubert, 136
Smith, Irby, 96, 154
Smith, Jack Martin, 139
Smith, Jeffrey, 144
Smith, John, 229
Smith, John Victor, 170
Smith, Joshua, 132
Smith, Kate, 229
Smith, Kent, 229
Smith, Kerry, 144
Smith, Lane, 102
Smith, Lelan, 18
Smith, Lois, 12, 13
Smith, Madeline, 210
Smith, Maggie, 50, 161, 229
Smith, Marty, 145
Smith, Marvin, 18
Smith, Maynard, 148
Smith, Milton, 141
Smith, Mitchell, 146
Smith, Pete, 161
Smith, Quinn, 28
Smith, Rainbeaux, 137, 138, 143, 144, 145
Smith, Roger, 229
Smith, Russel, 144
Smith, Rusty, 140
Smith, Stephen Houston, 126
Smith, Virginia, 120
Smith, Walter, 127
Smith, Wesson, 141
Smith, Wilbur, 197, 209
Smith, William, 139, 147
Smolen, Howard Don, 129
Sneers, Susan, 210
Snickowski, Bill, 97
Snodgrass, Carrie, 229
Snow, Susan, 204
Snowden, Leigh, 229
Snowy, Roy, 138
Snuff, 202
Sobel, Harold, 144
Soboloff, Arnold, 48, 114
Soker, Don, 150
Sokol, Marilyn, 82
Solaris, 213
Soldevilla, Laly, 212
Soles, P. J., 98
Solmo, Peter J., 127
Solomon, Joe, 143
Something to Hide, 202
Sommer, Elke, 209, 229
Sommer, M. Josef, 82
Sommers, Silky, 149

Sondergaard, Gale, 66, 67, 160
Sondheim, Stephen, 94
Song of Bernadette, The, 160
Song of the Thin Man, 134
Song Remains the Same, The, 213
Songsermvorakul, Supakorn, 133
Sonlinitsin, Anatoli, 213
Sonny, 229
Sopel, Stanley, 197
Soper, Gay, 214
Soper, Margarete, 174
Sorbello, Joe, 100
Sordi, Alberto, 229
Soref, Dan, 149
Sorel, Julia, 148
Sorel, Theodore, 102
Sorenson, Linda, 186
Soriano, Fred, Jr., 146
Soriano, Pepe, 207
Sorrells, Bill, 137
Sortino, Doug, 145
Sorvino, Paul, 130, 229
Sosa, Tomas, 210
Sosna, David O., 107
Sothern, Ann, 229
Soto, Helvio, 213
Soule, Olan, 118
Sound of Music, The, 161
Souperman, 149
Sousselier, Brigitte, 214
South, Leonard J., 24
Southwick, Larry, 129
Space, Arthur, 142
Spacek, Sissy, 98, 99, 153, 229
Spangler, Larry, 150
Spanish Fly, 211
Spanos, Yani, 209
Sparkle, 133
Sparkle, Susan, 145
Sparks, Bruce G., 213
Sparkuhl, Theodore, 206
Spartacus, 161
Spasma, 208
Spasmo, 208
Spathi, Tina, 133
Spatz, Linda, 135
Spaulding, Kathy, 84
Speare, Bob, 140
Special Delivery, 63
Speer, Darryl, 145
Speer, Jane, 212
Spelling, Aaron, 137
Spelvin, Georgiana, 128
Spence, Bruce, 139
Spence, Claude, 131
Spencer, Bud, 206
Spencer, James H., 100, 122
Spenser, Jeremy, 229
Sperber, Milo, 124
Sperling, Rae, 150
Spevack, Judith, 144
Spiegel, Sam, 104
Spierer, Chris, 201
Spies, Manfred, 203
Spiesser, Jacques, 198, 201
Spiga, Cyril, 206
Spikings, Barry, 180
Spinell, Joe, 22, 100
Spinello, Barry, 206
Spinetti, Victor, 124, 209
Spinks, James, 86
Spinnell, Joe, 8, 12
Spirit of Seventy-Sex, The, 148
Spirit of the Bee-Hive, The, 212
Spitaler, Ludwig, 204
Spitz, Joyce, 40
Sporting Proposition, A, 140
Spotts, Roger Hamilton, 128
Sprague, Richard, 143
Springer, Gary, 229
Sprinkle, Annie, 126, 136, 142, 145, 148, 149, 150, 214
Squirm, 141
St. Clair, Diana, 132, 144
St. Claire, Suzette, 194
St. Ives, 74
St. Jacques, Raymond, 148, 228
St. James, Cyril, 149
St. James, Susan, 228
St. John, Betta, 228
St. John, Jill, 228
St. John, Marco, 97
St. John, William, 10, 154
St. Pierre, Dominique, 150
Staab, Bruno, 192
Staats, Robert, 139
Stack, Robert, 229
Stacy, Michelle, 58
Stadlen, Lewis J., 229
Stafford, Ann, 140
Stafford, Langton, 131

Stafford, Robert, 64
Stagecoach, 160
Stagner, Rama, 149
Stalag 17, 161
Stallone, Frank, Jr., 100
Stallone, Sylvester, 4, 100, 101, 142, 152, 229
Stambaugh, David, 28
Stamp, Terence, 229
Stan Brock, 200
Stander, Lionel, 229
Stanford, Pamela, 202
Stang, Arnold, 229
Stanitsyn, Viktor, 236
Stanley, Frank, 86
Stanley, Jann, 31
Stanley, Kim, 229
Stannard, Roy, 167
Stanton, Harry Dean, 34
Stanwyck, Barbara, 229
Stapleford, George, 148
Stapleton, Jean, 229
Stapleton, Maureen, 229
Star, Monique, 137
Star, Morning, 143
Star is Born, A, 110
Starbird and Sweet William, 127
Stark, Ray, 50
Starkes, Jaison, 141
Starkey, Charles, 30
Starkey, Max, 127
Starlets, The, 149
Starr, Don, 30
Starr, Monique, 128, 142
Starr, Synthia, 149
Starrett, Jack, 143
Stateline Motel, 202
Stathis, Jim, 134
Stavrou, Aris, 133
Stay Hungry, 22
Steadman, John, 69, 134
Steckley, Doug, 143
Steel, Anthony, 229
Steele, Barbara, 141
Steele, Jeanne, 145
Steele, Karen, 141
Steele, Mike, 137
Steele, Tommy, 229
Stecle, Walter, 148
Steely, Mary, 145
Steen, Kristen, 138
Steffen, Anthony, 205
Steiger, Rod, 20, 21, 161, 212, 229
Stein, Ron, 114
Steinberg, Alberta, 140
Steinberg, Stewart, 107
Steinbert, Susan, 17
Steiner, John, 167
Stell, Aaron, 148
Stell, Frank, 128
Stellone, Al, 86
Stem, Kurt, 150
Stensvold, Alan, 132, 142
Stephan, Aram, 165
Stephanie, 126
Stephen, A. C., 149
Stephens, Harvey, 60
Stephens, Jack, 124
Sterling, Jan, 145, 229
Sterling, Robert, 229
Sterling, Tisha, 148
Stern, Guinella, 204
Sterne, Robert, 197
Stevens, Andrew, 127, 134, 144
Stevens, Carter, 130, 141, 146
Stevens, Connie, 147, 229
Stevens, George, 146, 160, 161
Stevens, Harvey, 60
Stevens, James, 201
Stevens, Jeffrey, 84
Stevens, Kaye, 229
Stevens, Kirdy, 144
Stevens, Marc, 127, 128, 130, 132, 135, 141, 142, 149, 205
Stevens, Mark, 229
Stevens, Rory, 98
Stevens, Stella, 114, 115, 127, 229
Stevens, Warren, 136
Stevenson, Houseley, 63
Stevenson, Parker, 55
Stevenson, Robert, 118
Stevenson, William M., 126
Stevinin, Jean-Francois, 192
Stewart, Alexandra, 229
Stewart, Bobby, 144
Stewart, Charles, 187
Stewart, Donald, 133
Stewart, Douglas, 72
Stewart, Elaine, 229
Stewart, Evelyne, 204
Stewart, James, 72, 160, 229
Stewart, Jaye, 18
Stewart, Lynn Marie, 143
Stewart, Martha, 229
Stewart, Nick, 112

Stewart, Paul, 20
Stewart, Peggy, 133
Stewart, Susan, 131
Stewart, Trish, 146
Stifflerin, Paul, 147
Stiglitz, Hugo, 210
Stiller, Jerry, 78, 79
Sting, The, 161
Stirling, Geoffrey, 201
Stitt, David, 149
Stock, Jennifer, 128
Stockmann, Hardy, 133
Stockton, Hope, 136
Stockwell, Dean, 229
Stohl, Hank, 136
Stoker, Austin, 148
Stokes, Barry, 213, 214
Stokowski, Leopold, 160
Stoler, Shirley, 162
Stone, Anton, 137
Stone, Bernard, 145
Stone, Christopher, 144
Stone, Dan, 144
Stone, Lively Andrew, 36, 112
Stone, Philip, 124
Stone, Tom, 136
Stone, Virginia, 144
Stoner, Solly, 206
Stoppelmoor, Cheryl, 144
Storch, Arthur, 144
Storm, Gale, 229
Storm, Howard, 143
Storm, Michael, 97
Story, Tom, 207
Story of a Sin, 213
Story of a Teenager, 129
Story of Louis Pasteur, The, 160
Stouck, Cassandra, 31
Stovall, Tom, 54
Strack, Gunter, 203
Stradling, Harry, Jr., 56, 62, 63
Straight, Beatrice, 102, 103, 161, 229
Strange Cargo, 39
Stranger and the Gunfighter, The, 205
Strasberg, Susan, 145, 229
Strasser, Pamela, 150
Straud, Don, 229
Straus, Thomas, 191
Strauss, Helen M., 196
Strauss, John, 120
Strauss, Peter, 104, 229
Strauss, Theodore, 146
Strawbridge, Larry, 30
Street, Tim, 206
Street People, 145
Streetcar Named Desire, A, 160
Streeter, Rhoden, 210
Streiner, Russell W., 145
Streisand, Barbra, 6, 110, 111, 161, 229
Strickland, Gail, 89, 122, 123
Stride, John, 60, 202
Strimpell, Stephen, 144
Stringer, Lance, 145
Stringer, Michael, 170
Strobel, Ulrich, 203
Strode, Woody, 229
Strohmeier, Tara, 144
Stroke, Big Sally, 142
Stroller, Louis, 98
Stromberg, Gary, 86
Strong, Adele, 124
Strosnider, Robin, 31
Stroud, Don, 148
Strozier, Henry, 31
Strudwick, Shepperd, 229
Struthers, Sally, 229
Stuart, Mary, 126, 127
Stud, Short, 148
Student Body, The, 136
Sturges, John, 203
Stuthman, Fred, 102
Styner & Jordan, 136, 140
Su, Louis, 126, 149
Suarez, Ramon, 206
Suben, Mark, 134
Subject Was Roses, The, 161
Subotsky, Milton, 204, 209
Sugimura, Haruko, 211
Sulistrowski, Zygmunt, 210
Sullivan, Barry, 229
Sullivan, Jean, 141
Sully, Frank, 229
Suly, William, 122
Sultana, L., 137
Sulton, Gene, 149
Summer of Laura, 131
Summers, David, 149
Summers, Elizabeth, 44
Summers, Leonora, 229
Summers, Robert, 148
Summers, Ronnie, 144
Summers, Shari, 28
Summers, Ward, 145
Sumner, Mary, 147

Sumner, Robert, 214
Sunday Woman, The, 189
Sundays and Cybele, 161
Sunset Boulevard, 150
Sunshine Boys, The, 158, 161
Super Dragon, 205
Super Seal, 132
Super Weapon, The, 206
Superbug, Super Agent, 213
Suprynowicz, Vincent, 150
Surfer Girls, 145
Surgere, Helene, 165
Surtees, Bruce, 14, 46, 72, 133
Surtees, Robert, 110
Survive!, 210, 211
Susan, Petrie, 141
Susanne, 150
Suschitzky, Wolfgang, 202
Suskind, David, 52
Suspicion, 160
Sussman, Barth Jules, 205
Sussman, Mark, 45
Sutherland, Donald, 229
Sutherland, Esther, 127
Sutherland, Julie, 137
Sutton, Carol, 147
Suzman, Janet, 124
Suzuki, Norifumi, 202, 211
Suzuki, Richard, 203
Svenson, Bo, 63, 152, 186, 229
Swan, Robert, 142
Swan Song, Inc., 213
Swanson, Gloria, 229
Swanson, Susan, 145
Swarthout, Glendon, 72
Swarthout, Miles Hood, 72
Swartz, Larry, 30
Swashbuckler, 68
Swaybill, Roger E., 186
Sweeney, Alfred, 112
Sweeny, Ann, 89
Sweet Bird of Youth, 161
Sweet Cakes, 144
Sweet Revenge, 43
Swenson, Inga, 26
Swinburne, Nora, 229
Swinging Coeds, The, 146
Swinging Swappers, The, 204
Swinging Teacher, 146, 147
Swink, Robert, 56
Swirnoff, Brad, 143
Swit, Loretta, 229
Swor, Ken, 107, 133
Sykes, Brenda, 143
Sykes, Gilly, 205
Sykes, Peter, 201, 214
Sykora, Jiri, 204
Sylbert, Paul, 120, 154
Sylvester, Harold, 147
Sylvester, William, 229
Sylwan, Karl, 178
Symington, Donald, 82
Symonds, Dusty, 78
Symptoms, 207
Syms, Sylvia, 229
Syne, Crystal, 138, 140, 149
System of Dr. Tarr and Prof. Feather, The, 203
Tabori, Kristoffer, 230
Tacchella, Jean-Charles, 184
Taffin, Tony, 213
Tait, Don, 118, 141
Takemitsu, Touru, 211
Talamonti, Rinaldo, 214
Talbot, Kenneth, 167
Talbot, Lyle, 230
Talbot, Michael, 98
Talbot, Nita, 230
Talr, Eddie, 45
Tamblyn, Russ, 140, 230
Tambornino, Jeff, 144
Tamburro, Charles, 114
Tandy, Jessica, 230
Tang, Yu, 213
Tangrea, Robert L., 100
Tanker, Andre, 213
Tannen, William, 237
Tanner, Alain, 214
Tanner, Clay, 20, 143
Tanner, Peter, 211
Tanya, 129
Tapestry of Passion, 149
Taplin, Terence, 206
Tappert, Horst, 213
Tarbes, Jean-Jacques, 210, 213
Tarbes, Monique, 198
Tari, Le, 145
Tarkovsky, Andrei, 213
Tarot, Didier, 206
Tarz & Jane & Boy & Cheeta, 126
Tarzan, 135
Taube-Henrikson, Aino, 178
Taurog, Norman, 160

253

Taxi Driver, 8
Tayback, Vic, 10, 62, 63, 118, 146
Taylor, Buck, 149
Taylor, C. D., 143
Taylor, Colin, 201
Taylor, Don, 134, 139, 230
Taylor, Dub, 69, 90, 131, 139, 141, 145, 149
Taylor, Edna, 72
Taylor, Elizabeth, 161, 207, 230
Taylor, Gilbert, 60
Taylor, Holland, 97
Taylor, Kent, 230
Taylor, Kurt, 143
Taylor, Lance, Sr., 127
Taylor, Leroy C., 148
Taylor, Marie, 145
Taylor, Peter, 88
Taylor, Richard, 210
Taylor, Robert, 38
Taylor, Robert Lewis, 141
Taylor, Rocky, 194
Taylor, Rod, 230
Taylor, Vaughn, 143
Taylor, Veronica, 147
Taylor, Wally, 143
Taylor, William, 148
Taylor-Young, Leigh, 230
Taylou, Pierre, 202
Taziner, Rik, 150
Te, Azure, 150
Teague, Anthony Skooter, 230
Teague, Jake, 150
Teal, Ray, 237
Tebber, Joseph, 149
Techine, Andre, 165
Tedesco, Paola, 212
Teen, Sammy, 126, 127
Teenage Sex Therapy, 130
Teenage Twins, 146
Teitel, Charles, 135
Telezynska, Isabella, 214
Tell Them Johnny Wadd Is Here, 147
Telleria, Isabel, 212
Temple, Shirley, 160, 161, 230
Tenant, The, 42
Tender Flesh, 141
Tenser, Marilyn J., 138
Tenser, S. Tony, 201
Terechova, Margareta, 207
Terranova, Osvaldo, 207
Terrell, Howard, 143
Terror from under the House, 204
Terror House, 142
Terry, Norbert, 206
Terry-Thomas, 210, 211, 230
Terzieff, Laurent, 172, 213, 230
Tessier, Valentine, 207
Testi, Fabio, 202
Tevis, Walter, 180
Teyssedre, Anne, 208
Thacher, Russell, 23
Thacker, Russ, 230
That Girl Is a Tramp, 214
That Lady from Rio, 148
Thatcher, Torin, 230
That's Entertainment, Part 2, 38
Thaxter, Phyllis, 230
Thayer, Michael, 131
Thea, Anna, 114
Thebaud, Marion, 203
Theiss, Manuella, 127
Theodore, Brother, 149
Thevenet, Virginia, 192
They Came from Within, 141
They Shoot Horses, Don't They?, 161
They're Coming to Get You, 210
Thiriot, Rick, 150
Thom, Robert, 128
Thomas, Albert, 213
Thomas, Andre, 214
Thomas, Betty, 133, 143, 145
Thomas, Bill, 58
Thomas, Cameron, 102
Thomas, Danny, 230
Thomas, Frank, 129
Thomas, Jack W., 40
Thomas, Jeremy, 212
Thomas, Marlo, 230
Thomas, Melody, 72
Thomas, Mike, 145
Thomas, Paul, 132, 145
Thomas, Philip, 133, 230
Thomas, Richard, 230
Thomas, Ted, 206
Thomas, William C., 140
Thomerson, Timothy, 86
Thompson, Claude, 116
Thompson, Donald G., 146

Thompson, Elizabeth, 20, 21
Thompson, Galen, 146
Thompson, J. Lee, 74
Thompson, Jack, 212, 230
Thompson, Jay, 44
Thompson, Jim, 148
Thompson, John, 135
Thompson, Marshall, 230
Thompson, Rex, 230
Thompson, Sada, 230
Thomson, Dorri, 149
Thorent, Andre, 203
Thornberg, Billy, 131, 132, 149
Thorndike, Dame Sybil, 237
Thorne, Dyanne, 130, 131
Thorne, Ken, 78, 133
Thornton, Chuck, 144
Thornton, Frank, 210
Thorpe, Sharon, 126, 127, 128, 132, 135, 137, 144, 149
Thousand Clowns, A, 161
3 A.M., 128
Three Faces of Eve, The, 161
Three Shades of Flesh, 140
Thring, Frank, 212
Through a Glass Darkly, 161
Through the Looking Glass, 145
Thulin, Ingrid, 172, 230
Thunderbuns, Mark, 149
Thurman, Bill, 131, 145
Thursday Morning Murders, The, 144
Thurston, Ellen, 147
Tibbs, Casey, 32
Tichy, Gerard, 213
Tidy, Patricia, 89
Tidyman, Ernest, 145
Tiemens, Fred, 147
Tierney, Gene, 230
Tierney, Lawrence, 230
Tiffany Jones, 210
Tiffin, Pamela, 230
Til, Roger, 44
Tin, Hui, 209
Ting-hung, Kuo, 210
Tint, Francine, 144
Tinti, Gabriele, 209, 213
Tiplitsky, Lee, 30
Tippit, Wayne, 106
To Each His Own, 160
To Kill a Mockingbird, 161
To The Devil a Daughter, 214
Tobalina, Carlos, 147
Tobey, Kenneth, 20, 137
Tobin, Matthew, 82
Todd, Bob, 214
Todd, Richard, 230
Toei Co., 211
Toffolo, Lino, 210
Tognazzi, Ugo, 210
Togni, Alex, 204
Toho-Eizo, 205
Tokar, Norman, 10
Toland, John, 148
Toldeo, Jose, 133
Toles, Jackie, 86
Toll, Pamela, 143
Tolman, Jennifer, 176
Tolo, Marilu, 230
Tolu, Maria, 206
Tom Jones, 161
Tom Thumb, 208
Tomak, Erich, 203
Tomblin, David, 60
Tomkins, Ann-May, 130
Tomkins, Mary, 145
Tomlin, Lily, 230
Ton Ton, Won, 40
Toney, Theadore, 147
Tongue, 128
Tonkin, Phil, 140
Too Hot to Handle, 148
Topkapi, 161
Topol, 230
Topor, Roland, 42
Topper, Burt, 142
Torday, Terry, 203
Torn, Rip, 31, 180, 181, 230
Tornade, Pierre, 209
Torreni, Ana, 212
Torrens, Tania, 192
Torres, Liz, 230
Tors, David, 200
Tors, Ivan, 200
Tors, Peter, 200
Tors, Steven, 200
Tosi, Mario, 98
Totten, Robert, 149
Totter, Audrey, 230
Touch of Class, A, 161
Toulose, Bran, 214
Toure, Moustapha, 211
Tove, Birte, 210
Tovoli, Luciano, 189, 208
Towers, Harry Alan, 206
Townsend, Bud, 138, 142

Townsend, Jill, 94, 206
Townsend, Jim, 144
Tozzi, Fausto, 145, 203
Tracey, Ray, 148
Trackdown, 134
Tracy, Spencer, 38, 160
Trager, Pam, 18
Tramer, Bennett, 36
Tramunti, Alexis, 136
Trap of Cougar Mountain, The, 141
Travanti, Daniel J., 74
Travernier, Bertrand, 208
Travers, Bill, 206, 211, 230
Travers, Sy, 120
Travino, Tony, 139
Travis, Michael, 30, 77
Travis, Richard, 230
Travolta, John, 98, 99, 153, 230
Traynor, Peter S., 129
Treadwell, Liz, 126
Treasure of Matecumbe, 141
Treasure of the Sierra Madre, The, 160
Tree, Beerbohm, 148
Trelos, Tony, 128
Tremayne, Les, 230
Trend, Jean, 201
Trent, Jackie, 209
Trent, John, 212
Trentham, Barbara, 131
Treu, Wolfgang, 205
Trevor, Claire, 160
Triche, Bernard, 150
Triesault, Jon, 128
Trikonis, Gus, 131, 136
Tringham, David, 124
Trintignant, Jean-Louis, 189, 213, 230
Tristan, Dorothy, 68
Trixi, Helga, 214
Troldmyr, Susan, 211
Tropea, Paul, 176, 177
Trost, Carol, 18
Trostle, Ed, 230
Trouble with Young Stuff, The, 149
Troughton, Patrick, 60
Trovaioli, Armando, 201, 213
Troy, Lisa, 128
True, Andrea, 127, 128, 136
True Grit, 161
Trueblood, Guerdon, 23
Trueman, Paula, 46
Truffaut, Eva, 192
Truffaut, Francois, 192
Truffaut, Laura, 192
Trumbo, Dalton, 237
Trumper, John, 206, 214
Trumplay, Henry, 140
Trussell, Christopher, 133
Trustman, Alan, 97
Tryon, Tom, 230
Tsengoles, Sue, 138
Tsengoles, Tony, 138
Tsopei, Corinna, 230
Tsu, Irene, 133
Tube, Sandy, 175
Tubor, Morton, 134, 142
Tucci, Ugo, 208
Tucker, Bob, 135
Tucker, Forrest, 144, 230
Tucker, Phil, 140
Tugsmith, Chief Elmer, 114
Tumelty, Bob, 139
Tumelty, Karen, 139
Tung, Al, 205
Tunnelvision, 143
Turkel, Joseph, 127
Turman, Glynn, 134, 141
Turner, John, 194
Turner, Ken, 137
Turner, Lana, 39, 89, 230
Turpin, Turk, 129, 145
Turquand, Todd, 90
Tushingham, Rita, 230
Tutin, Dorothy, 230
Tuttle, Lurene, 230
Tuttle, William, 161
Twelve O'Clock High, 160
Twiggy, 230
Two Against the Law, 210
Two Women, 161
Two-Minute Warning, 107
Tyler, Beverly, 230
Tyler, Walter, 56
Tyne, George, 130
Tyner, Charles, 24
Tyrrell, Susan, 148, 230
Tyson, Cicely, 134, 207, 230
Ugarte, Julian, 205
Uggams, Leslie, 230
Ullmann, Liv, 178, 179, 230
Ultimate Warrior, The, 139
Ultramax, 145
Umbas, Stitch, 144

Umeki, Miyoshi, 161
Uncle Rudy, 110
Underground, 137
Underwood, Ray, 144
Unger, Bertil, 114
Unger, Gustar, 114
Unitas, Johnny, 64
Uno, Jukichi, 211
Unsworth, Geoffrey, 88
UP (RHM), 146
Upmalis, Mike, 207
Upson, John, 145
Urago, Bento, 206
Urioste, Frank J., 56
Ursin, Nick, 150
Urtel, Peter Martin, 204
Ustinov, Peter, 58, 141, 161, 230
Vacaryova, Magda, 204
Vaccaro, Brenda, 230
Vadim, Roger, 203
Valdes, Ghuy, 149
Valdez, Jorge, 84
Valdez Horses, The, 203
Valentine, 100
Valentine, Anthony, 214
Valette, Michel, 206
Valino, Joe, 127
Vallacher, Kitty, 142
Vallee, Rudy, 230
Valli, Alida, 166, 209, 230
Vallier, Alain, 210
Vallone, Raf, 230
Valmence, Jean, 203
Van, Bobby, 230
Van, Frankie, 100
Van Cleef, Lee, 205, 207, 212, 230
Van Clief, Rene, 140
Van Clief, Ron, 206
Van Damme, Alain, 210
van de Ven, Monique, 212, 230
Van Den Beemt, Peter, 128
van der Heyde, Nikolai, 214
Van Der Linden, Paul, 213
van der Linden, Sandy, 214
Van Devere, Trish, 230
Van Doren, Mamie, 230
Van Dyke, Dick, 230
Van Fleet, Jo, 42, 161, 230
Van Noy, George, 150
van Oterloo, Roger, 212
Van Pallandt, Nina, 133
Van Patten, Dick, 64, 118, 141, 230
Van Patten, Joyce, 28, 29, 120, 230
Van Patten, Vincent, 203
Van Runkle, Theadora, 114
Van Scott, Mickel, 135
Vandernberg, Gerard, 214
Vane, Norman Thaddeus, 190
Vanni, Massimo, 204
Vanzina, Stefano, 213
Varconi, Victor, 237
Vaughan, Peter, 207
Vaughan, Rhiannon, 135
Vaughn, Ben, 30
Vaughn, Robert, 230
Vaughn, Roger, 136
Vaughn, Skeeter, 127
Veber, Francis, 214
Vega, Isela, 143, 150, 230
Veillot, Claude, 208
Vejar, Mike, 148
Velvet Smooth, 140
Venantini, Venantino, 202, 213
Veniero, Kathalina, 129
Ventura, Lino, 206, 230
Venture, Richard, 18
Venus, Brenda, 150
Venuta, Venay, 230
Vera-Ellen, 230
Verano, Roberto, 132
Verber, Francis, 205
Verbois, Jack, 114
Verderame, Steve, 135
Verdi, Giuseppe, 208
Verdon, Gwen, 230
Verdugo, Ana, 139
Vereen, Ben, 230
Vereneti, Laura, 135
Verhoeven, Paul, 212
Veril, Don, 126
Verley, Milton, 137
Verley, Renaud, 206, 209
Verlox, Catherine, 184
Vernon, Howard, 202
Vernon, John, 46
Vernon, Richard, 199
Verona, Stephen, 106
Veronique or the Summer of My 13th Year, 208
Verschueren, Gust, 214
Vertue, Beryl, 133
VeSota, Bruno, 237
Viala, Laura, 214
Viale, Oscar, 207
Vickers, Mike, 201, 209

Viera, Ana, 124
Vigilante Force, 134
Vigran, Herb, 30, 118
Vilers, Vania, 202
Villa, Ed E., 43
Villanueva, Edd, 149
Villareal, Valentine, 148
Villars, Felix, 213
Villasante, Jose, 212
Villeret, Jacques, 209
Vincent, Diane, 127
Vincent, Francois, Paul and the Others, 204
Vincent, Frank, 148
Vincent, Horst, 206
Vincent, Jan-Michael, 7, 134, 137, 190, 230
Vincent, Virginia, 141
Vint, Jesse, 133
Violet, Ultra, 230
V.I.P's, The, 161
Viramontes, Jerry, 148
Virgin and the Lover, 205
Virgin Snow, 136
Virgin Spring, The, 161
Virility, 206
Visconti, Luchino, 212, 237
Viskin, Robert, 203
Vitale, Enzo, 162
Vitale, Milly, 230
Vitarelli, Arthur J., 10
Vitte, Ray, 86
Vitti, Monica, 214
Vitzin, George, 207
Viva Zapata, 160
Vlok, Ben, 209
Vogel, Daniel, 207
Vogel, Jesse, 201
Vogler, Karl Michael, 197
Vohrer, Alfred, 213
Vohs, Joan, 230
Voight, Jon, 182, 230
Volgova, Robert, 136
Volkmann, Elizabeth, 204
Volonte, Gian Maria, 230
Volz, Benjamin, 209
Von Bergdorfe, Enjil, 142, 144
Von Eaton, E., 148
Von Essen, Desiree, 150
Von Hellen, M. C., 149
Von Kleist, Heinrich, 191
Von Leer, Hunter, 34
von Noe, Margarethe Schell, 182
von Schereler, Sasha, 102
von Schumacher, Augustus, 40
Von Shrokehardt, Eric, 126, 127
von Sydow, Max, 124, 139, 230
Von Treuberg, Franz, 209
Von Zerneck, Frank, 143
Von-Davis, Tia, 146
Voujargol, Paul, 213
Voulzy, Laurent, 206
Voyage of the Damned, 124
Voyette, Marie-Josephe, 207
Vukotic, Milena, 168
Vulpiano, Mario, 209
Vye, Murvyn, 237
W. C. Fields and Me, 20
Wachta, Edward, 207
Wackiest Wagon Train in the West, The, 144
Waddell, Florilyn, 124
Wadsworth, Derek, 150
Wagenheim, Charles, 34
Wagner, George, 142
Wagner, Leon, 36
Wagner, Lindsay, 230
Wagner, Robert, 56, 57, 230
Waite, Genevieve, 230
Waiting for Fidel, 201
Walberg, Gary, 137
Walcott, Gregory, 56
Walczewski, Marek, 213
Waldberg, Garry, 107
Walden, Robert, 18
Walders, Joe, 139
Waldman, Frank, 199
Walken, Christopher, 12, 13, 230
Walker, Charles, 127
Walker, Clint, 150, 230
Walker, Esther, 132
Walker, Hal, 149
Walker, Joseph A., 134
Walker, Nancy, 50, 230
Walker, Pete, 214
Walker Brothers, 208
Wallace, Jack, 145
Wallace, Tommy, 148
Wallace, Trevor, 213
Wallach, Eli, 202, 230
Wallis, Shani, 230
Wallner, Herman, 135
Walls of Malapaga, The, 160

Walsh, David M., 20, 50, 112
Walsh, M. Emmet, 114, 120
Walsh, Shaun, 138
Walsh, Terry, 205
Walston, Ray, 112, 231
Walter, Chuck, 147
Walter, Ernest, 207
Walter, Jessica, 231
Walter, Michael, 204
Walter, Pennie, 140
Walters, Hugh, 206
Walters, Penni, 131
Walters, Robert D., 149
Wanamaker, Sam, 124, 125, 231
Wang, T. C., 133
Wanger, Walter, 160
Wannberg, Ken, 89
War and Peace, 161
Warburton, Cotton, 10, 141
Ward, Burt, 231
Ward, Simon, 231
Warden, Jack, 18, 19, 231
Warfield, Joe, 114
Warfield, Marlene, 102, 103
Warner, David, 60, 61, 204
Warner, Harry M., 160
Warner, Richard, 201
Warnick, Allan, 41
Warren, Carol, 129
Warren, Jennifer, 231
Warren, Kenneth J., 201
Warren, Lesley Ann, 44, 231
Warren, Michael, 30, 77, 153
Warrick, Ruth, 231
Warschilka, Edward, 62
Washbourne, Mona, 207, 231
Washington, Ken, 140
Washington, Ned, 237
Watch on the Rhine, 160
Watch Out, We're Mad, 206
Waterkotte, Mike, 145
Waterman, Dennis, 211
Waters, Bob, 140
Waters, Ethel, 231
Waters, Ralph, 150
Waters, Robert E., 140
Waters, Tom, 149
Waterston, Sam, 43, 213, 231
Watkin, David, 170, 214
Watkins, James Louis, 141
Watkins, Linda, 237
Watkins, Michael, 148, 207
Watkins, Miles, 144
Watkins, Peter, 211
Watling, Jack, 231
Watson, Douglass, 231
Watson, Earl, Jr., 132
Watson, Mills, 141
Watson, Owen, 140
Watson, Vernee, 77
Watt, Reuben, 14
Watts, Bobby, 190
Waugh, Claire, 144
Waugh, Donald, 84
Waxman, Harry, 199, 213
Way of All Flesh, The, 160
Wayne, Anthony, 210
Wayne, David, 231
Wayne, John, 6, 72, 73, 161, 231
Wayne, Patrick, 131, 231
Weathers, Carl, 100, 101
Weaver, Dennis, 231
Weaver, Fritz, 92
Weaver, Marjorie, 231
Webb, Alan, 231
Webb, Jack, 231
Webber, Robert, 56, 231
Weber, Sharon, 55
Webster, Ferris, 46, 108
Webster, June, 138
Weck, Peter, 205
Wedgeworth, Ann, 16, 31
Weed, Mike, 150
Weekend Girls, 207
Weeks, Linda, 136
Wei-Min, Chan, 201
Weiner, Sol, 145
Weinert, Jim, 145
Weintraub, Fred, 133, 134, 139, 146
Weir, James, 30
Weir, Peter, 139
Weisenfeld, Joel, 207
Weissman, Richard, 149
Weissmuller, Johnny, 135, 231
Welch, Niles, 237
Welch, Raquel, 41, 231
Welch, Tin, 154
Welcome to Arrow Beach, 141
Weld, Tuesday, 231
Weldon, Charles, 134
Weldon, Joan, 231
Weldon, Mike, 142
Welles, Gwen, 231

Welles, Jennifer, 126, 127, 130, 140, 144, 148, 205
Welles, Orson, 124, 125, 161, 231
Wellington, Y. B., 131
Wellman, William, 110
Wells, Danny, 118
Wells, H. G., 54
Wells, J. C., 140
Wells, Richard, 36
Wells, Tiny, 30
Wendkos, Paul, 63
Wepper, Fritz, 212
Werner, Carlos, 209
Werner, Oskar, 124, 125, 231
Werner, Peter, 210
Werris, Snag, 126
Wertheim, Ronald, 145
Wertmuller, Lina, 162, 164, 188
Wesman, Paul, 147
West, Alan, 145
West, Cindy, 127, 128
West, Genevieve, 124
West, John, 107
West, Mae, 231
West, Martin, 24, 148
West, Melody, 132
West Side Story, 161
Westbrook, Jenny, 207
Westby, Geir, 211
Westerfield, Jim, 45
Westerner, The, 160
Westman, James A., 128
Weston, Armand, 130
Weston, Bill, 146
Weston, Cecil, 237
Weston, Jack, 69, 78, 79, 231
Weston, Jay, 20
Weston, Ned, 130
Weston, Steve, 112
Wetherall, Virginia, 201
Wexler, Haskell, 122, 137, 154
Wexler, Norman, 143
Weyand, Ronald, 17
Weysom, Samantha, 78
Whalen, James, 132
What Changed Charley Farthing?, 201
Wheatley, Dennis, 214
Wheeler, John, 144
Wheeler, Paul, 68, 202
Wheelwright, Ernie, 134
Whigham, P. J., 143
Whipple, Rod, 142
Whitaker, Johnny, 231
Whitaker, Len, 148
White, Billy Vance, 136
White, Carol, 231
White, Carol Ita, 106, 137
White, Charles, 231
White, Cheryl Ann, 130
White, David, 176
White, Frank, 202
White, Garry Michael, 131
White, Gene, 147
White, Jesse, 127, 131, 231
White, Jonathan, 186
White, Lloyd, 112
White, Onna, 161
White, Roy, 109
White, Sheila, 206
White Slavery in New York, 126
Whiteaker, Joe, 31
Whitehead, E. A., 187
Whitelaw, Billie, 60, 61
Whitely, Jon, 161
Whiteman, George, 146
Whitemore, Hugh, 207
Whitfield, Karen J., 144, 145
Whitfield, Marshall C., 144, 145
Whitfield, Norman, 86
Whitman, Stuart, 127, 141, 231
Whitmore, James, 231
Whitmore, Stanford, 137
Who's Afraid of Virginia Woolf?, 161
Whose Child Am I?, 201
Wicki, Bernhard, 174
Wicking, Christopher, 201, 214
Widdoes, Kathleen, 231
Wideman, David, 207
Widmark, Richard, 214, 231
Wienand, Jannie, 200
Wilbor, Robert, 135
Wilbur, Frank, 139
Wilcox, John, 211
Wilcox, Larry, 23
Wilcox, Mary, 62
Wilcox, Ralph, 154
Wilcox-Horne, Colin, 231
Wilcoxon, Henry, 149, 231

Wild, Arnold, 207
Wild Goose Chase, The, 210
Wildcat Women, 142
Wilde, Brian, 206
Wilde, Cornel, 231
Wilde, Billy, 160, 161
Wilder, Gene, 7, 112, 113, 231
Wilder, Glen, 58, 107
Wilder, Yvonne, 48
Wilding, Michael, 231
Wilensky, Moshe, 209
Wiley, Margaret, 106
Wilhelmi, Roman, 213
Wilkerson, Cathy, 137
Wilkinson, C. T., 78
Willard, Fred, 112, 149
Willens, Bill, 18
Williams, Arnold, 41
Williams, Arthur, 144
Williams, Bart, 143
Williams, Bert, 76
Williams, Billy, 124
Williams, Billy Dee, 7, 36, 37, 148, 231
Williams, Brian, 150
Williams, Christine, 149
Williams, Cindy, 131, 231
Williams, Diahn, 17
Williams, Dick A., 17, 140
Williams, Dwight, 135
Williams, Emlyn, 231
Williams, Esther, 231
Williams, Grant, 231
Williams, J. Terry, 24, 129
Williams, Janine, 86
Williams, Jason, 138
Williams, John, 10, 11, 24, 34, 56, 84, 231
Williams, Liberty, 64
Williams, Oscar, 133
Williams, Paul, 55, 84
Williams, Polly, 194
Williams, Ralph, 10
Williams, Sammy, 148
Williams, Simon, 196
Williams, Sylvia Kuumba, 70
Williams, Thomas, 129
Williams, Treat, 11, 78, 79
Williams, Trevor, 80
Williamson, Fred, 126, 127, 136, 137, 150, 231
Williamson, Jeff, 137
Williamson, Nicol, 94, 95, 170, 171
Willingham, Nobel, 148
Willis, Gordon, 18
Willis, Helen, 145
Willison, Walter, 44
Willoughby, Marlene, 132, 148, 149, 150
Wills, Bob, 131
Wills, Frank, 18
Wills, Henry, 143
Wills, John, 131
Wilmer, Douglas, 196
Wilrich, Rudolph, 82
Wilson, Bruce, 147
Wilson, Burtrust T., 149
Wilson, Demond, 231
Wilson, Flip, 231
Wilson, Frank Arthur, 148
Wilson, Freddie, 172
Wilson, George, 201, 211
Wilson, Howard, 207
Wilson, James, 136, 140
Wilson, John G., 46
Wilson, Johnny, 131
Wilson, Lester, 133
Wilson, Lydia, 102
Wilson, Nancy, 231
Wilson, Paul, 78
Wilson, Scott, 231
Wilson, Theodore, 134
Wilson, Trey, 136
Winde, Beatrice, 133, 231
Windom, William, 134, 231
Winds of Autumn, The, 139
Windsor, Marie, 231
Windsor, Ty, 126
Winer, Harry S., 126
Winetrobe, Maury, 76, 143
Winfield, Paul, 210, 231
Wing Woo, James, 92
Winger, Debra, 145
Wingert, Donna Lee, 149
Wingert, Jim, 149
Wings, 160
Winitsky, Alex, 94, 182
Winkeler, Fanny, 214
Winkler, Henry, 231
Winkler, Irwin, 100, 114, 126
Winkler, Lee B., 126, 127
Winkler, Margo, 126
Winn, Kitty, 126, 231
Winner, Andrew, 114
Winner, Jeffrey, 144
Winner, Michael, 40
Winslow, Dick, 40, 72, 107
Winslow, Susan, 150
Winston, Helene, 118

Winter, Catherine, 209
Winter, Edward, 63
Winter, Judy, 213
Winter, Vincent, 161
Winter Heat, 135
Winters, David, 110, 144
Winters, Howar, 136
Winters, Jonathan, 231
Winters, Ralph E., 116
Winters, Roland, 231
Winters, Shelley, 12, 42, 161, 202, 213, 231
Winwood, Estelle, 50, 51, 231
Wise, Alfie, 68
Wise, Robert, 161
Wiseman, Joseph, 213
Wisenor, Eugene, 139
Wislocki, George, 17
Wisman, Ron, 183
Witch Who Came from the Sea, The, 128
Withers, Googie, 231
Withers, Jane, 231
Witta, Jacques, 203
Wodehouse, Scott, 94
Wolcott, Robbie, 129
Wolf, David M., 97
Wolf, Emanuel, 210
Wolfberg, Lee, 44
Wolfe, Francis X., 210
Wolfe, Joseph, 210
Wolfe, Kedric, 135
Wolfe, Robert L., 18
Wolff, Ruth, 196
Wolfson, Martin, 120
Wolman, Dan, 205
Woman in the Rain, 145
Women in Love, 161
Won Ton Ton, the Dog Who Saved Hollywood, 40
Wong, Arthur, 133
Wong, Catherine, 129
Wong, Joe, 142
Wong, Linda, 137, 144, 146
Woo, Joe, Jr., 148
Wood, Douglas, 145, 148
Wood, Forrest, 107
Wood, Janet, 142, 145, 146
Wood, Natalie, 126, 231
Wood, Peggy, 231
Wood, Ward, 146
Woodlawn, Holly, 231
Woods, Bob, 144
Woods, James, 96, 231
Woods, Jeril, 137
Woods, Ren, 86
Woods, Roberta, 126
Woodvine, John, 133
Woodward, Bob, 18
Woodward, Ian, 206
Woodward, Joanne, 161, 231
Woodward, Morgan, 129, 143
Woodworth, Ed, 132
Wooland, Norman, 231
Wooley, Chuck, 144
Wooley, Peter, 133
Woolf, Charles, 137
Woolley, Robert, 97
Woolsey, Ralph, 41, 55
Words, Syl, 127
Worker, Robert, 126
Workman, Carl, 137
Worley, Jo Anne, 118
Woronov, Mary, 133, 142, 231
Wray, Fay, 231
Wrenn, Trevor, 207
Wright, Alvin, 30
Wright, Arthur, 147
Wright, Ebony, 147
Wright, Harland, 30
Wright, Heather, 197, 211
Wright, Herbert J., 190
Wright, Jackie, 131
Wright, Jenny Lee, 194
Wright, Johan, 175
Wright, Nory, 140
Wright, Patrick, 137, 142, 150
Wright, Stanley, 133
Wright, Teresa, 160, 231
Wright, Wendell, 18
Write, P. James, 144
Written on the Wind, 161
Wurtzel, Stuart, 97
Wyatt, Jane, 141, 231
Wyatt, Sonja, 139
Wyler, William, 160, 161
Wylie, Meg, 26
Wyman, Bob, 58
Wyman, Jane, 160, 231
Wymore, Patrice, 231
Wyn, Michel, 206
Wyner, George, 18
Wynn, David, 126
Wynn, Dianne, 199
Wynn, Keenan, 118, 119, 139, 148, 210, 231

Wynn, May, 231
Wynter, Dana, 231
Xala, 211
Yablans, Frank, 112
Yaccelini, Alberto, 214
Yaegermann, Kelly, 140
Yamaguchi, Kazuhiko, 211
Yamamoto, Kei, 211
Yankee Doodle Dandy, 160
Yankowitz, Phil, 145
Yarbrough, Camille, 97
Yarvet, Youri, 213
Yates, Peter, 41
Yee, Chang Shun, 201
Yee, Chang Sing, 201
Yeh, Karen, 205
Yesterday, Today and Tomorrow, 161
Yeung, K. M., 147
Yiu Lan, Chan, 206
Yoder, Aly, 133
Yonemoto, Bruce, 150
Yonemoto, Norman, 161
York, Dick, 231
York, Michael, 58, 59, 231
York, Susannah, 131, 231
You Can't Take It with You, 160
Young, Alan, 150, 231
Young, Bill Eld, 147
Young, Brooke, 144, 146
Young, Buck, 107
Young, Burt, 44, 100, 101
Young, Darryl, 147
Young, Ericka, 147
Young, Freddie, 207
Young, Gig, 161, 231
Young, J. B., 144
Young, John, 150
Young, Keone, 137
Young, Kiki, 148
Young, Kris, 148
Young, Lisa, 135
Young, Loretta, 160, 231
Young, Robert, 231
Young, Stephanie, 145
Young, Stephen, 55, 186
Young, Taylor, 144, 146
Young, Terence, 204
Youngblood, T. J., 140, 143
Youngblood, Zachary, 140
Younger, Margo, 131
Youngman, Henny, 48
Your Heaven, My Hell, 211
Youssov, Vadim, 213
Yu, Albert, 213
Yu, Jimmy Wang, 205, 209
Yulin, Harris, 74
Yung, Hsieh Hsiu, 141
Yung-Yu, Chen, 210
Z, 161
Zacha, Jac, 139
Zaentz, Saul, 154
Zagon, Marty, 130
Zak, Sharri, 107
Zakka, Richard, 97
Zaleski, Ann, 147
Zaloom, Joe, 97
Zapata, Carmen, 130
Zappala, Joseph, 89, 127
Zapponi, Bernardo, 208
Zaubmann, Maurizio, 145
Zebrowski, Jon, 84
Zehetgruber, Rudolf, 213
Zeitler, William A., 145
Zeleny, Muriel, 192
Zelnik, George, 206
Zelnik, Jerzy, 213
Zenker, Fred, 214
Zepplin, Led, 213
Zetterling, Mai, 231
Zeyn, Eva, 203
Zidi, Claude, 210
Ziegler, Helga, 203
Ziesmer, Jerry, 44
Zietsman, Frank, 175
Zim, Cazander, 128
Zimbalist, Efrem, Jr., 231
Zimet, Mohamed, 209
Zimmer, Laurie, 148
Zimmerman, Jack, 207
Zimmerman, Vernon, 133
Zinnemann, Fred, 161
Zinnenberg, Monica, 213
Zinner, Peter, 110
Zito, Louis, 136
Zodiacs, The, 149
Zorba the Greek, 161
Zorich, Louis, 20
Zorrilla, China, 207
Zouzou, 131, 208
Zsigmond, Vilmos, 43, 70, 140
Zukerman, Pinchas, 182
Zukor, Adolph, 160, 237